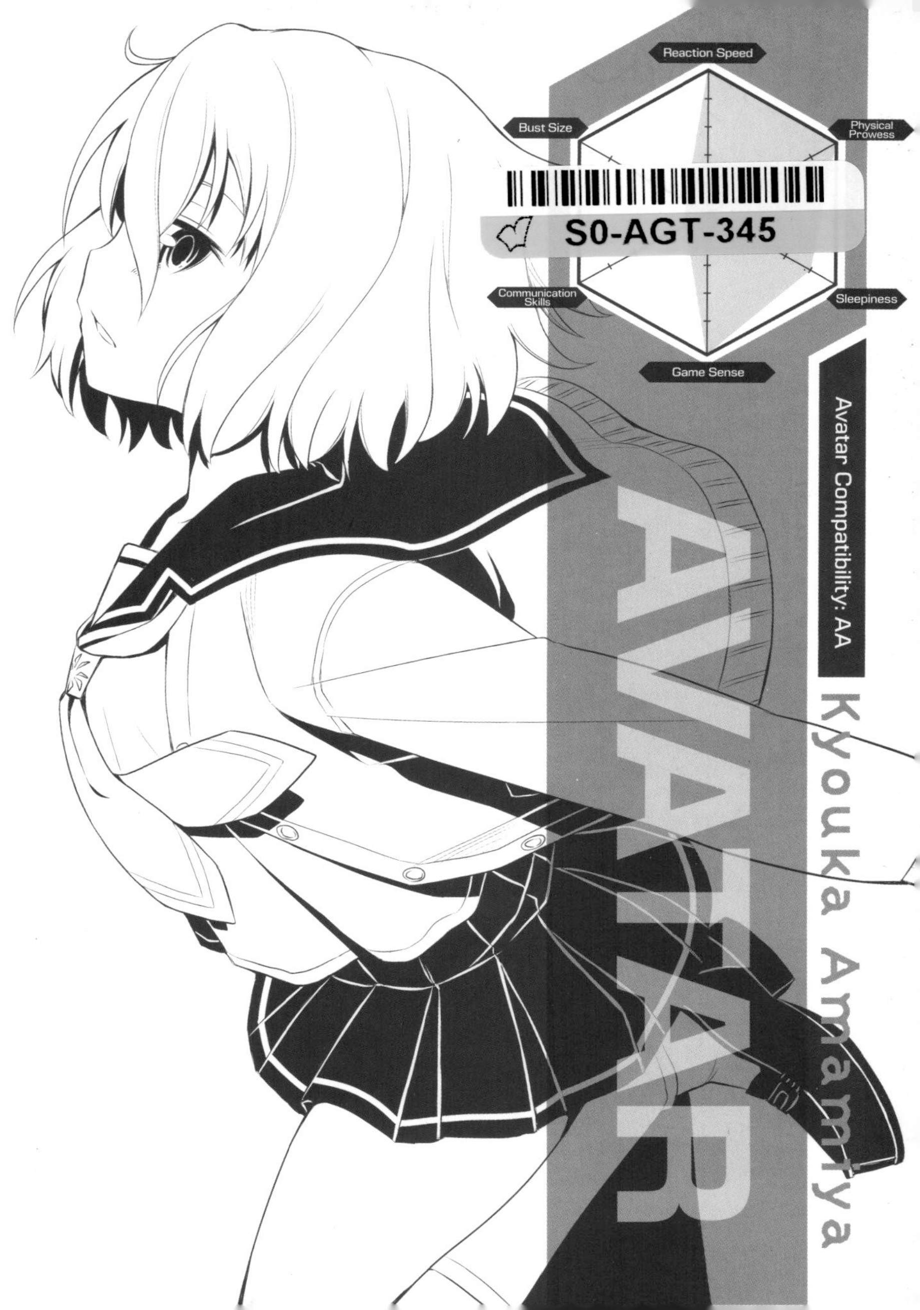
Reaction Speed
Bust Size
Physical Prowess
Communication Skills
Sleepiness
Game Sense
Avatar Compatibility: AA
AVATAR
Kyouka Amamiya

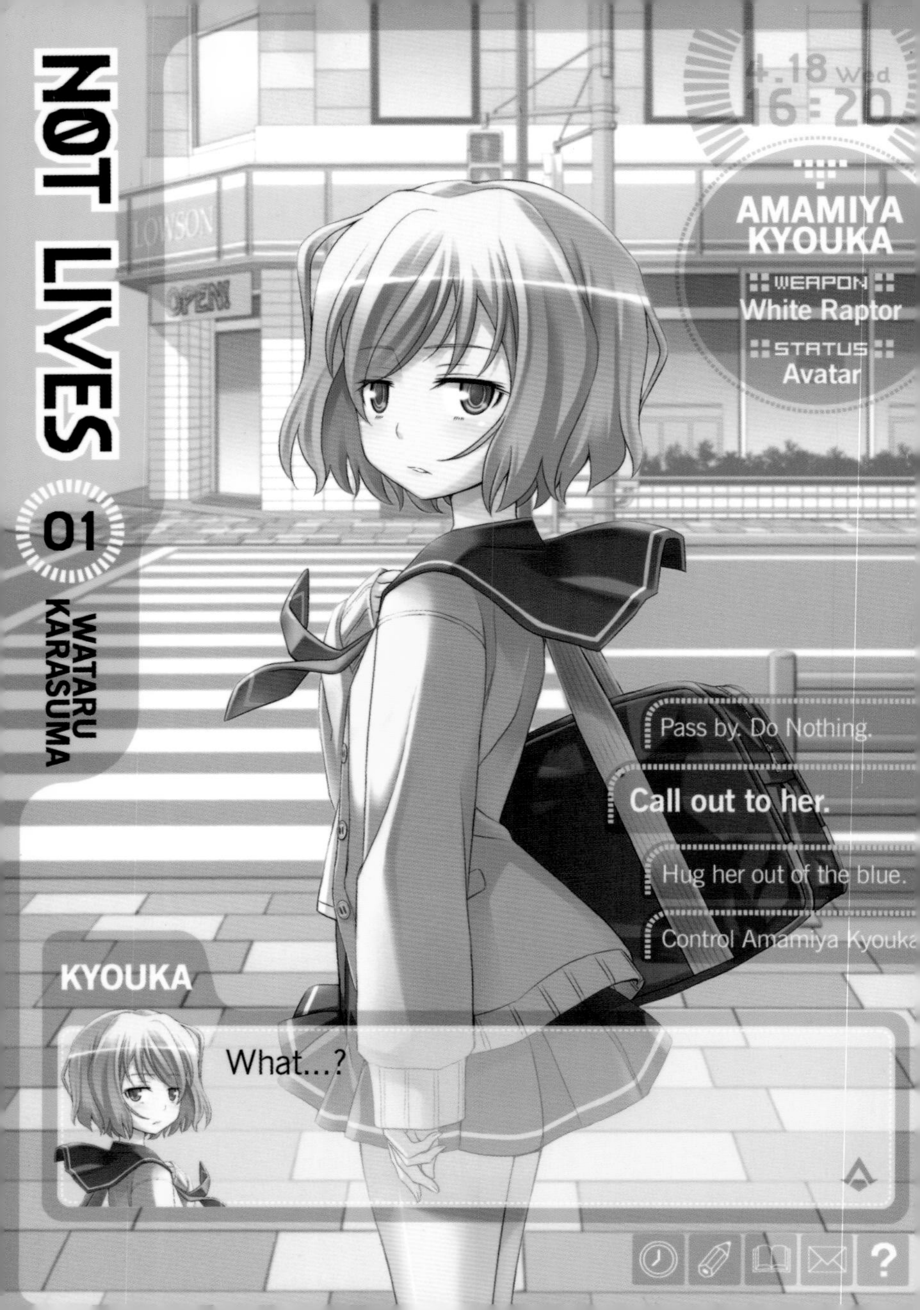
NOT LIVES
01
WATARU KARASUMA
LOWSON
OPEN
4.18 Wed
16:20
AMAMIYA KYOUKA
WEAPON
White Raptor
STATUS
Avatar
Pass by. Do Nothing.
Call out to her.
Hug her out of the blue.
Control Amamiya Kyouka
KYOUKA
What...?

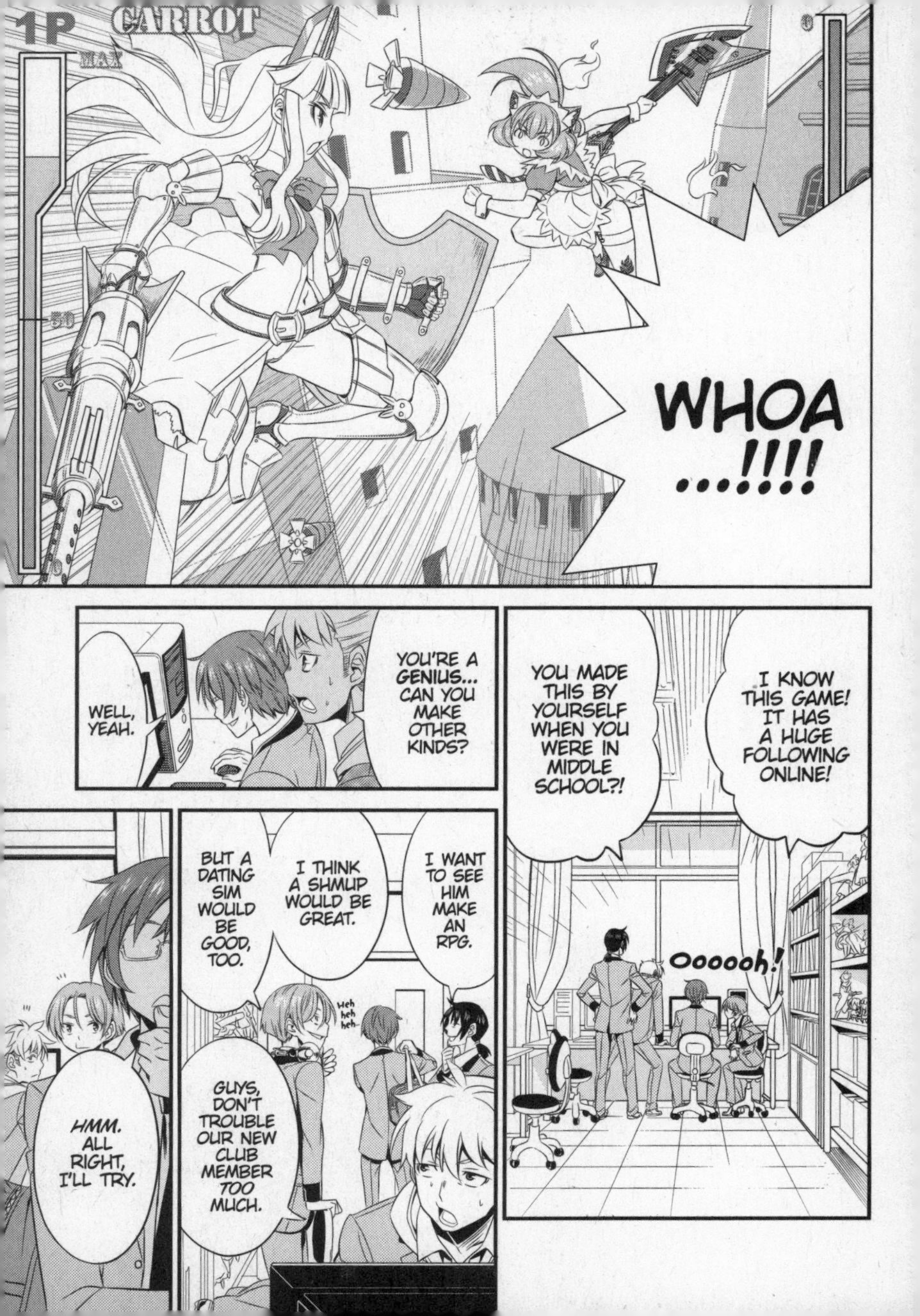

1P
CARROT
MAX
50
WHOA ....!!!!
I KNOW THIS GAME! IT HAS A HUGE FOLLOWING ONLINE!
YOU MADE THIS BY YOURSELF WHEN YOU WERE IN MIDDLE SCHOOL?!
Oooooh!
YOU'RE A GENIUS... CAN YOU MAKE OTHER KINDS?
WELL, YEAH.
I WANT TO SEE HIM MAKE AN RPG.
I THINK A SHMUP WOULD BE GREAT.
BUT A DATING SIM WOULD BE GOOD, TOO.
Heh heh heh
GUYS, DON'T TROUBLE OUR NEW CLUB MEMBER *TOO* MUCH.
HMM. ALL RIGHT, I'LL TRY.

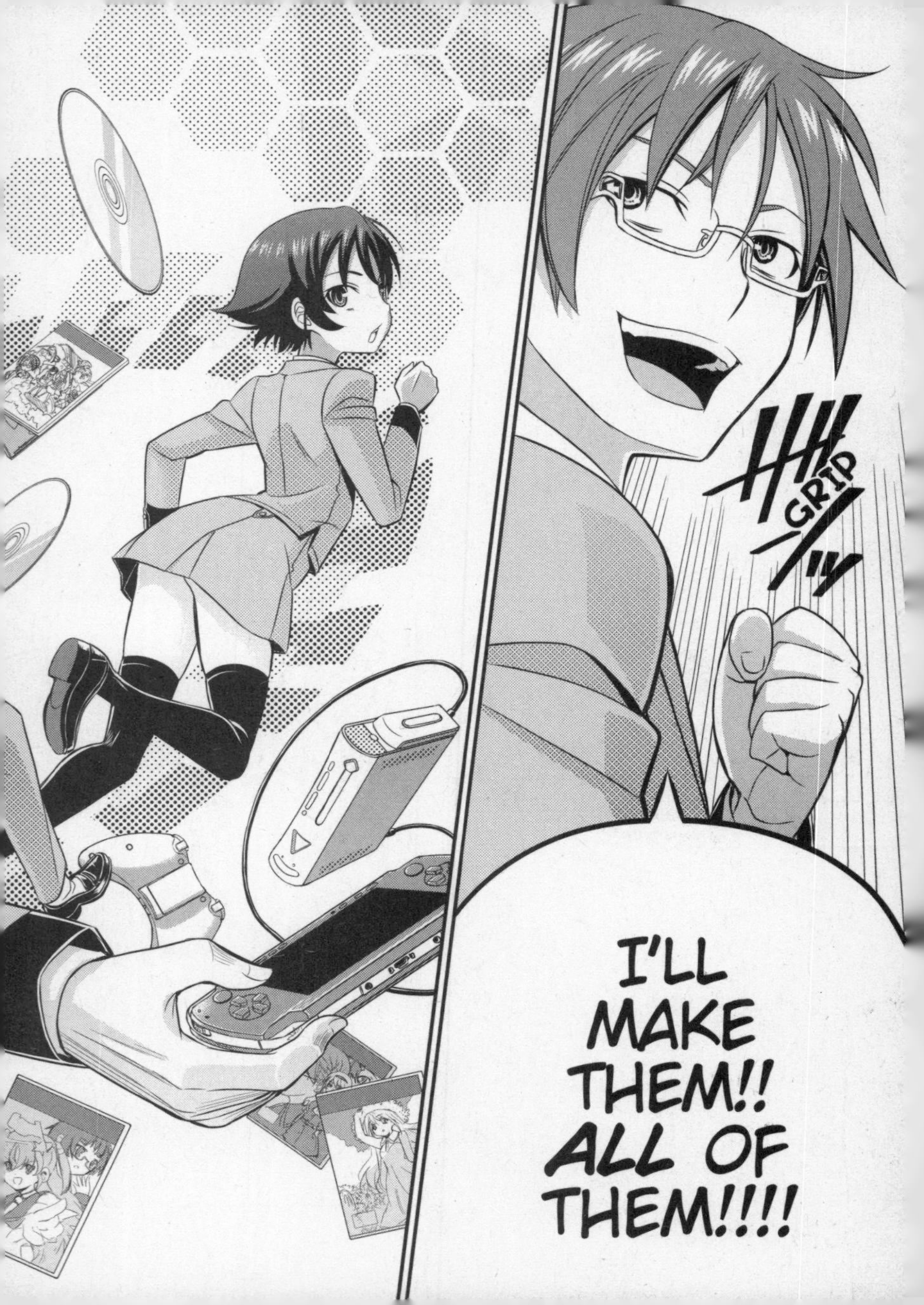
GRIP
I'LL MAKE THEM!! ALL OF THEM!!!!

CHAPTER 1

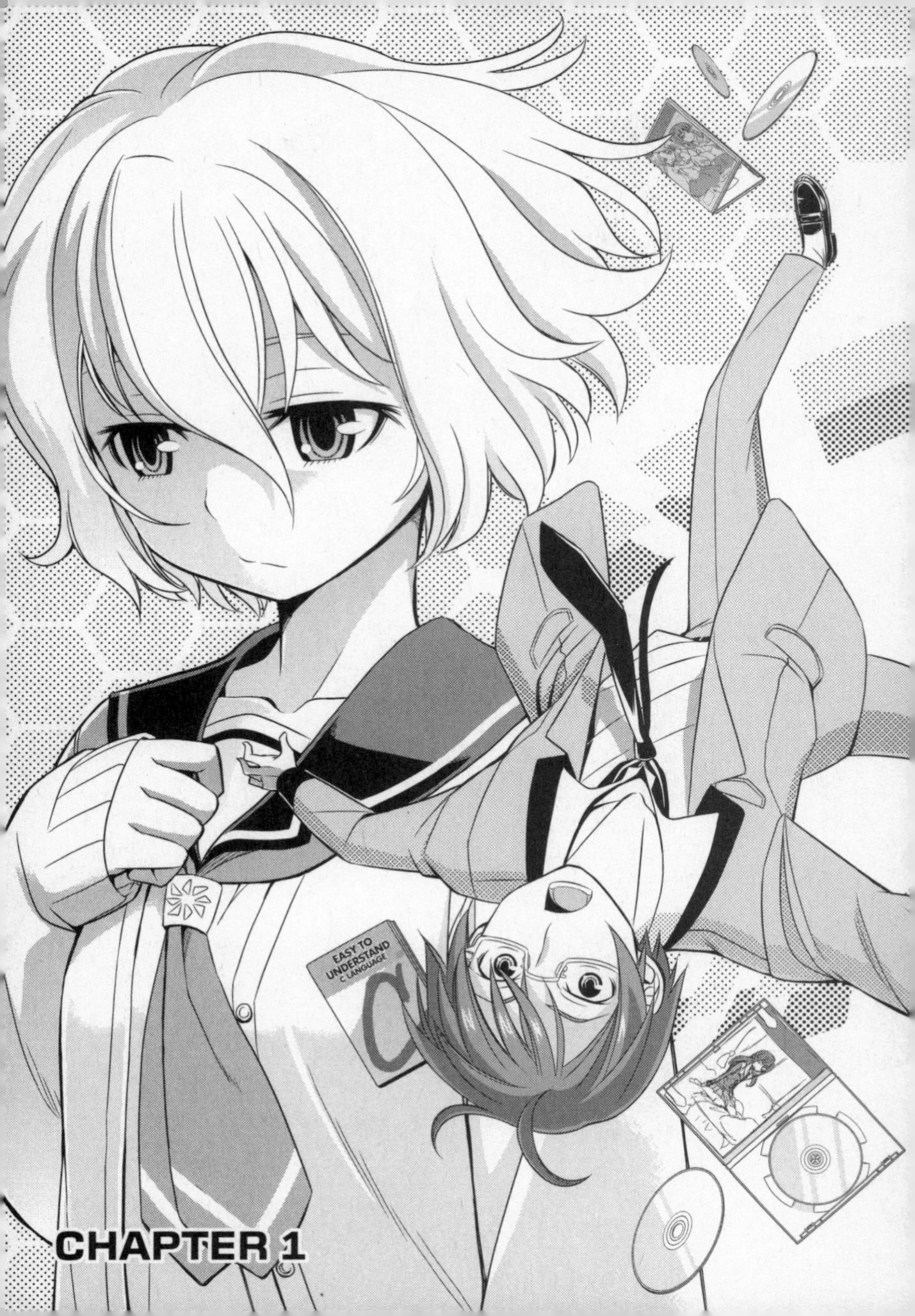
EASY TO UNDERSTAND C LANGUAGE

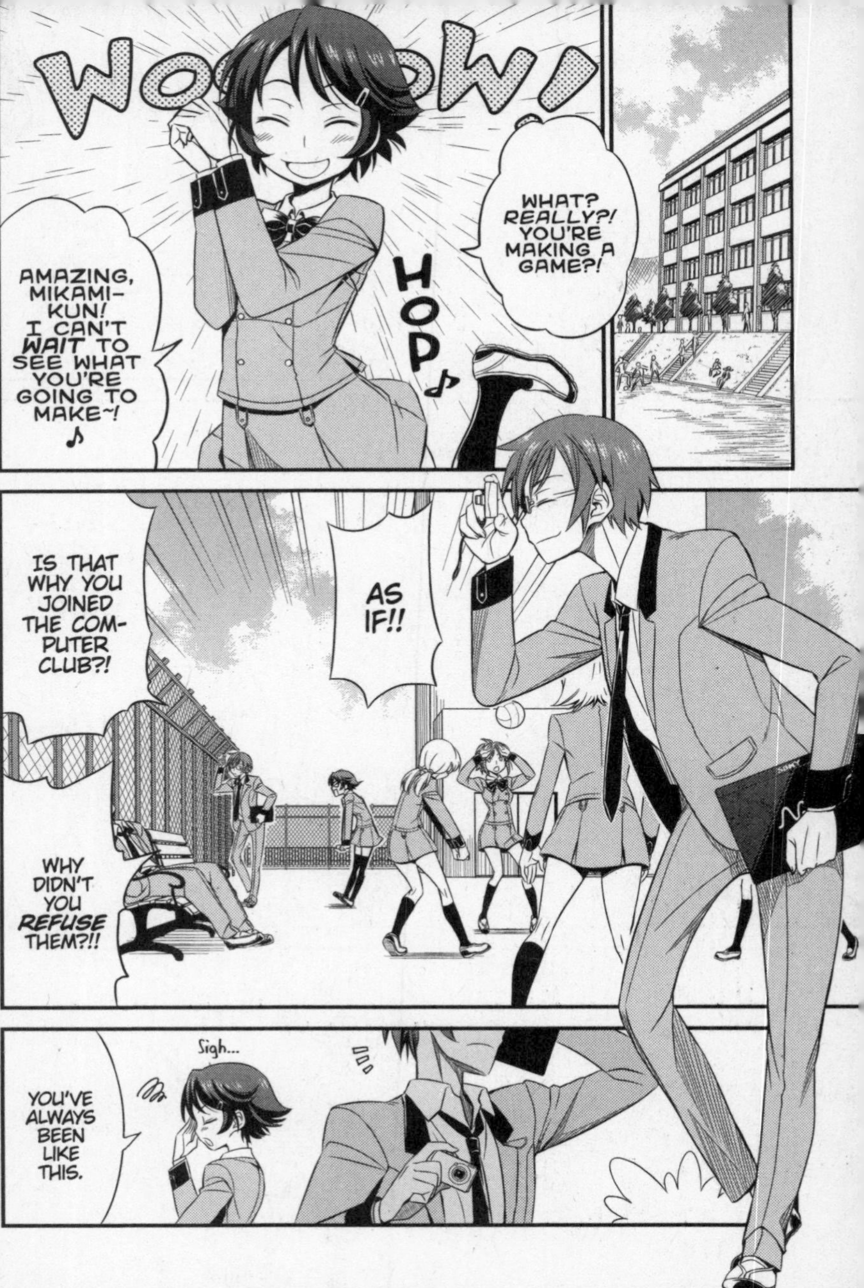
WOOOW!
WHAT? REALLY?! YOU'RE MAKING A GAME?!
HOP♪
AMAZING, MIKAMI-KUN! I CAN'T *WAIT* TO SEE WHAT YOU'RE GOING TO MAKE~! ♪
AS IF!!
IS THAT WHY YOU JOINED THE COMPUTER CLUB?!
WHY DIDN'T YOU *REFUSE* THEM?!!
Sigh...
YOU'VE ALWAYS BEEN LIKE THIS.

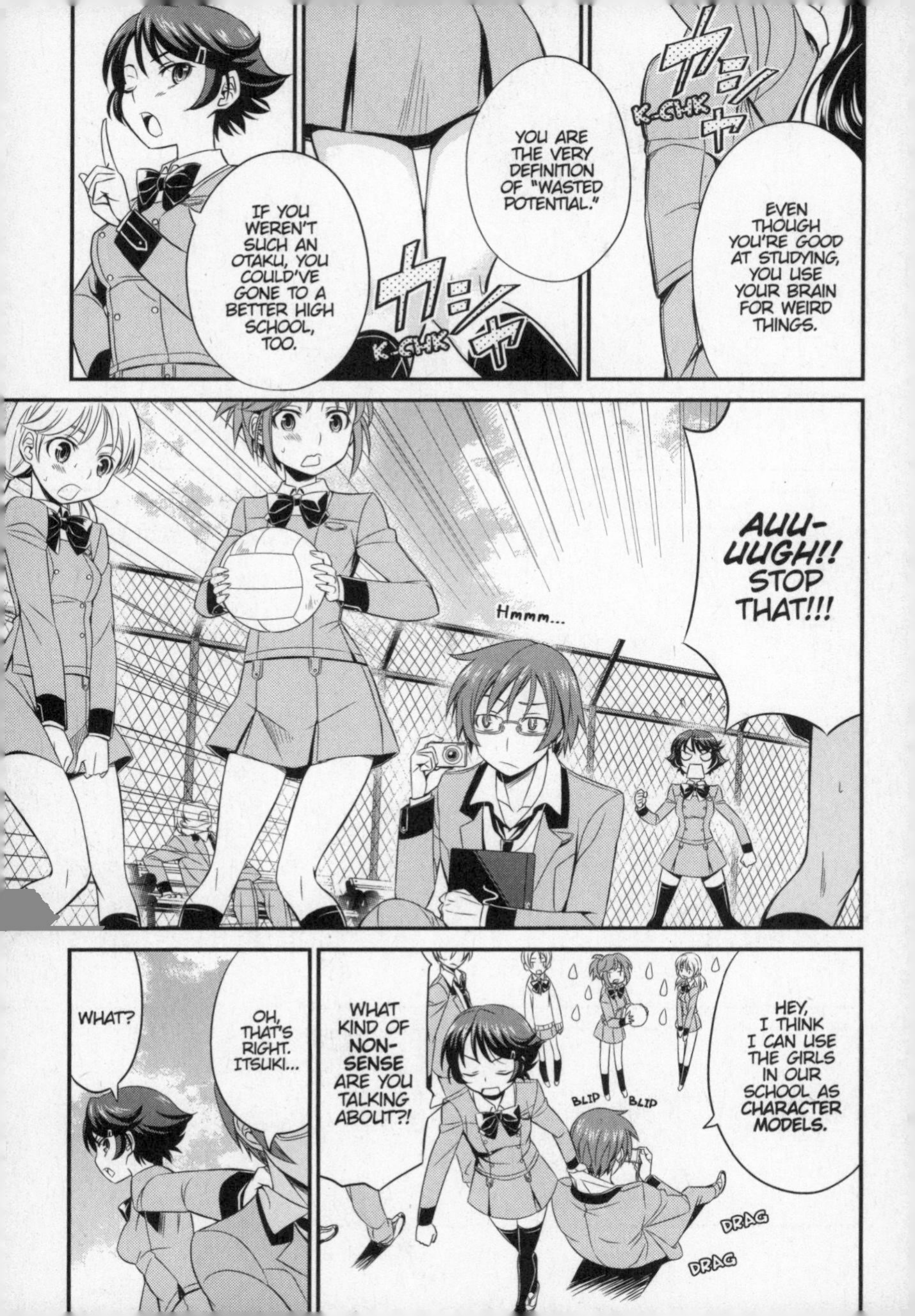
EVEN THOUGH YOU'RE GOOD AT STUDYING, YOU USE YOUR BRAIN FOR WEIRD THINGS.
K-CHK
YOU ARE THE VERY DEFINITION OF "WASTED POTENTIAL."
K-CHK
IF YOU WEREN'T SUCH AN OTAKU, YOU COULD'VE GONE TO A BETTER HIGH SCHOOL, TOO.
AUUU-UUGH!! STOP THAT!!!
Hmmm...
HEY, I THINK I CAN USE THE GIRLS IN OUR SCHOOL AS CHARACTER MODELS.
BLIP
BLIP
WHAT KIND OF NON-SENSE ARE YOU TALKING ABOUT?!
DRAG
DRAG
OH, THAT'S RIGHT. ITSUKI...
WHAT?

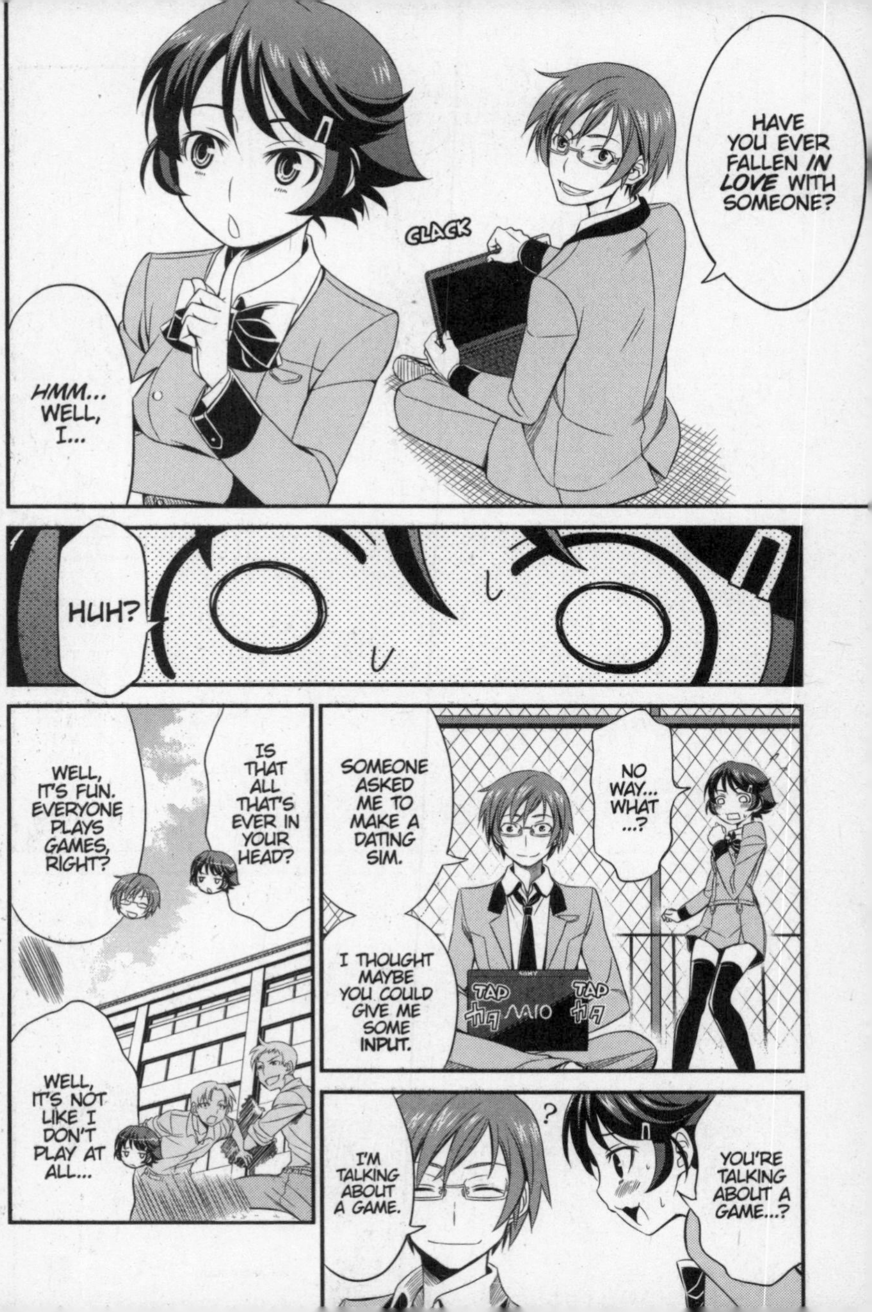
HAVE YOU EVER FALLEN *IN LOVE* WITH SOMEONE?
CLACK
HMM... WELL, I...
HUH?
NO WAY... WHAT ...?
SOMEONE ASKED ME TO MAKE A DATING SIM.
I THOUGHT MAYBE YOU COULD GIVE ME SOME INPUT.
TAP カタ
TAP カタ
YOU'RE TALKING ABOUT A GAME...?
I'M TALKING ABOUT A GAME.
IS THAT ALL THAT'S EVER IN YOUR HEAD?
WELL, IT'S FUN. EVERYONE PLAYS GAMES, RIGHT?
WELL, IT'S NOT LIKE I DON'T PLAY AT ALL...

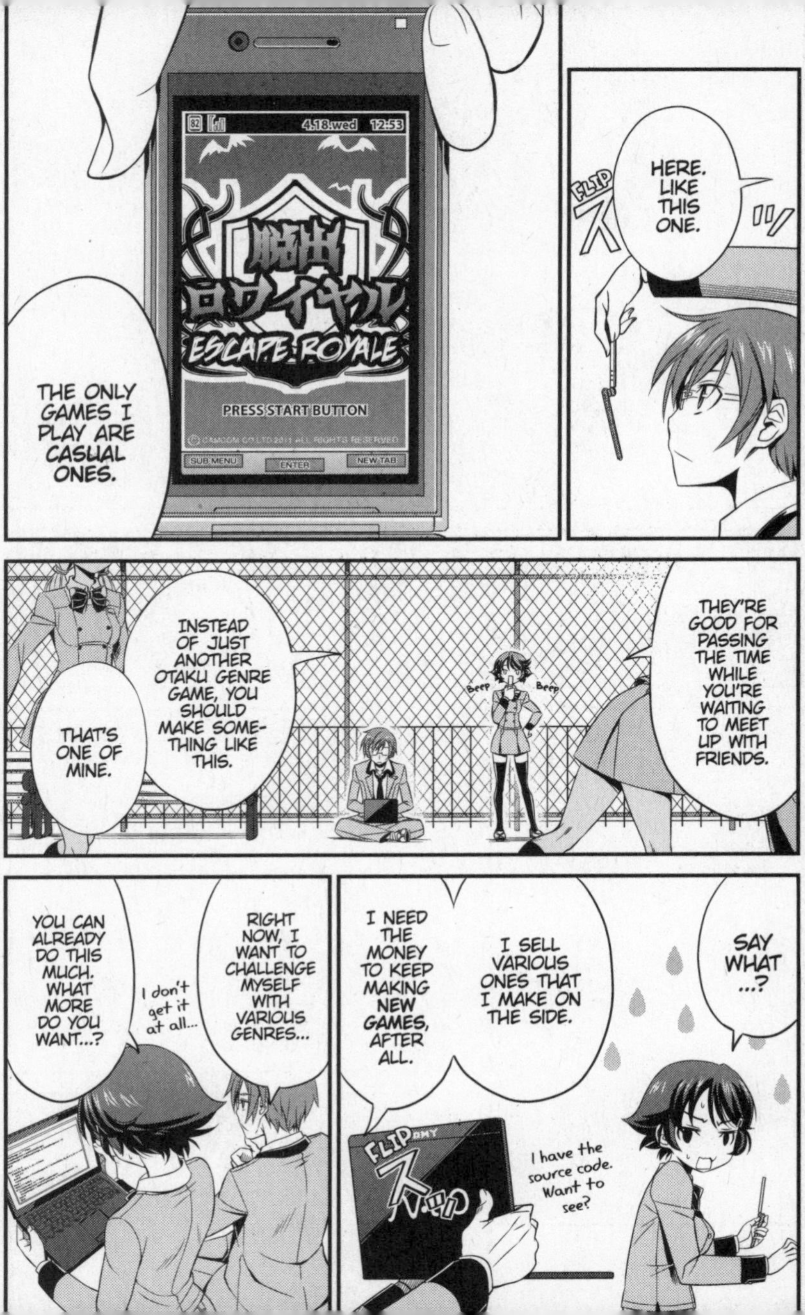
FLIP
HERE. LIKE THIS ONE.
4.18.wed 12:53
脱出ロワイヤル
ESCAPE ROYALE
PRESS START BUTTON
SUB MENU
ENTER
NEW TAB
THE ONLY GAMES I PLAY ARE CASUAL ONES.
THEY'RE GOOD FOR PASSING THE TIME WHILE YOU'RE WAITING TO MEET UP WITH FRIENDS.
Beep
Beep
INSTEAD OF JUST ANOTHER OTAKU GENRE GAME, YOU SHOULD MAKE SOME-THING LIKE THIS.
THAT'S ONE OF MINE.
SAY WHAT ...?
I SELL VARIOUS ONES THAT I MAKE ON THE SIDE.
I NEED THE MONEY TO KEEP MAKING NEW GAMES, AFTER ALL.
FLIP
I have the source code. Want to see?
RIGHT NOW, I WANT TO CHALLENGE MYSELF WITH VARIOUS GENRES...
I don't get it at all...
YOU CAN ALREADY DO THIS MUCH. WHAT MORE DO YOU WANT...?

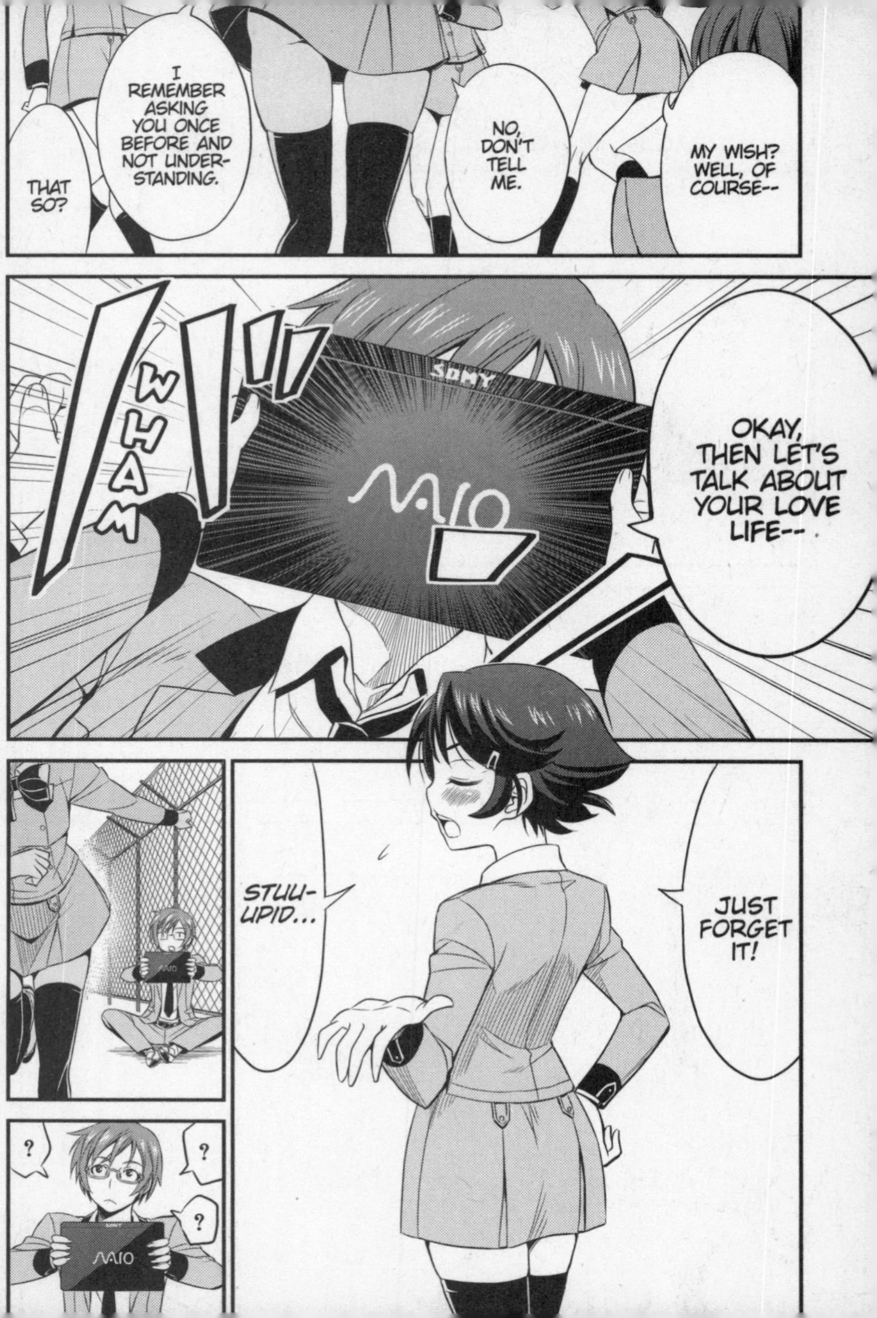
MY WISH? WELL, OF COURSE--
NO, DON'T TELL ME.
I REMEMBER ASKING YOU ONCE BEFORE AND NOT UNDER-STANDING.
THAT SO?
OKAY, THEN LET'S TALK ABOUT YOUR LOVE LIFE--.
WHAM
JUST FORGET IT!
STUU-UPID...
?
?
?

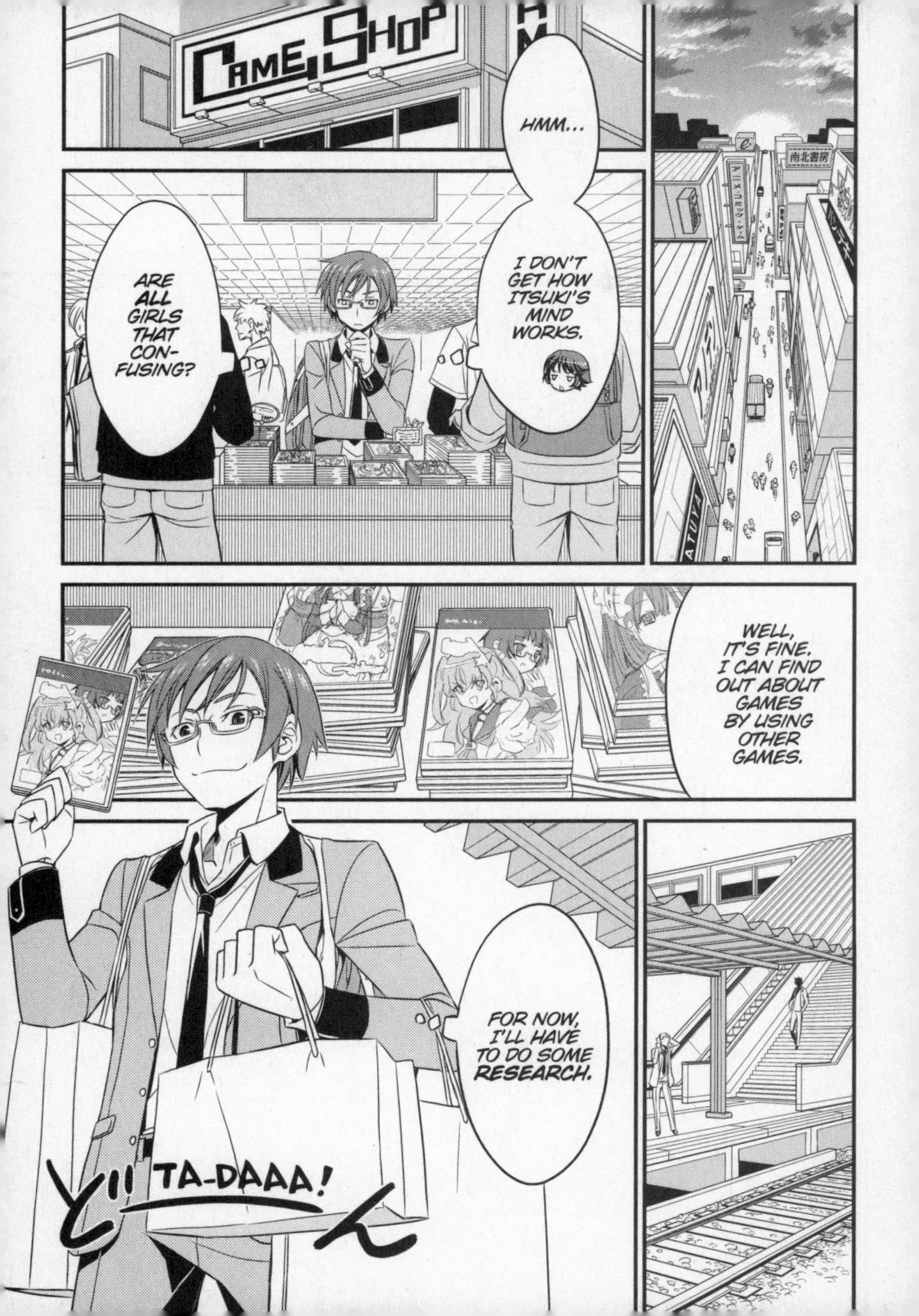
GAME SHOP
HMM...
I DON'T GET HOW ITSUKI'S MIND WORKS.
ARE ALL GIRLS THAT CON-FUSING?
WELL, IT'S FINE. I CAN FIND OUT ABOUT GAMES BY USING OTHER GAMES.
FOR NOW, I'LL HAVE TO DO SOME RESEARCH.
TA-DAAA!

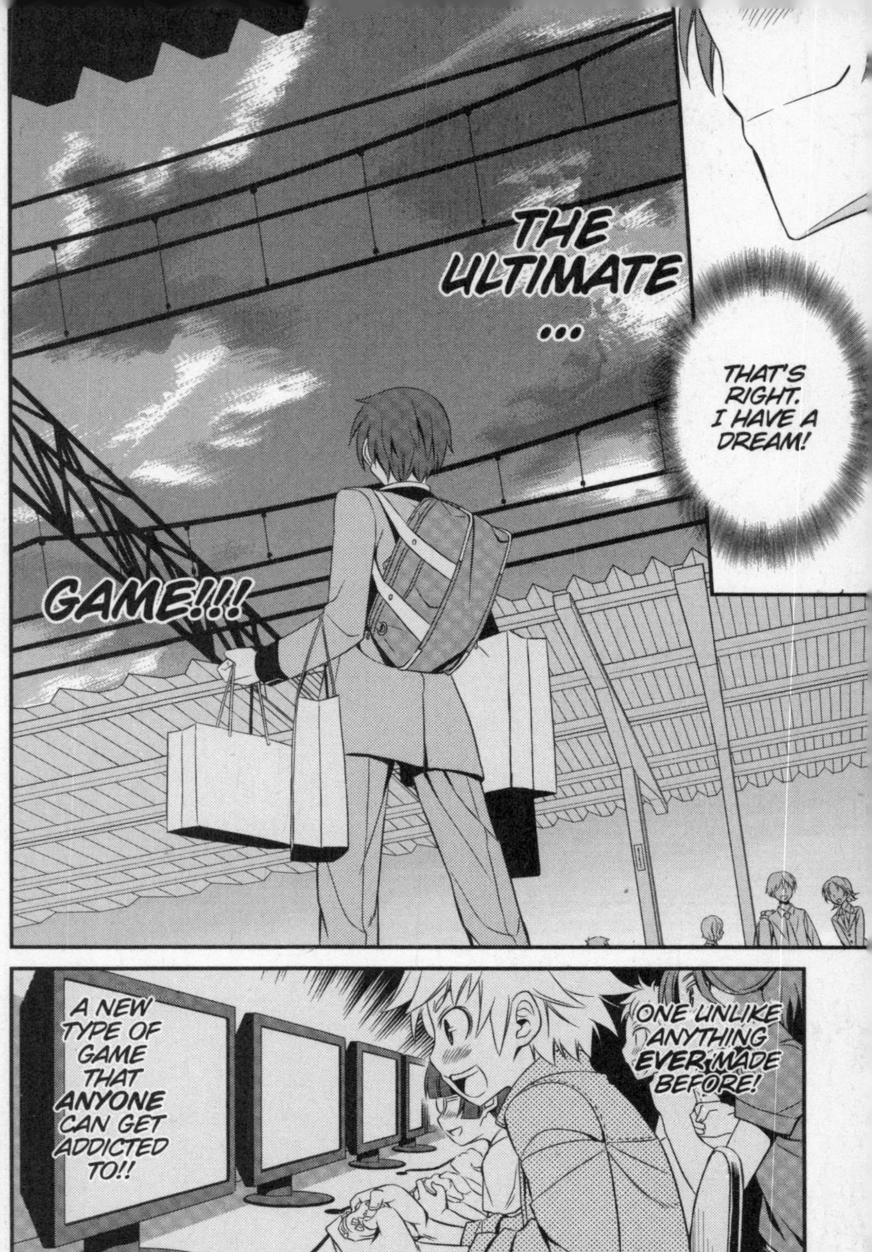
THAT'S RIGHT. I HAVE A DREAM!
THE ULTIMATE ...
GAME!!!
ONE UNLIKE ANYTHING EVER MADE BEFORE!
A NEW TYPE OF GAME THAT ANYONE CAN GET ADDICTED TO!!

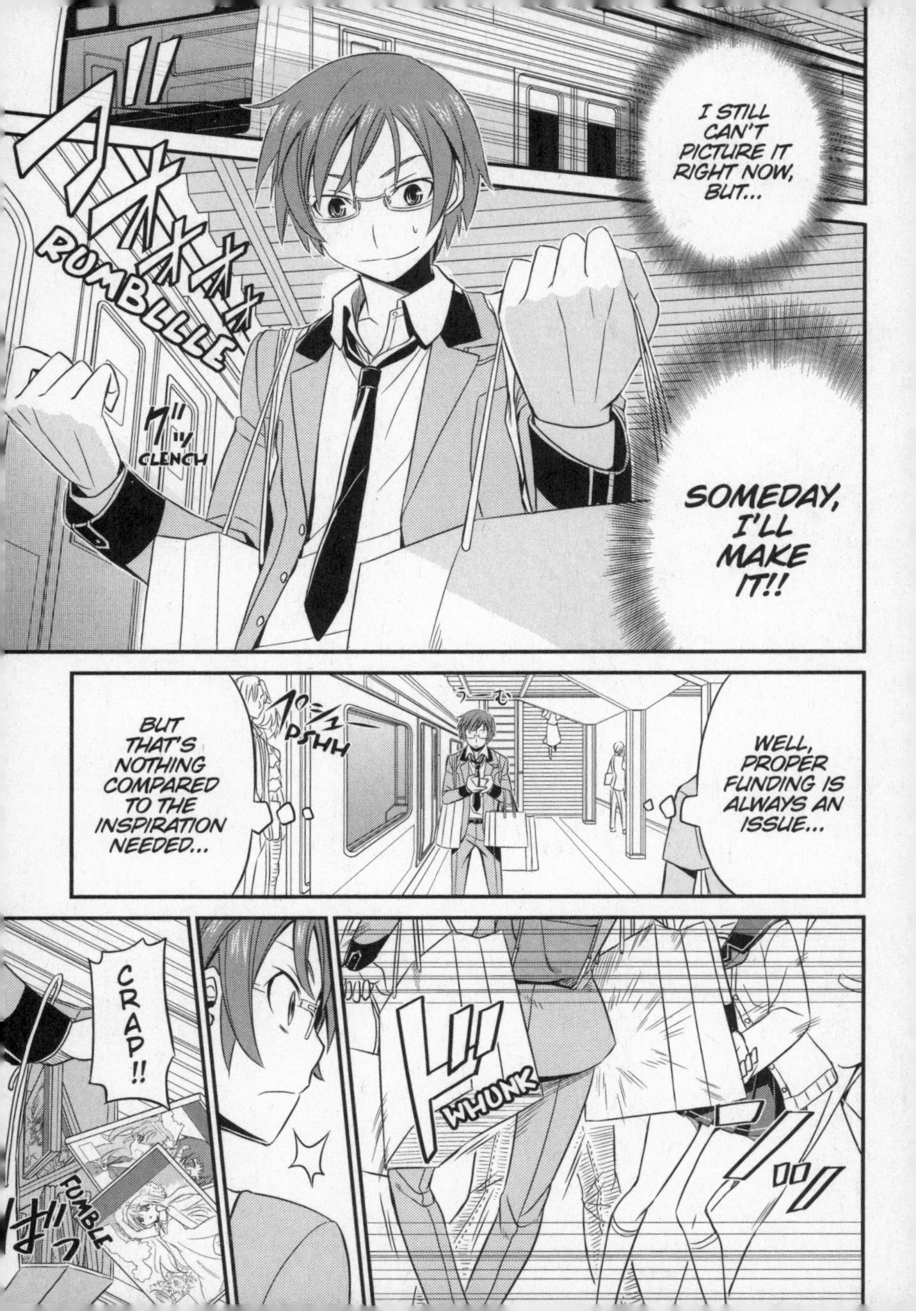
I STILL CAN'T PICTURE IT RIGHT NOW, BUT...
SOMEDAY, I'LL MAKE IT!!
RUMBLLLE
CLENCH
WELL, PROPER FUNDING IS ALWAYS AN ISSUE...
PSHH
BUT THAT'S NOTHING COMPARED TO THE INSPIRATION NEEDED...
WHUNK
CRAP!!
FUMBLE

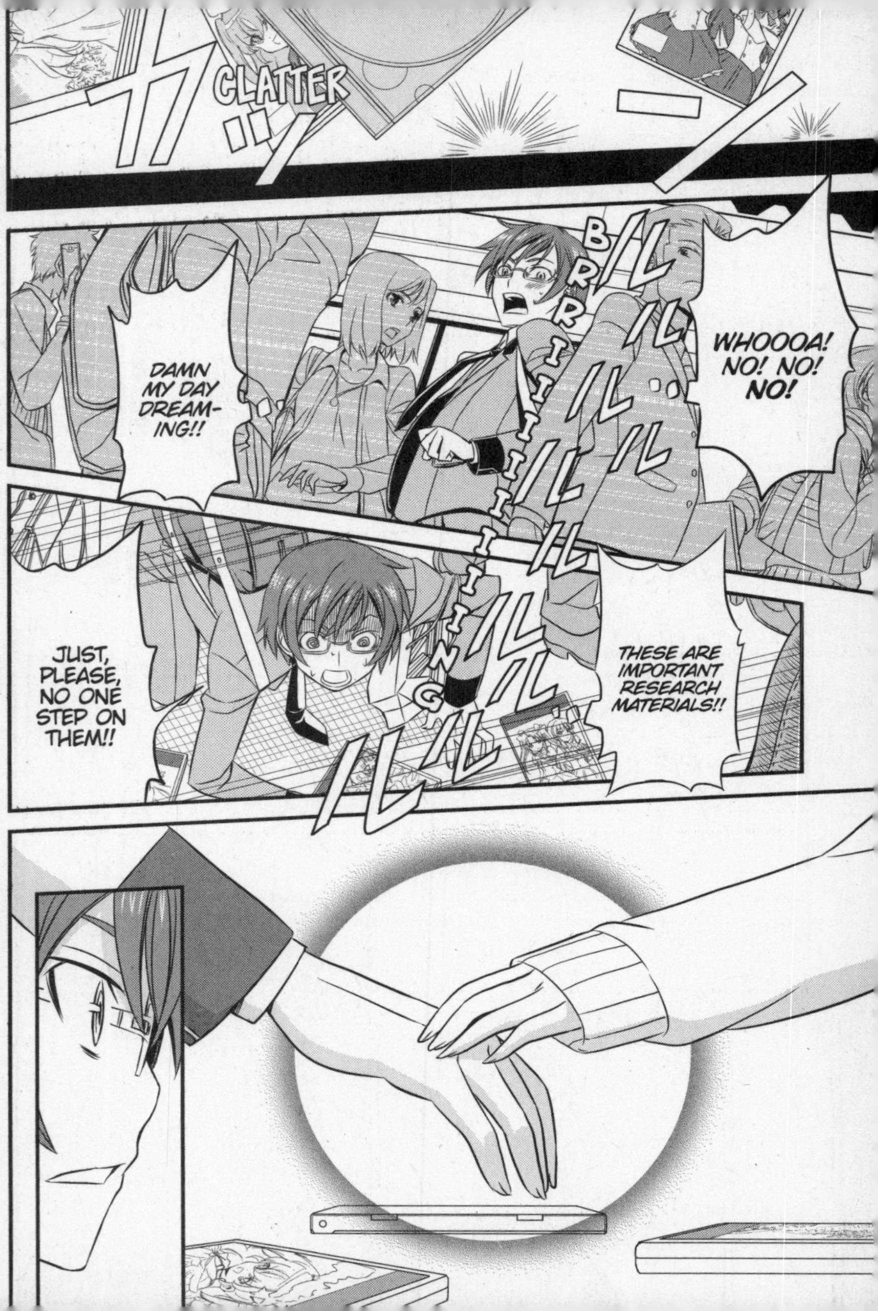
CLATTER
WHOOOA! NO! NO! NO!
BRRIIIIIIIIING
DAMN MY DAY DREAMING!!
THESE ARE IMPORTANT RESEARCH MATERIALS!!
JUST, PLEASE, NO ONE STEP ON THEM!!

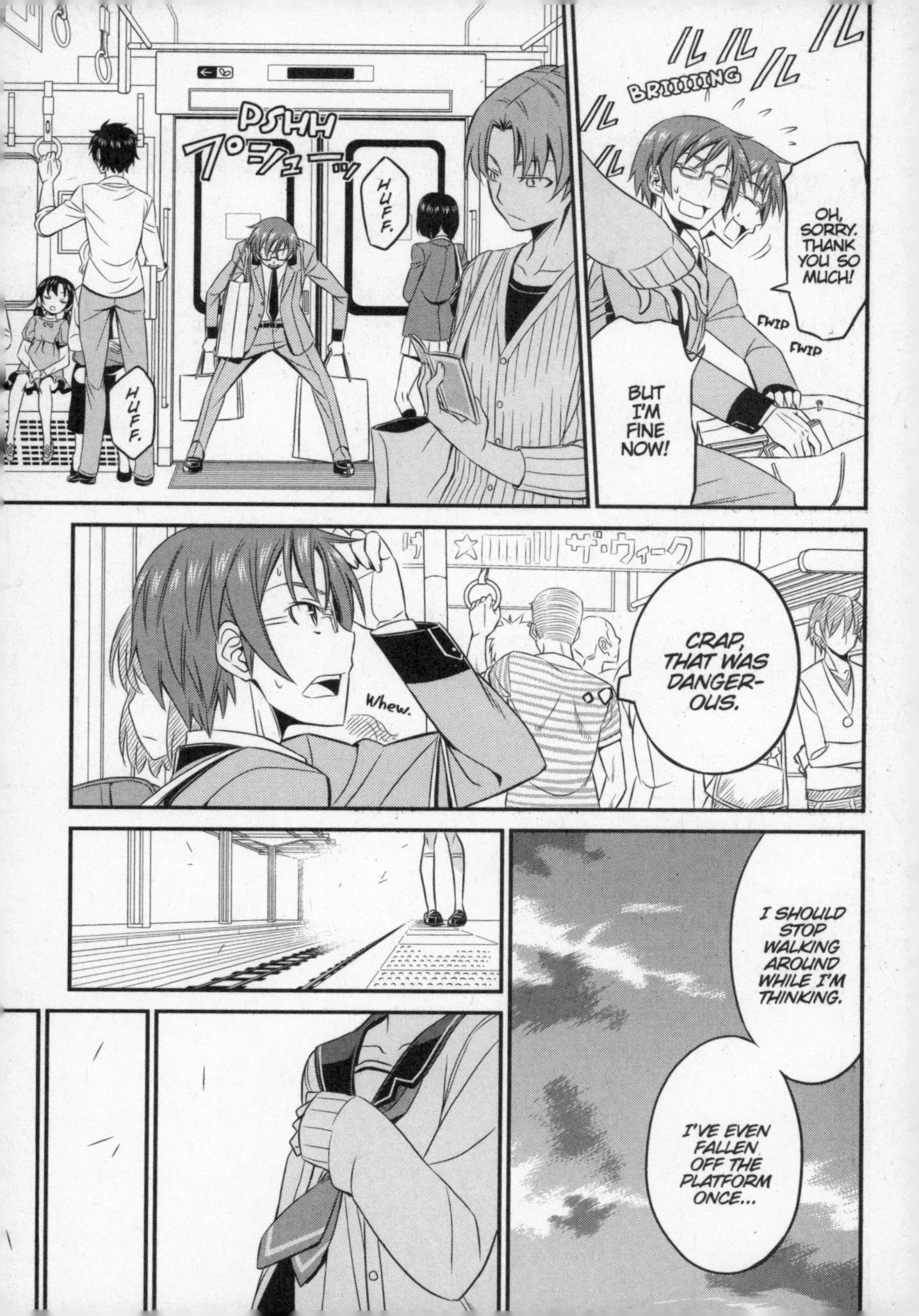
BRIIIIIING
OH, SORRY. THANK YOU SO MUCH!
FWIP
FWIP
BUT I'M FINE NOW!
PSHH
プシュー
HUFF.
HUFF.
CRAP, THAT WAS DANGER-OUS.
Whew.
I SHOULD STOP WALKING AROUND WHILE I'M THINKING.
I'VE EVEN FALLEN OFF THE PLATFORM ONCE...

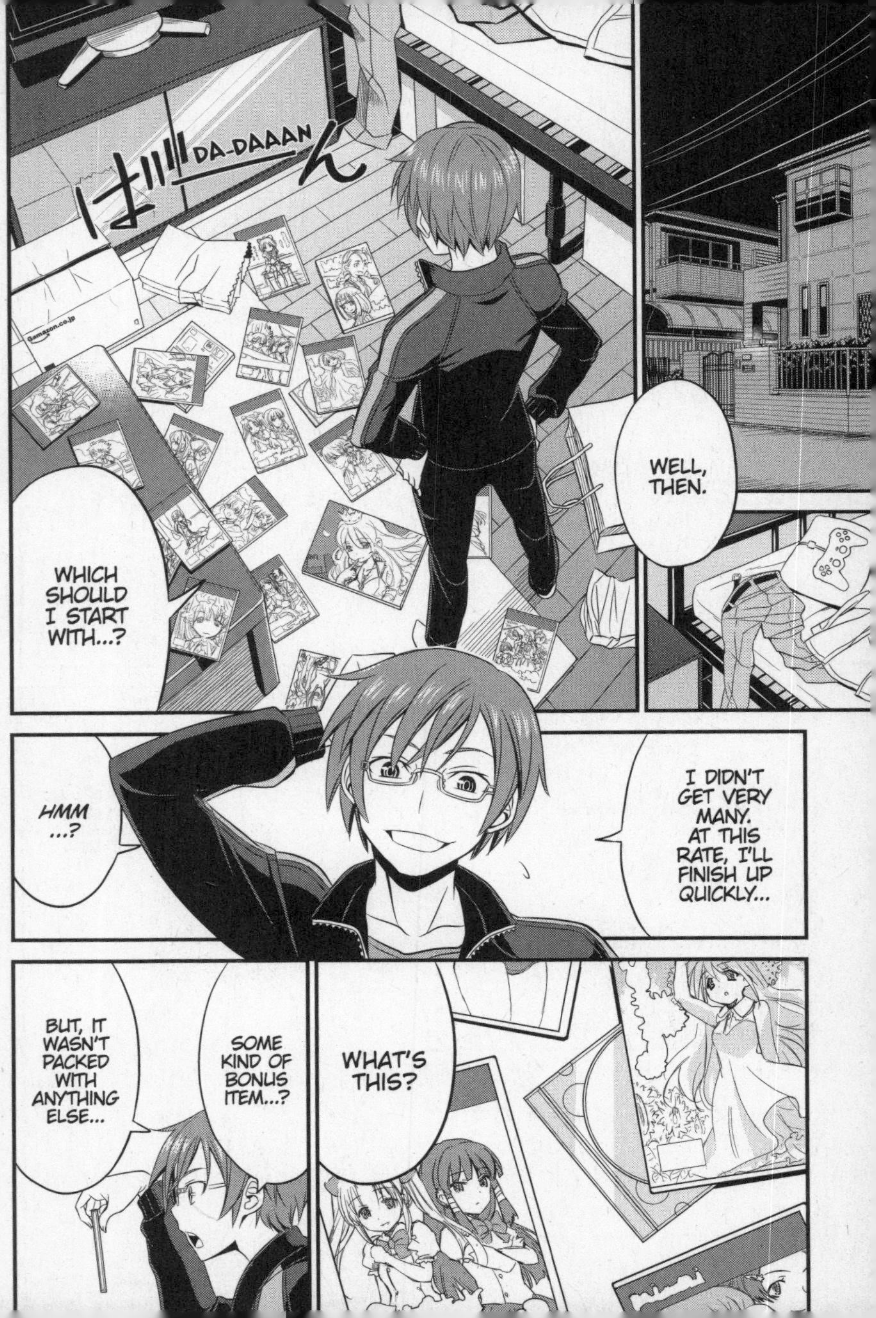
WELL, THEN.
DA-DAAAN
WHICH SHOULD I START WITH...?
I DIDN'T GET VERY MANY. AT THIS RATE, I'LL FINISH UP QUICKLY...
HMM ...?
WHAT'S THIS?
SOME KIND OF BONUS ITEM...?
BUT, IT WASN'T PACKED WITH ANYTHING ELSE...

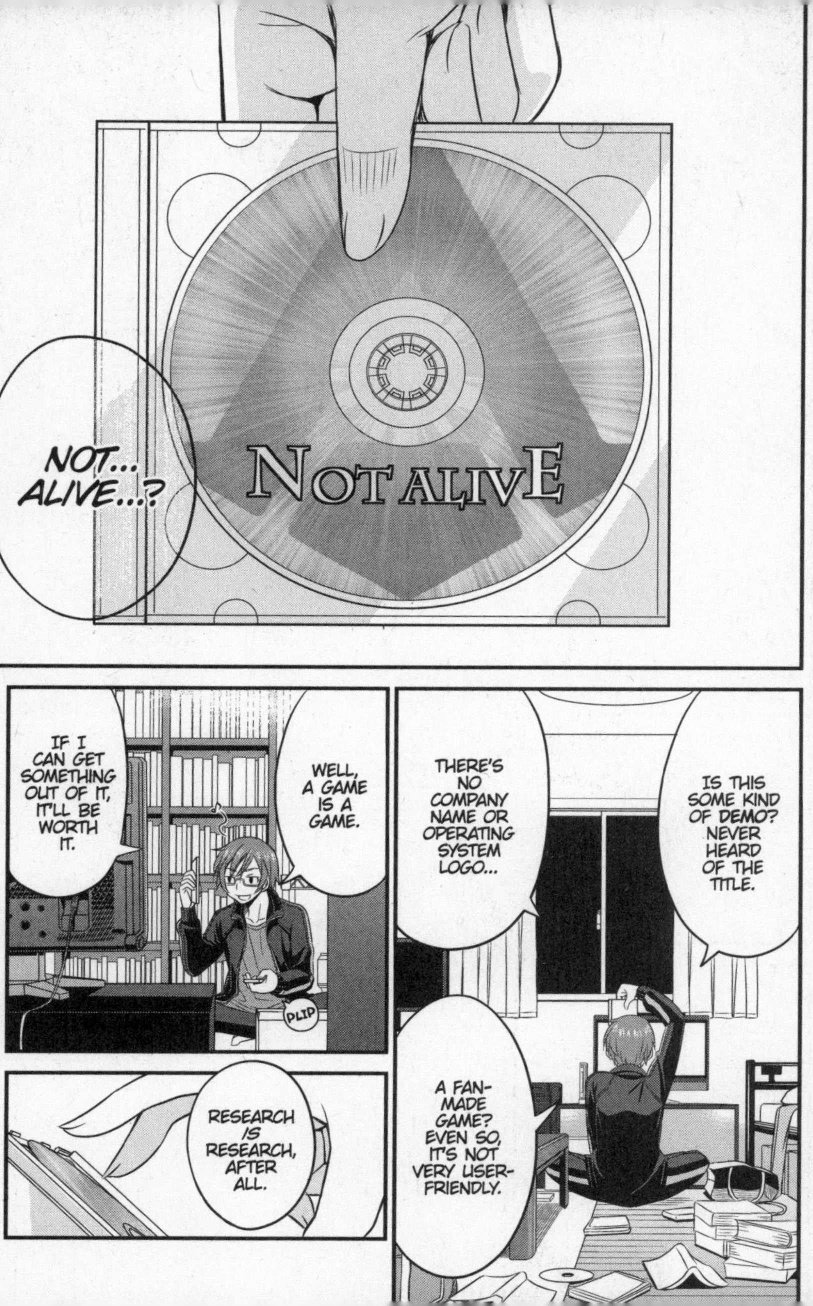
NOT ALIVE
NOT... ALIVE...?
IS THIS SOME KIND OF DEMO? NEVER HEARD OF THE TITLE.
THERE'S NO COMPANY NAME OR OPERATING SYSTEM LOGO...
A FAN-MADE GAME? EVEN SO, IT'S NOT VERY USER-FRIENDLY.
WELL, A GAME IS A GAME.
IF I CAN GET SOMETHING OUT OF IT, IT'LL BE WORTH IT.
PLIP
RESEARCH IS RESEARCH, AFTER ALL.

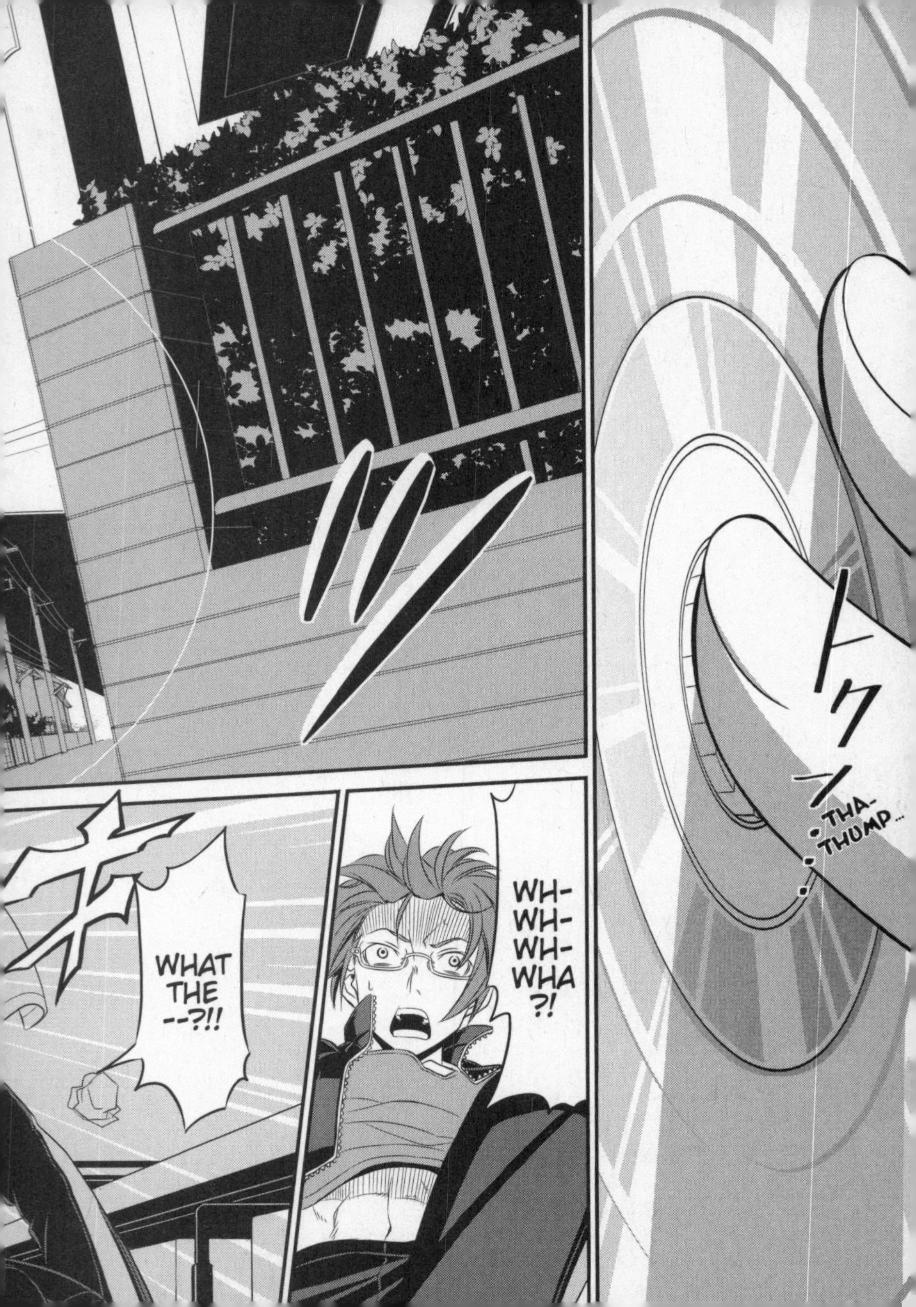

トクン
THA-THUMP...
WH-WH-WH-WHA?!
WHAT THE--?!!

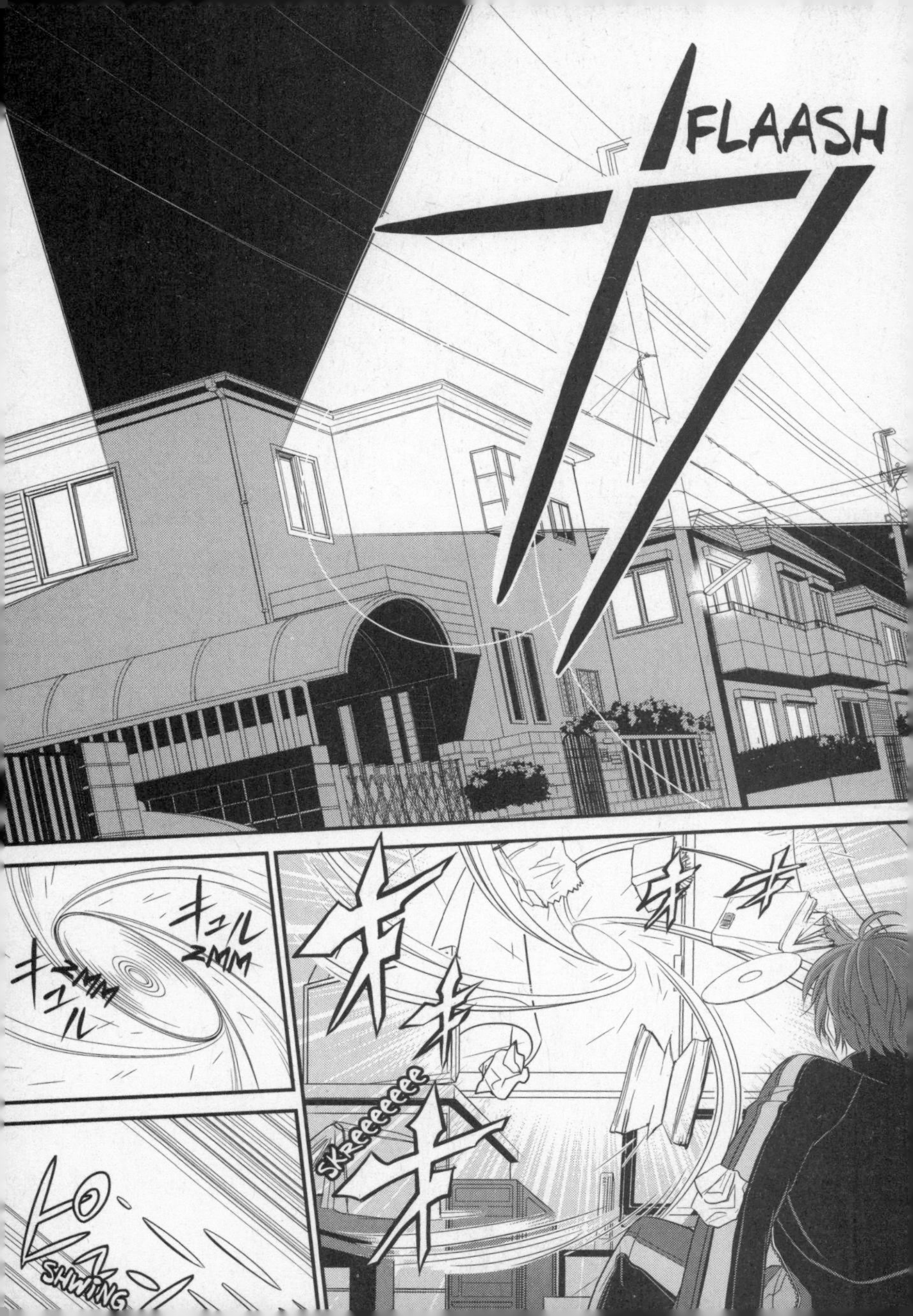
FLAASH
SKREEEEEEE
キュル
ZMM
キュル
ZMM
SHWING

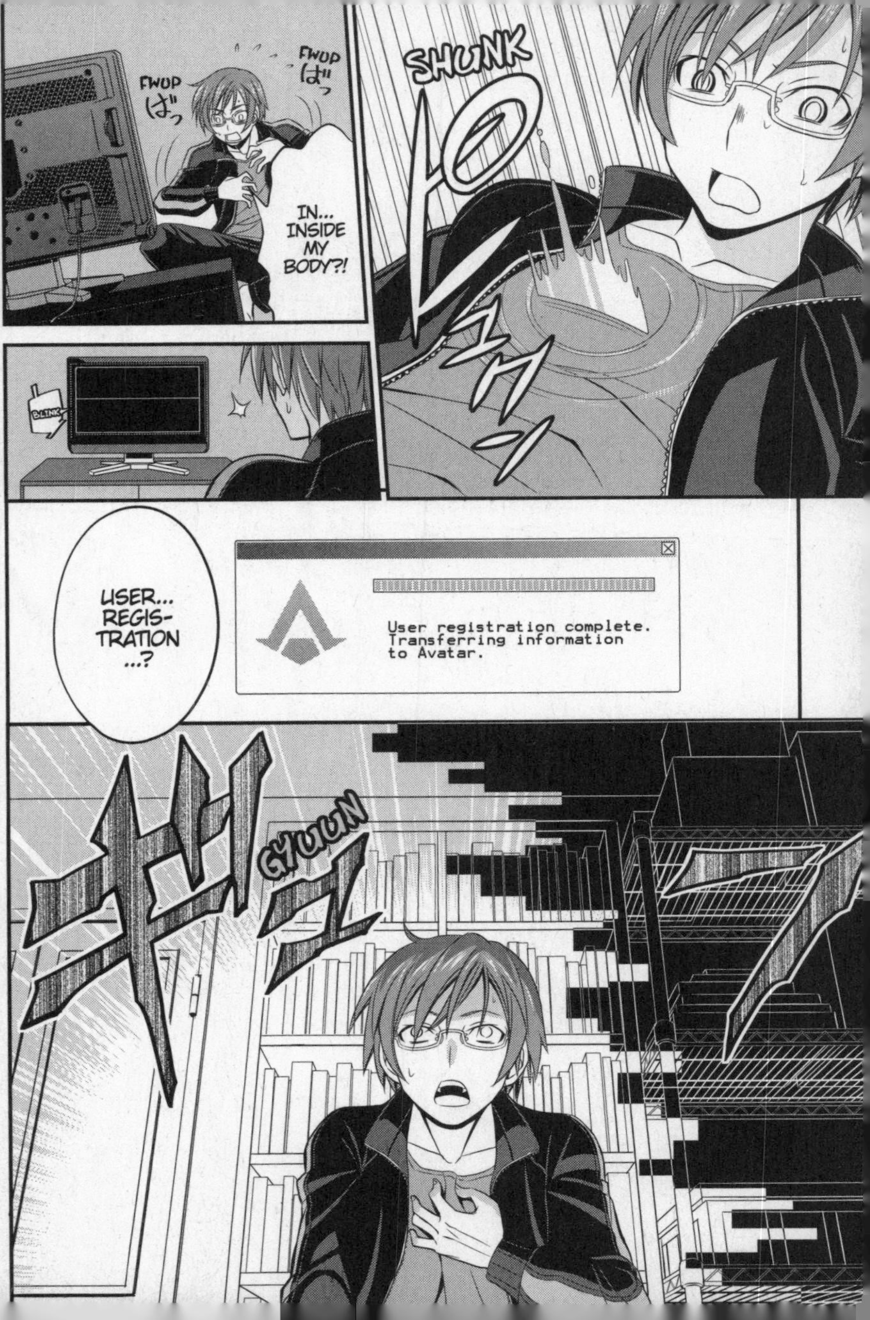
SHUNK
FWUP ばっ
FWUP ばっ
IN... INSIDE MY BODY?!
BLINK
User registration complete. Transferring information to Avatar.
USER... REGIS-TRATION ...?
GYUUN

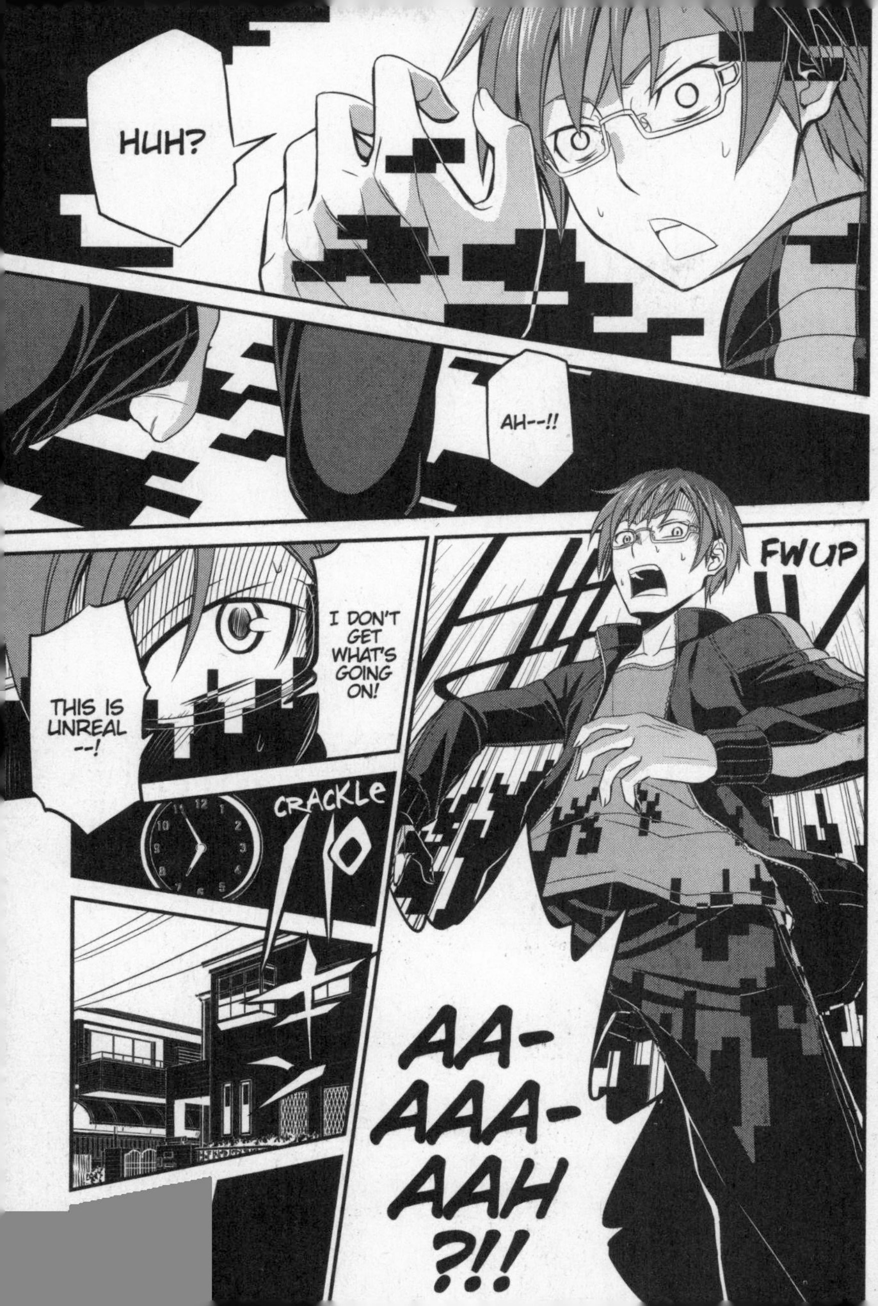
HUH?
AH--!!
FWUP
AA-AAA-AAH?!!
I DON'T GET WHAT'S GOING ON!
THIS IS UNREAL--!
CRACKLE

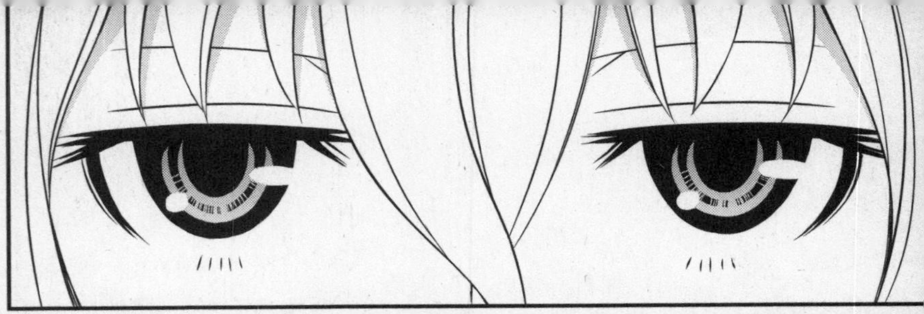
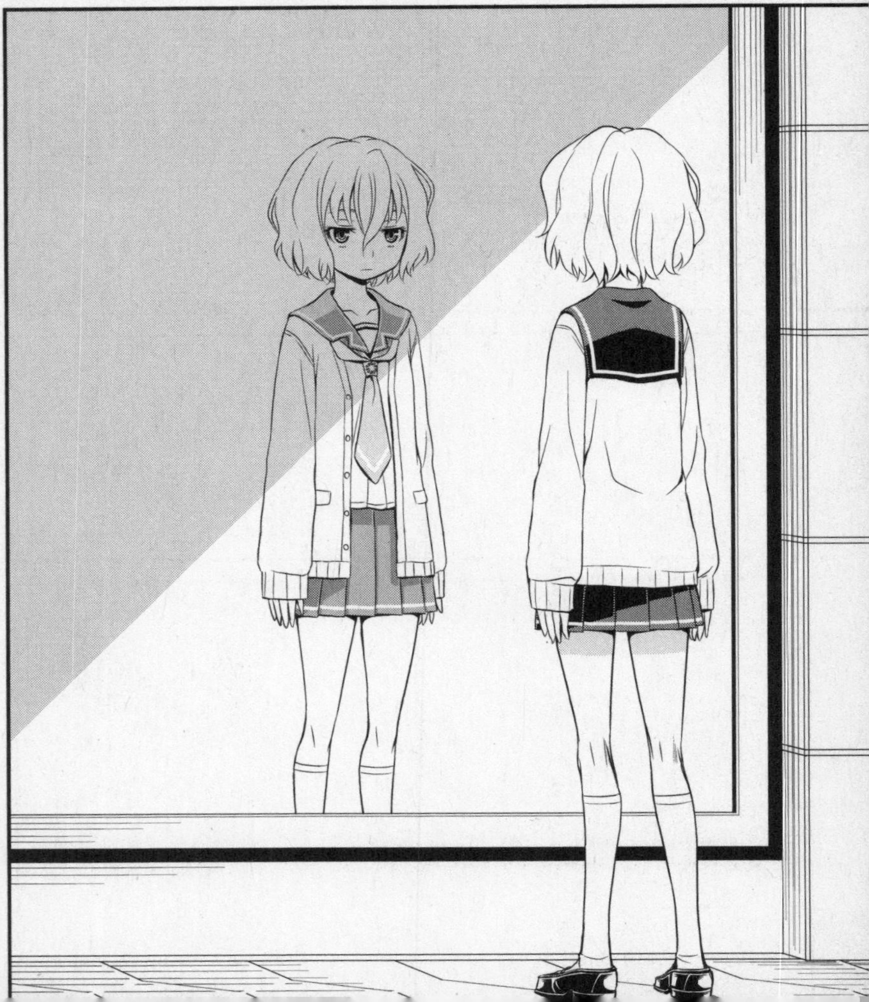

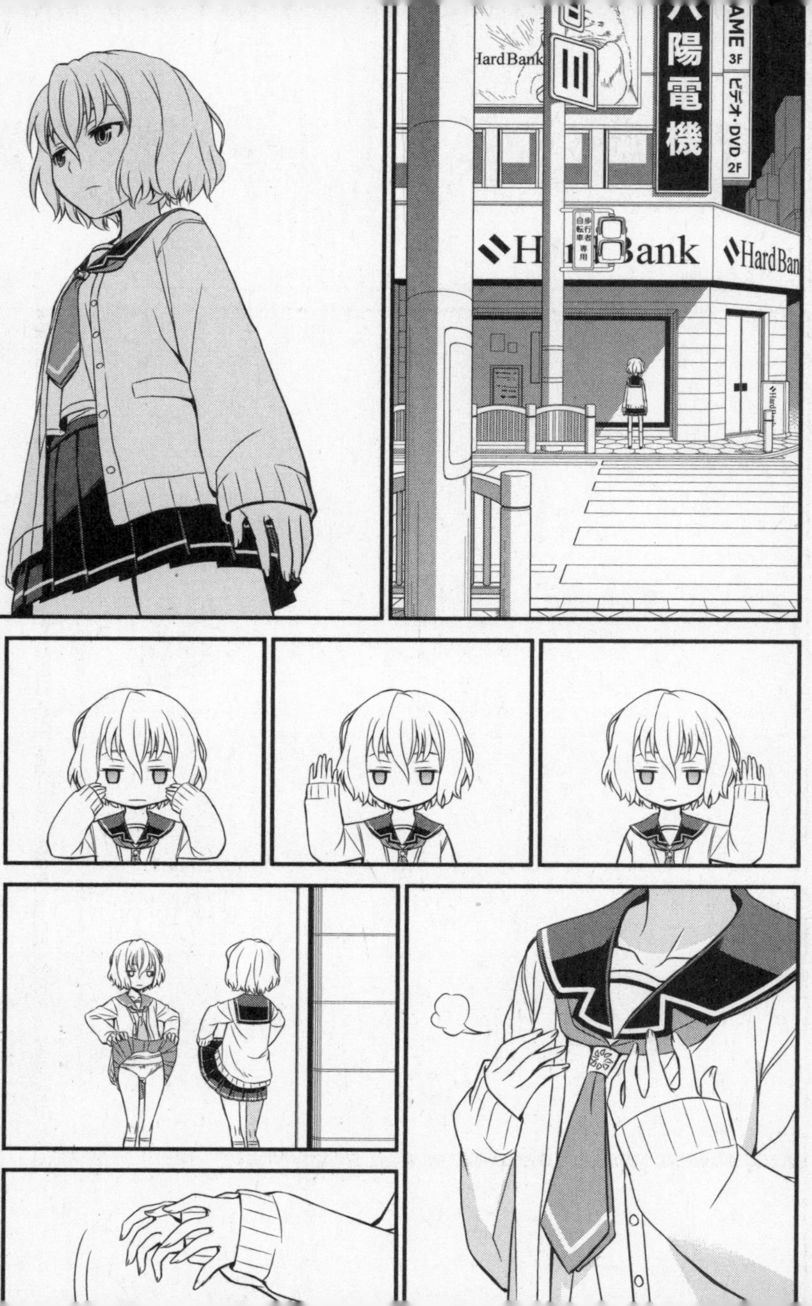
陽電機
AME 3F
ビデオ・DVD 2F
HardBank
歩行者自転車専用
HardBank
HardBan

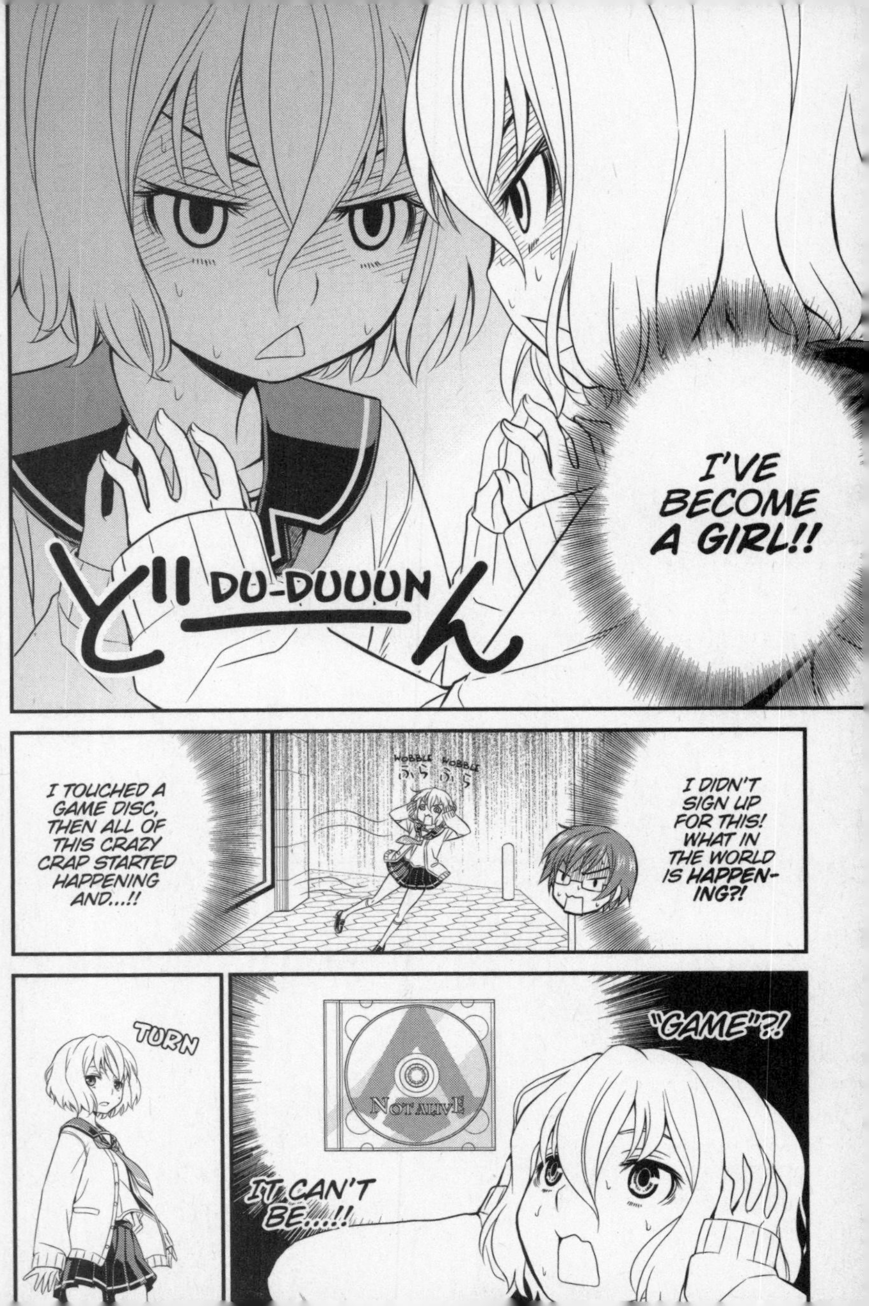

I'VE BECOME A GIRL!!
DU-DUUUN
I DIDN'T SIGN UP FOR THIS! WHAT IN THE WORLD IS HAPPENING?!
WOBBLE WOBBLE
I TOUCHED A GAME DISC, THEN ALL OF THIS CRAZY CRAP STARTED HAPPENING AND...!!
"GAME"?!
NOT ALIVE
IT CAN'T BE...!!
TURN

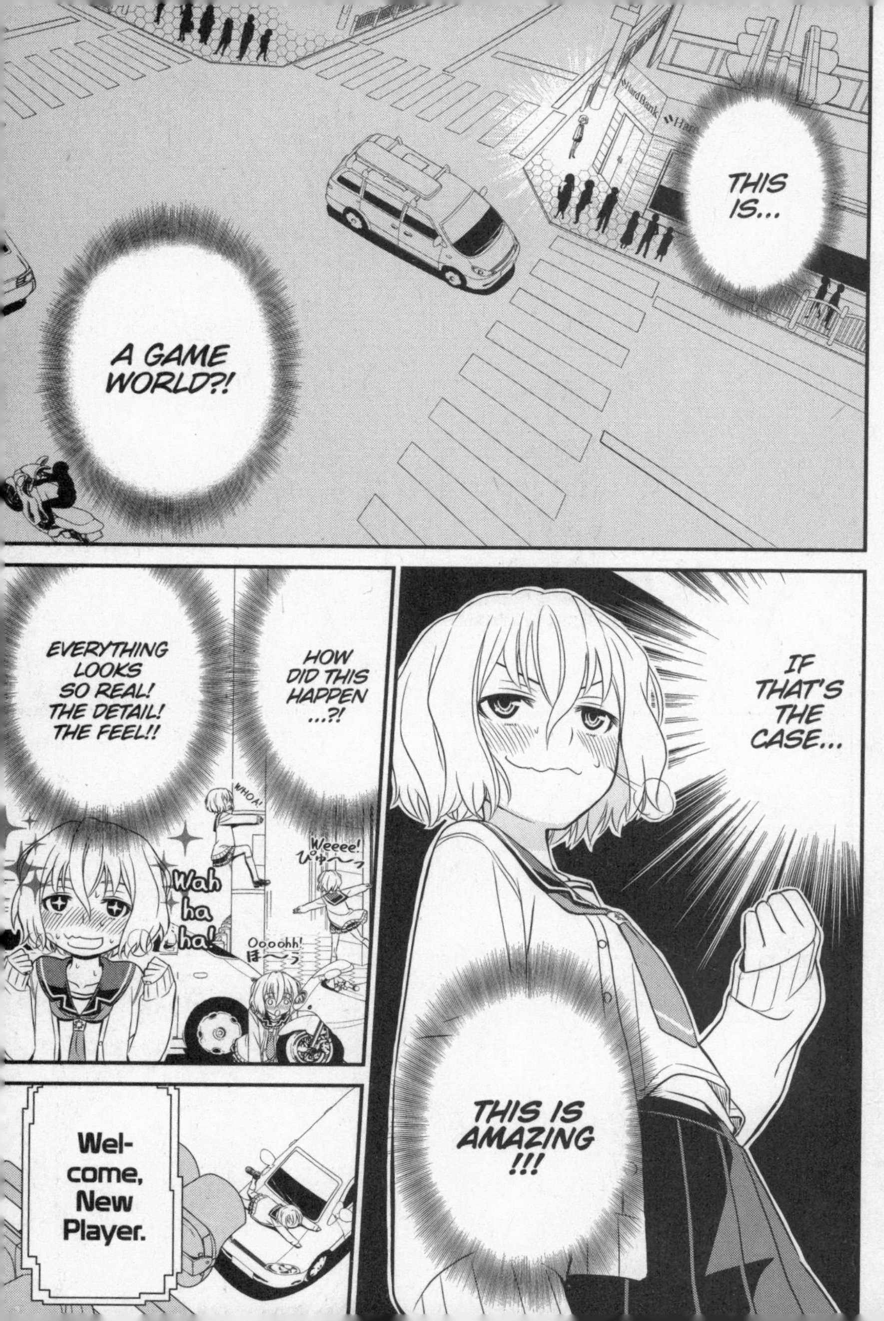
THIS IS...
A GAME WORLD?!
IF THAT'S THE CASE...
THIS IS AMAZING!!!
HOW DID THIS HAPPEN ...?!
EVERYTHING LOOKS SO REAL! THE DETAIL! THE FEEL!!
WHOA!
Weeee! ぴゅ〜っ
Wah ha ha!
Ooooohh! ほ〜っ
Wel-come, New Player.

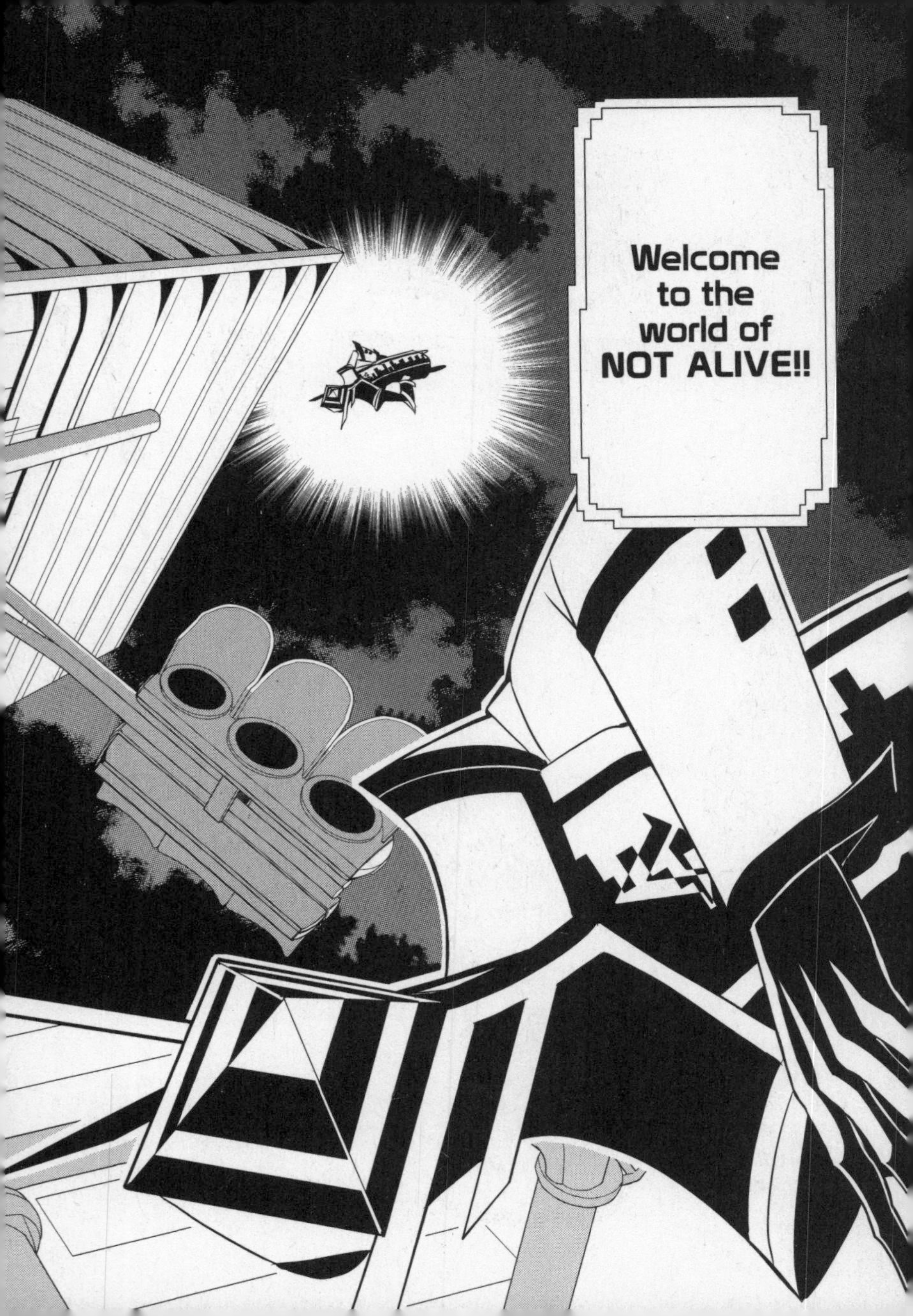
Welcome to the world of NOT ALIVE!!

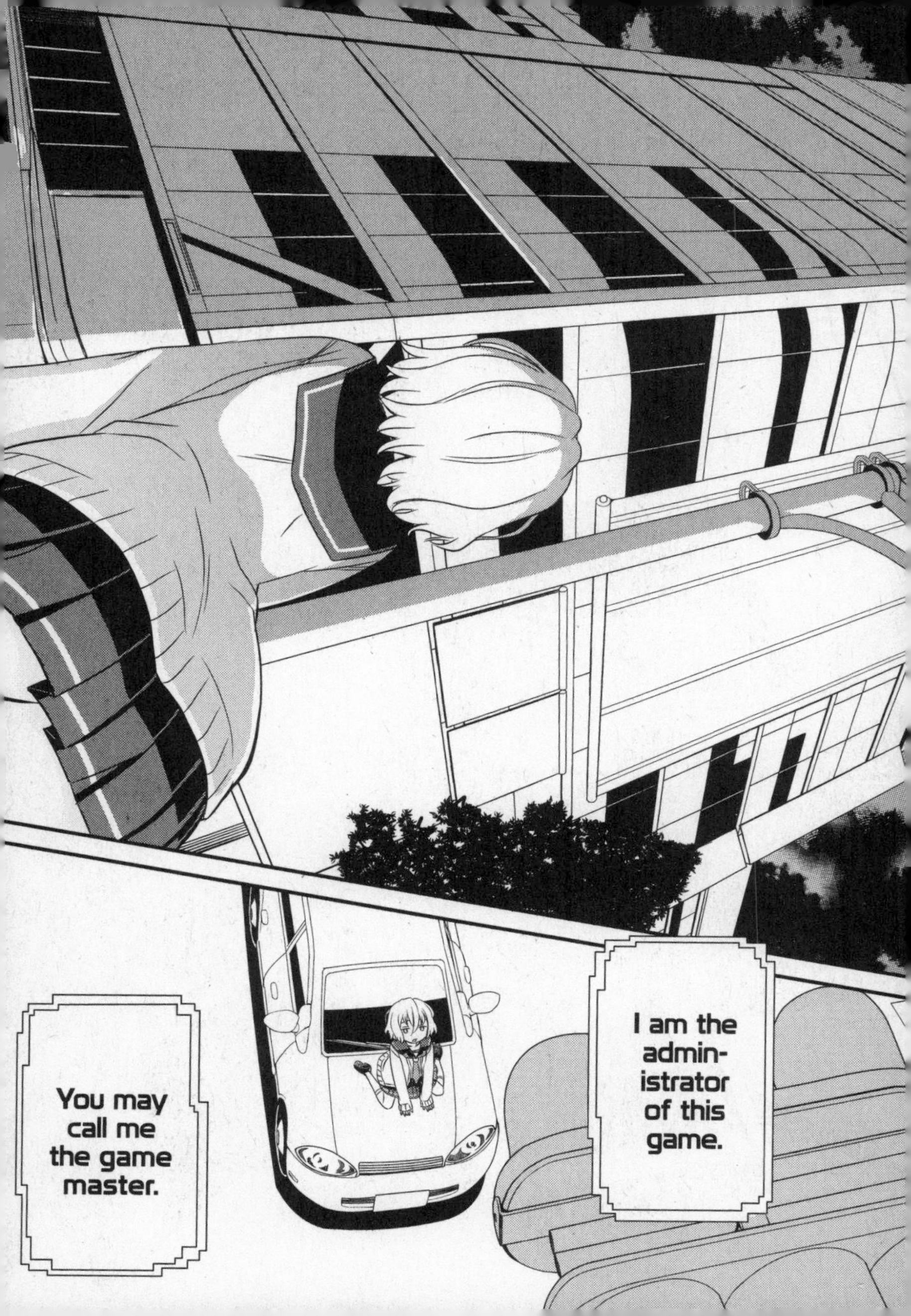
I am the admin-istrator of this game.
You may call me the game master.

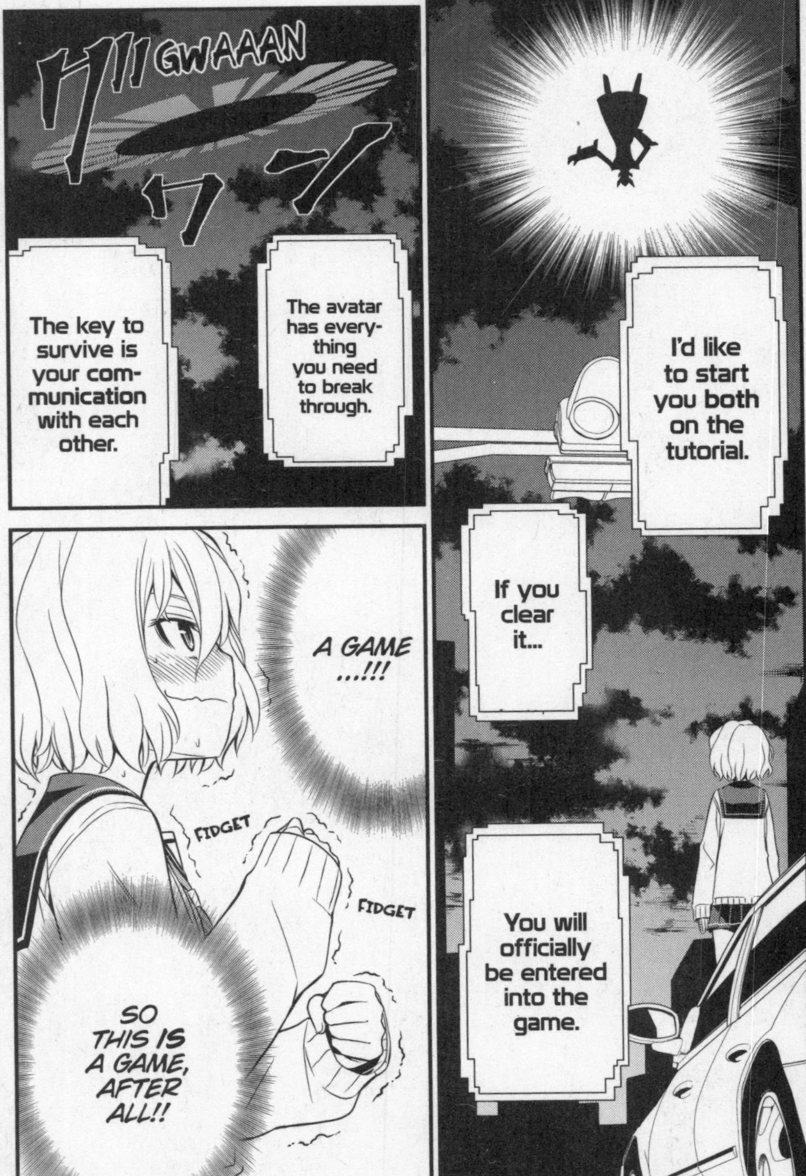
I'd like to start you both on the tutorial.
If you clear it...
You will officially be entered into the game.
GWAAAN
The avatar has everything you need to break through.
The key to survive is your communication with each other.
A GAME ...!!!
FIDGET
FIDGET
SO THIS IS A GAME, AFTER ALL!!

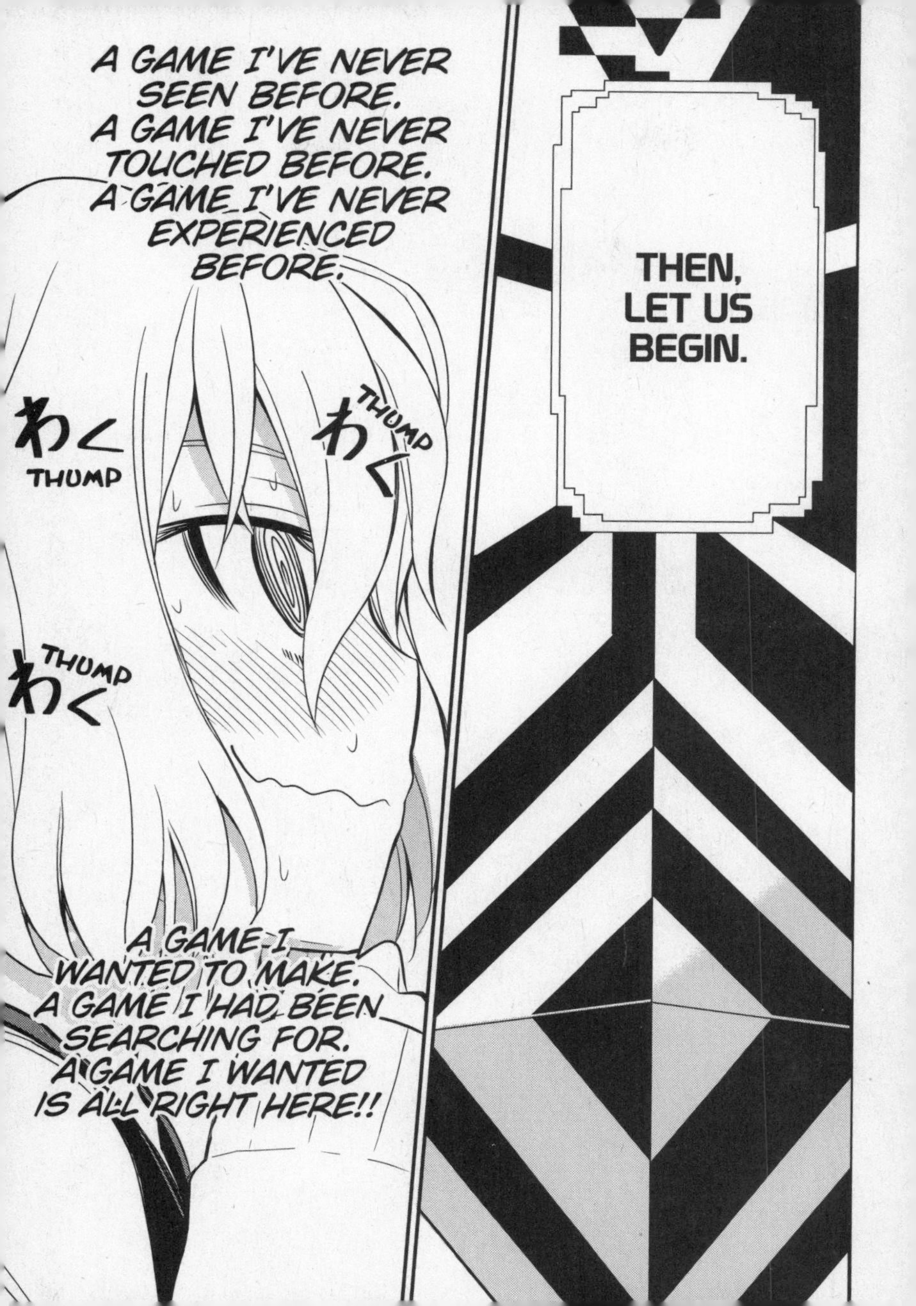
THEN, LET US BEGIN.
A GAME I'VE NEVER SEEN BEFORE. A GAME I'VE NEVER TOUCHED BEFORE. A GAME I'VE NEVER EXPERIENCED BEFORE.
わく THUMP
わく THUMP
わく THUMP
A GAME I WANTED TO MAKE. A GAME I HAD BEEN SEARCHING FOR. A GAME I WANTED IS ALL RIGHT HERE!!

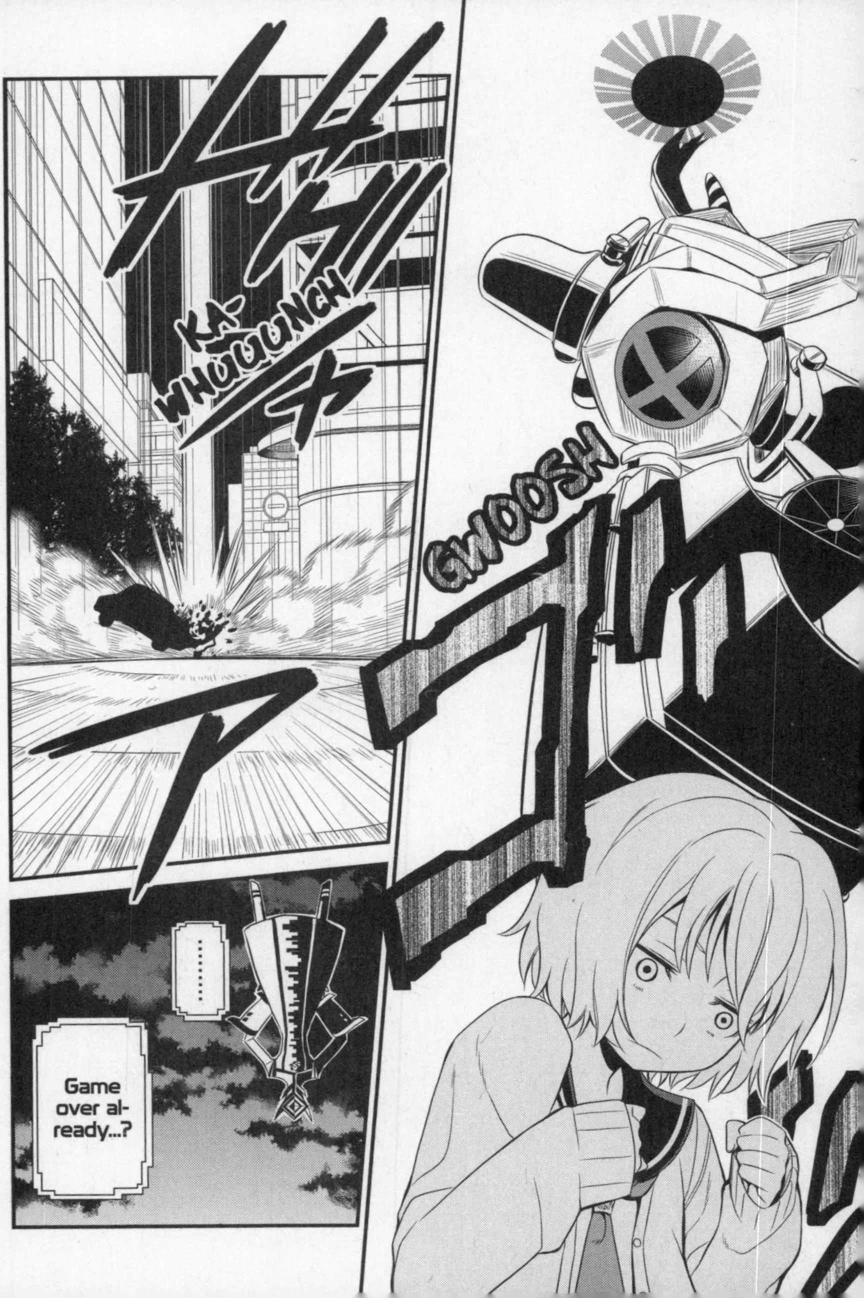
GWOOSH
KA-WHUUUNCH
......
Game over al-ready...?

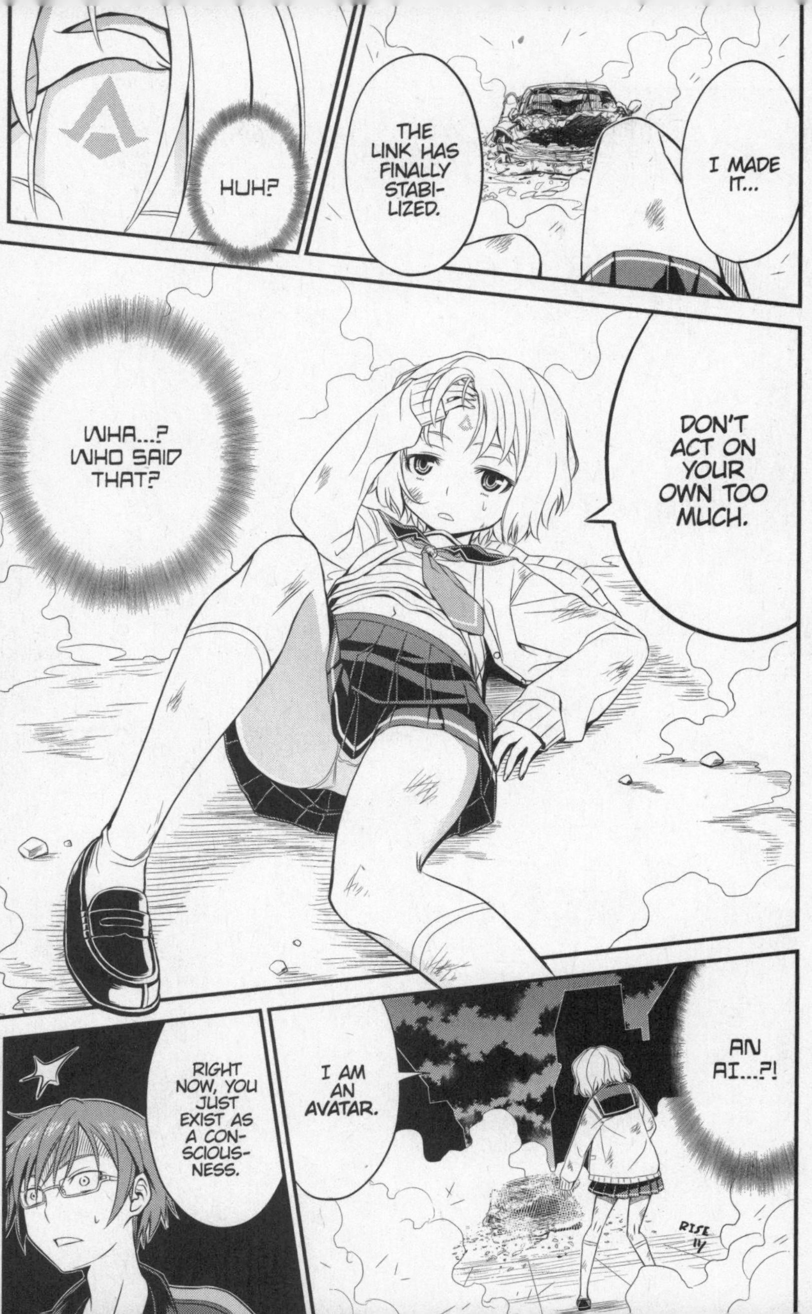
I MADE IT...
THE LINK HAS FINALLY STABILIZED.
HUH?
DON'T ACT ON YOUR OWN TOO MUCH.
WHA...? WHO SAID THAT?
AN AI...?!
I AM AN AVATAR.
RISE
RIGHT NOW, YOU JUST EXIST AS A CONSCIOUSNESS.

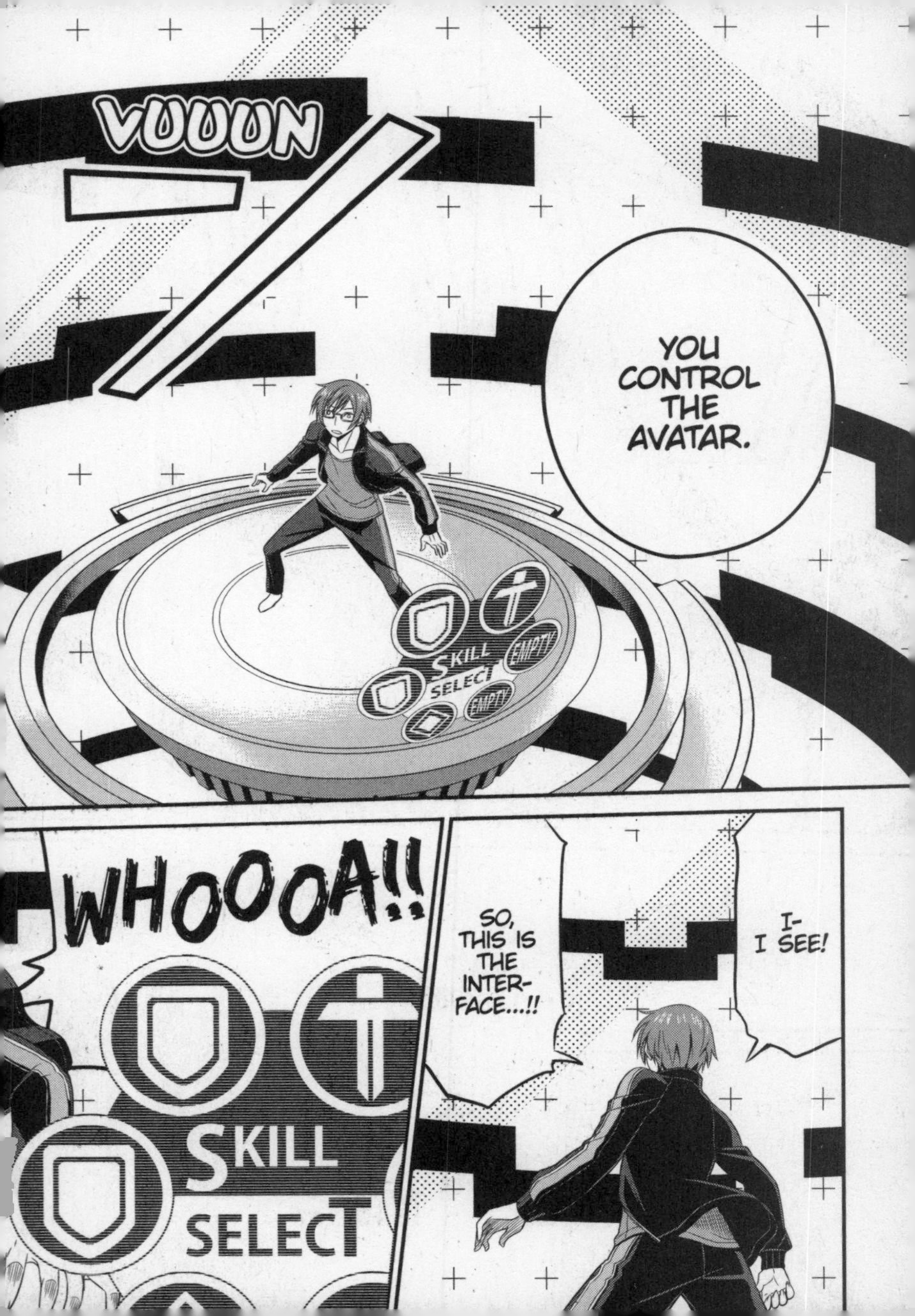
VUUUN
YOU CONTROL THE AVATAR.
SKILL SELECT
EMPTY
EMPTY
I- I SEE!
SO, THIS IS THE INTER-FACE...!!
WHOOOA!!
SKILL SELECT

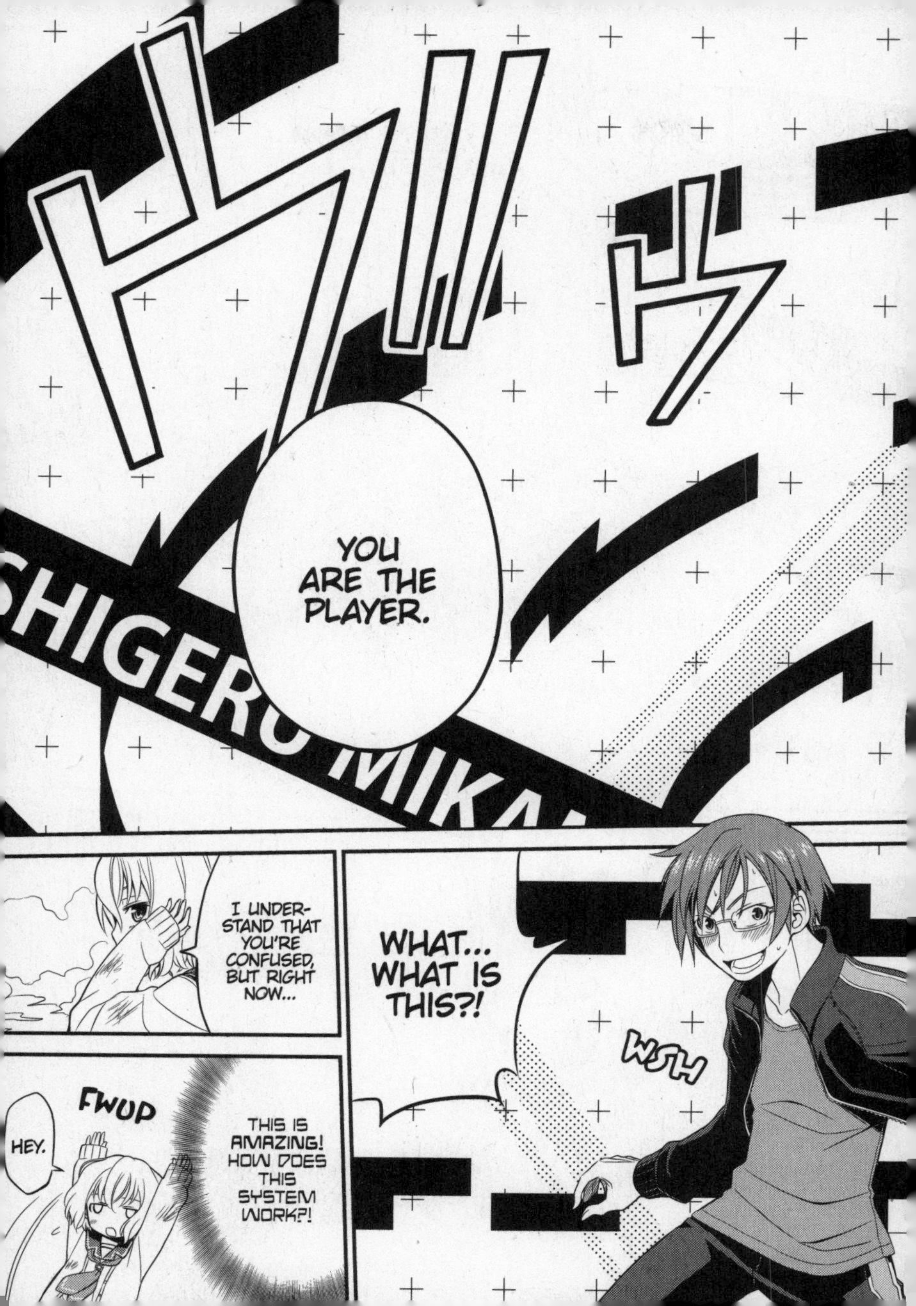
SHIGERU MIKA
YOU ARE THE PLAYER.
WHAT... WHAT IS THIS?!
WSH
I UNDERSTAND THAT YOU'RE CONFUSED, BUT RIGHT NOW...
THIS IS AMAZING! HOW DOES THIS SYSTEM WORK?!
FWUP
HEY.

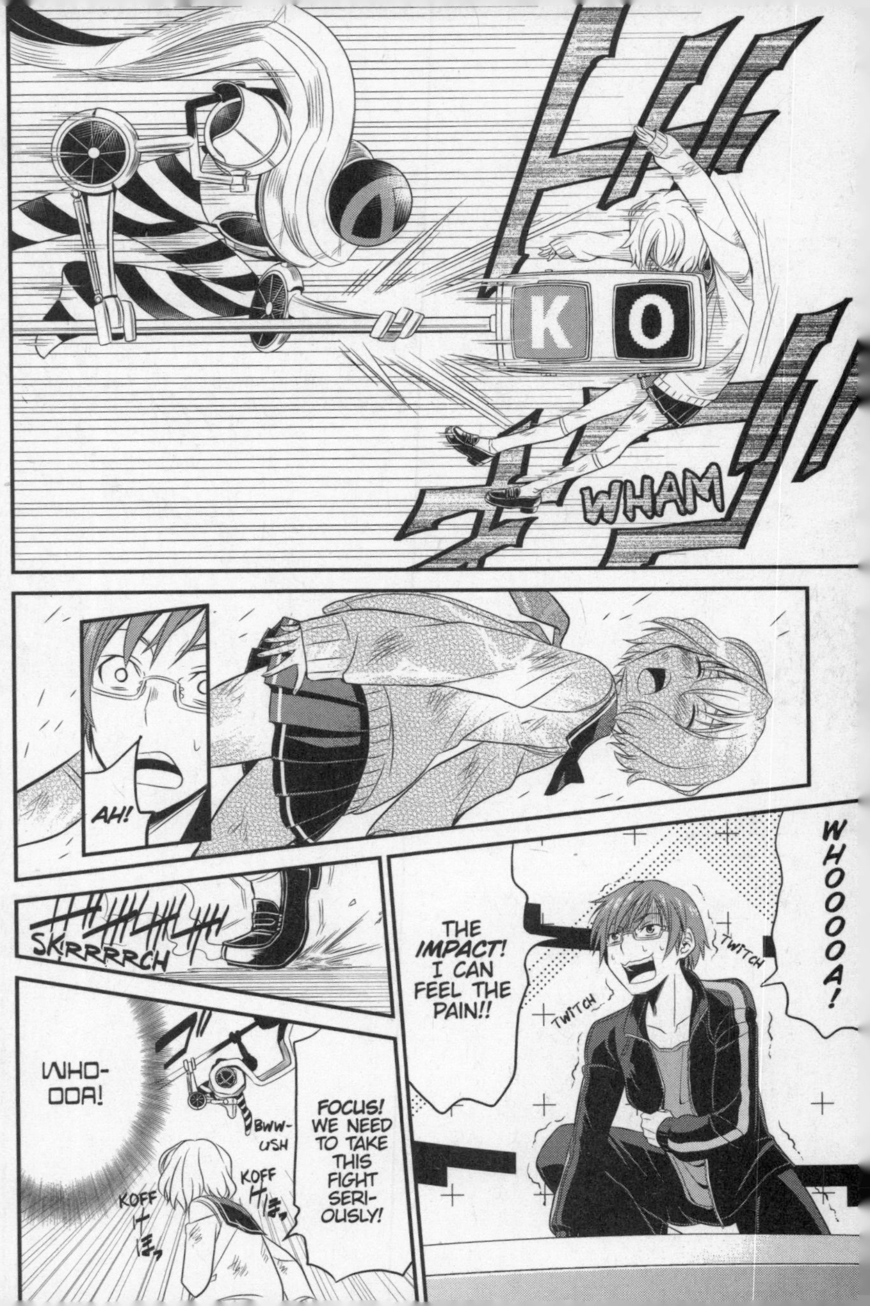
K O
WHAM
AH!
WHOOOOOA!
THE IMPACT! I CAN FEEL THE PAIN!!
TWITCH
TWITCH
SKRRRRCH
FOCUS! WE NEED TO TAKE THIS FIGHT SERIOUSLY!
WHO-OOA!
BWW-USH
KOFF
KOFF

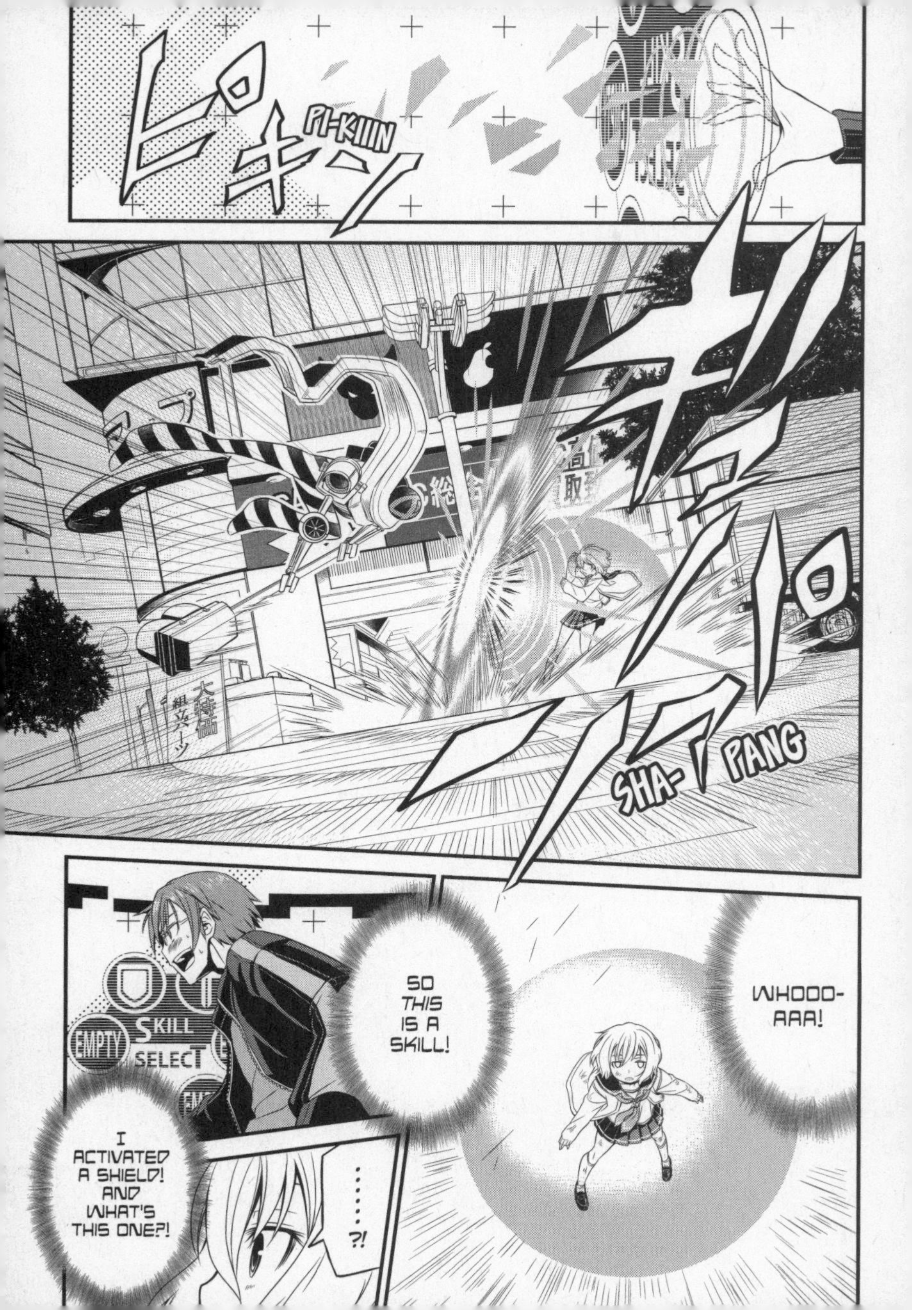
PI-KIIIN
SHA-PANG
WHOOD-AAA!
SO THIS IS A SKILL!
EMPTY
SKILL SELECT
I ACTIVATED A SHIELD! AND WHAT'S THIS ONE?!
......?!

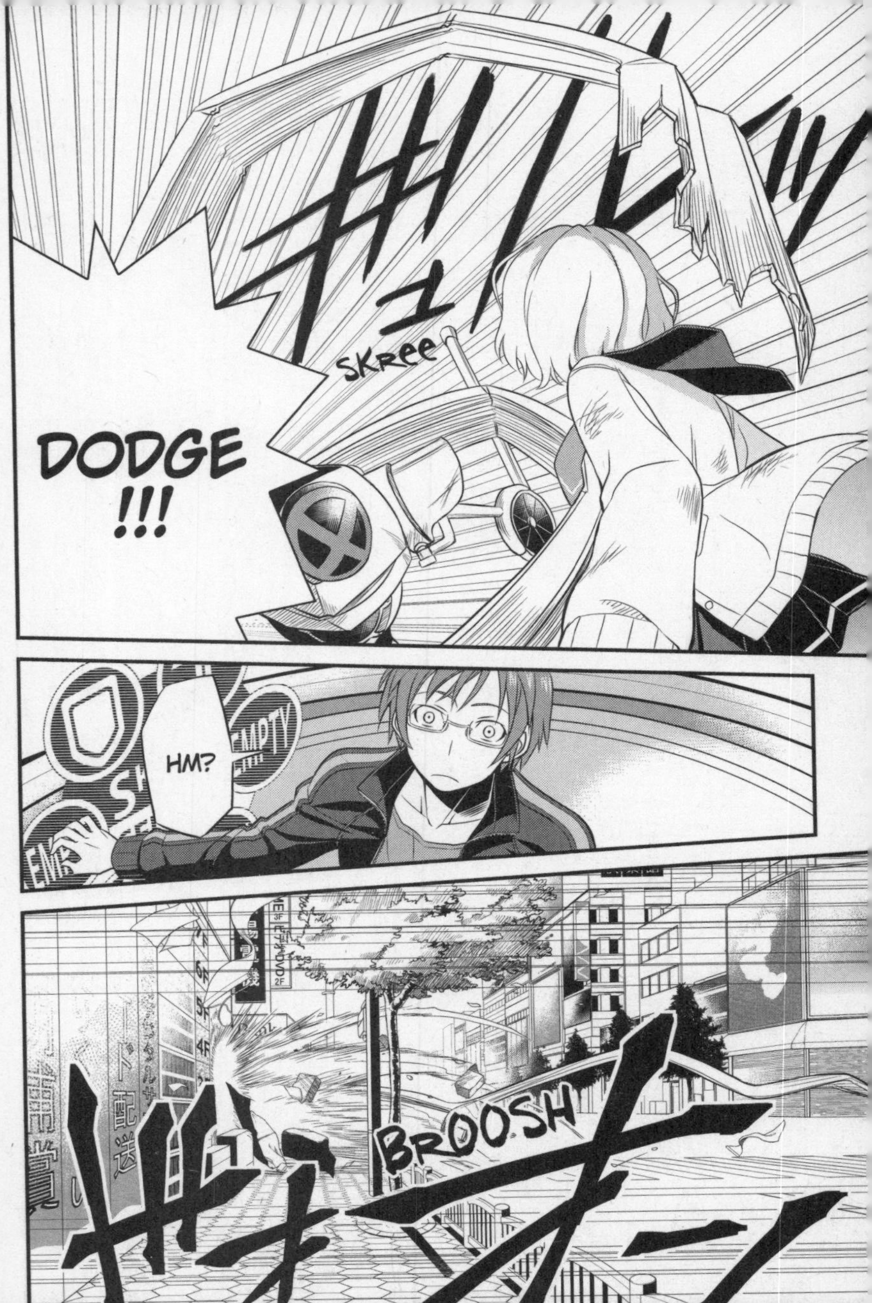

SKree
DODGE !!!
HM?
EMPTY
BROOSH

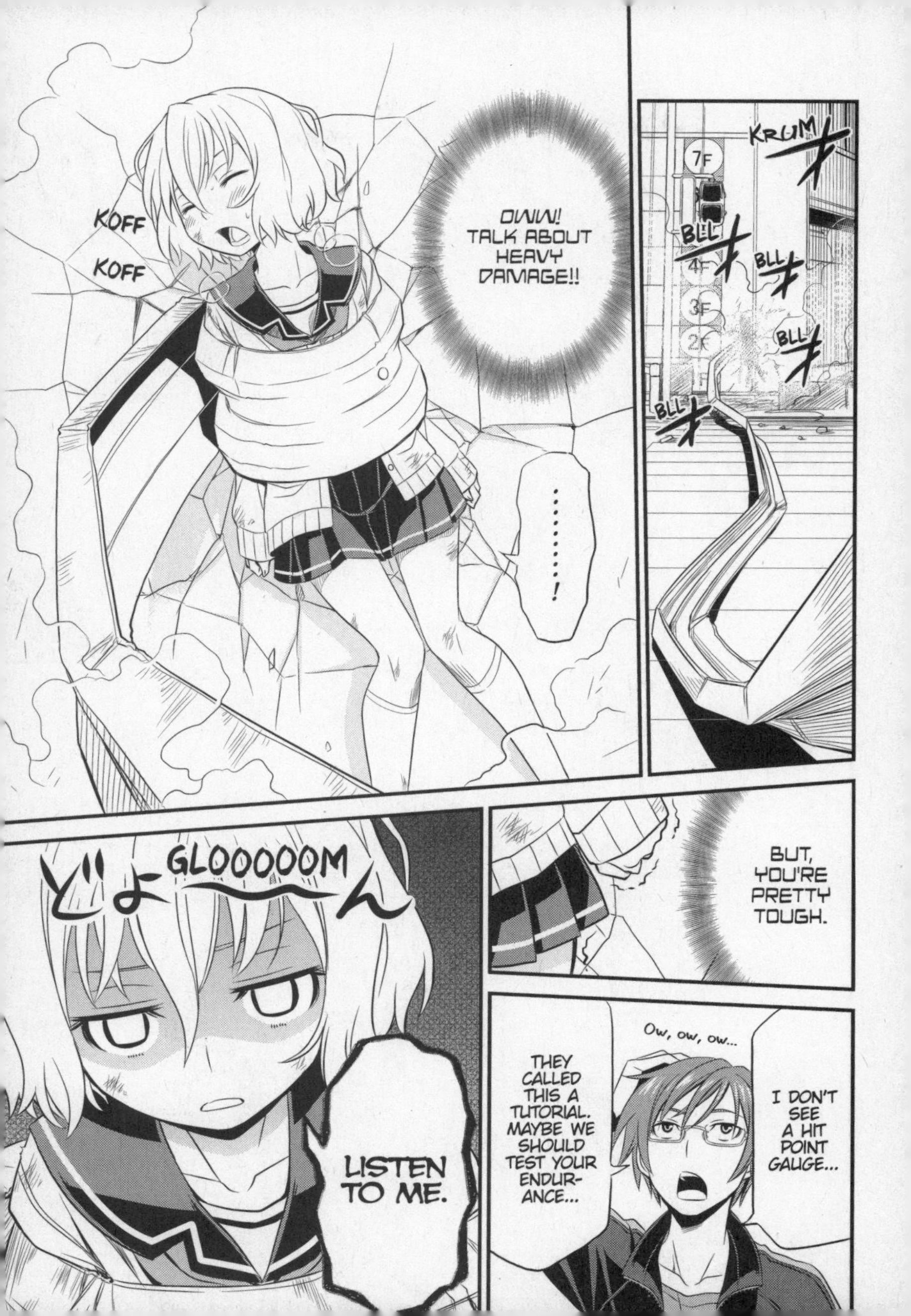
KRUM
7F
BLL
BLL
BLL
BLL
KOFF
KOFF
OWW! TALK ABOUT HEAVY DAMAGE!!
......!
BUT, YOU'RE PRETTY TOUGH.
Ow, ow, ow...
I DON'T SEE A HIT POINT GAUGE...
THEY CALLED THIS A TUTORIAL. MAYBE WE SHOULD TEST YOUR ENDUR-ANCE...
どよ～～ん
GLOOOOOM
LISTEN TO ME.

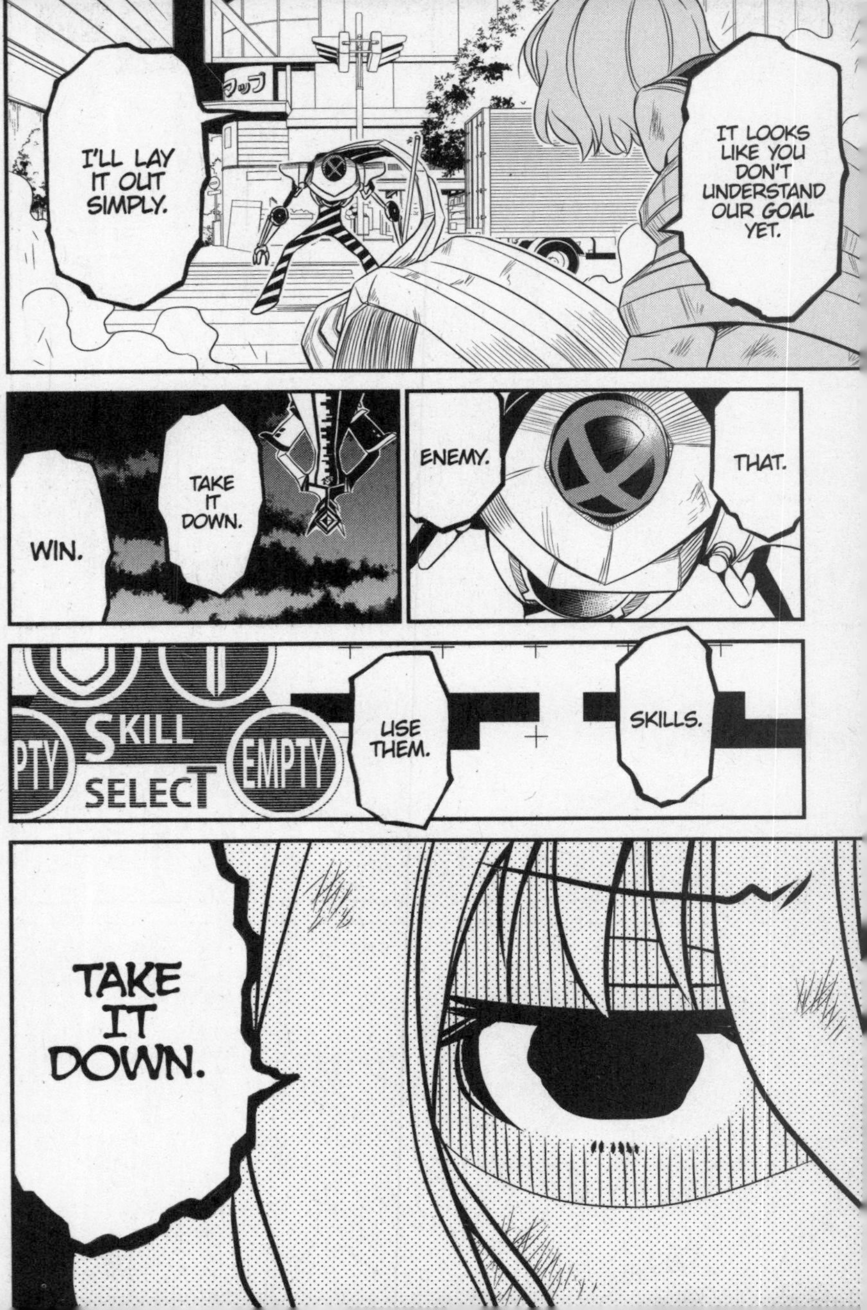
IT LOOKS LIKE YOU DON'T UNDERSTAND OUR GOAL YET.
I'LL LAY IT OUT SIMPLY.
THAT.
ENEMY.
TAKE IT DOWN.
WIN.
SKILLS.
USE THEM.
EMPTY
SKILL SELECT
TAKE IT DOWN.

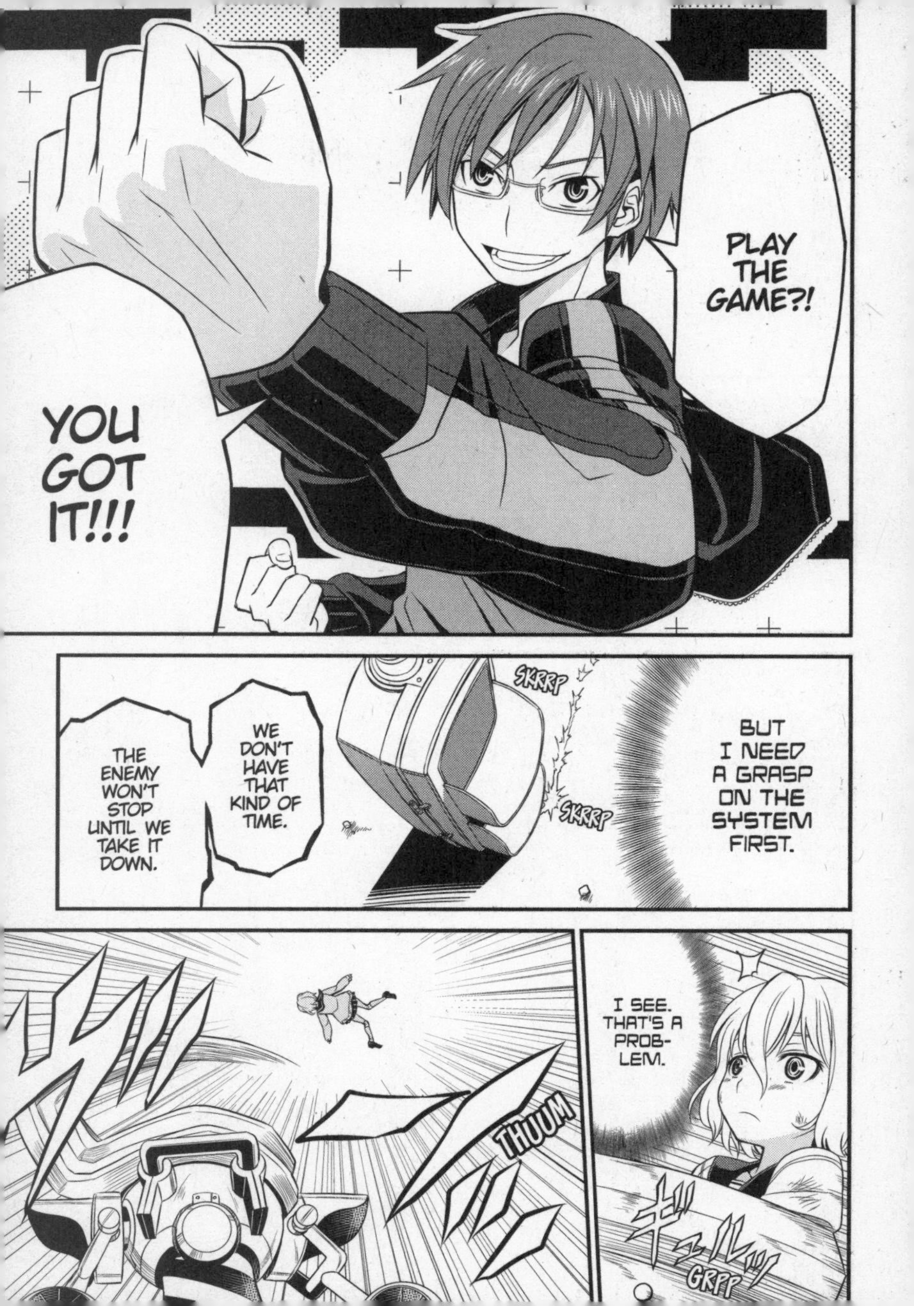
PLAY THE GAME?!
YOU GOT IT!!!
BUT I NEED A GRASP ON THE SYSTEM FIRST.
SKRRP
SKRRP
WE DON'T HAVE THAT KIND OF TIME.
THE ENEMY WON'T STOP UNTIL WE TAKE IT DOWN.
I SEE. THAT'S A PROB-LEM.
ギュルッ
GRPP
THUUM

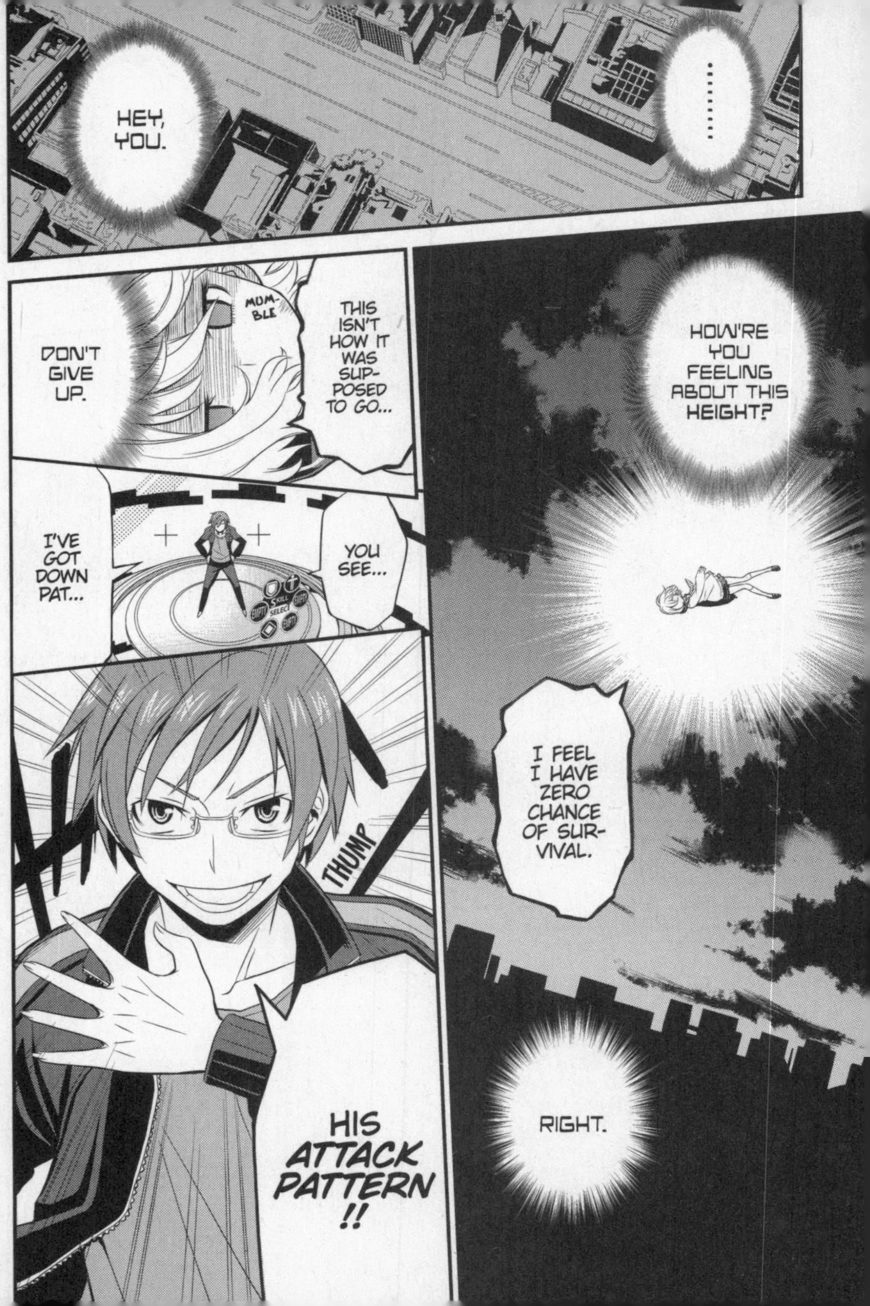
......
HEY, YOU.
HOW'RE YOU FEELING ABOUT THIS HEIGHT?
I FEEL I HAVE ZERO CHANCE OF SURVIVAL.
RIGHT.
THIS ISN'T HOW IT WAS SUPPOSED TO GO...
MUMBLE
DON'T GIVE UP.
YOU SEE...
I'VE GOT DOWN PAT...
THUMP
HIS *ATTACK PATTERN* !!

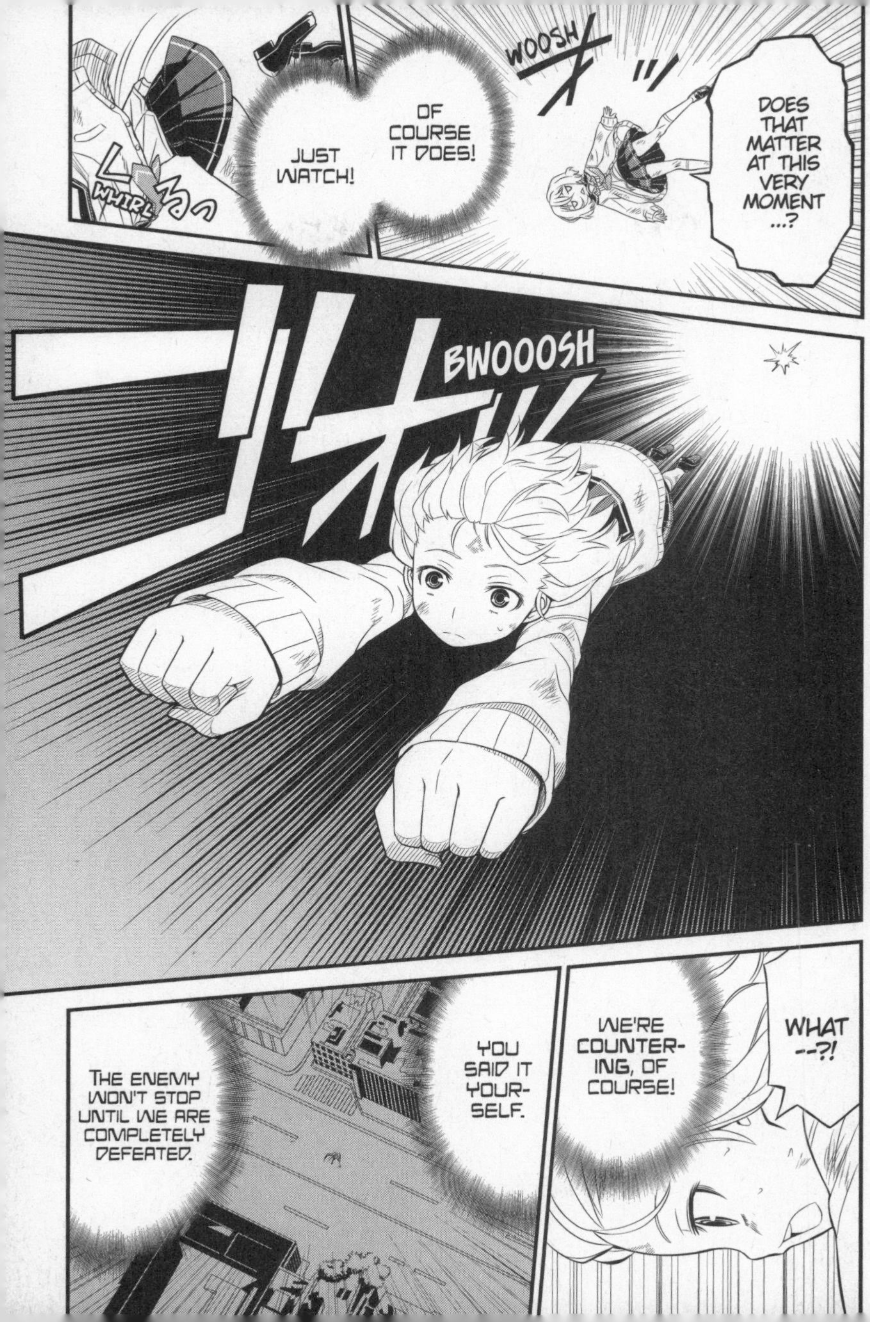
WOOSH
DOES THAT MATTER AT THIS VERY MOMENT ...?
OF COURSE IT DOES!
JUST WATCH!
WHIRL
BWOOOSH
WHAT --?!
WE'RE COUNTER-ING, OF COURSE!
YOU SAID IT YOUR-SELF.
THE ENEMY WON'T STOP UNTIL WE ARE COMPLETELY DEFEATED.

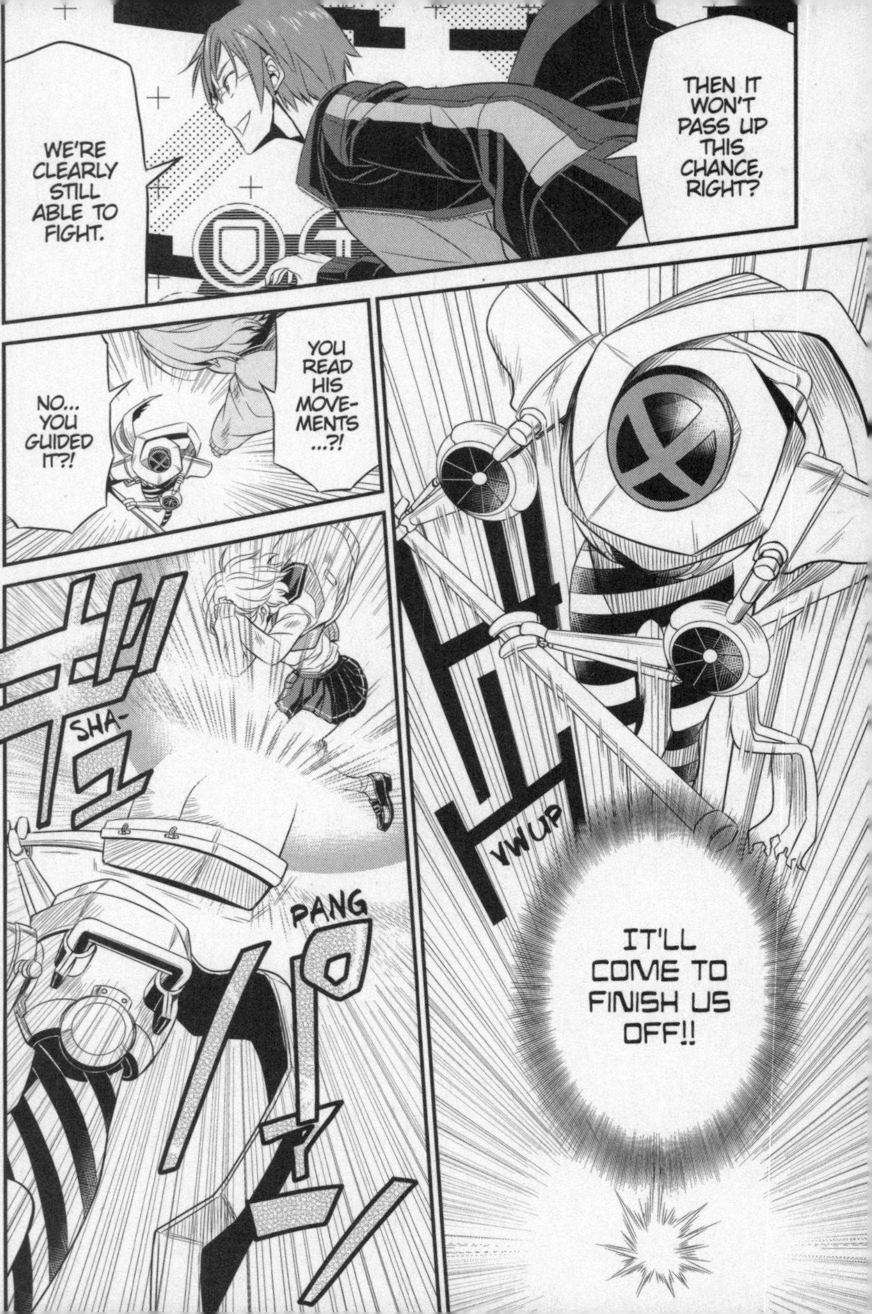
THEN IT WON'T PASS UP THIS CHANCE, RIGHT?
WE'RE CLEARLY STILL ABLE TO FIGHT.
VWUP
IT'LL COME TO FINISH US OFF!!
YOU READ HIS MOVEMENTS ...?!
NO... YOU GUIDED IT?!
SHA-
PANG

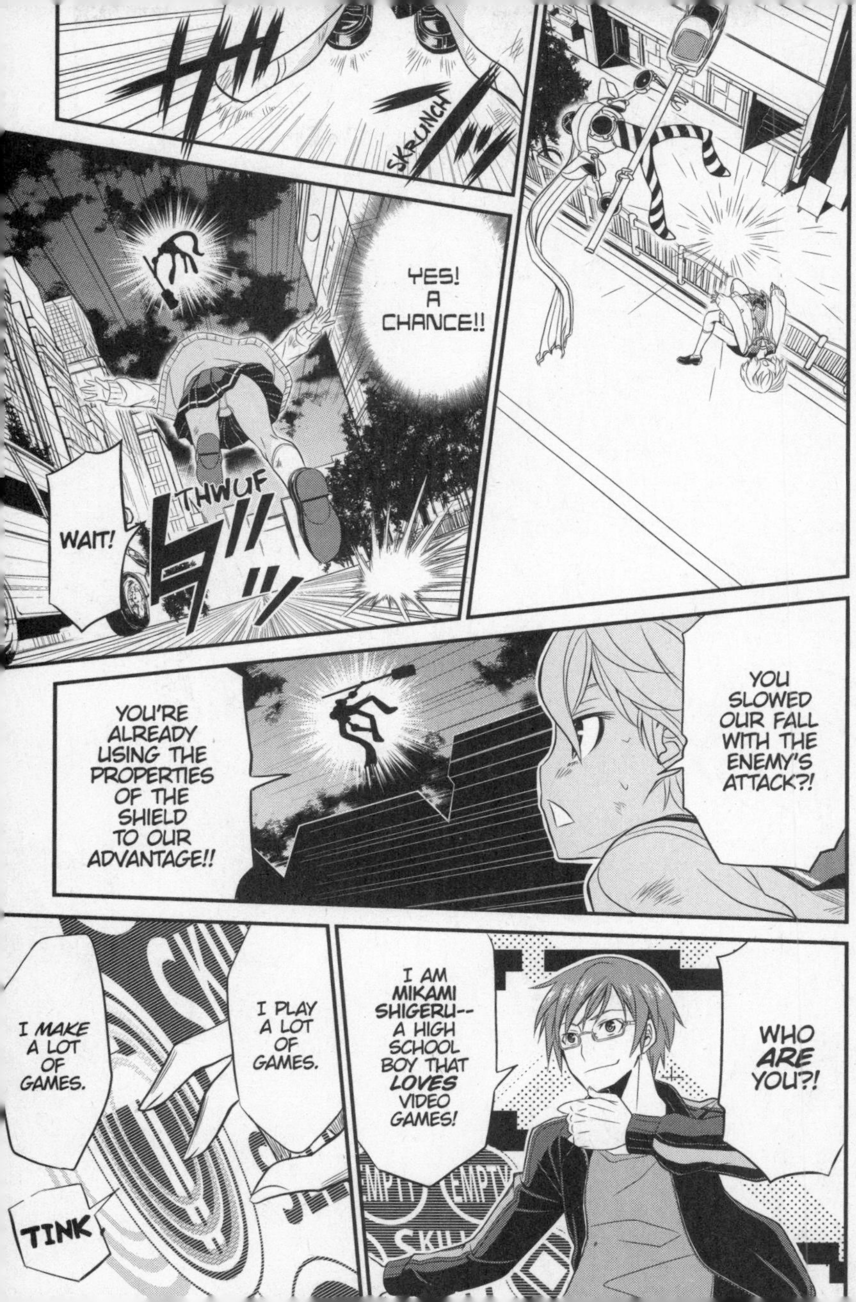
SKRUNCH
YES! A CHANCE!!
THWUF
WAIT!
YOU SLOWED OUR FALL WITH THE ENEMY'S ATTACK?!
YOU'RE ALREADY USING THE PROPERTIES OF THE SHIELD TO OUR ADVANTAGE!!
WHO *ARE* YOU?!
I AM MIKAMI SHIGERU-- A HIGH SCHOOL BOY THAT ***LOVES*** VIDEO GAMES!
I PLAY A LOT OF GAMES.
I *MAKE* A LOT OF GAMES.
TINK
EMPTY
EMPTY
SKILL

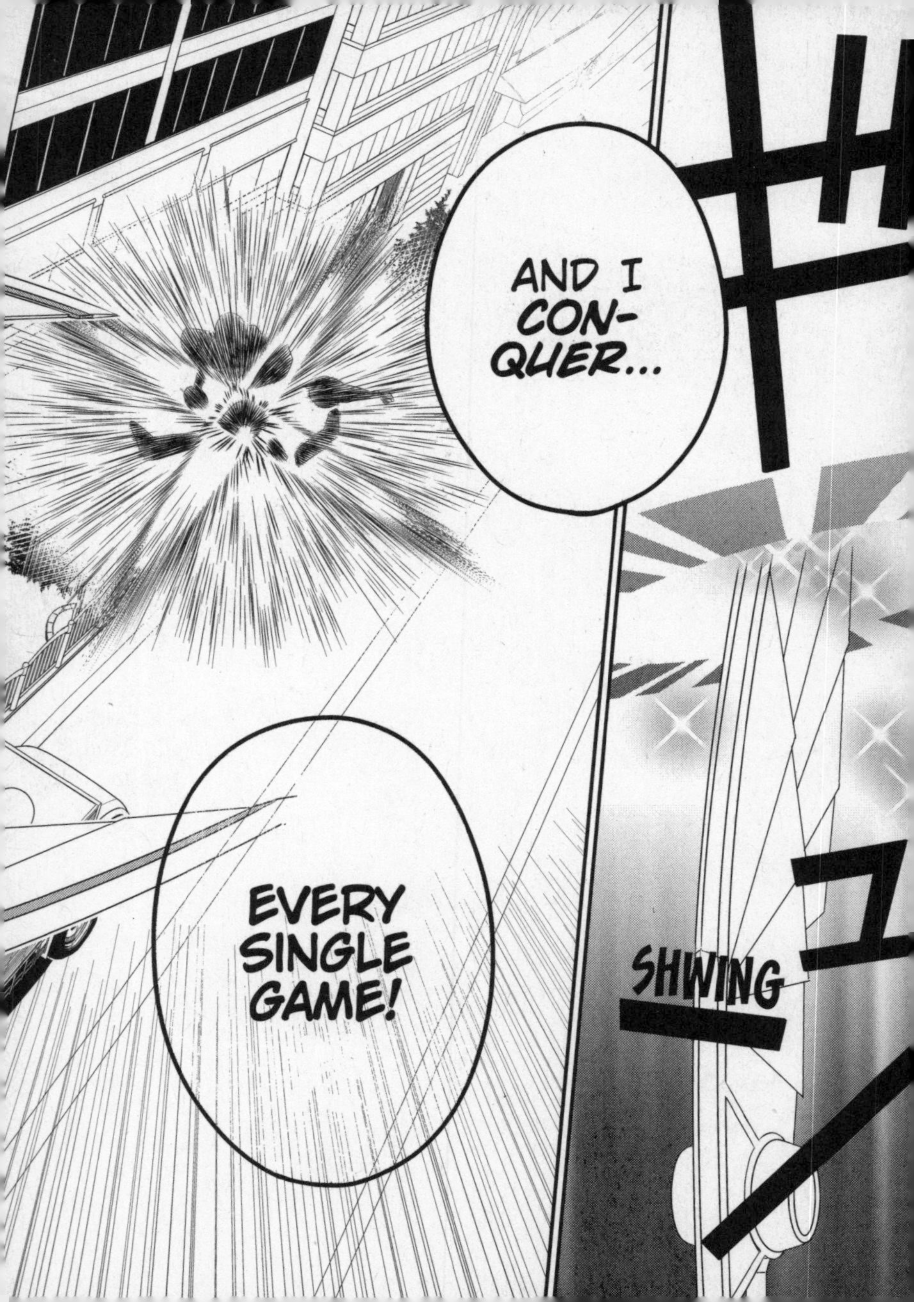
AND I CON-QUER...
EVERY SINGLE GAME!
SHWING

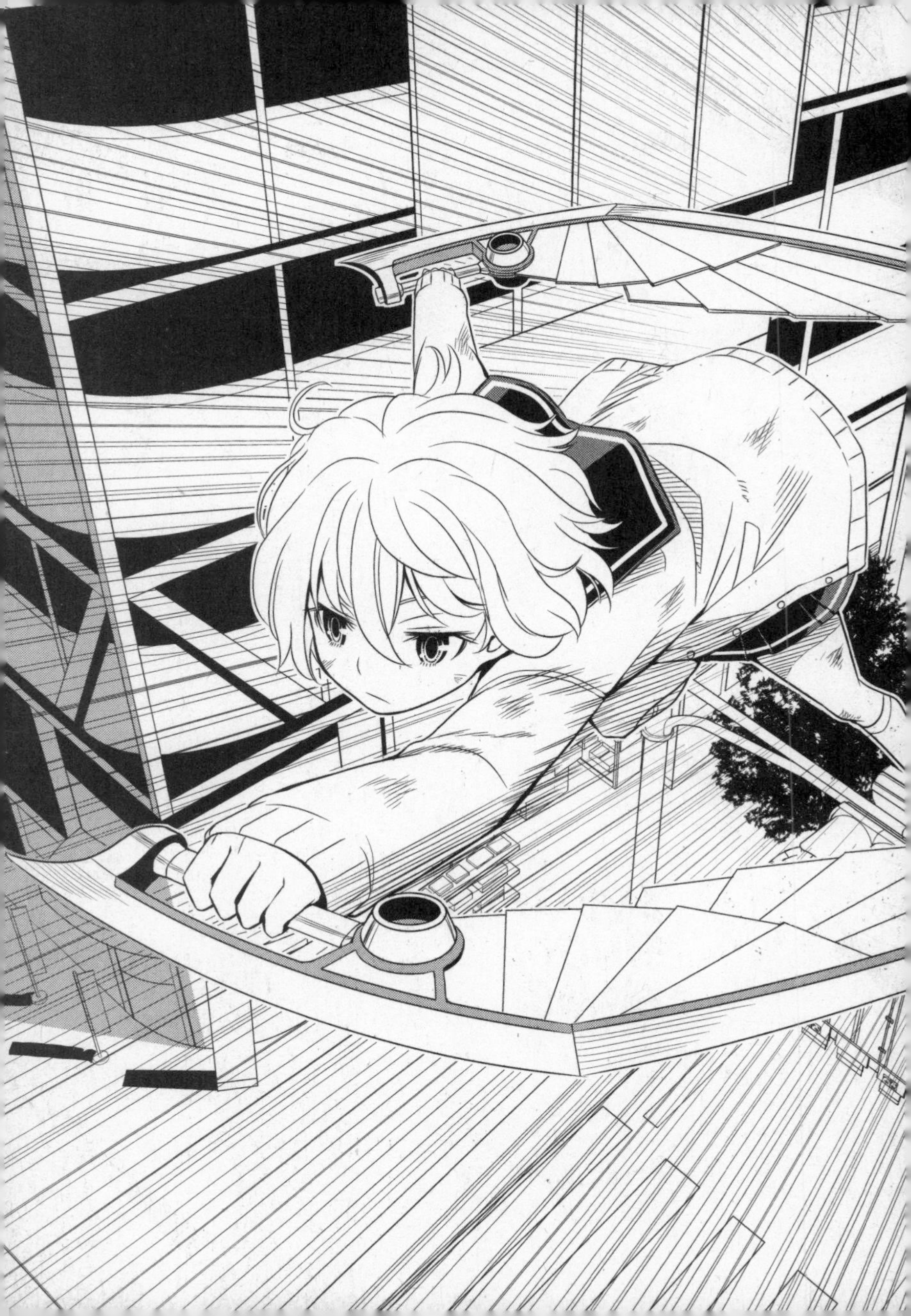

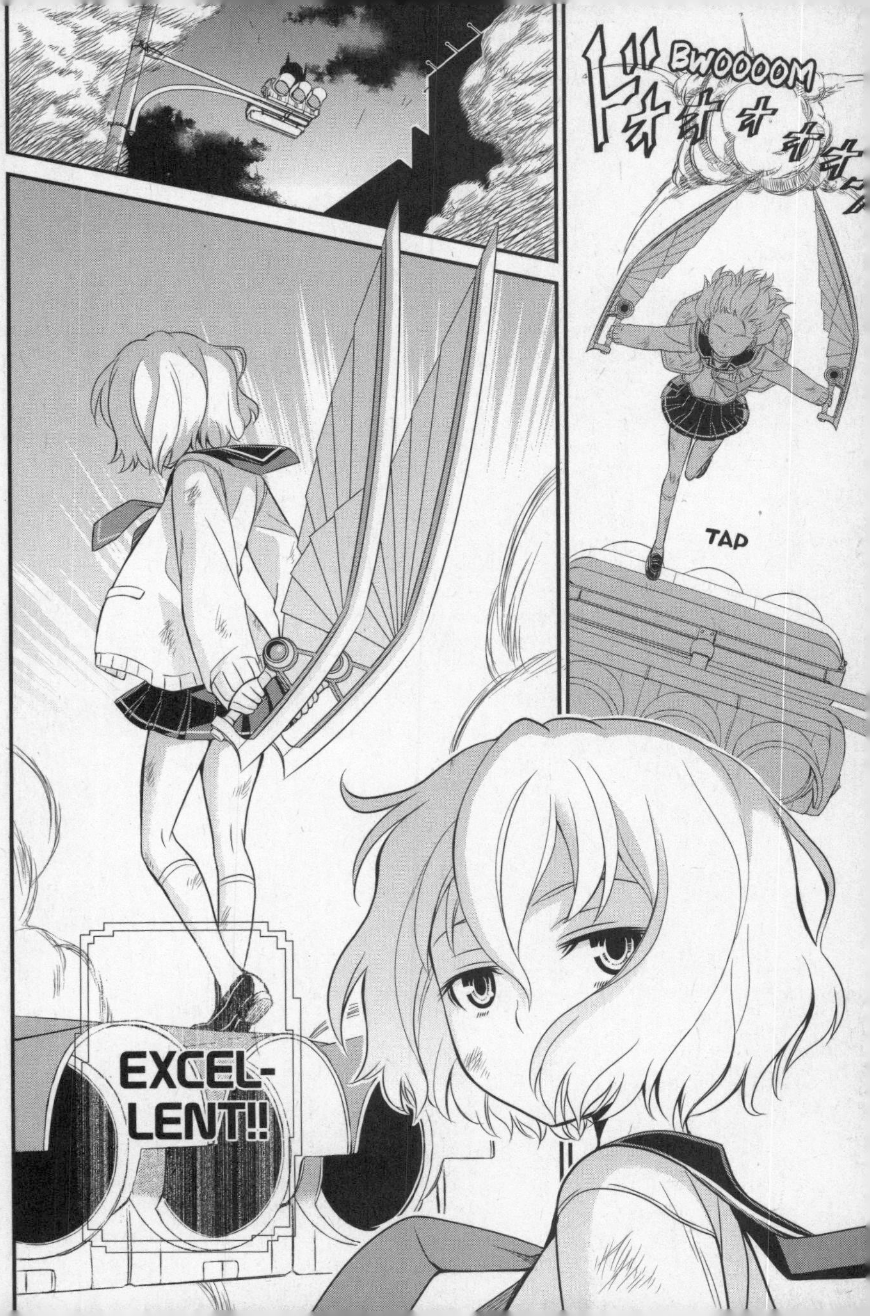
BWOOOOM
ドオォォォォッ
TAP
EXCEL-
LENT!!

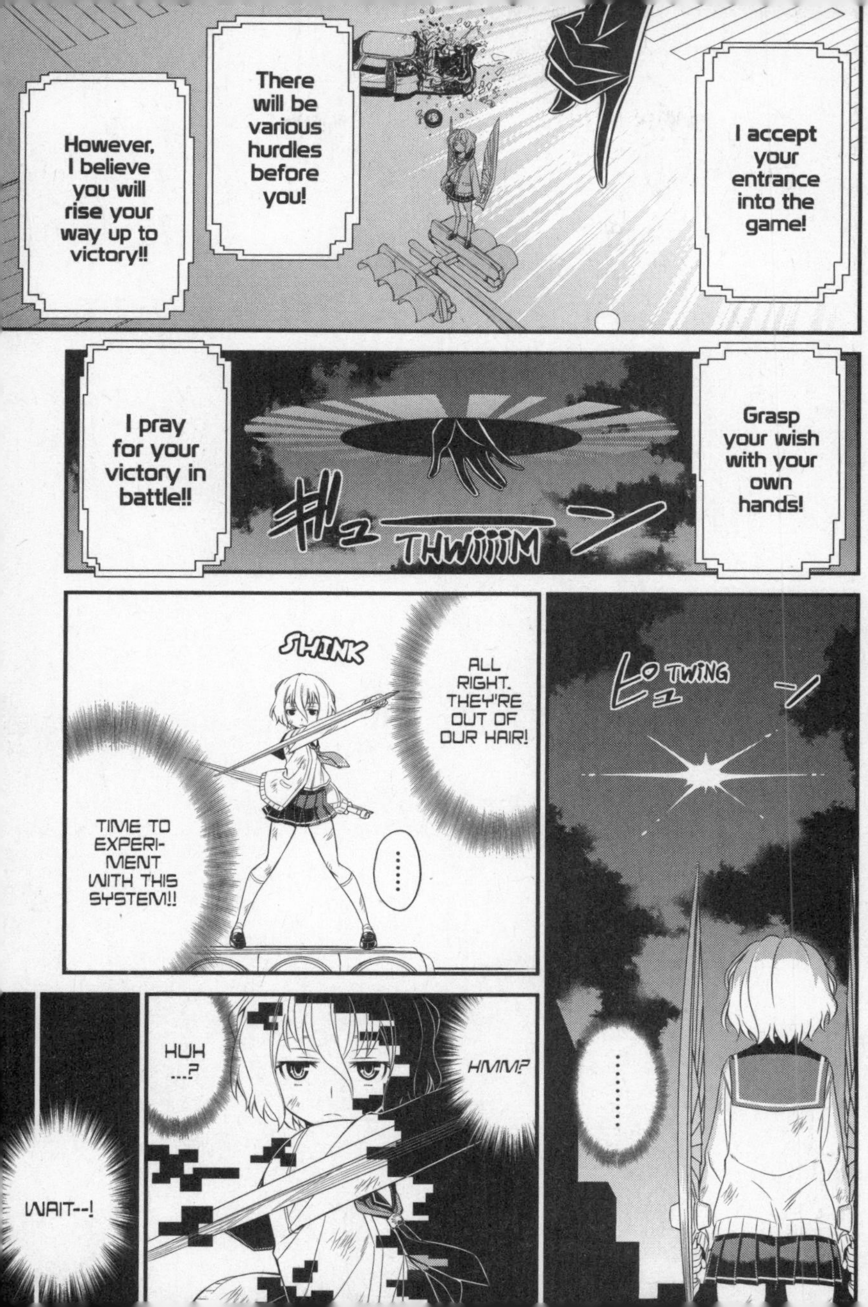
I accept your entrance into the game!
There will be various hurdles before you!
However, I believe you will rise your way up to victory!!
Grasp your wish with your own hands!
THWiiiiM
I pray for your victory in battle!!
TWING
......
SHINK
ALL RIGHT. THEY'RE OUT OF OUR HAIR!
......
TIME TO EXPERIMENT WITH THIS SYSTEM!!
HMM?
HUH ...?
WAIT--!

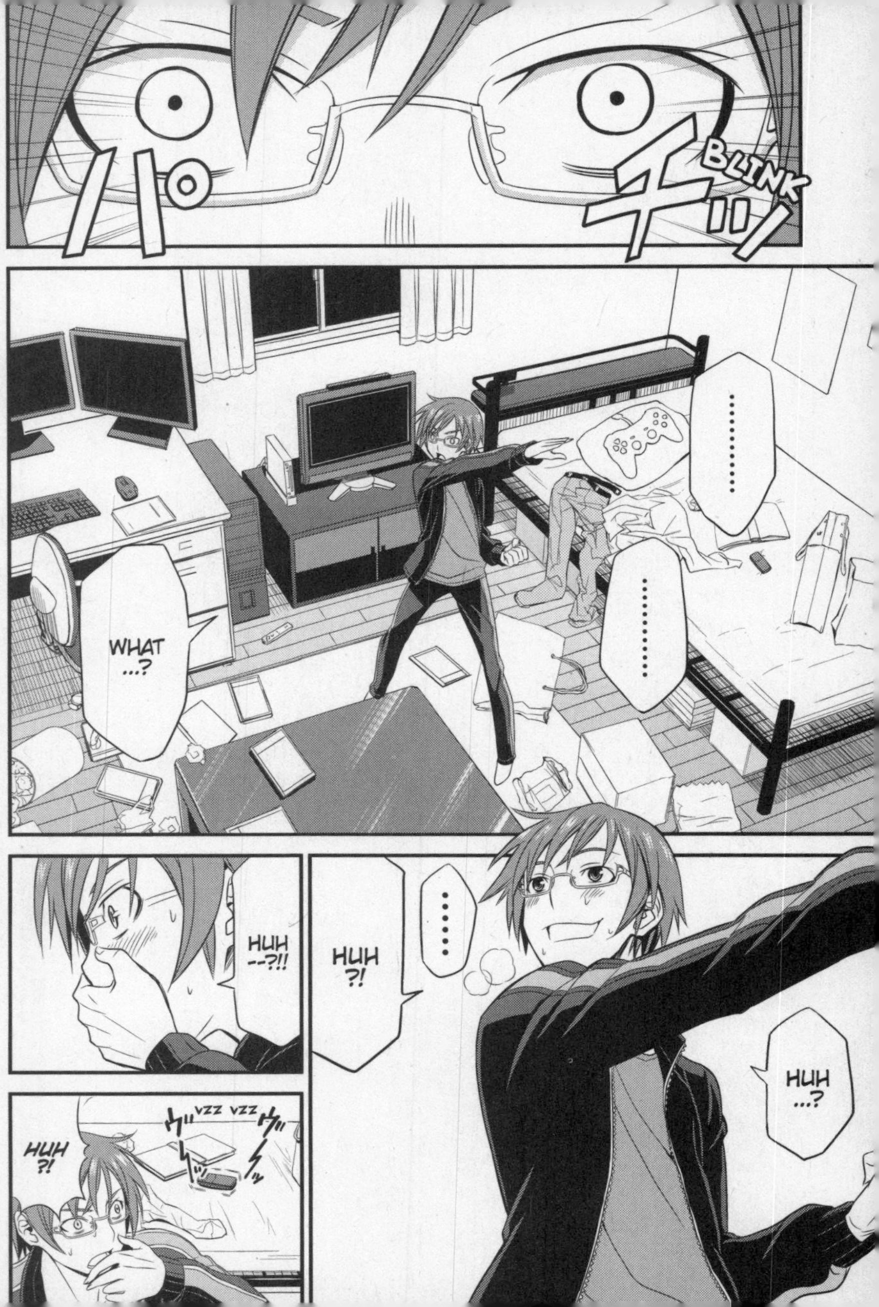

BLINK
....
....
WHAT ...?
......
HUH ...?
HUH ?!
HUH --?!!
VZZ VZZ
HUH ?!

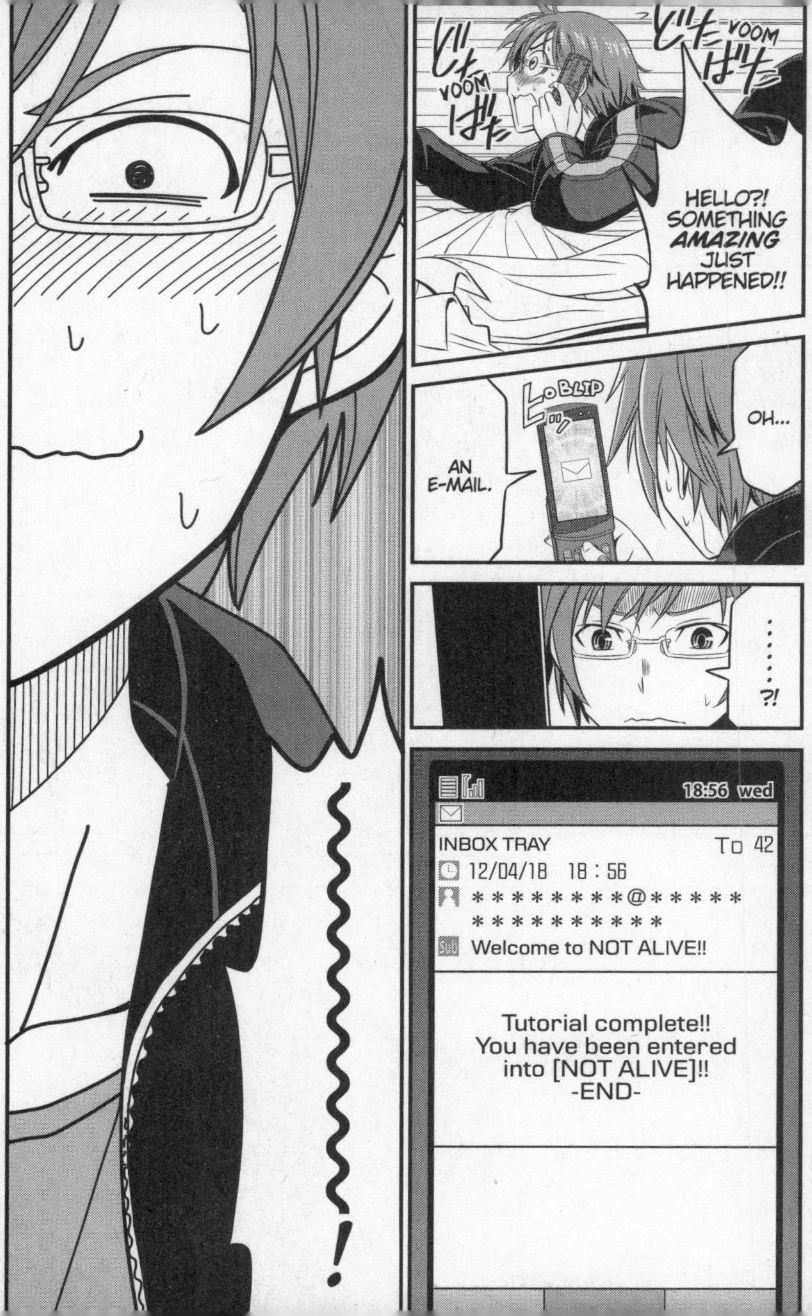
VOOM
HELLO?! SOMETHING AMAZING JUST HAPPENED!!
VOOM
OH...
BLIP
AN E-MAIL.
......
?!
18:56 wed
INBOX TRAY
To 42
12/04/18 18 : 56
********@*****
****
Welcome to NOT ALIVE!!
Tutorial complete!!
You have been entered
into [NOT ALIVE]!!
-END-
!

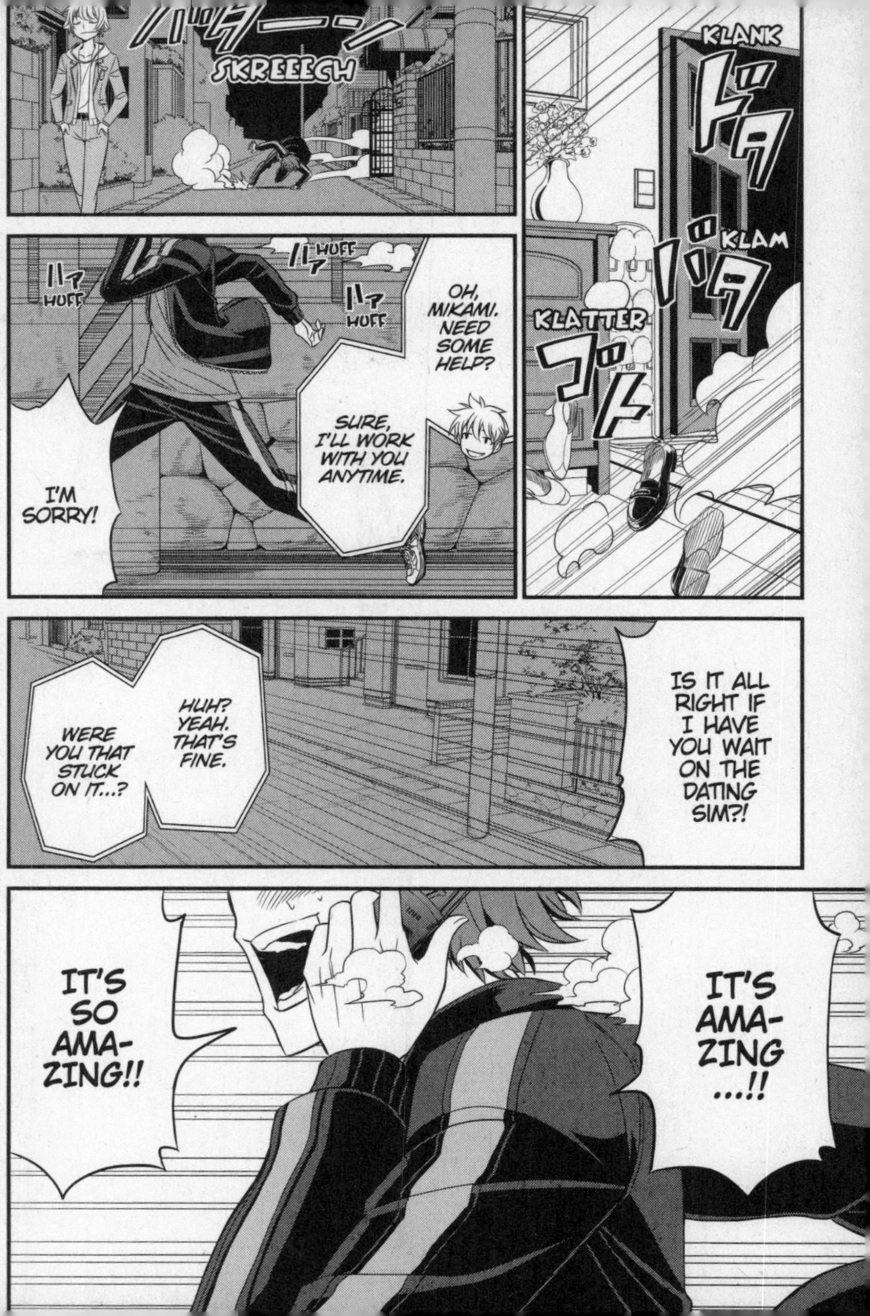
KLANK
KLAM
KLATTER
SKREEECH
HUFF
HUFF
HUFF
OH, MIKAMI. NEED SOME HELP?
SURE, I'LL WORK WITH YOU ANYTIME.
I'M SORRY!
IS IT ALL RIGHT IF I HAVE YOU WAIT ON THE DATING SIM?!
HUH? YEAH. THAT'S FINE.
WERE YOU THAT STUCK ON IT...?
IT'S AMA-ZING...!!
IT'S SO AMA-ZING!!

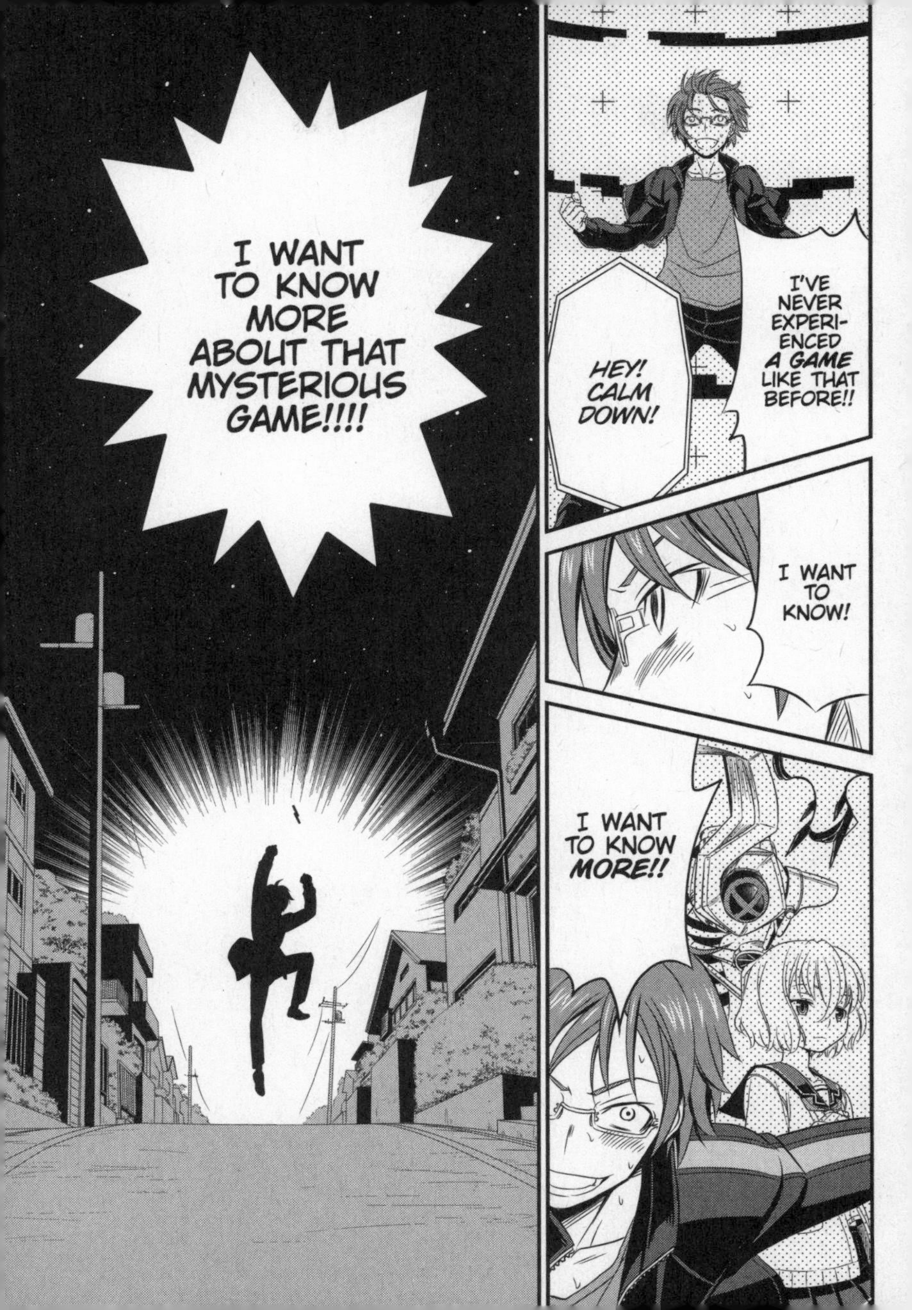
I'VE NEVER EXPERIENCED *A GAME* LIKE THAT BEFORE!!
HEY! CALM DOWN!
I WANT TO KNOW!
I WANT TO KNOW *MORE!!*
I WANT TO KNOW MORE ABOUT THAT MYSTERIOUS GAME!!!!

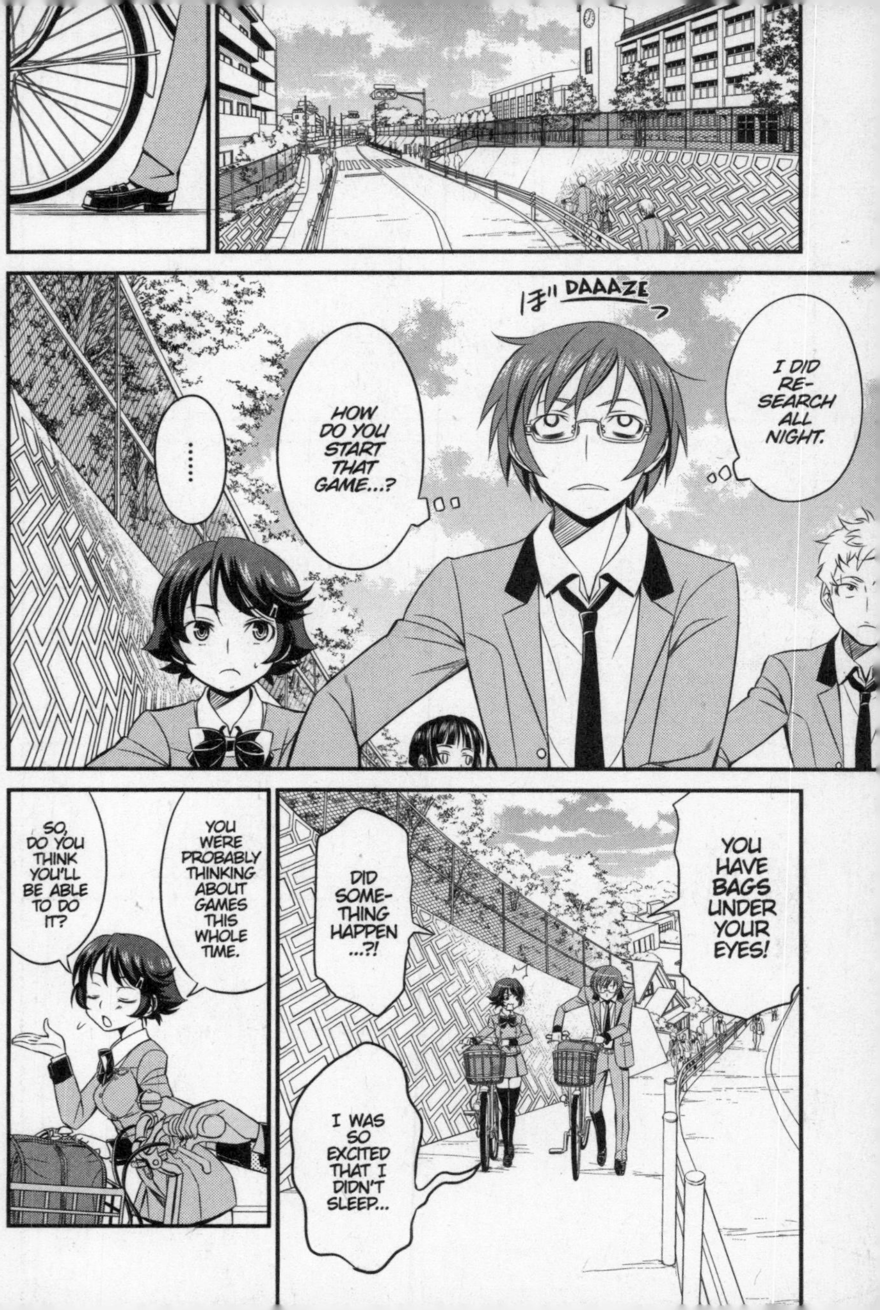
ぼ DAAAZE
I DID RE-SEARCH ALL NIGHT.
HOW DO YOU START THAT GAME...?
......
YOU HAVE BAGS UNDER YOUR EYES!
DID SOME-THING HAPPEN...?!
I WAS SO EXCITED THAT I DIDN'T SLEEP...
YOU WERE PROBABLY THINKING ABOUT GAMES THIS WHOLE TIME.
SO, DO YOU THINK YOU'LL BE ABLE TO DO IT?

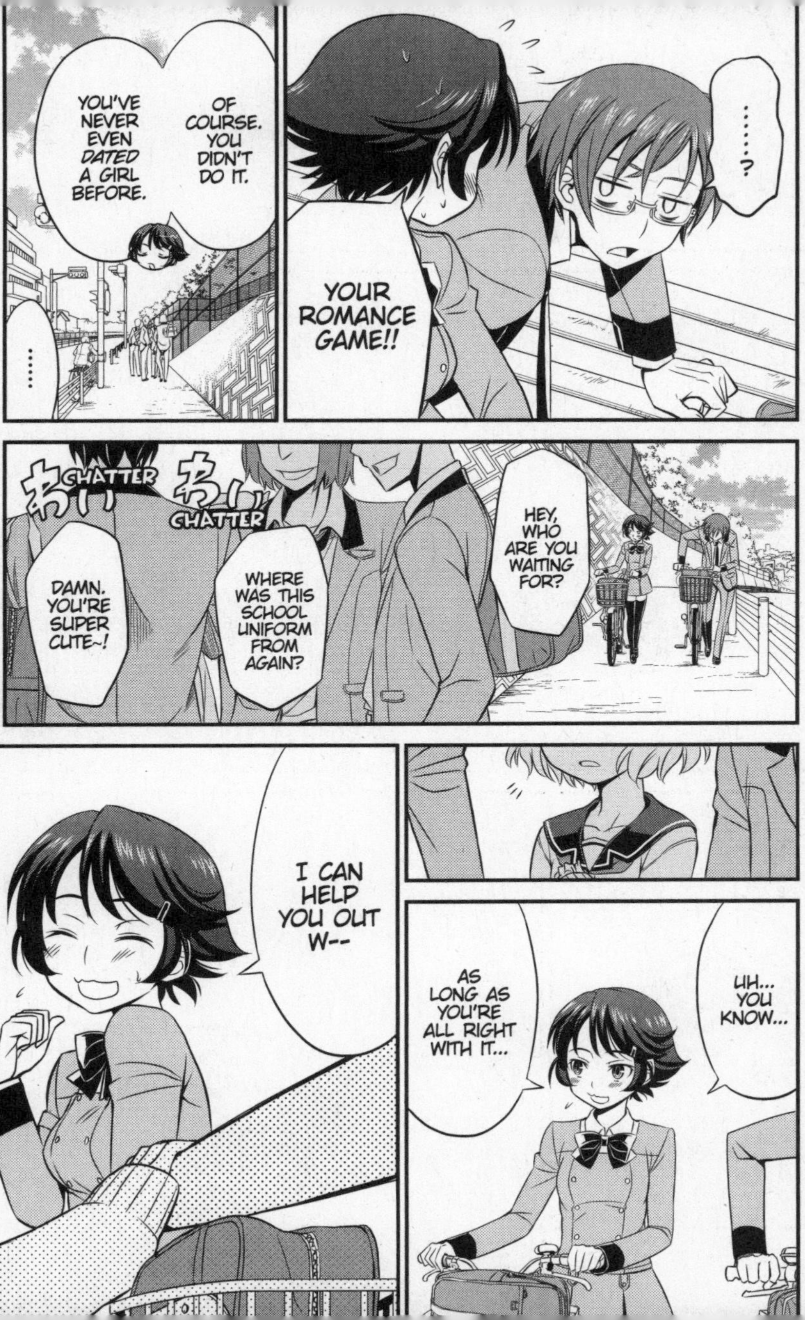
......?
YOUR ROMANCE GAME!!
OF COURSE. YOU DIDN'T DO IT.
YOU'VE NEVER EVEN *DATED* A GIRL BEFORE.
......
HEY, WHO ARE YOU WAITING FOR?
CHATTER
WHERE WAS THIS SCHOOL UNIFORM FROM AGAIN?
CHATTER
DAMN. YOU'RE SUPER CUTE~!
UH... YOU KNOW...
AS LONG AS YOU'RE ALL RIGHT WITH IT...
I CAN HELP YOU OUT W--

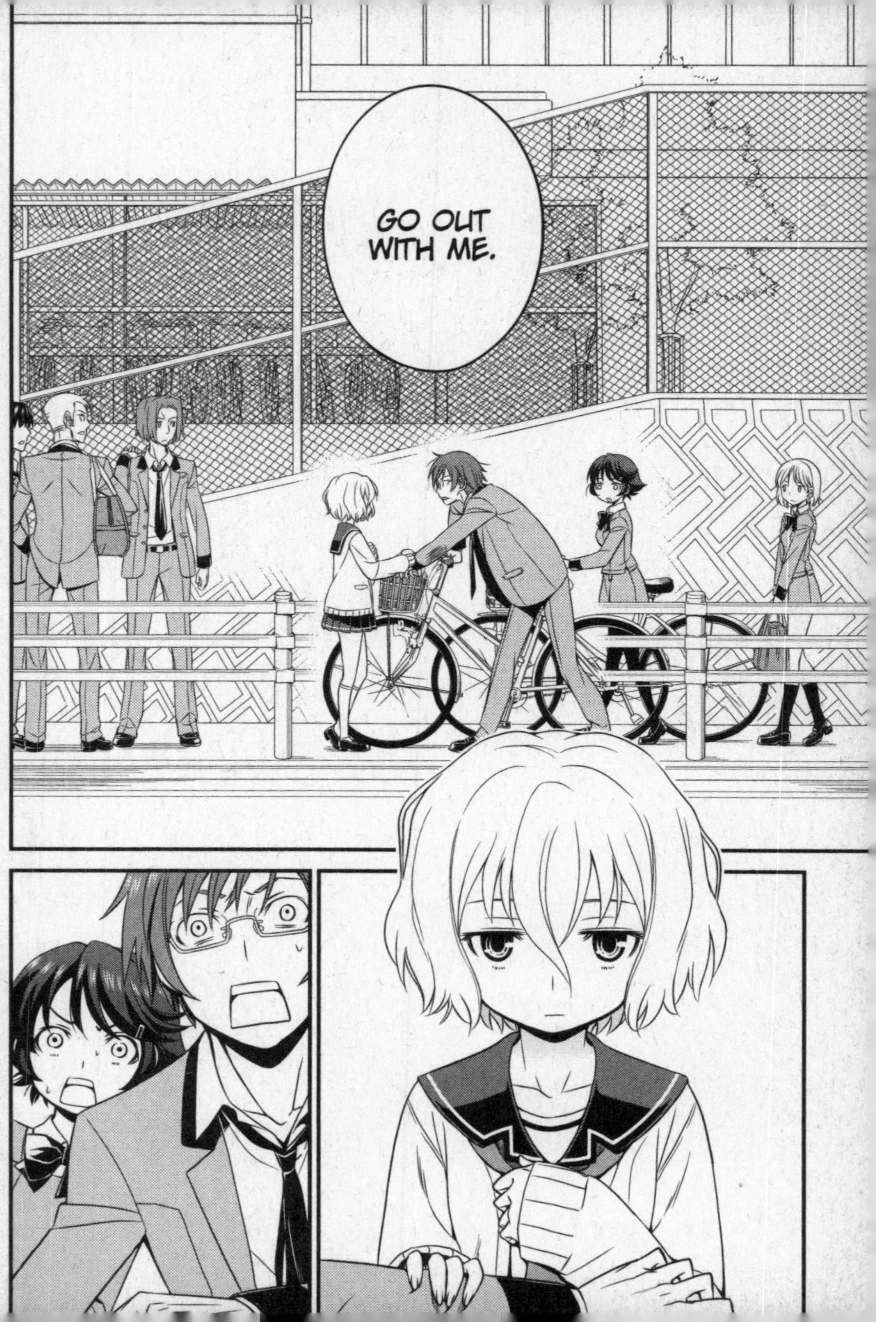
GO OUT WITH ME.

NOT LIVES

ノットライヴス

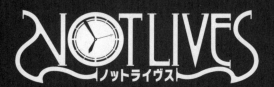

NOT ALIVE

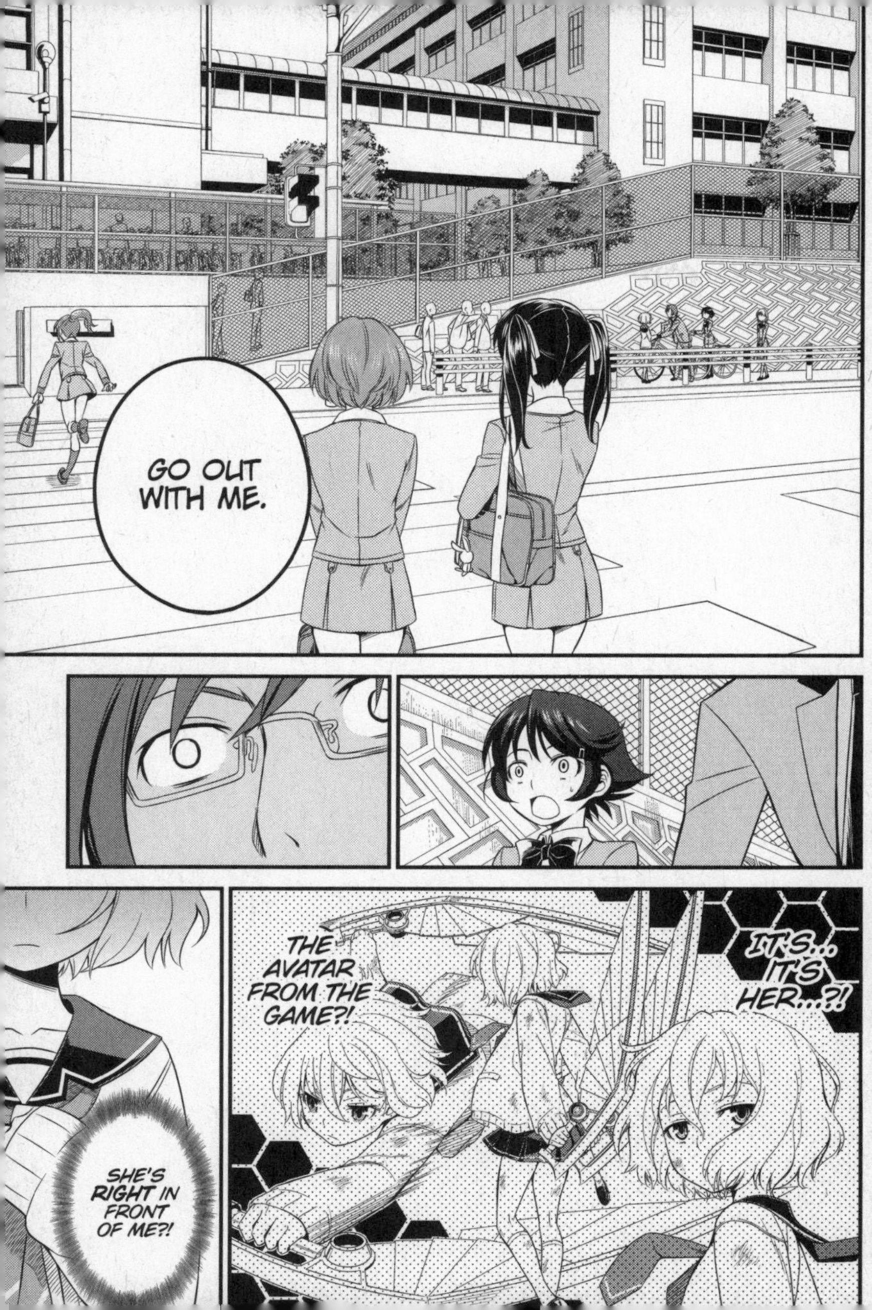
GO OUT WITH ME.
IT'S... IT'S HER...?!
THE AVATAR FROM THE GAME?!
SHE'S RIGHT IN FRONT OF ME?!

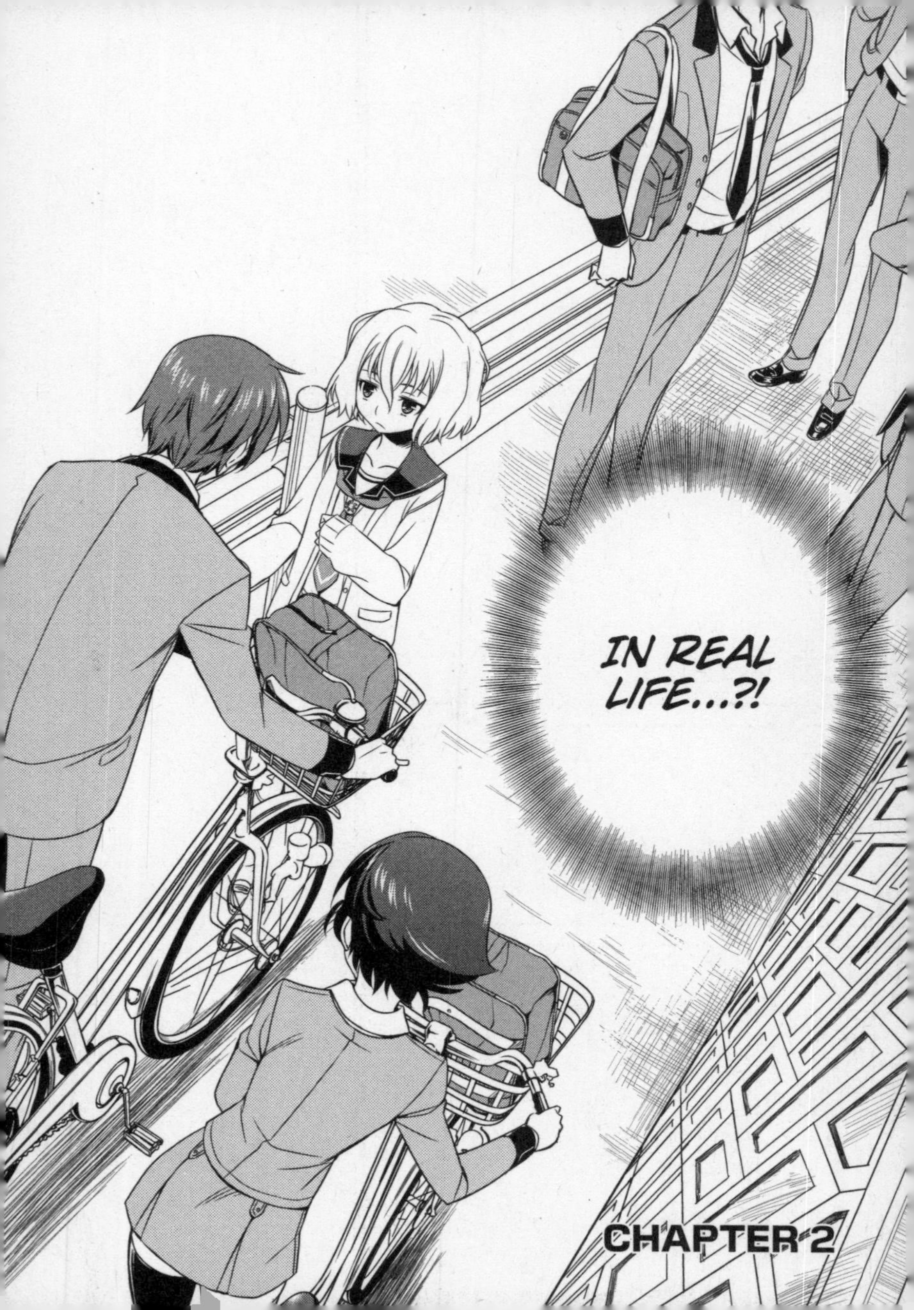
IN REAL LIFE...?!
CHAPTER 2

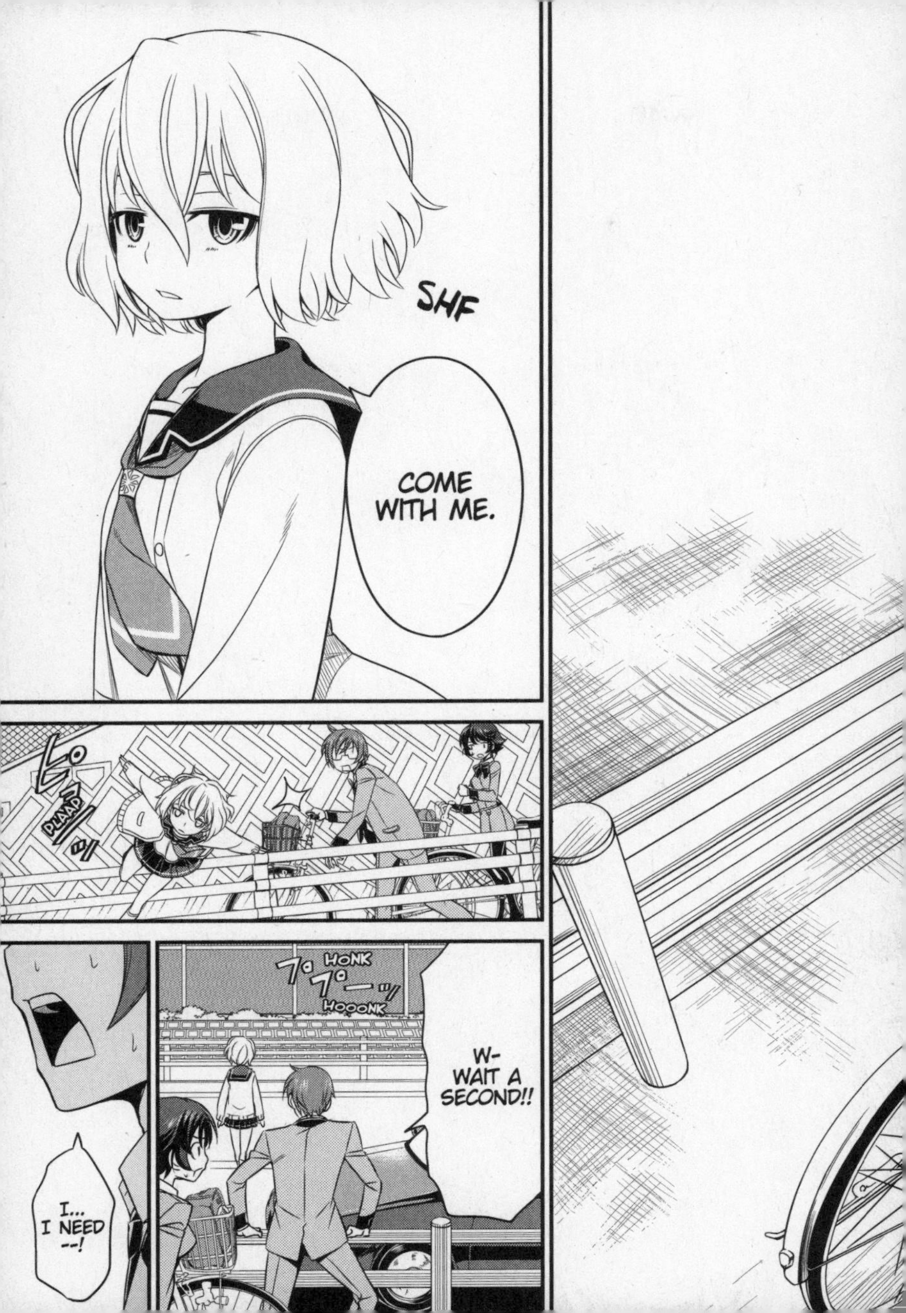
SHF
COME WITH ME.
PLAAP
HONK
HOOONK
W- WAIT A SECOND!!
I... I NEED --!

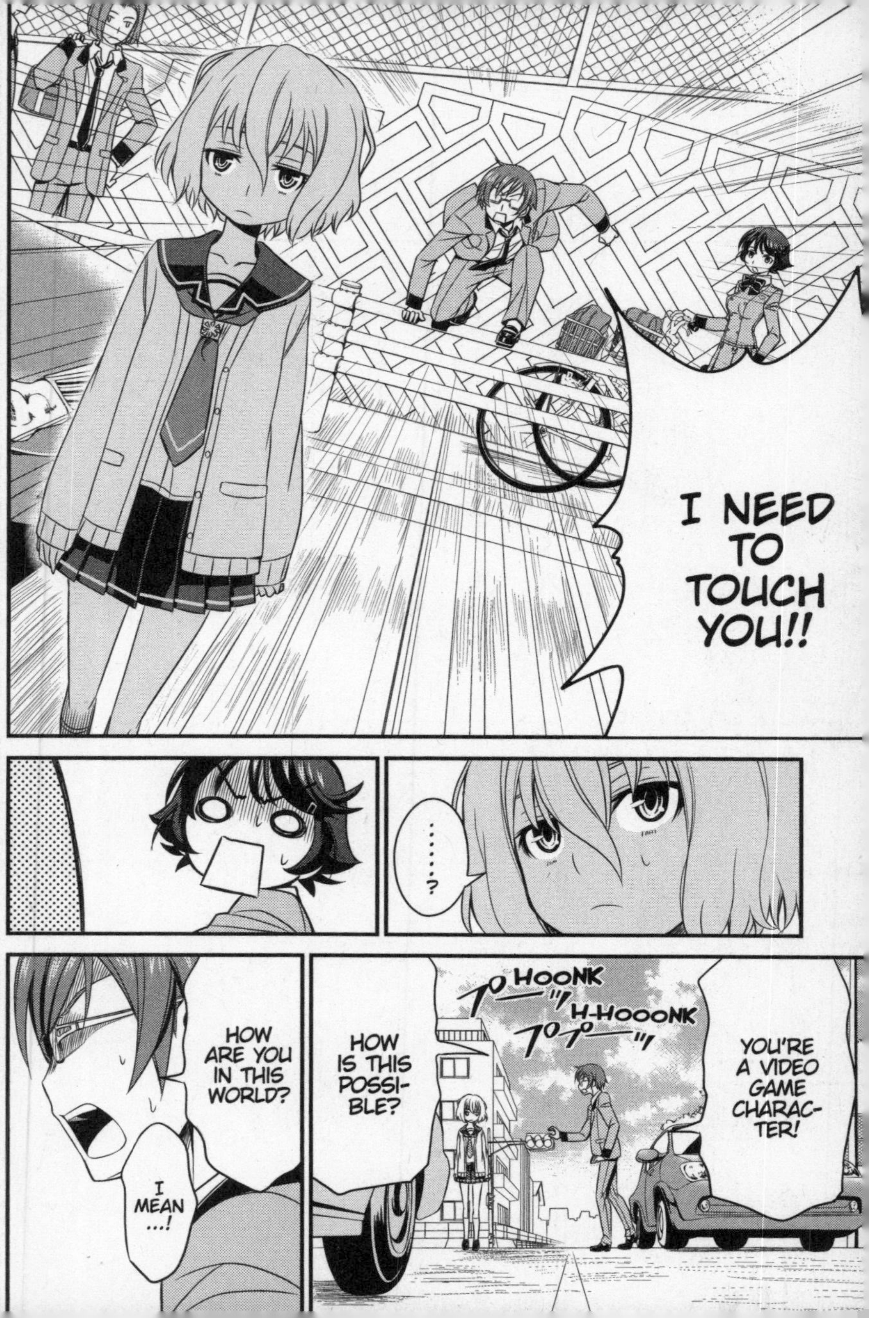
I NEED TO TOUCH YOU!!
......?
YOU'RE A VIDEO GAME CHARACTER!
HOONK
H-HOOONK
HOW IS THIS POSSIBLE?
HOW ARE YOU IN THIS WORLD?
I MEAN...!

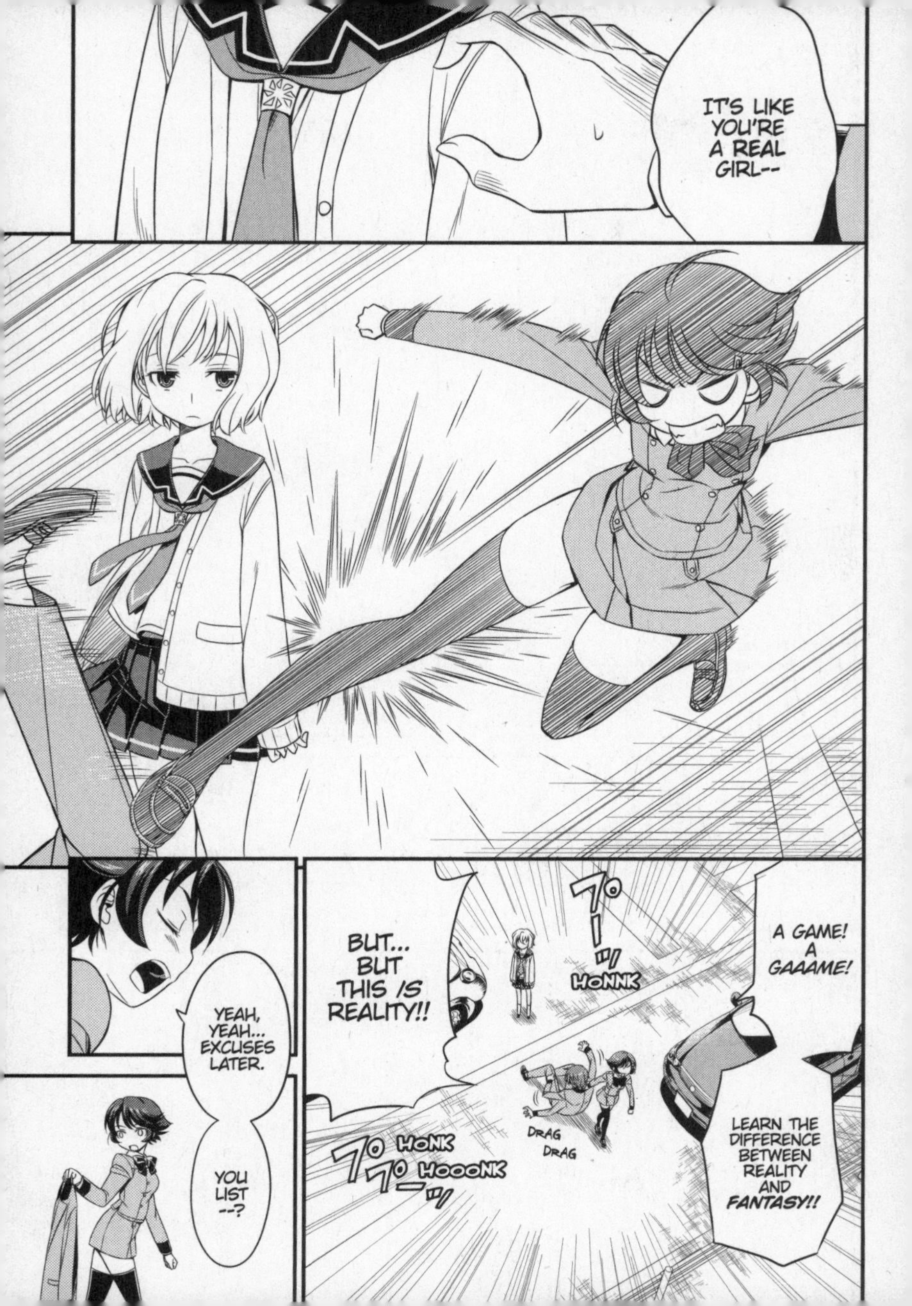
IT'S LIKE YOU'RE A REAL GIRL--
A GAME! A GAAAME!
HONNK
BUT... BUT THIS *IS* REALITY!!
LEARN THE DIFFERENCE BETWEEN REALITY AND *FANTASY*!!
DRAG DRAG
HONK
HOOOONK
YEAH, YEAH... EXCUSES LATER.
YOU LIST --?

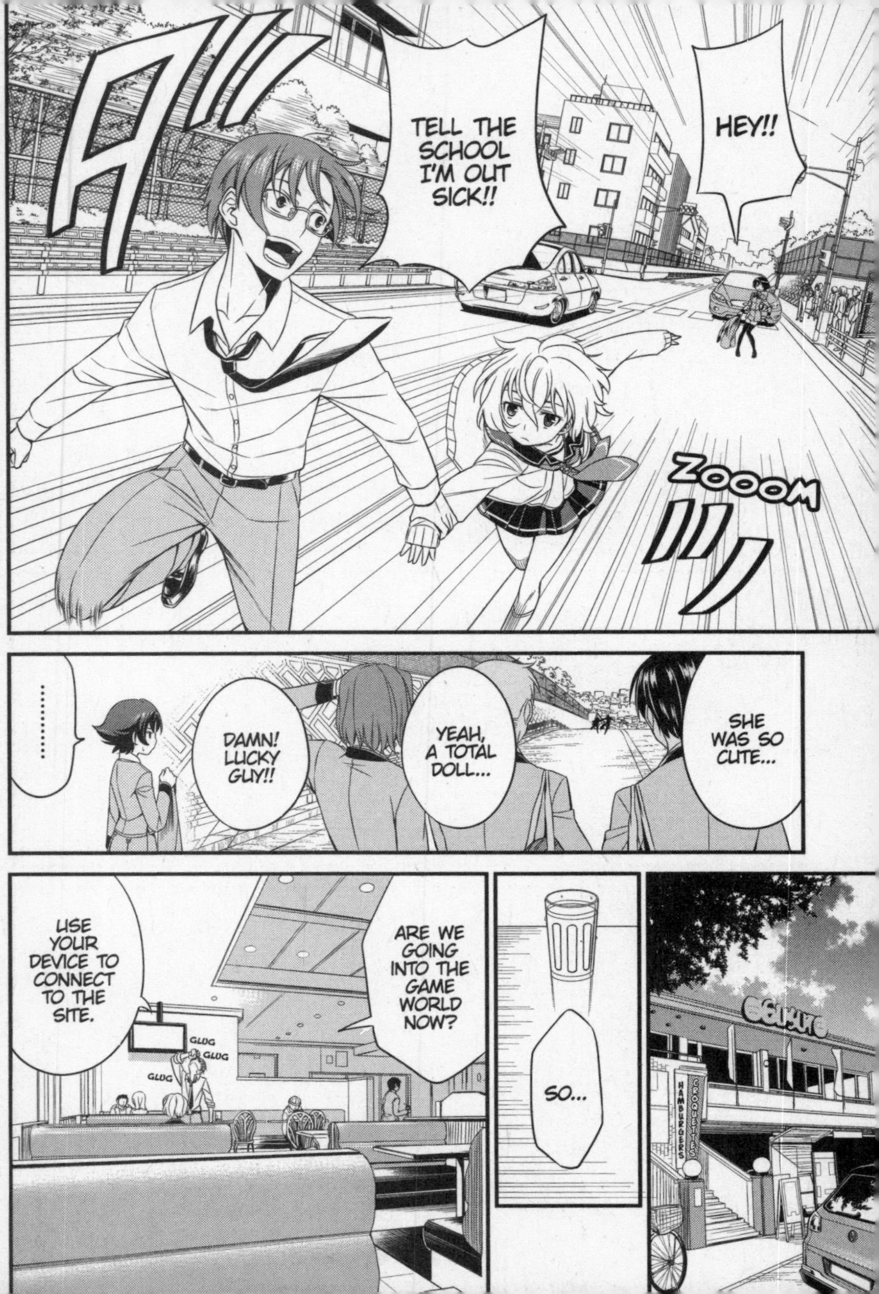
HEY!!
TELL THE SCHOOL I'M OUT SICK!!
ZOOOM
SHE WAS SO CUTE...
YEAH, A TOTAL DOLL...
DAMN! LUCKY GUY!!
......
HAMBURGERS
CROQUETTES
SO...
ARE WE GOING INTO THE GAME WORLD NOW?
USE YOUR DEVICE TO CONNECT TO THE SITE.
GLUG
GLUG
GLUG

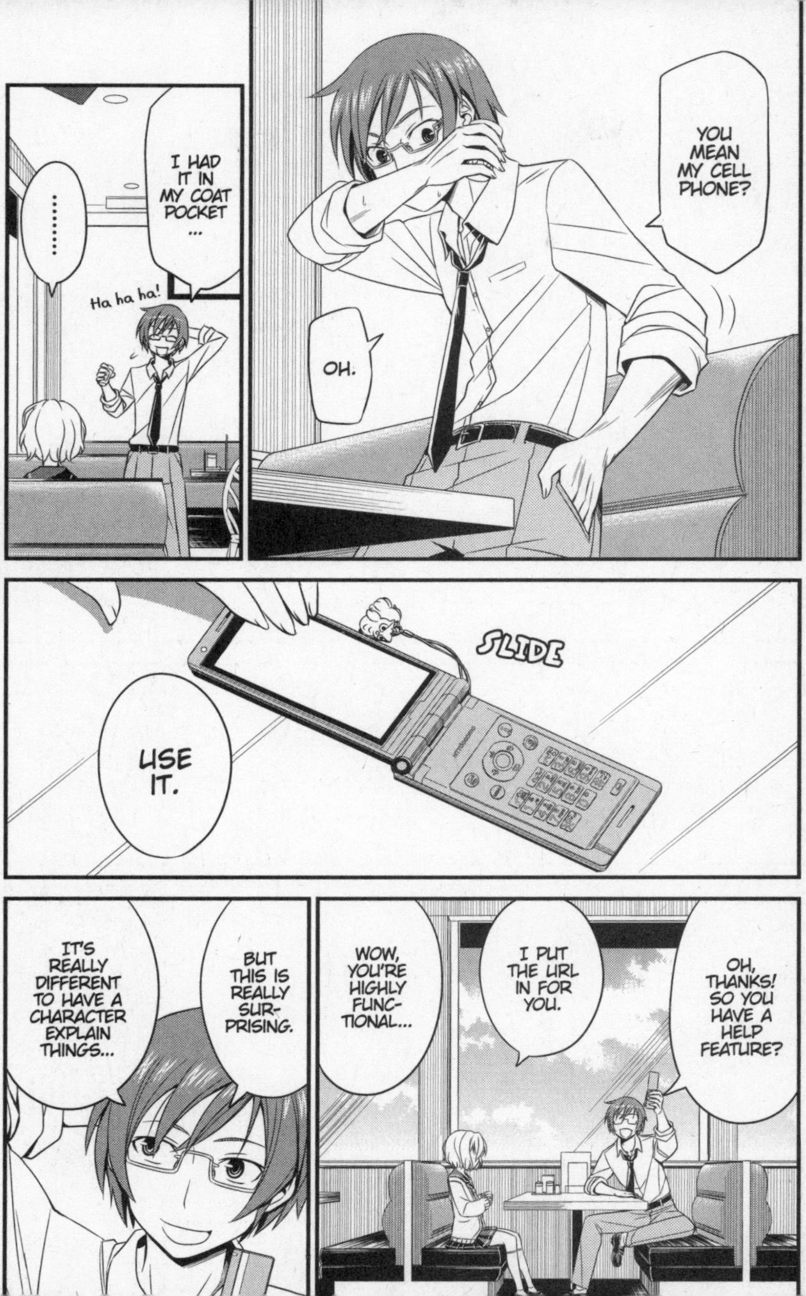
YOU MEAN MY CELL PHONE?
OH.
I HAD IT IN MY COAT POCKET ...
......
Ha ha ha!
SLIDE
USE IT.
OH, THANKS! SO YOU HAVE A HELP FEATURE?
I PUT THE URL IN FOR YOU.
WOW, YOU'RE HIGHLY FUNC-TIONAL...
BUT THIS IS REALLY SUR-PRISING.
IT'S REALLY DIFFERENT TO HAVE A CHARACTER EXPLAIN THINGS...

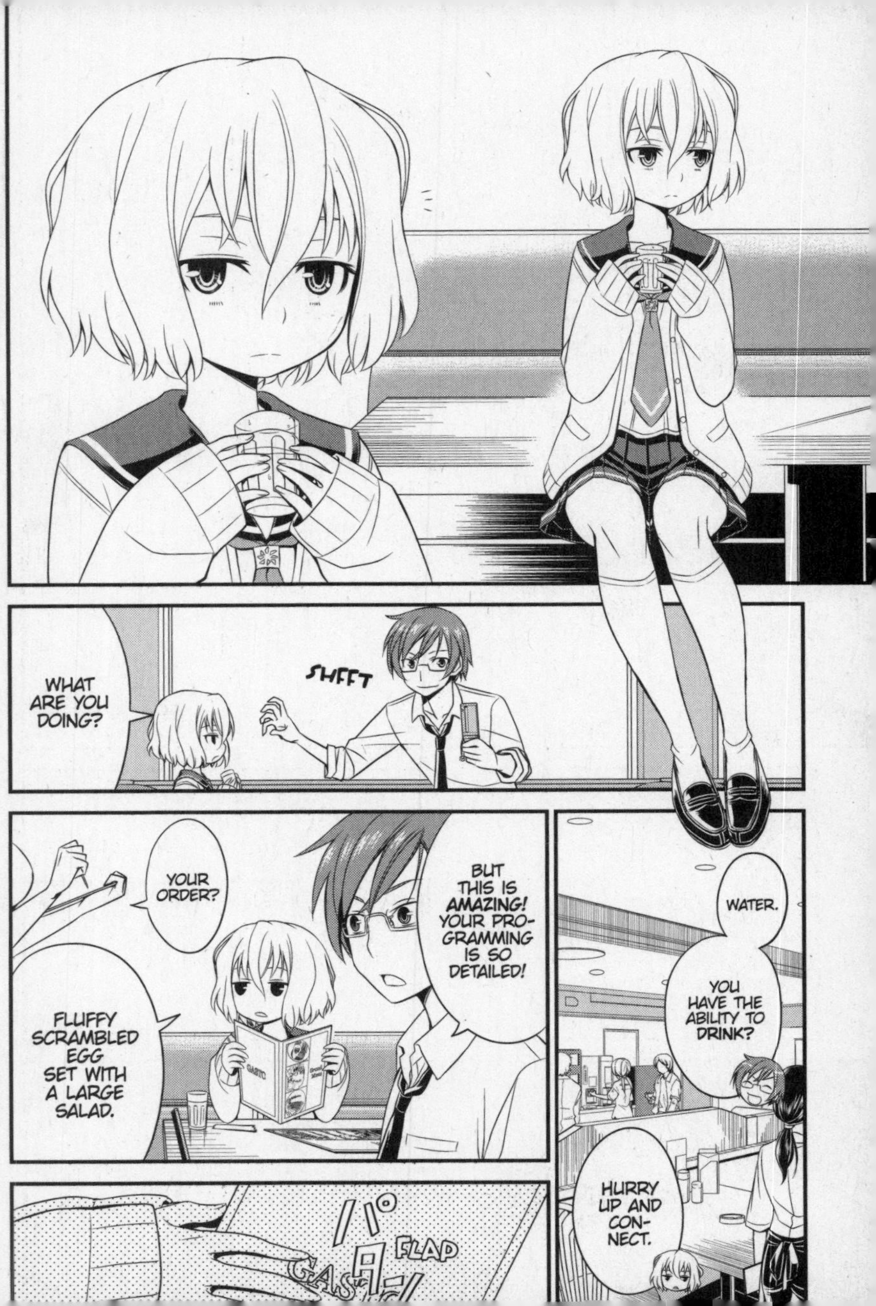
SHFFT
WHAT ARE YOU DOING?
WATER.
YOU HAVE THE ABILITY TO DRINK?
HURRY UP AND CON-NECT.
BUT THIS IS AMAZING! YOUR PRO-GRAMMING IS SO DETAILED!
YOUR ORDER?
FLUFFY SCRAMBLED EGG SET WITH A LARGE SALAD.
FLAP

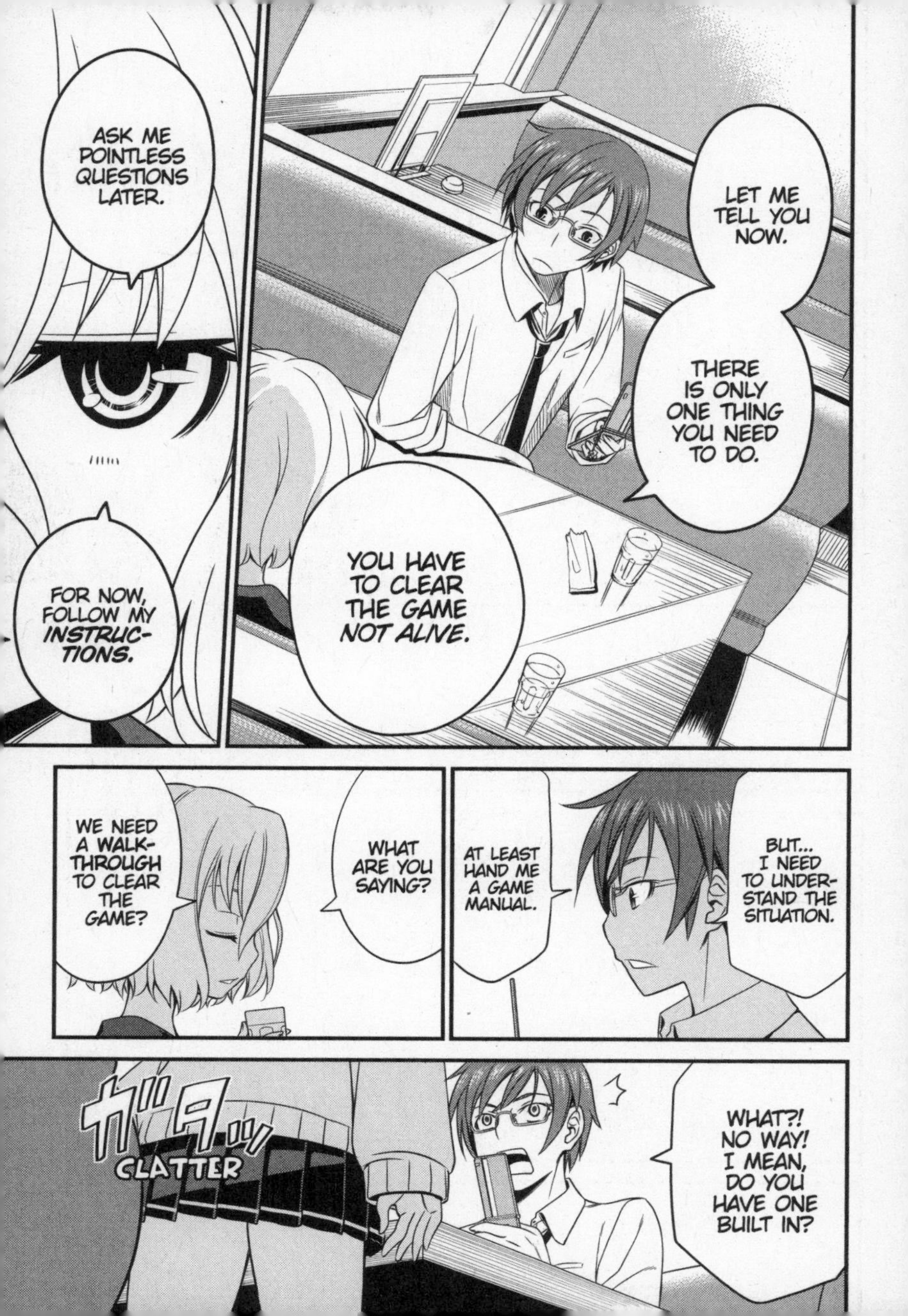
LET ME TELL YOU NOW.
THERE IS ONLY ONE THING YOU NEED TO DO.
YOU HAVE TO CLEAR THE GAME *NOT ALIVE.*
ASK ME POINTLESS QUESTIONS LATER.
FOR NOW, FOLLOW MY *INSTRUCTIONS.*
BUT... I NEED TO UNDERSTAND THE SITUATION.
AT LEAST HAND ME A GAME MANUAL.
WHAT ARE YOU SAYING?
WE NEED A WALK-THROUGH TO CLEAR THE GAME?
WHAT?! NO WAY! I MEAN, DO YOU HAVE ONE BUILT IN?
ガタッ
CLATTER

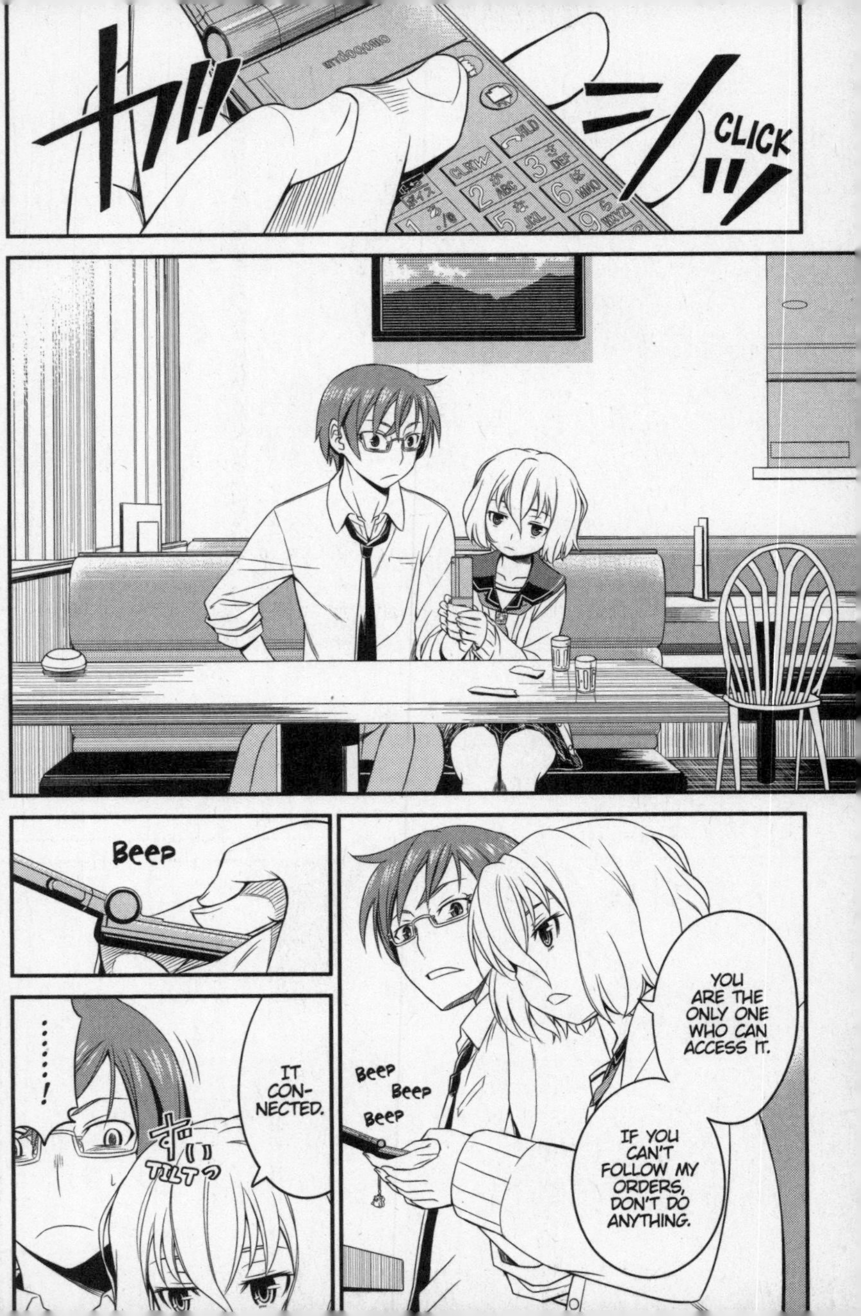
CLICK
YOU ARE THE ONLY ONE WHO CAN ACCESS IT.
IF YOU CAN'T FOLLOW MY ORDERS, DON'T DO ANYTHING.
Beep Beep Beep
Beep
IT CON-NECTED.
TILT
......!

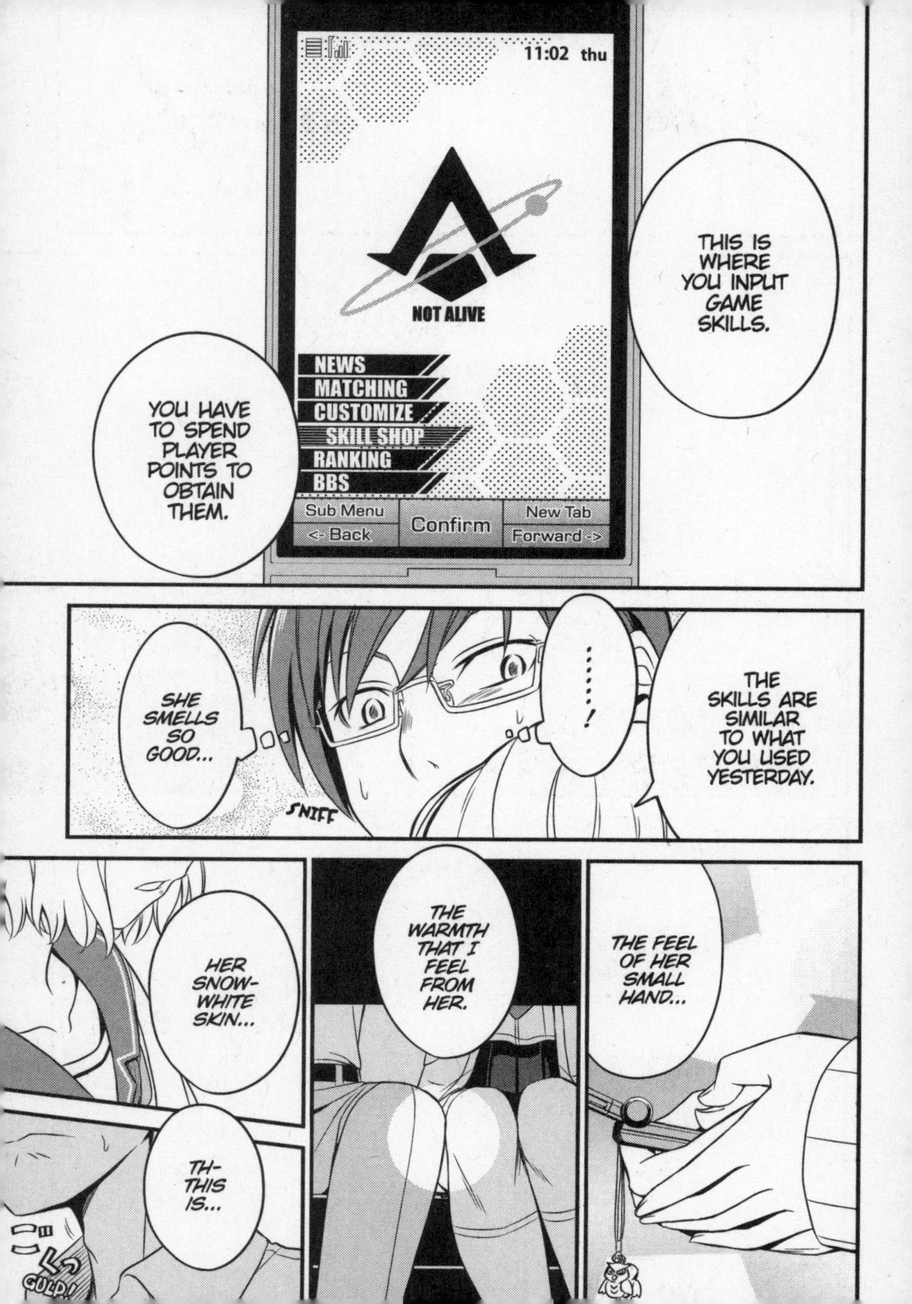
THIS IS WHERE YOU INPUT GAME SKILLS.
11:02 thu
NOT ALIVE
NEWS
MATCHING
CUSTOMIZE
SKILL SHOP
RANKING
BBS
Sub Menu
<- Back
Confirm
New Tab
Forward ->
YOU HAVE TO SPEND PLAYER POINTS TO OBTAIN THEM.
THE SKILLS ARE SIMILAR TO WHAT YOU USED YESTERDAY.
......!
SHE SMELLS SO GOOD...
SNIFF
THE FEEL OF HER SMALL HAND...
THE WARMTH THAT I FEEL FROM HER.
HER SNOW-WHITE SKIN...
TH-THIS IS...
GULP!

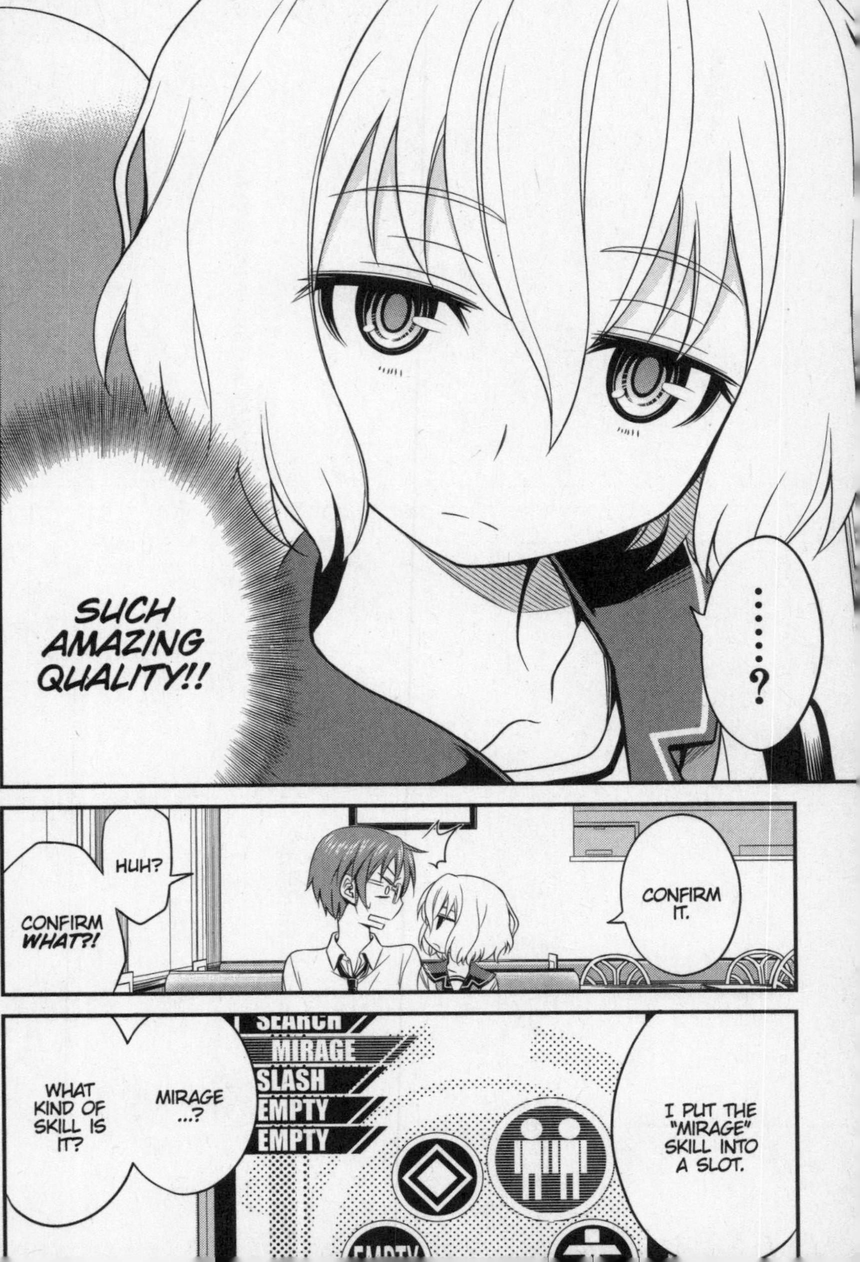
......?
SUCH AMAZING QUALITY!!
CONFIRM IT.
HUH?
CONFIRM WHAT?!
I PUT THE "MIRAGE" SKILL INTO A SLOT.
SEARCH
MIRAGE
SLASH
EMPTY
EMPTY
MIRAGE ...?
WHAT KIND OF SKILL IS IT?

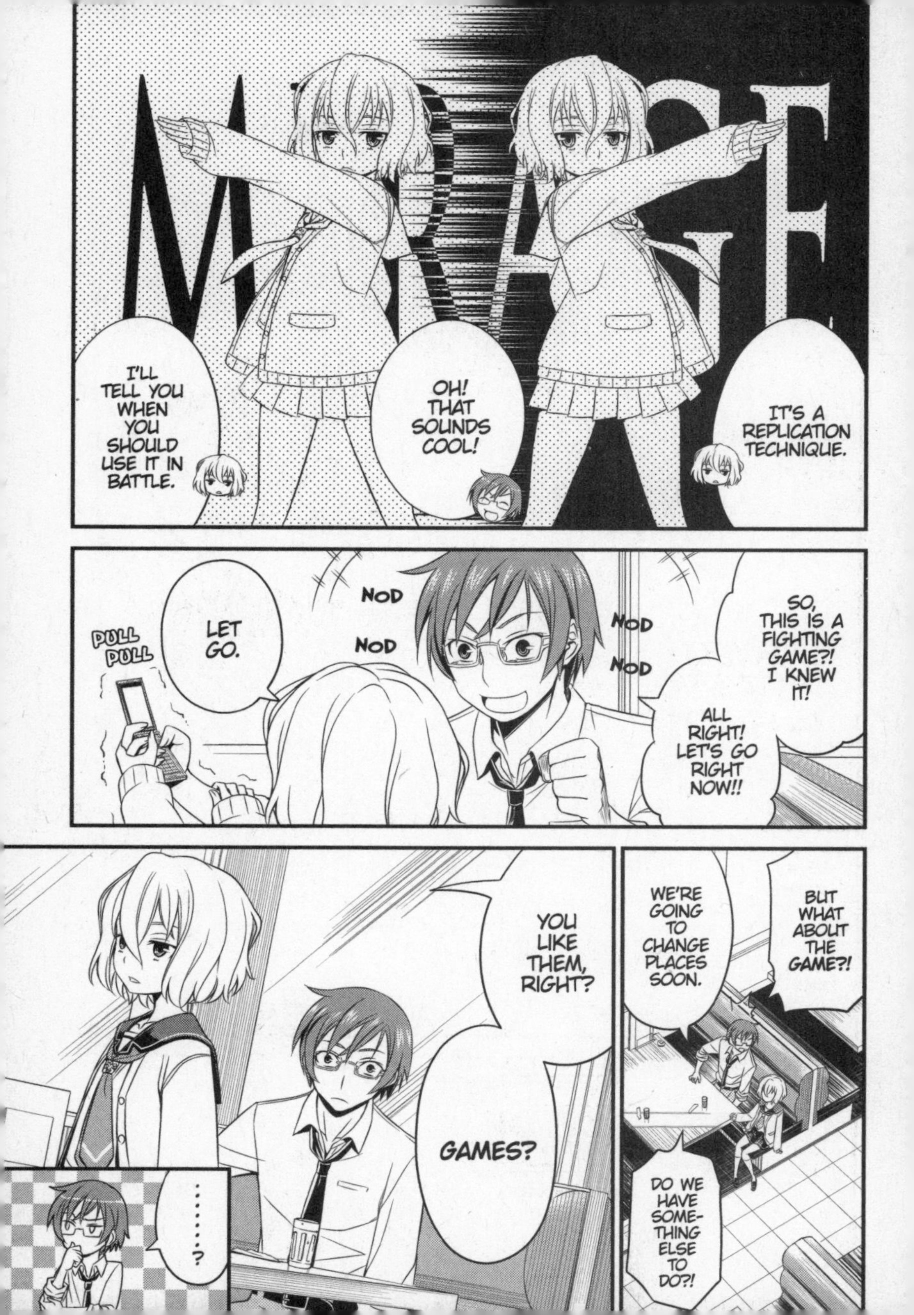
IT'S A REPLICATION TECHNIQUE.
OH! THAT SOUNDS COOL!
I'LL TELL YOU WHEN YOU SHOULD USE IT IN BATTLE.
SO, THIS IS A FIGHTING GAME?! I KNEW IT!
ALL RIGHT! LET'S GO RIGHT NOW!!
NOD
NOD
NOD
NOD
LET GO.
PULL PULL
BUT WHAT ABOUT THE GAME?!
WE'RE GOING TO CHANGE PLACES SOON.
DO WE HAVE SOMETHING ELSE TO DO?!
YOU LIKE THEM, RIGHT?
GAMES?
......?

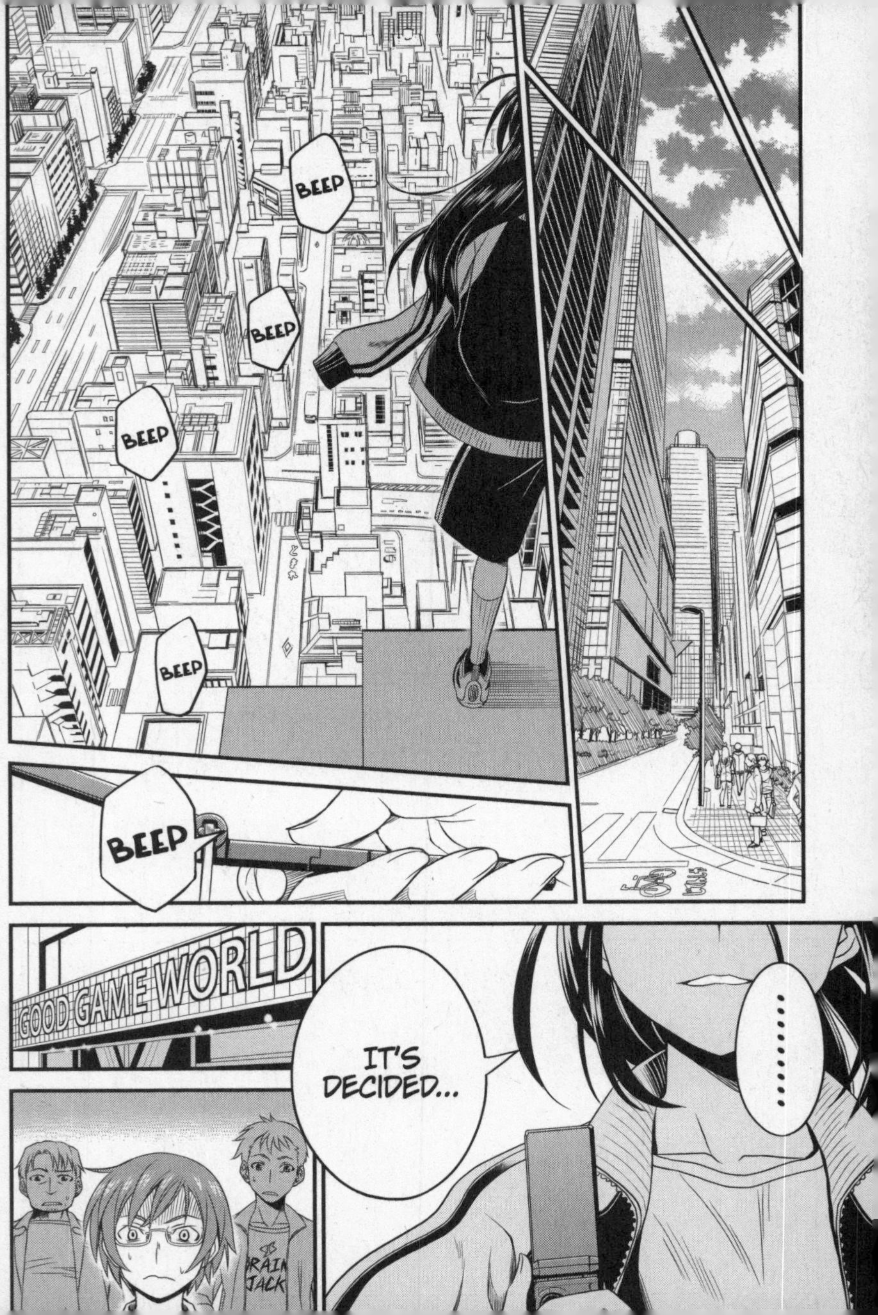

BEEP
BEEP
BEEP
BEEP
BEEP
......
IT'S DECIDED...
GOOD GAME WORLD
BRAIN JACK

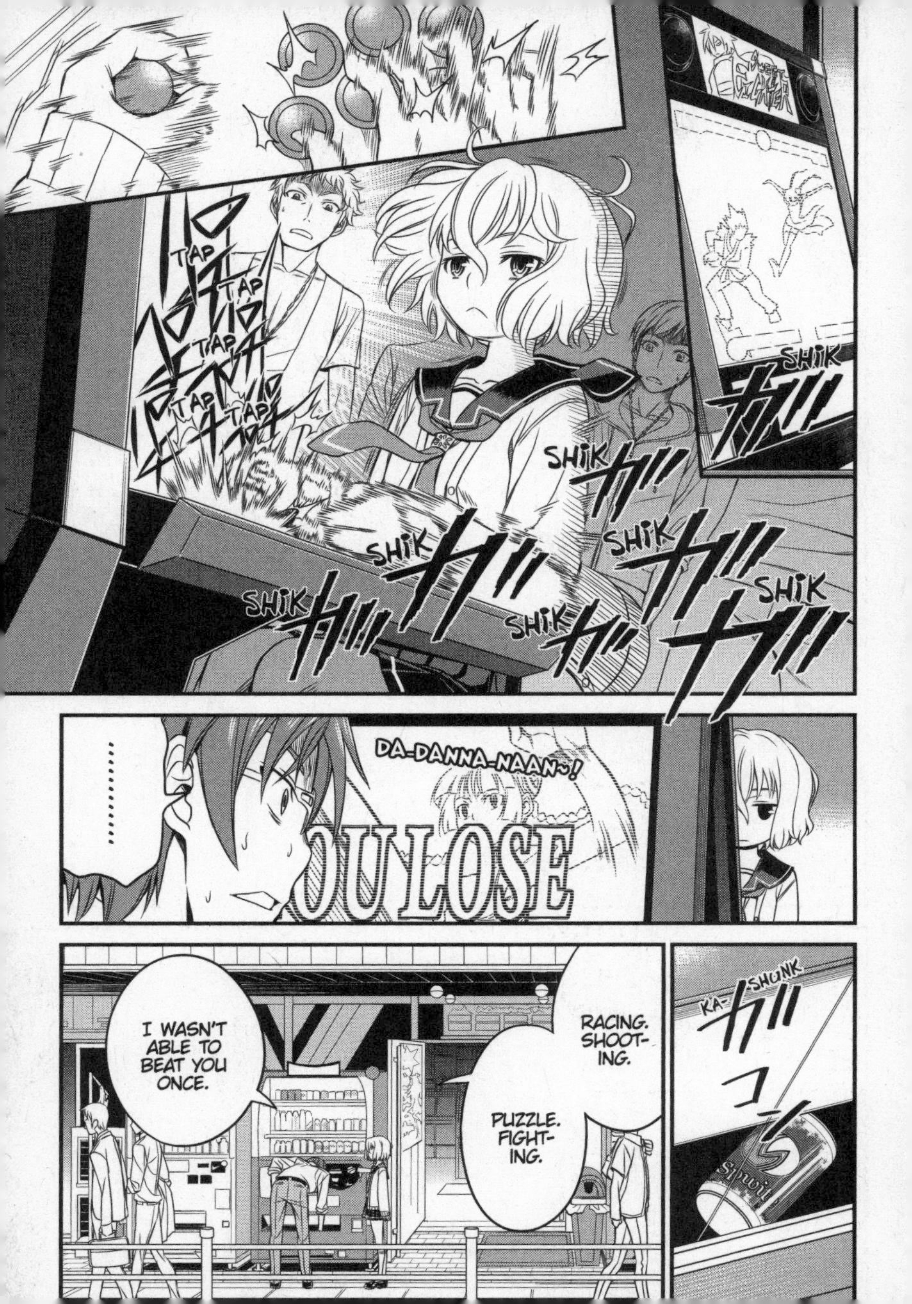

TAP
TAP
TAP
TAP
TAP
SHIK
SHIK
SHIK
SHIK
SHIK
SHIK
DA-DANNA-NAAN~!
OU LOSE
......
KA-SHUNK
RACING. SHOOT-ING.
PUZZLE. FIGHT-ING.
I WASN'T ABLE TO BEAT YOU ONCE.

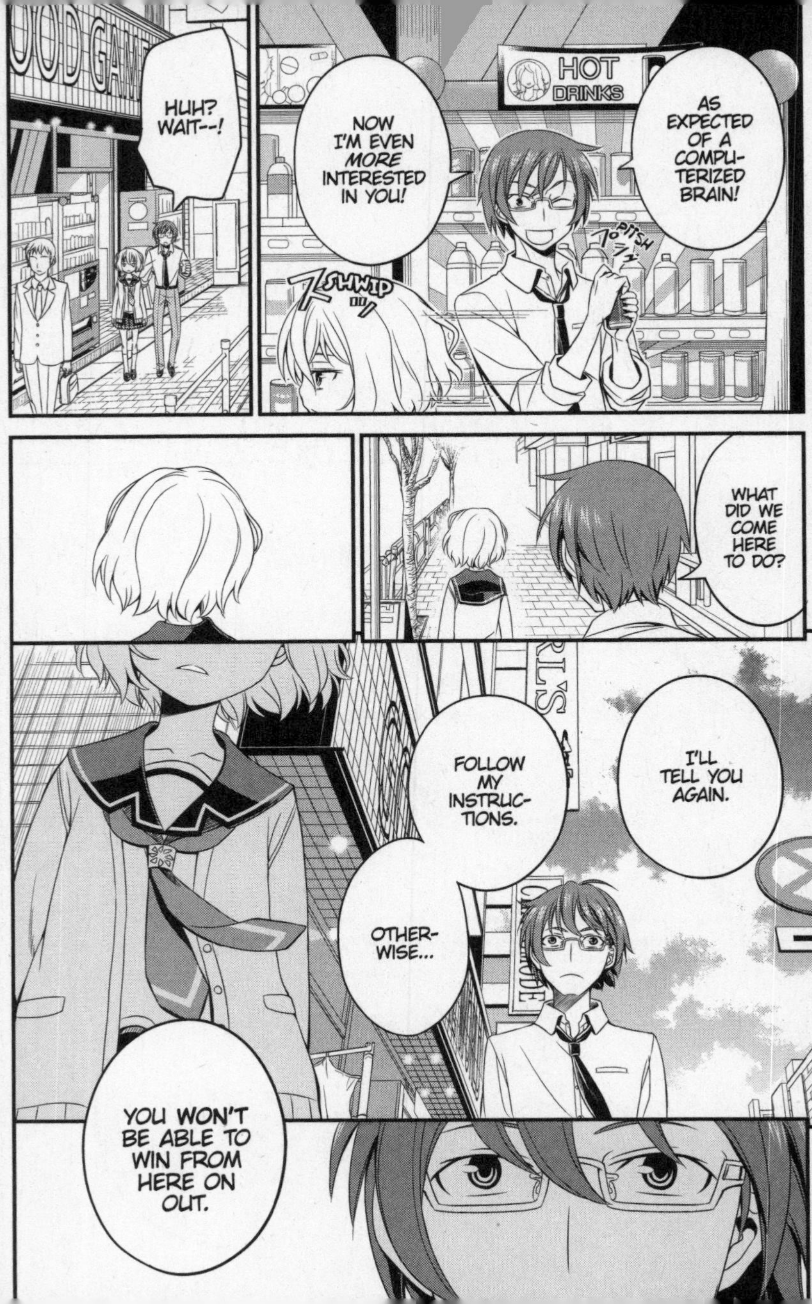
HOT DRINKS
AS EXPECTED OF A COMPUTERIZED BRAIN!
PITSH
NOW I'M EVEN *MORE* INTERESTED IN YOU!
SHWIP
HUH? WAIT--!
WHAT DID WE COME HERE TO DO?
I'LL TELL YOU AGAIN.
FOLLOW MY INSTRUCTIONS.
OTHERWISE...
YOU WON'T BE ABLE TO WIN FROM HERE ON OUT.

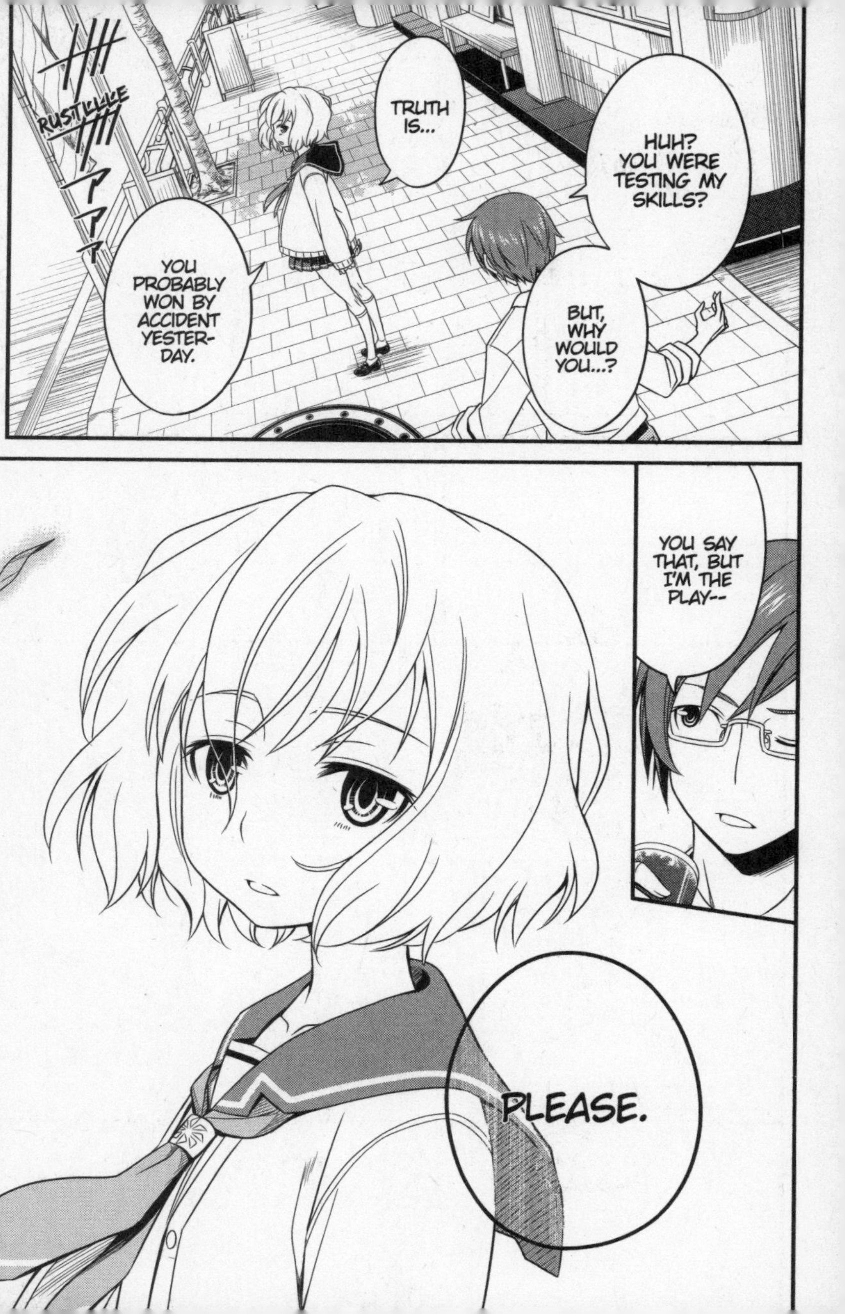
HUH? YOU WERE TESTING MY SKILLS?
BUT, WHY WOULD YOU...?
TRUTH IS...
YOU PROBABLY WON BY ACCIDENT YESTER-DAY.
RUSTLLLE
YOU SAY THAT, BUT I'M THE PLAY--
PLEASE.

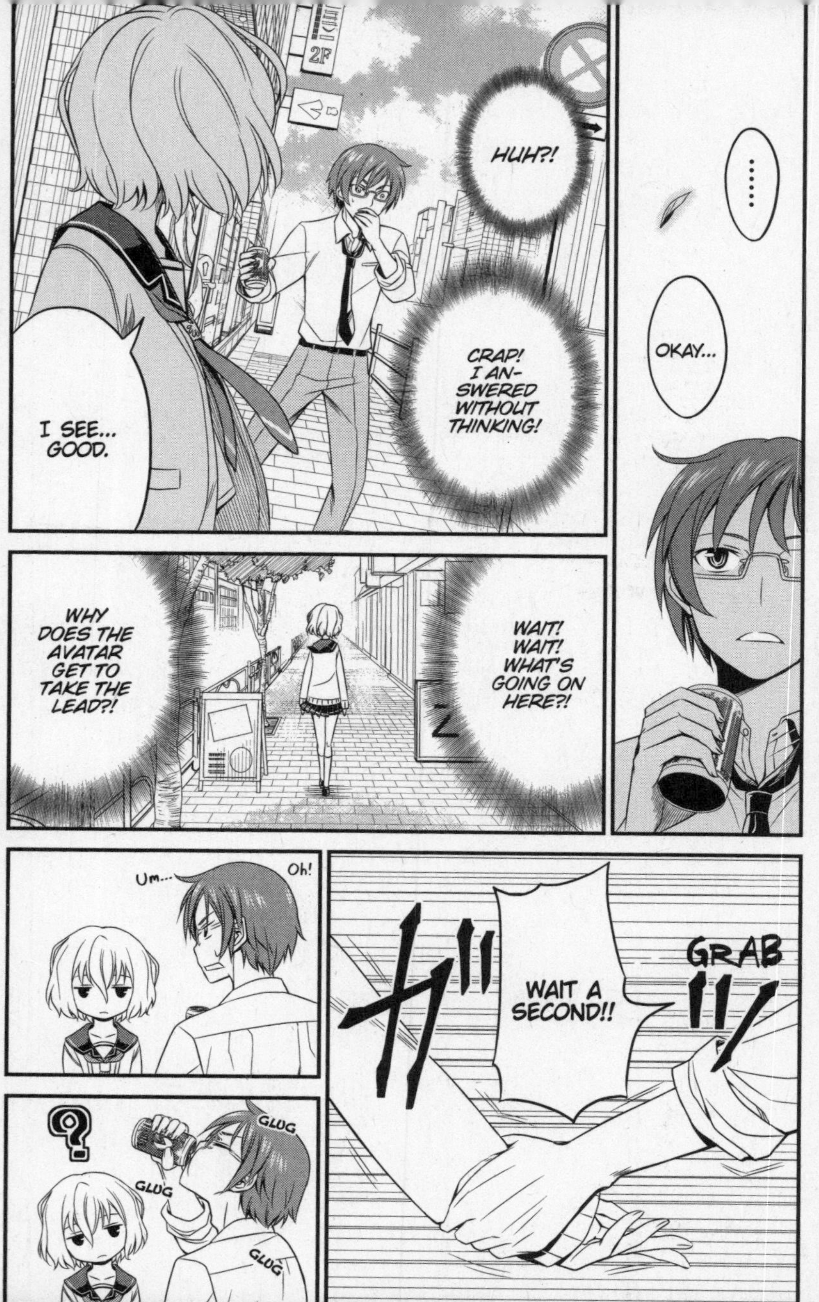
......
OKAY...
HUH?!
CRAP! I AN-SWERED WITHOUT THINKING!
I SEE... GOOD.
WAIT! WAIT! WHAT'S GOING ON HERE?!
WHY DOES THE AVATAR GET TO TAKE THE LEAD?!
GRAB
ガッ
WAIT A SECOND!!
Oh!
Um...
GLUG
GLUG
GLUG

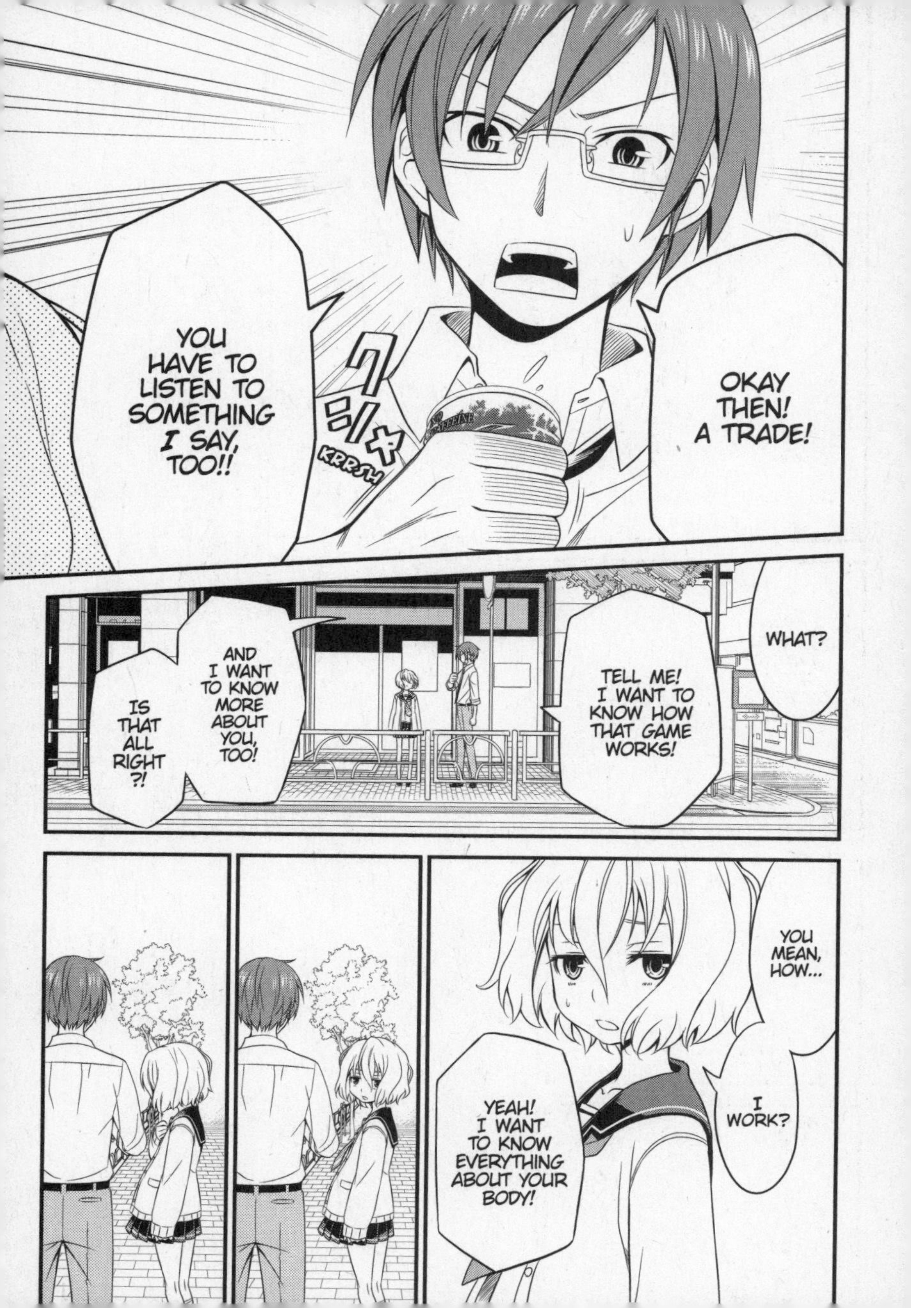
OKAY THEN! A TRADE!
KRRSH
YOU HAVE TO LISTEN TO SOMETHING I SAY, TOO!!
WHAT?
TELL ME! I WANT TO KNOW HOW THAT GAME WORKS!
AND I WANT TO KNOW MORE ABOUT YOU, TOO!
IS THAT ALL RIGHT?!
YOU MEAN, HOW...
I WORK?
YEAH! I WANT TO KNOW EVERYTHING ABOUT YOUR BODY!

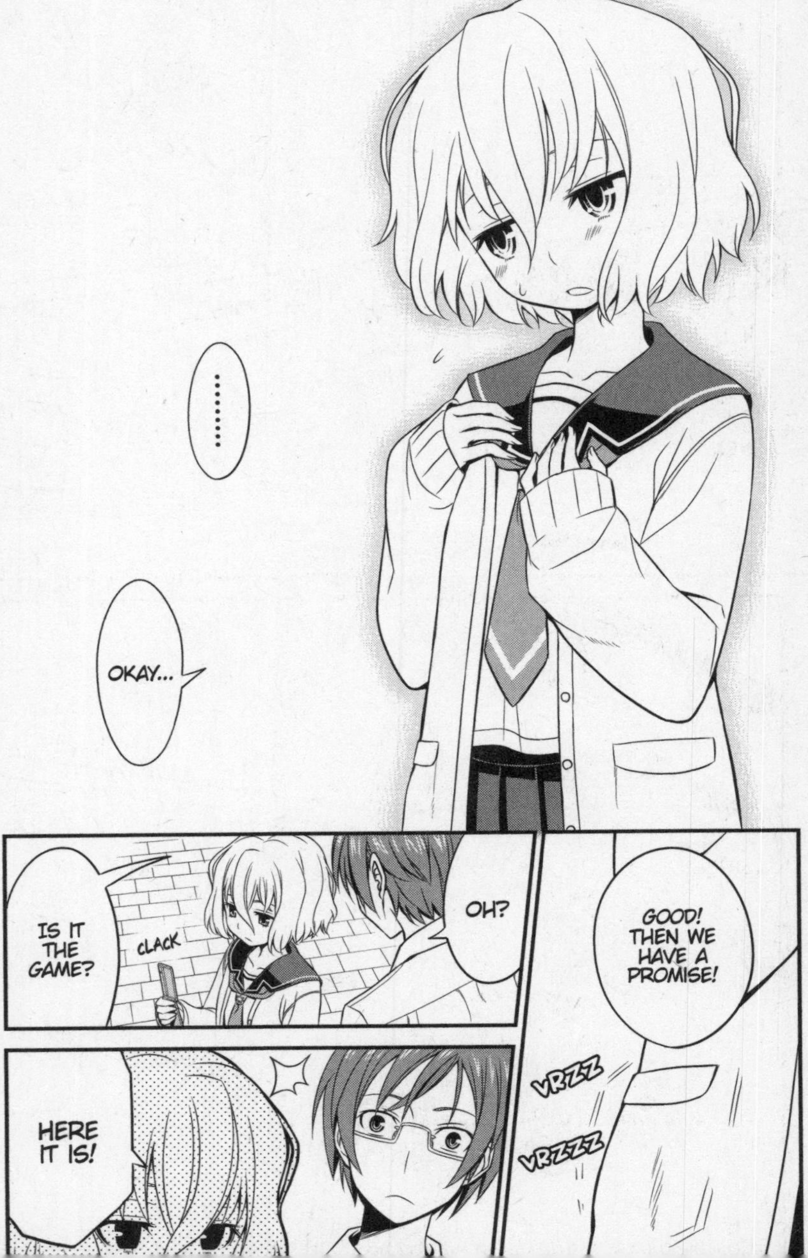
......
OKAY...
GOOD! THEN WE HAVE A PROMISE!
VRZZ
VRZZZ
OH?
IS IT THE GAME?
CLACK
HERE IT IS!

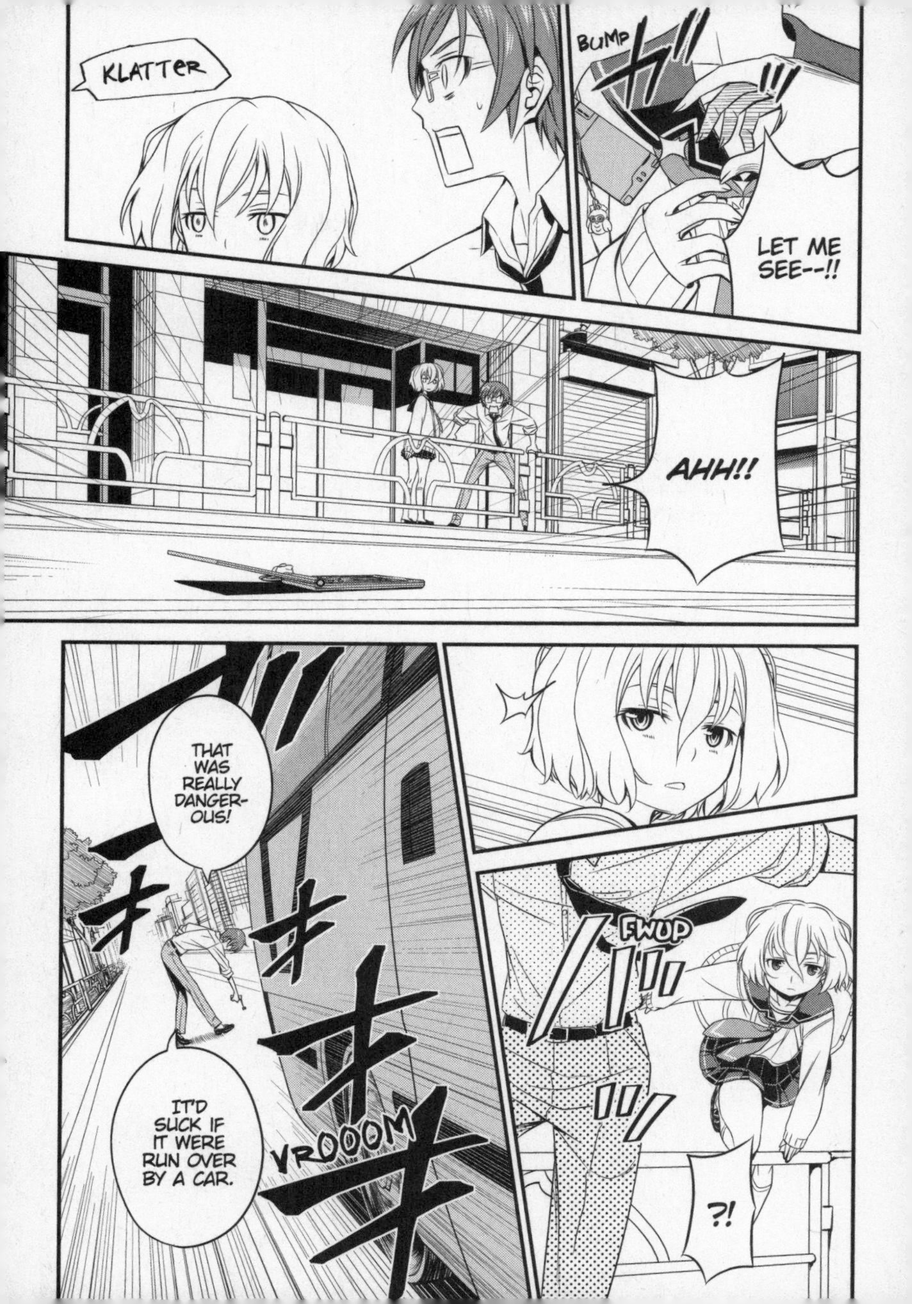
BUMP
LET ME SEE--!!
KLATTER
AHH!!
FWUP
?!
THAT WAS REALLY DANGER-OUS!
IT'D SUCK IF IT WERE RUN OVER BY A CAR.
VROOOM

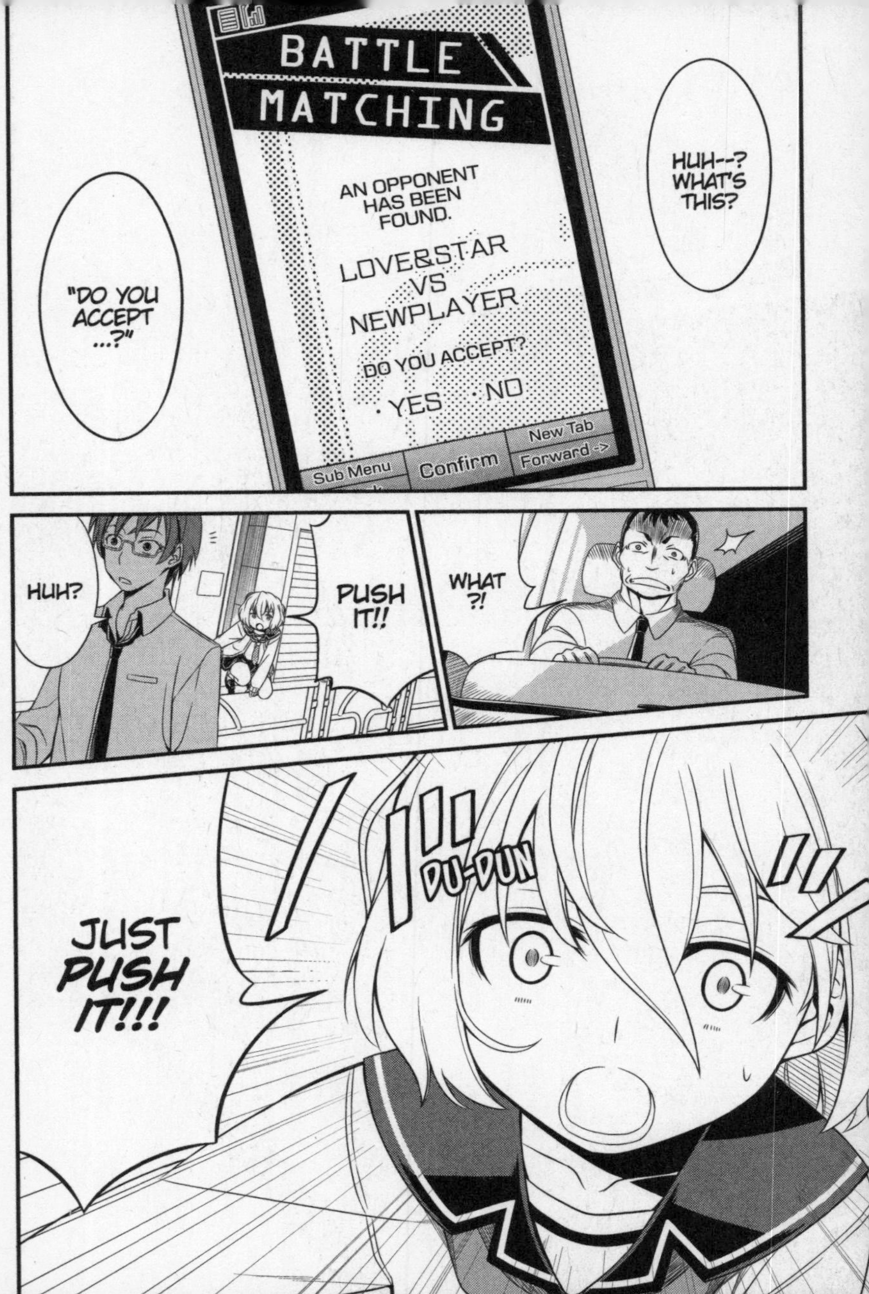
HUH--? WHAT'S THIS?
BATTLE MATCHING
AN OPPONENT HAS BEEN FOUND.
LOVE&STAR VS NEWPLAYER
DO YOU ACCEPT?
· YES · NO
New Tab
Forward ->
Confirm
Sub Menu
"DO YOU ACCEPT ...?"
WHAT ?!
PUSH IT!!
HUH?
DU-DUN
JUST PUSH IT!!!

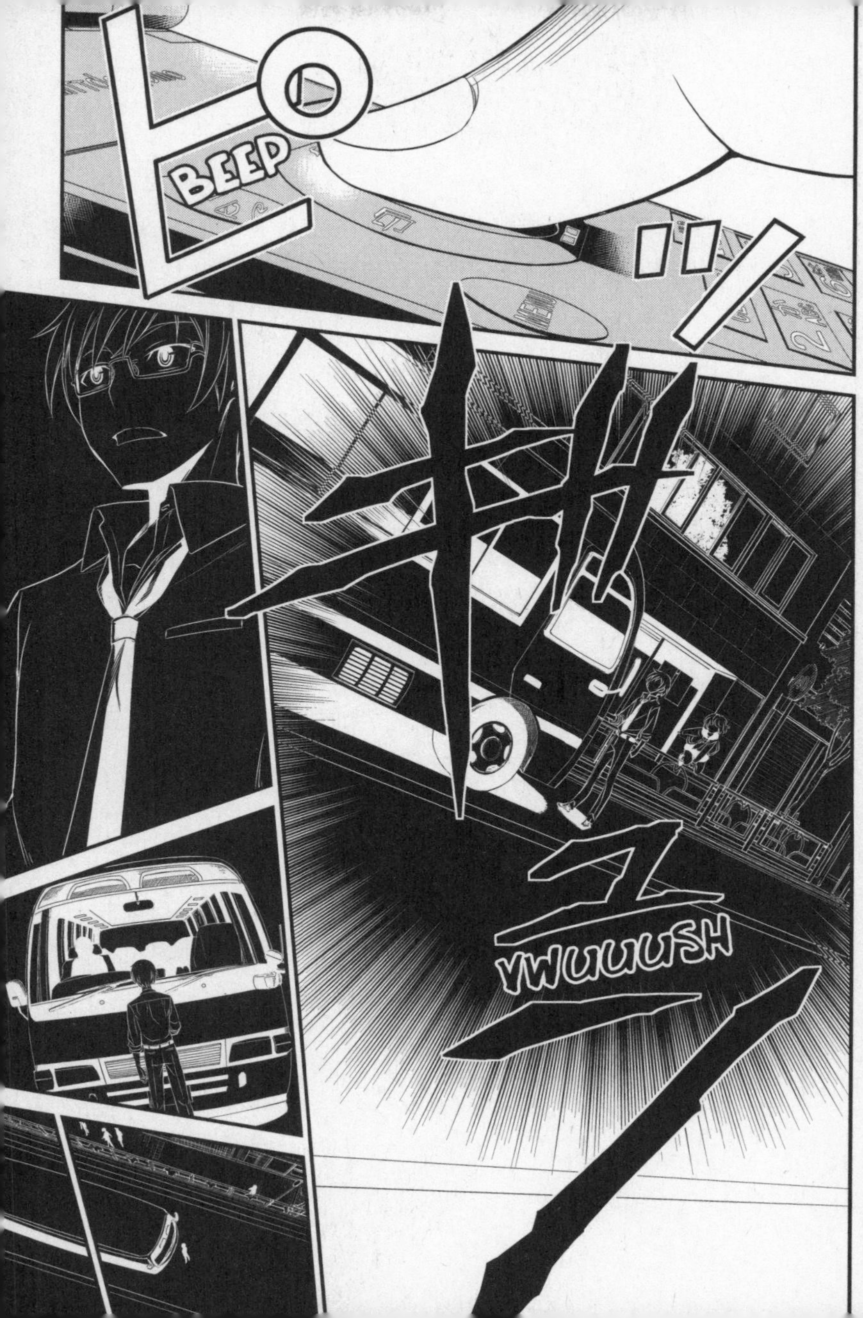
ピッ
BEEP
キュ
YWUUUSH

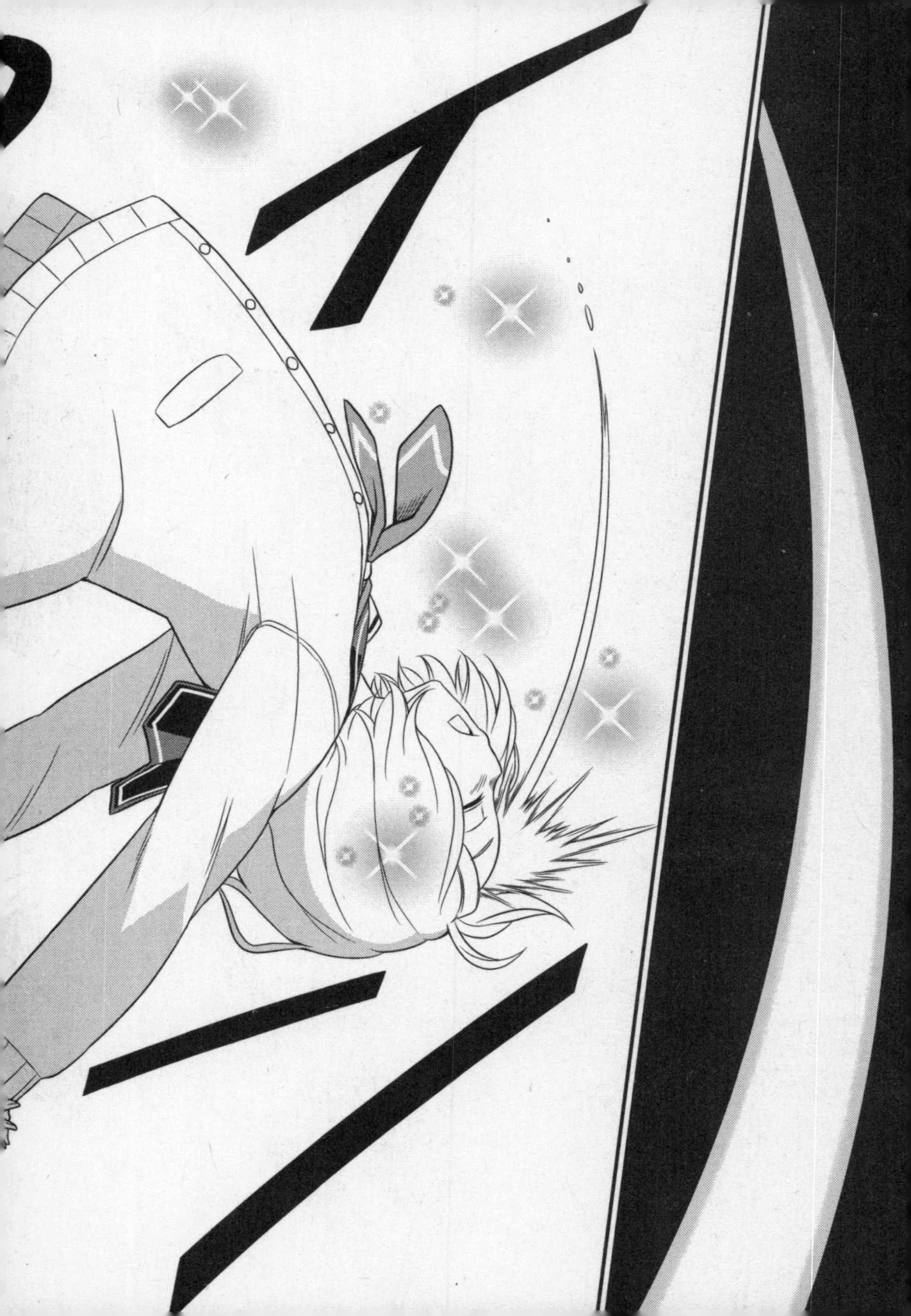

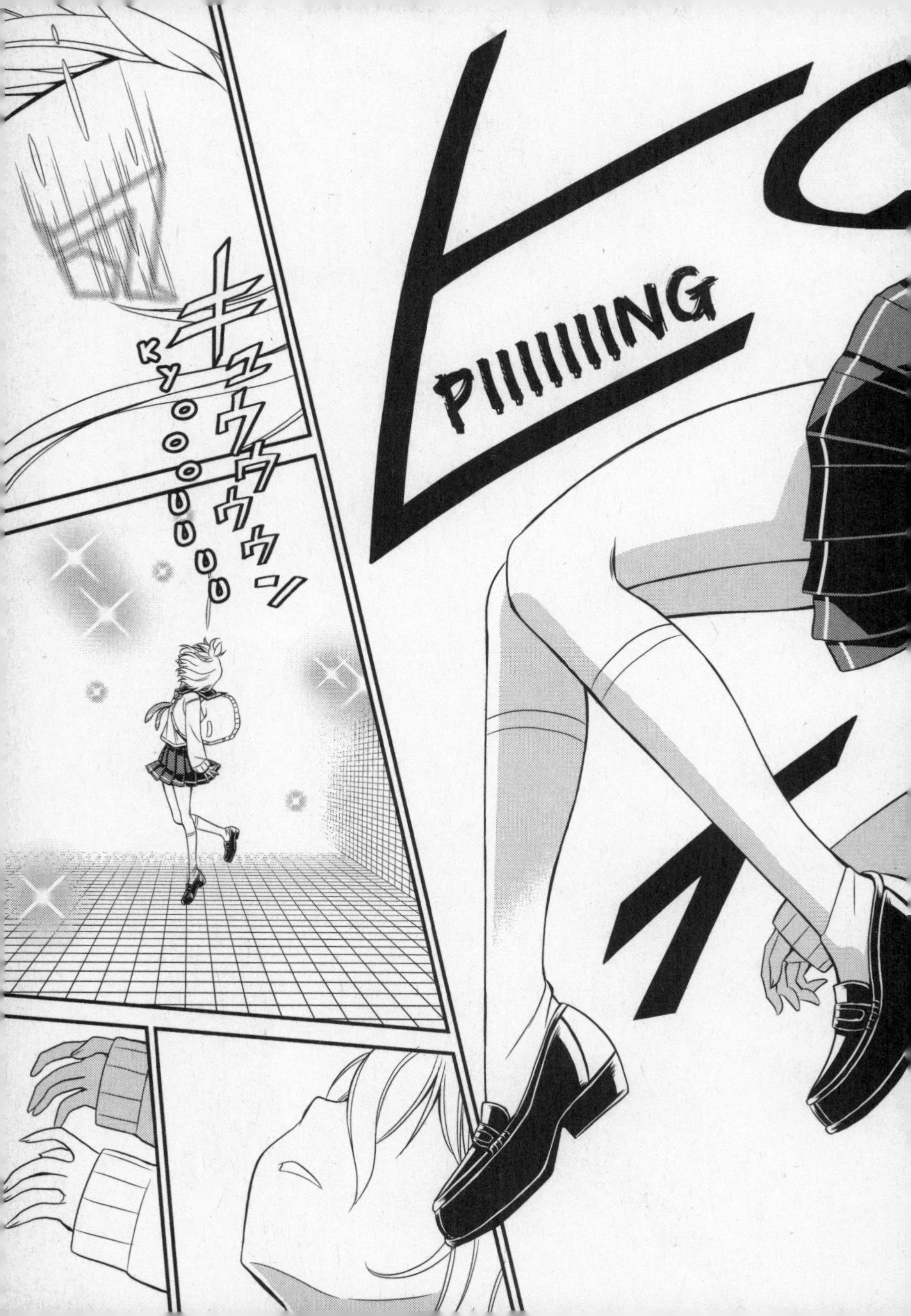
PIIIIIING
キュウウウウウーッ
KYOOOOUUUUU

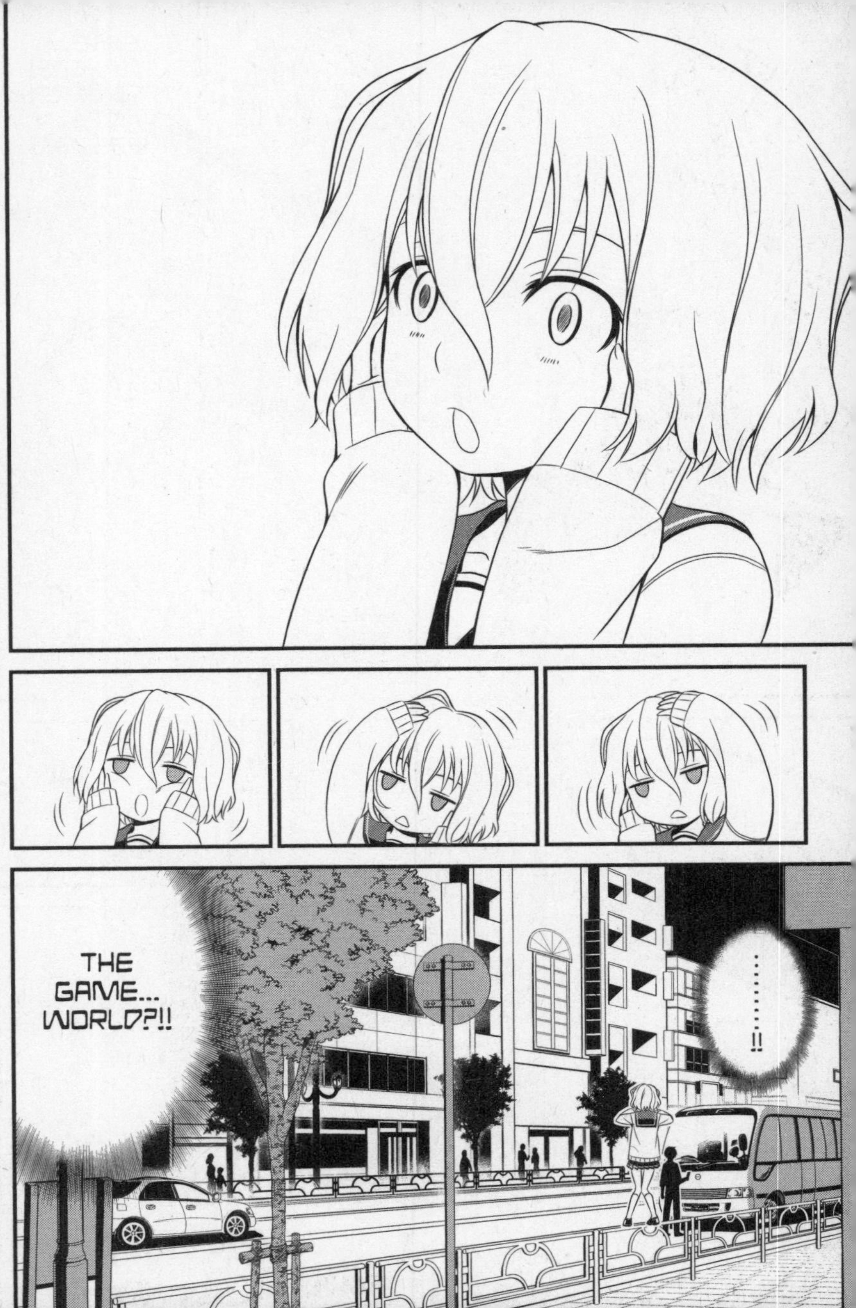
........!!
THE GAME... WORLD?!!

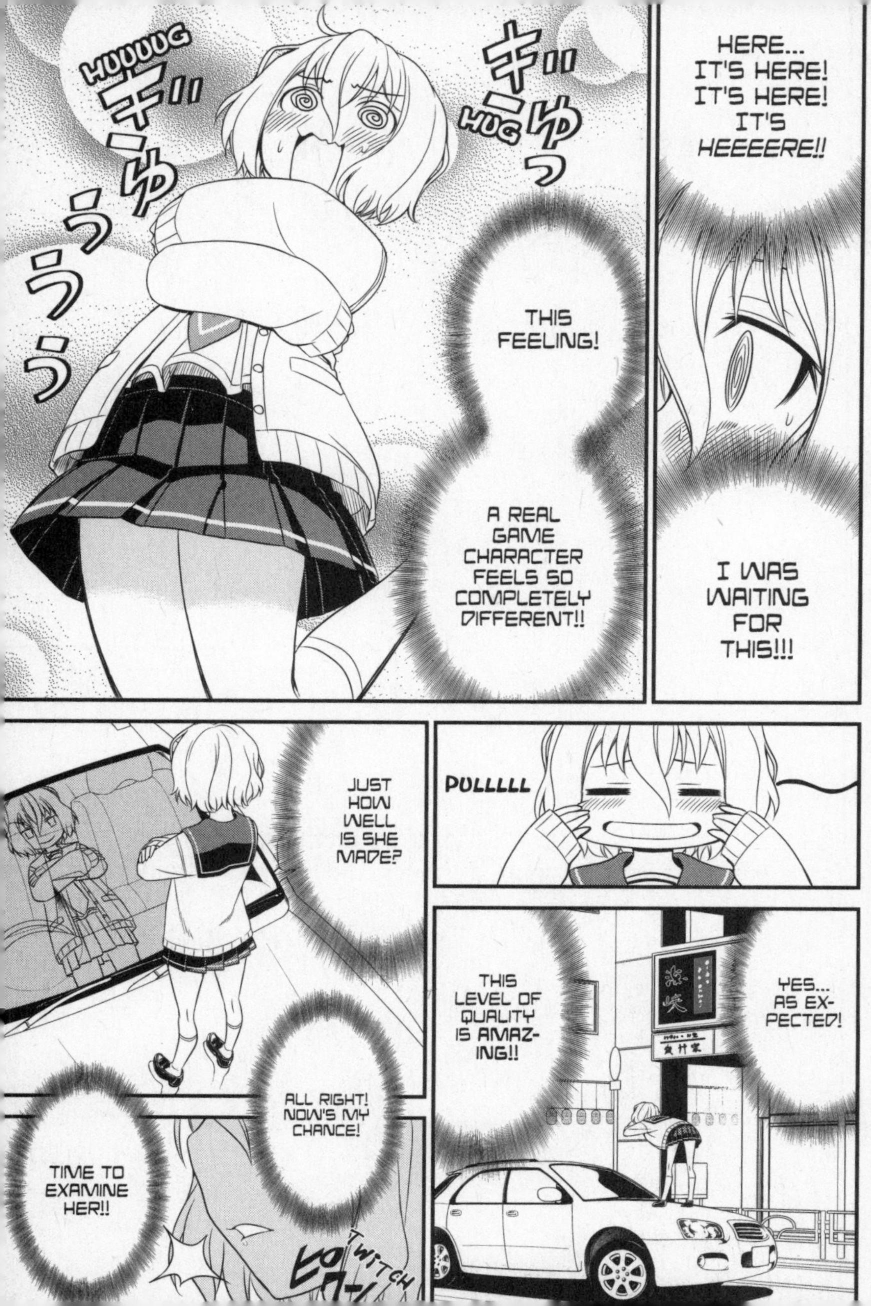
HERE... IT'S HERE! IT'S HERE! IT'S HEEEEERE!!
I WAS WAITING FOR THIS!!!
HUUUUG
HUG
THIS FEELING!
A REAL GAME CHARACTER FEELS SO COMPLETELY DIFFERENT!!
PULLLLL
JUST HOW WELL IS SHE MADE?
YES... AS EX-PECTED!
THIS LEVEL OF QUALITY IS AMAZ-ING!!
ALL RIGHT! NOW'S MY CHANCE!
TIME TO EXAMINE HER!!
TWITCH

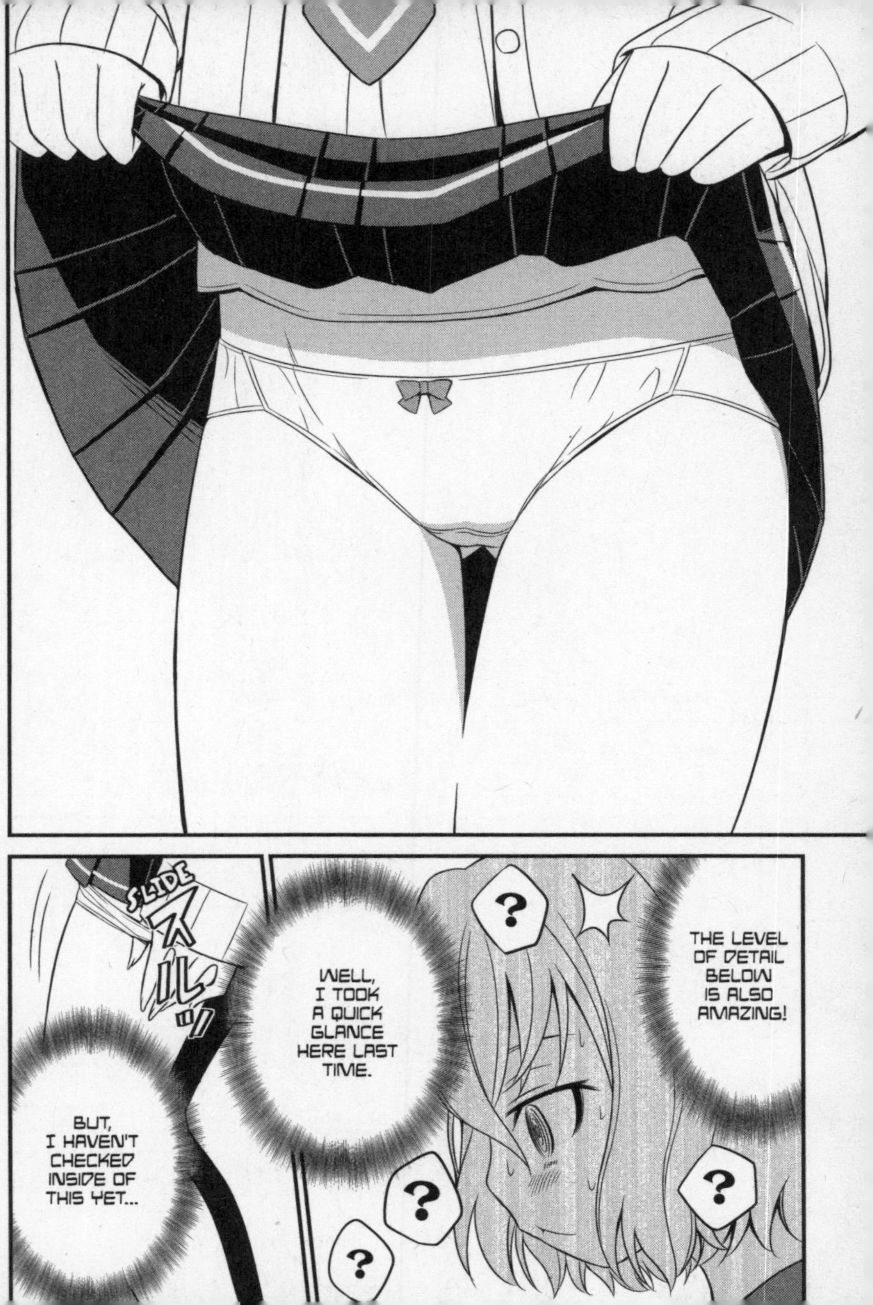
THE LEVEL OF DETAIL BELOW IS ALSO AMAZING!
WELL, I TOOK A QUICK GLANCE HERE LAST TIME.
BUT, I HAVEN'T CHECKED INSIDE OF THIS YET...
SLIDE

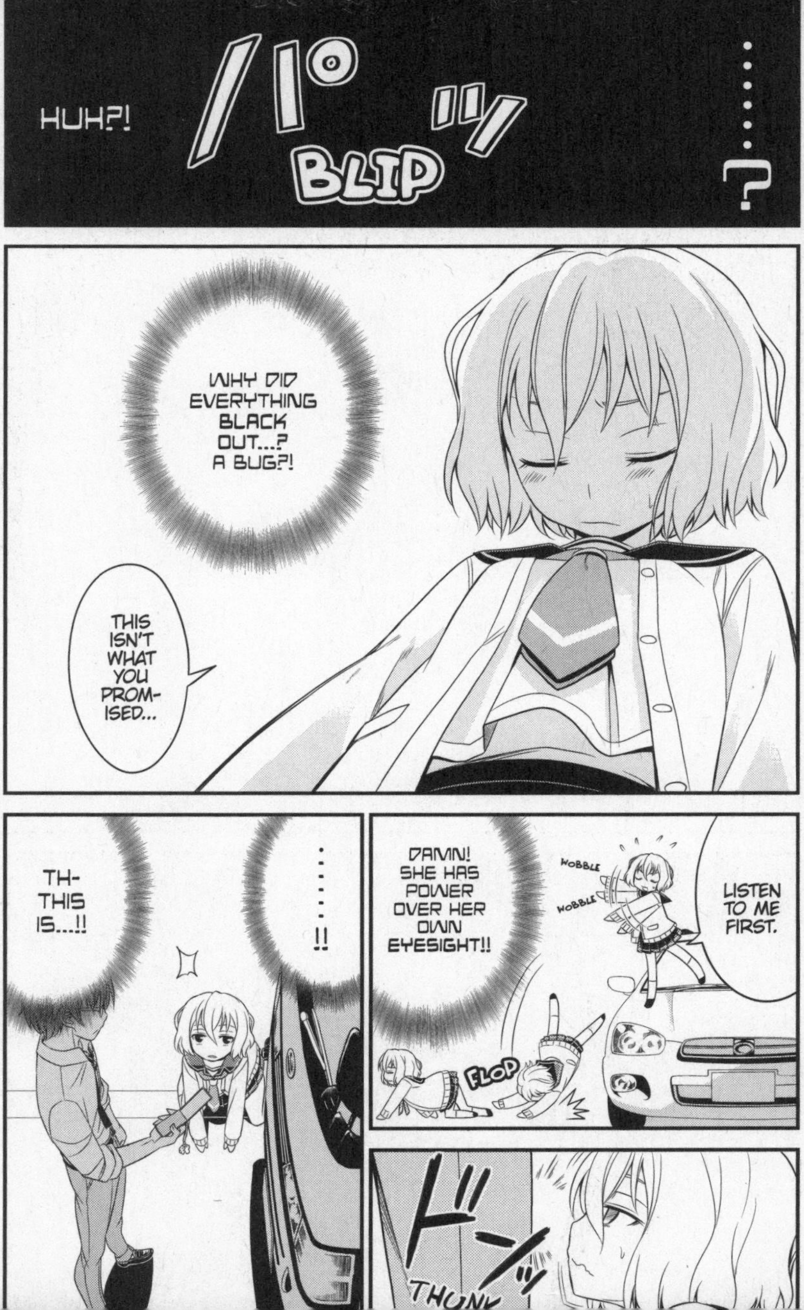
......?
パッ
BLIP
HUH?!
WHY DID EVERYTHING BLACK OUT...? A BUG?!
THIS ISN'T WHAT YOU PROMISED...
LISTEN TO ME FIRST.
WOBBLE
WOBBLE
DAMN! SHE HAS POWER OVER HER OWN EYESIGHT!!
FLOP
THUNK
......!!
TH- THIS IS...!!

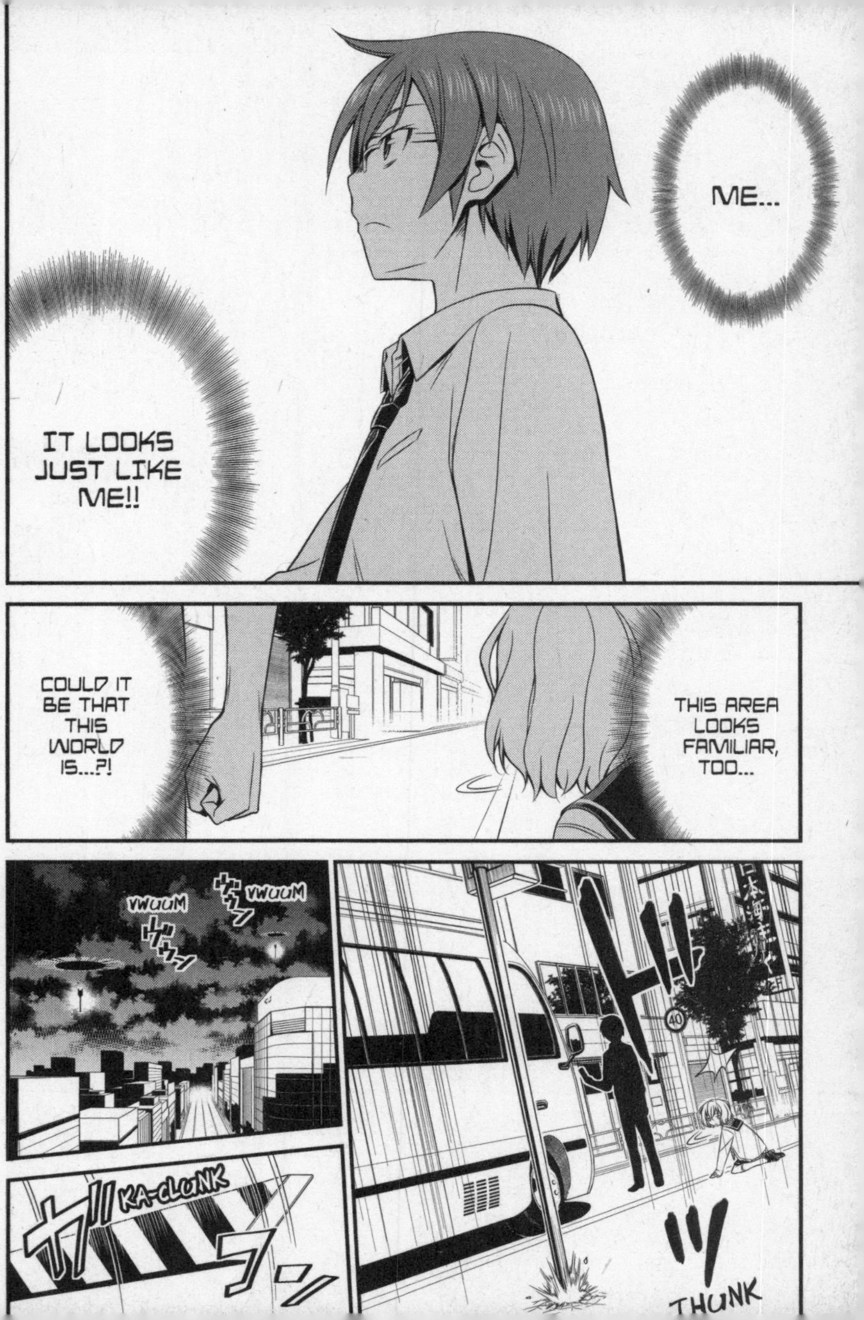
ME...
IT LOOKS JUST LIKE ME!!
THIS AREA LOOKS FAMILIAR, TOO...
COULD IT BE THAT THIS WORLD IS...?!
40
THUNK
VWUUM
VWUUM
KA-CLUNK

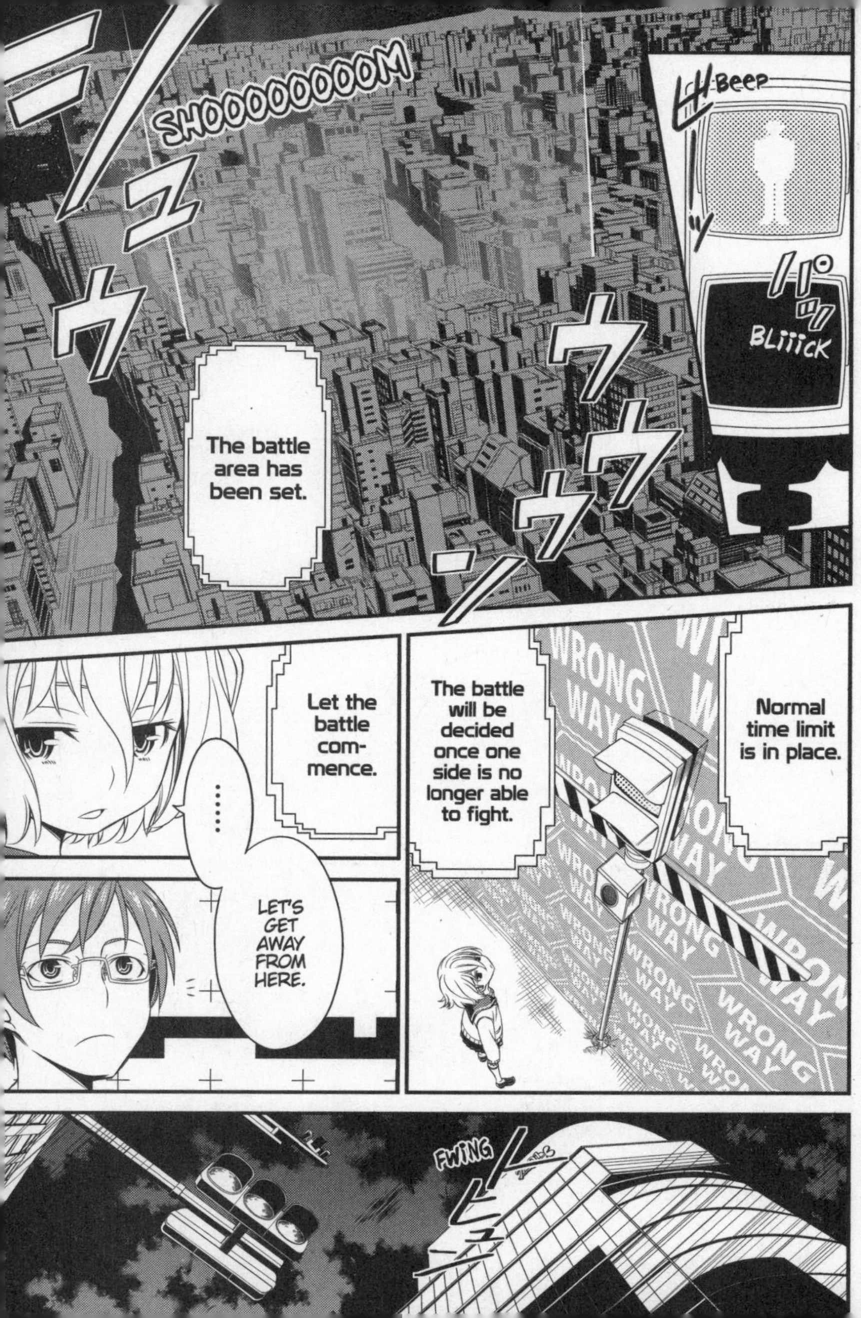
Beep
BLiiick
SHOOOOOOOOM
The battle area has been set.
Normal time limit is in place.
WRONG WAY
The battle will be decided once one side is no longer able to fight.
Let the battle com-mence.
......
LET'S GET AWAY FROM HERE.
FWING

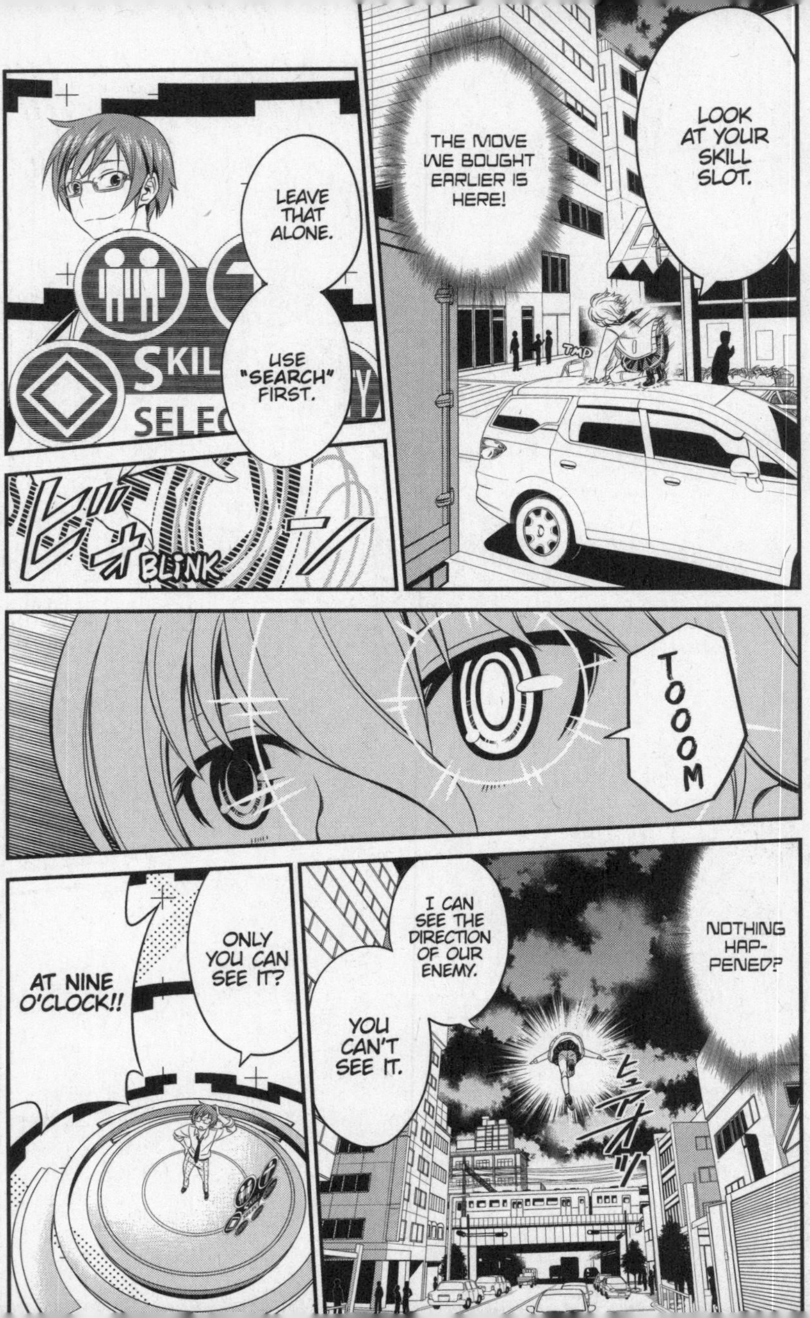
LOOK AT YOUR SKILL SLOT.
THE MOVE WE BOUGHT EARLIER IS HERE!
TMP
LEAVE THAT ALONE.
USE "SEARCH" FIRST.
BLINK
TOOOM
NOTHING HAP-PENED?
I CAN SEE THE DIRECTION OF OUR ENEMY.
YOU CAN'T SEE IT.
ONLY YOU CAN SEE IT?
AT NINE O'CLOCK!!

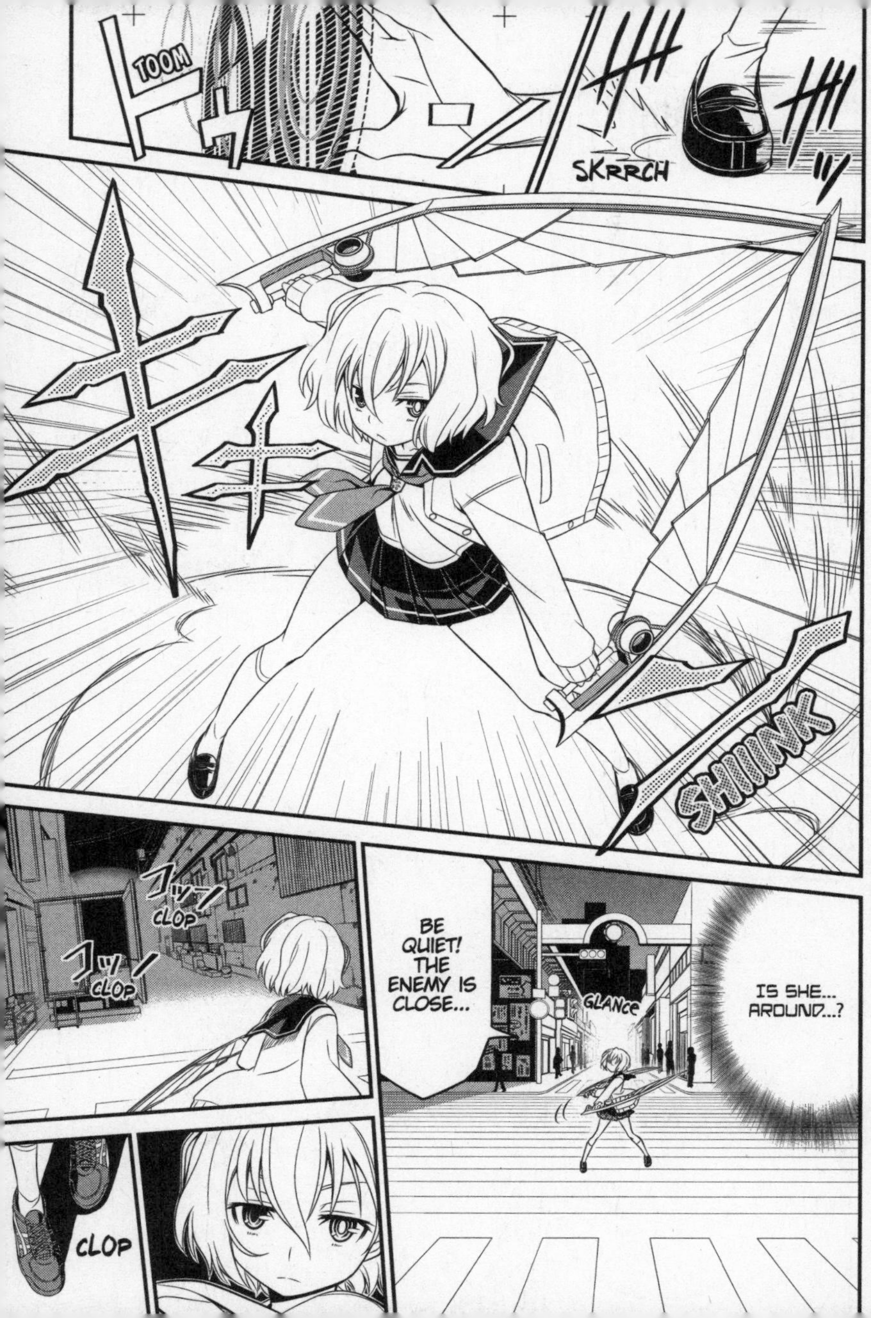
SKRRCH
TOOM
SHIINK
IS SHE... AROUND...?
BE QUIET! THE ENEMY IS CLOSE...
GLANCE
コッ
CLOP
コッ
CLOP
CLOP

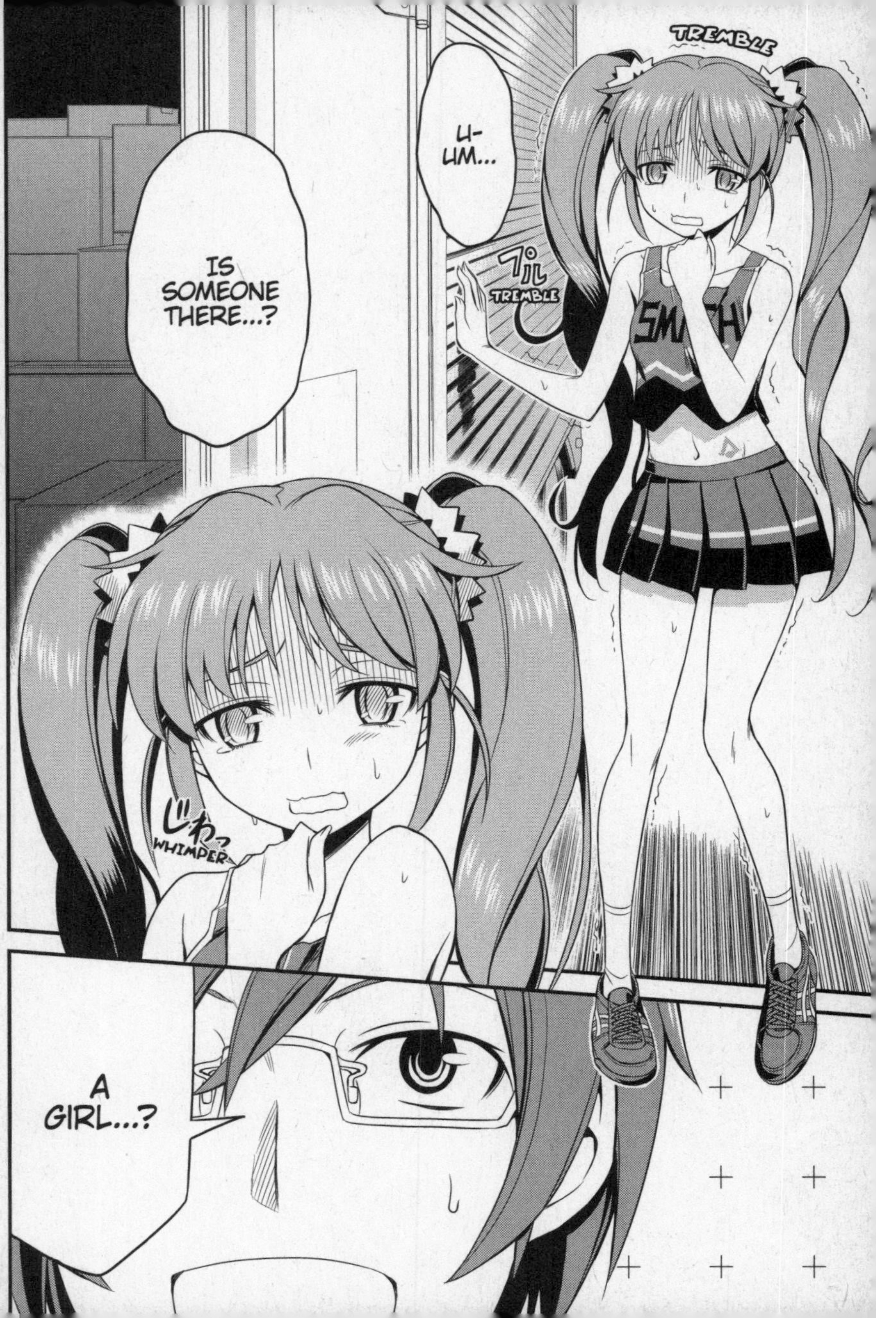
TREMBLE
U-UM...
プル
TREMBLE
IS SOMEONE THERE...?
じわっ
WHIMPER
A GIRL...?

NOT LIVES

ノットライヴス

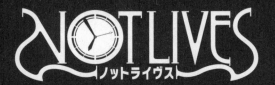

NOT ALIVE

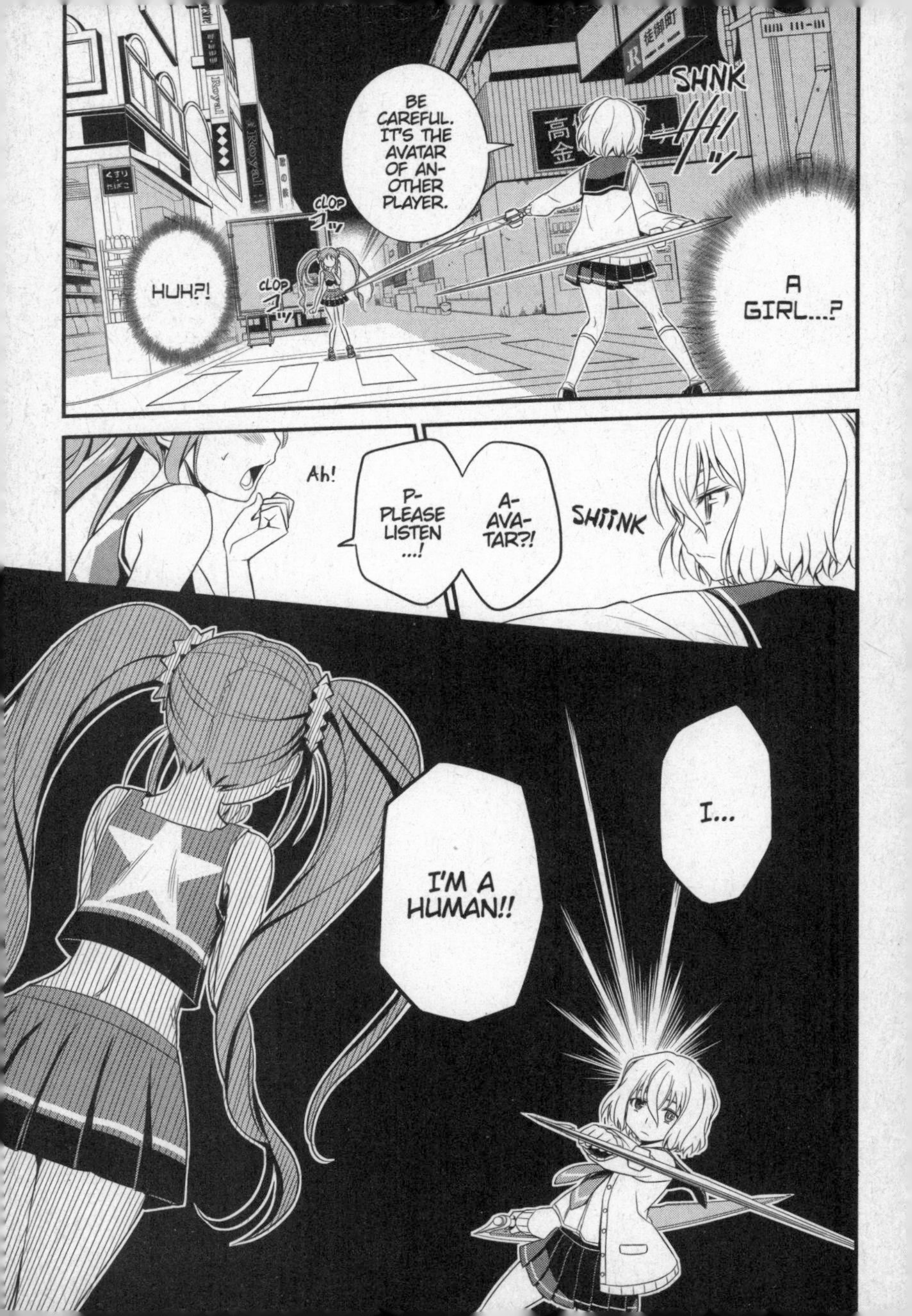
SHNK
A GIRL...?
BE CAREFUL. IT'S THE AVATAR OF AN-OTHER PLAYER.
CLOP
ゴッ
CLOP
ゴッ
HUH?!
SHIIINK
A- AVA- TAR?!
P- PLEASE LISTEN ...!
Ah!
I...
I'M A HUMAN!!

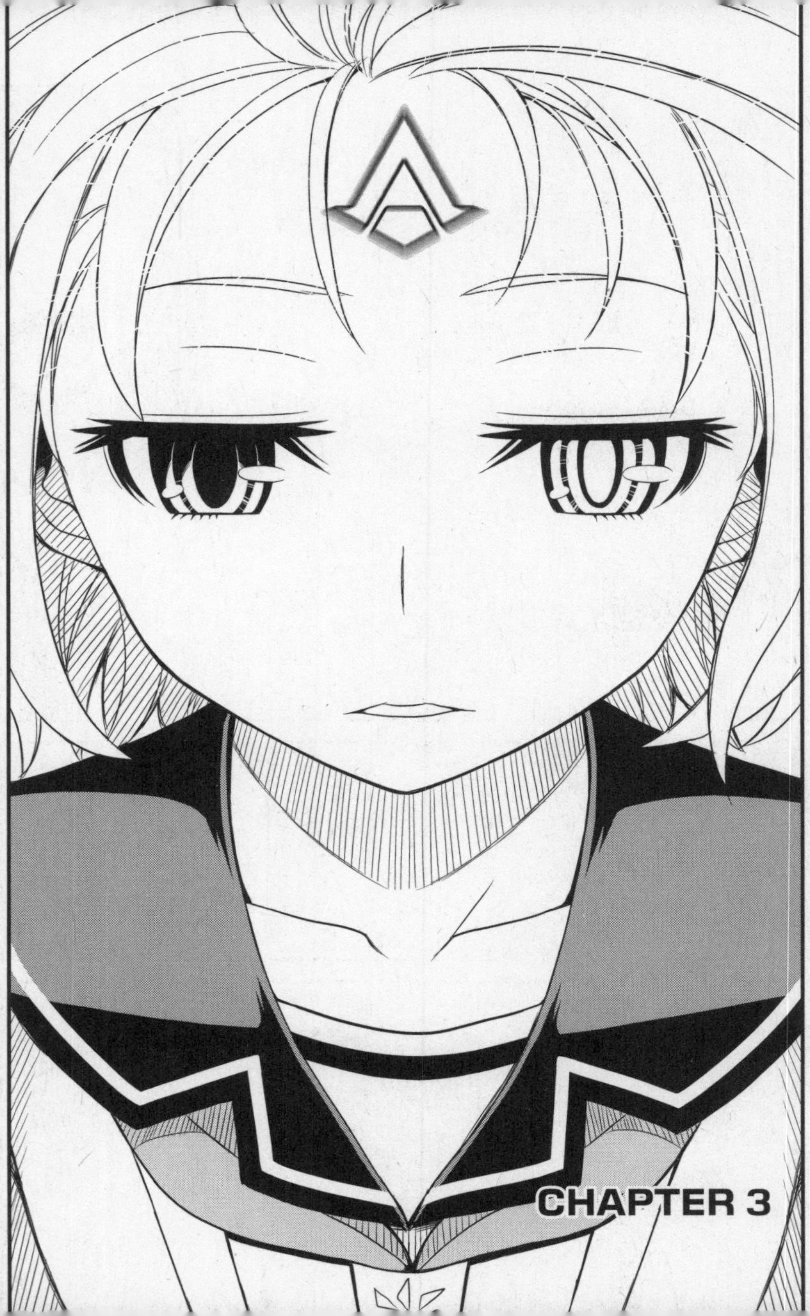
CHAPTER 3

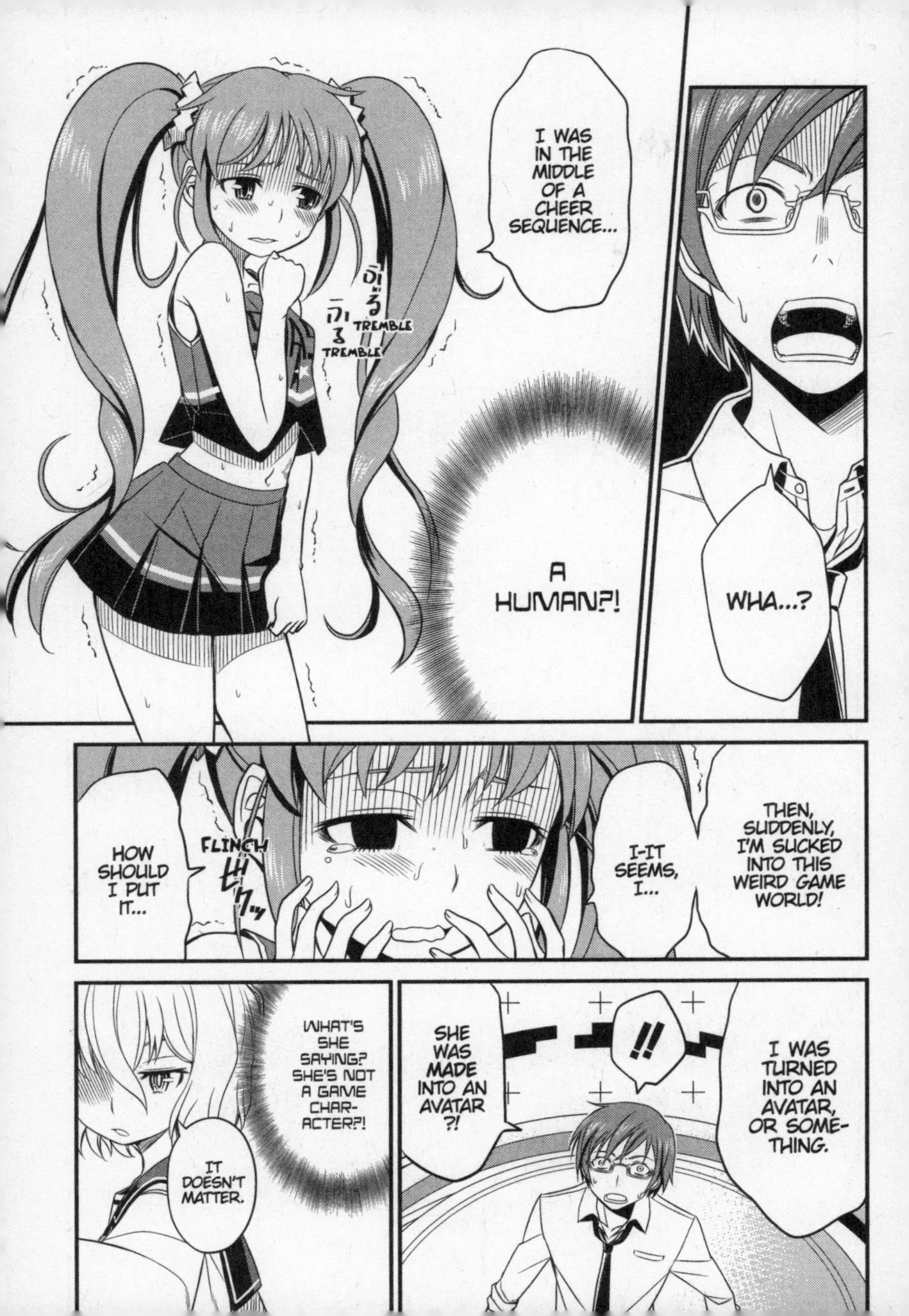
WHA...?
I WAS IN THE MIDDLE OF A CHEER SEQUENCE...
TREMBLE
TREMBLE
A HUMAN?!
THEN, SUDDENLY, I'M SUCKED INTO THIS WEIRD GAME WORLD!
I-IT SEEMS, I...
FLINCH
HOW SHOULD I PUT IT...
I WAS TURNED INTO AN AVATAR, OR SOME-THING.
!!
SHE WAS MADE INTO AN AVATAR?!
WHAT'S SHE SAYING? SHE'S NOT A GAME CHAR-ACTER?!
IT DOESN'T MATTER.

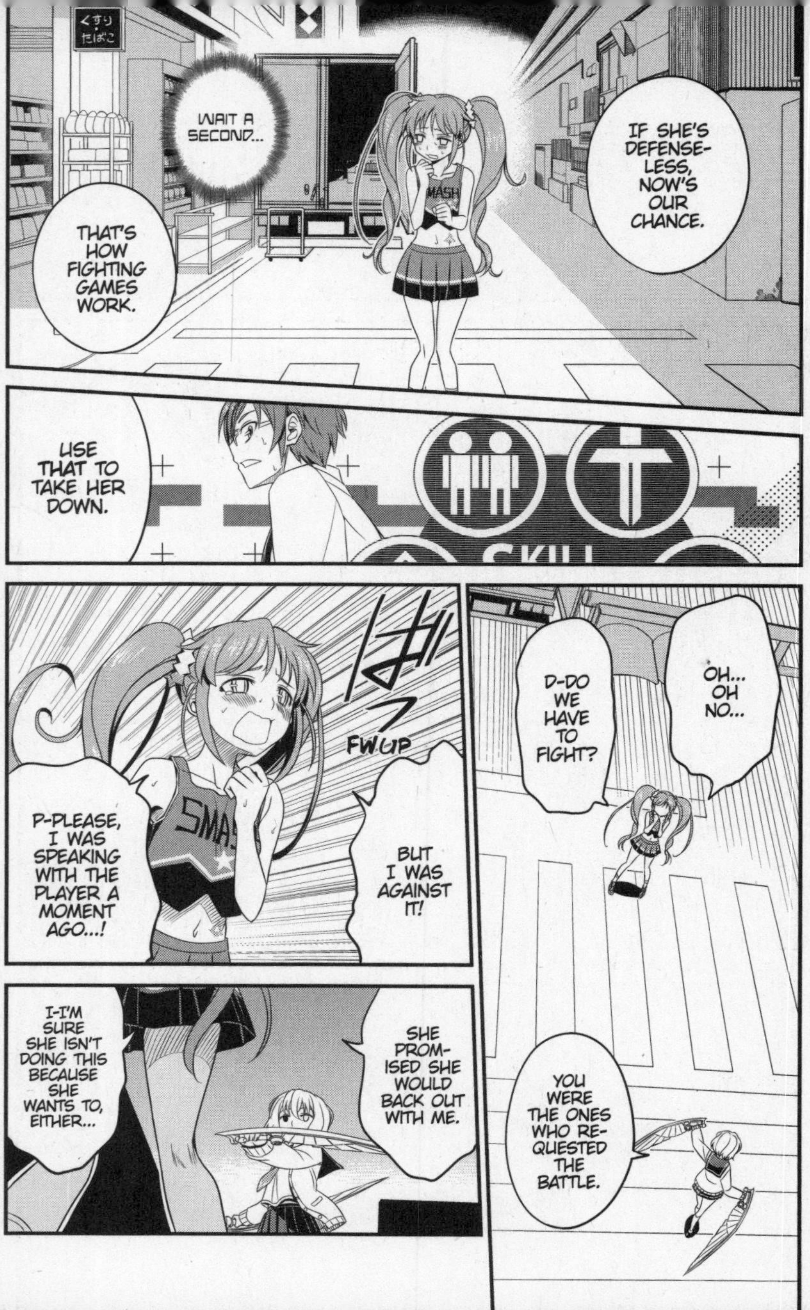
くすり
たばこ
IF SHE'S DEFENSE-LESS, NOW'S OUR CHANCE.
WAIT A SECOND...
THAT'S HOW FIGHTING GAMES WORK.
USE THAT TO TAKE HER DOWN.
OH... OH NO...
D-DO WE HAVE TO FIGHT?
YOU WERE THE ONES WHO RE-QUESTED THE BATTLE.
FWUP
BUT I WAS AGAINST IT!
P-PLEASE, I WAS SPEAKING WITH THE PLAYER A MOMENT AGO...!
SHE PROM-ISED SHE WOULD BACK OUT WITH ME.
I-I'M SURE SHE ISN'T DOING THIS BECAUSE SHE WANTS TO, EITHER...

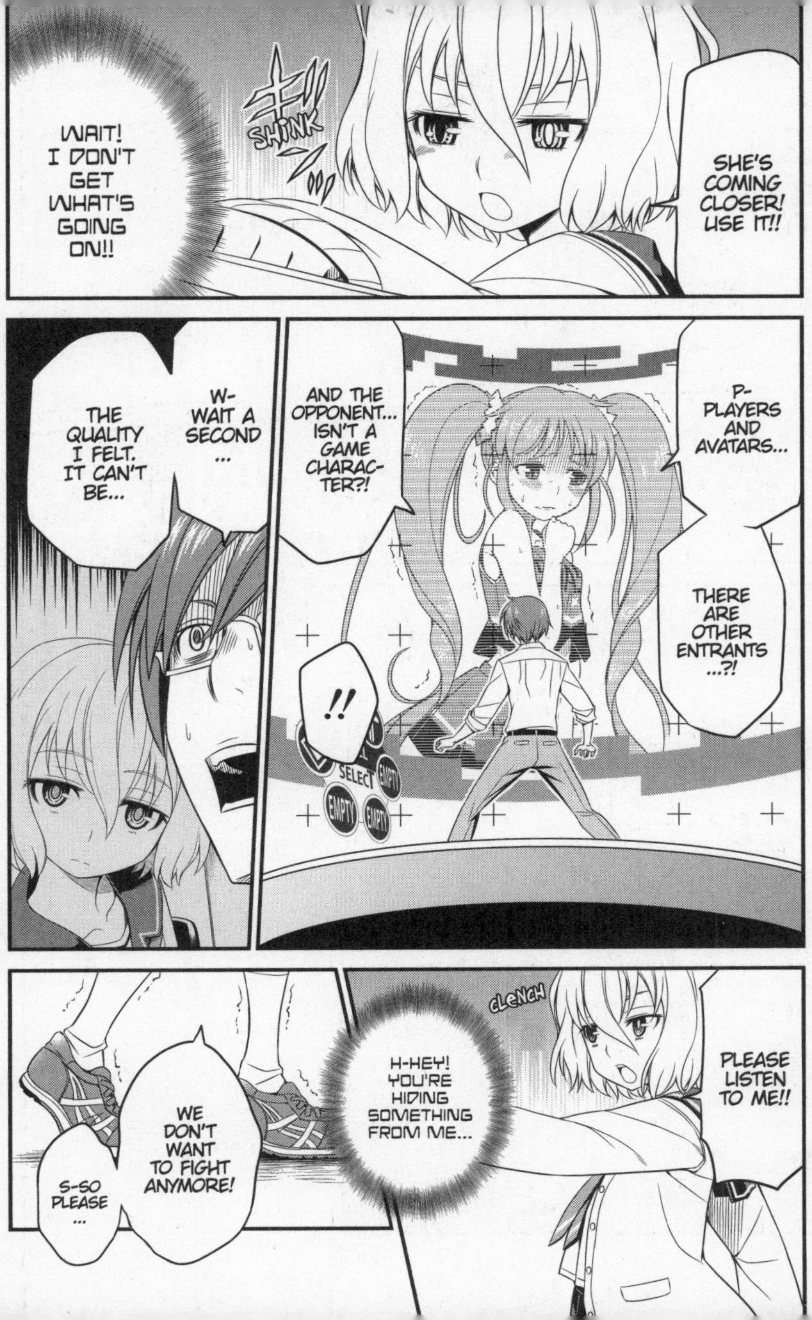
SHE'S COMING CLOSER! USE IT!!
SHINK
WAIT! I DON'T GET WHAT'S GOING ON!!
P-PLAYERS AND AVATARS...
AND THE OPPONENT... ISN'T A GAME CHARACTER?!
THERE ARE OTHER ENTRANTS ...?!
!!
SELECT
EMPTY
EMPTY
EMPTY
W-WAIT A SECOND ...
THE QUALITY I FELT. IT CAN'T BE...
PLEASE LISTEN TO ME!!
CLENCH
H-HEY! YOU'RE HIDING SOMETHING FROM ME...
WE DON'T WANT TO FIGHT ANYMORE!
S-SO PLEASE ...

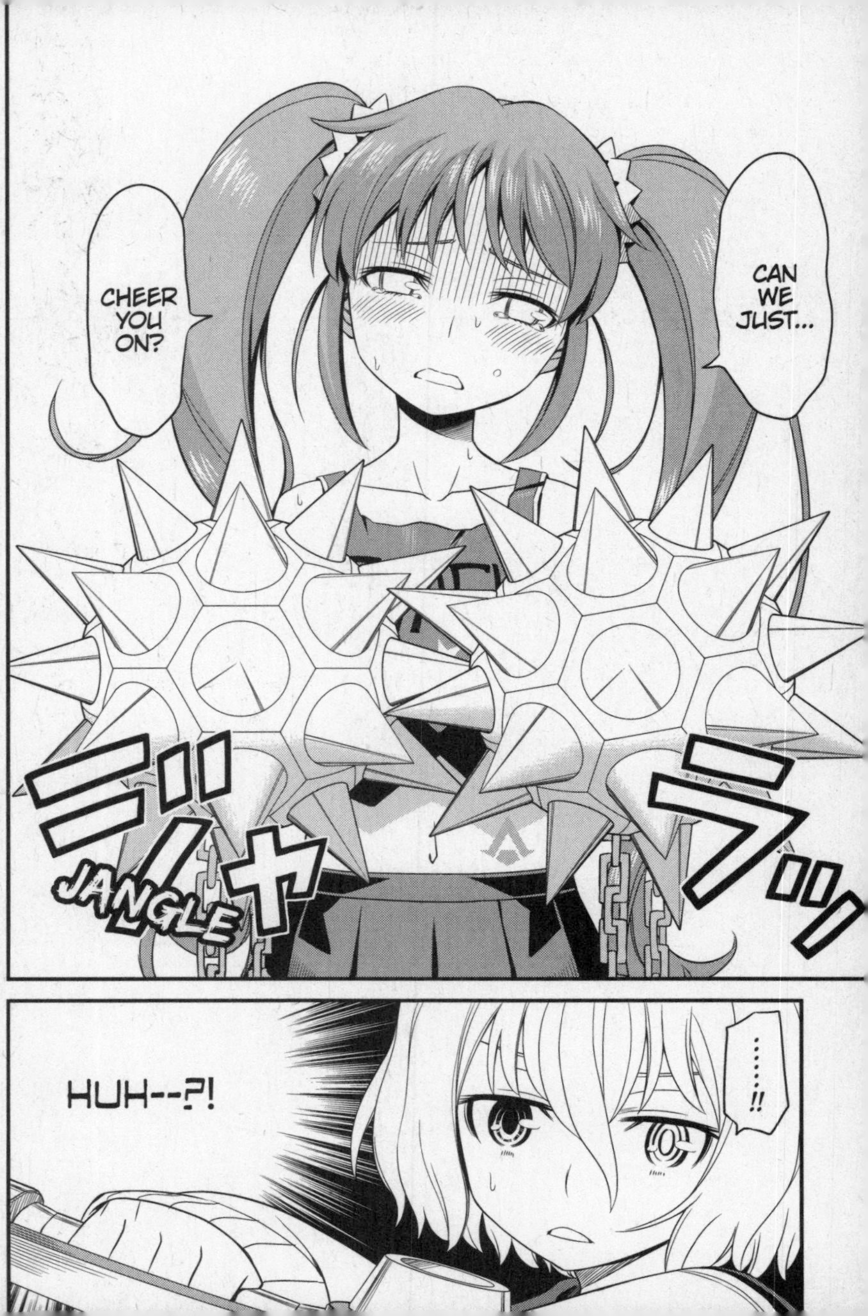
CAN WE JUST...
CHEER YOU ON?
JANGLE
......!!
HUH--?!

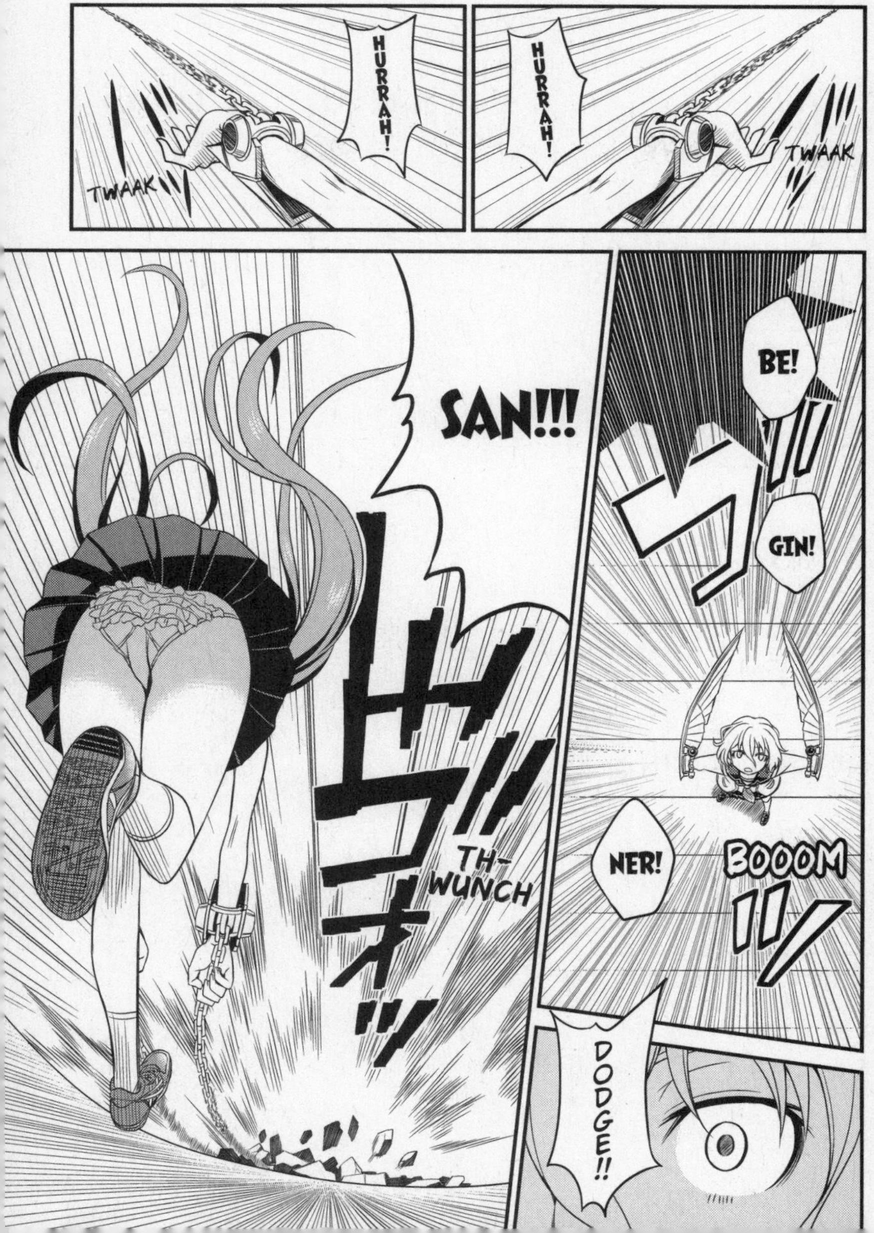
HURRAH!
TWAAK
HURRAH!
TWAAK
BE!
GIN!
NER!
BOOOM
DODGE!!
SAN!!!
TH-WUNCH

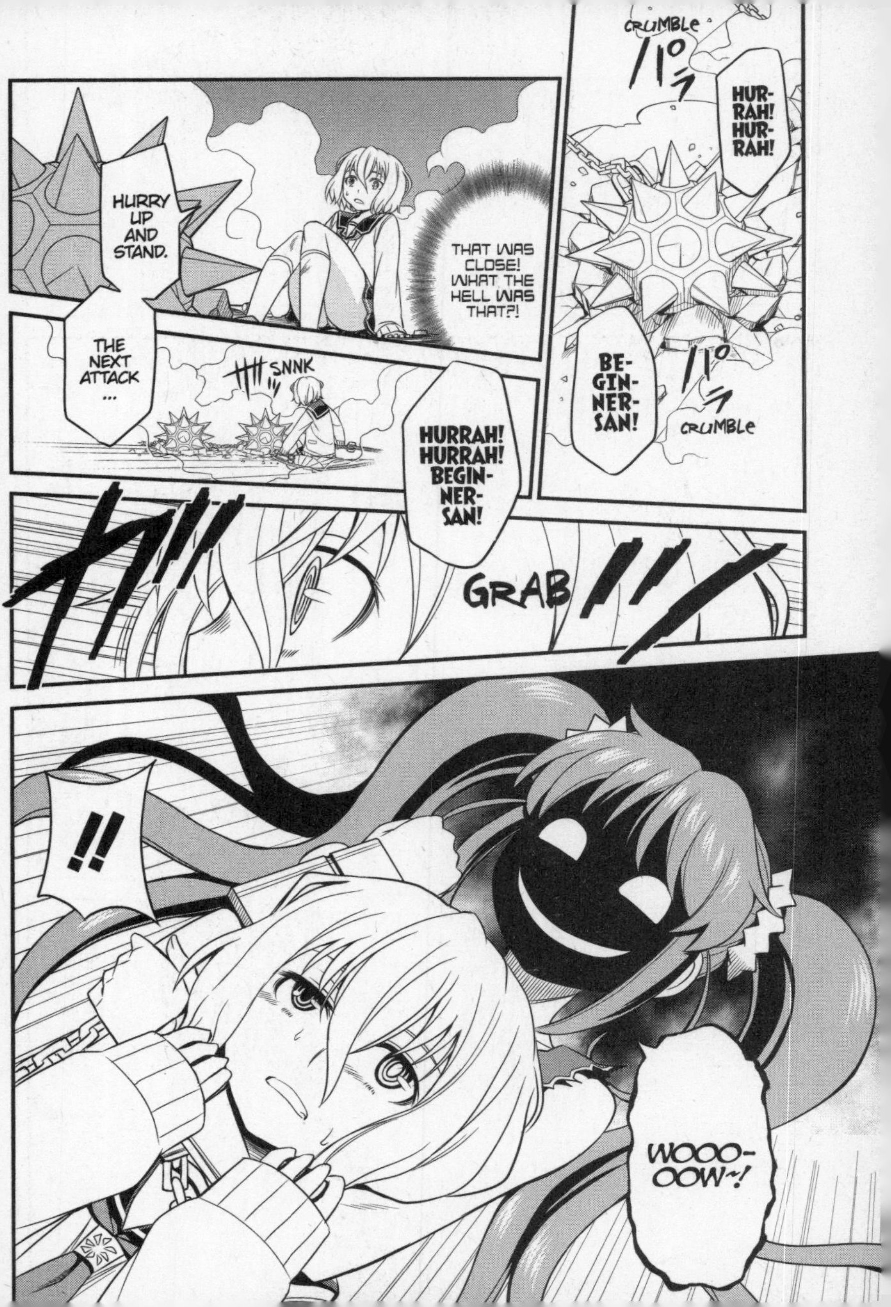

CRUMBLE
HUR-RAH! HUR-RAH!
BE-GIN-NER-SAN!
CRUMBLE
THAT WAS CLOSE! WHAT THE HELL WAS THAT?!
HURRY UP AND STAND.
HURRAH! HURRAH! BEGIN-NER-SAN!
SNNK
THE NEXT ATTACK ...
GRAB
WOOO-OOW~!
!!

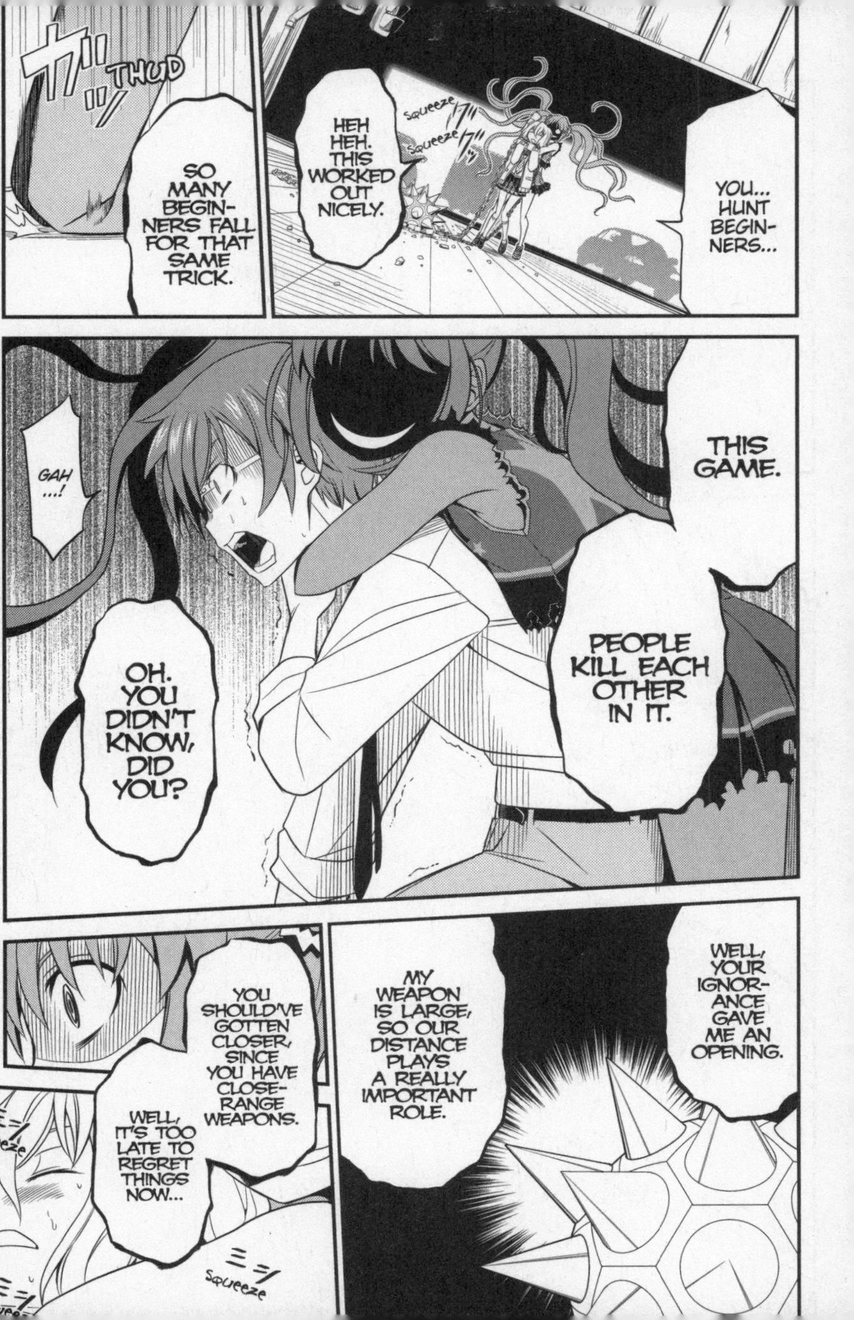
YOU... HUNT BEGINNERS...
HEH HEH. THIS WORKED OUT NICELY.
Squeeze
Squeeze
THUD
SO MANY BEGINNERS FALL FOR THAT SAME TRICK.
THIS GAME.
PEOPLE KILL EACH OTHER IN IT.
GAH ...!
OH. YOU DIDN'T KNOW, DID YOU?
WELL, YOUR IGNORANCE GAVE ME AN OPENING.
MY WEAPON IS LARGE, SO OUR DISTANCE PLAYS A REALLY IMPORTANT ROLE.
YOU SHOULD'VE GOTTEN CLOSER, SINCE YOU HAVE CLOSE-RANGE WEAPONS.
WELL, IT'S TOO LATE TO REGRET THINGS NOW...
Squeeze
Squeeze

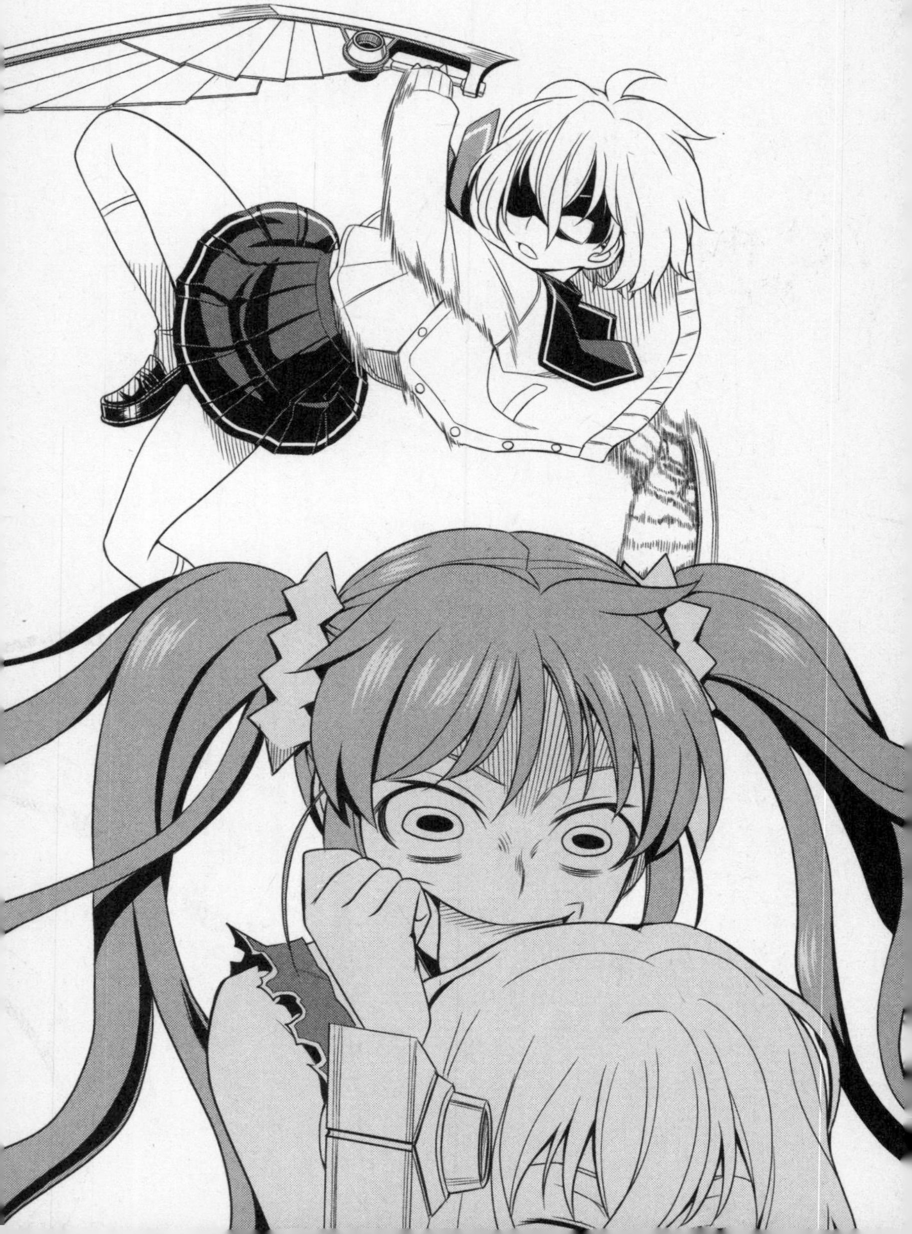

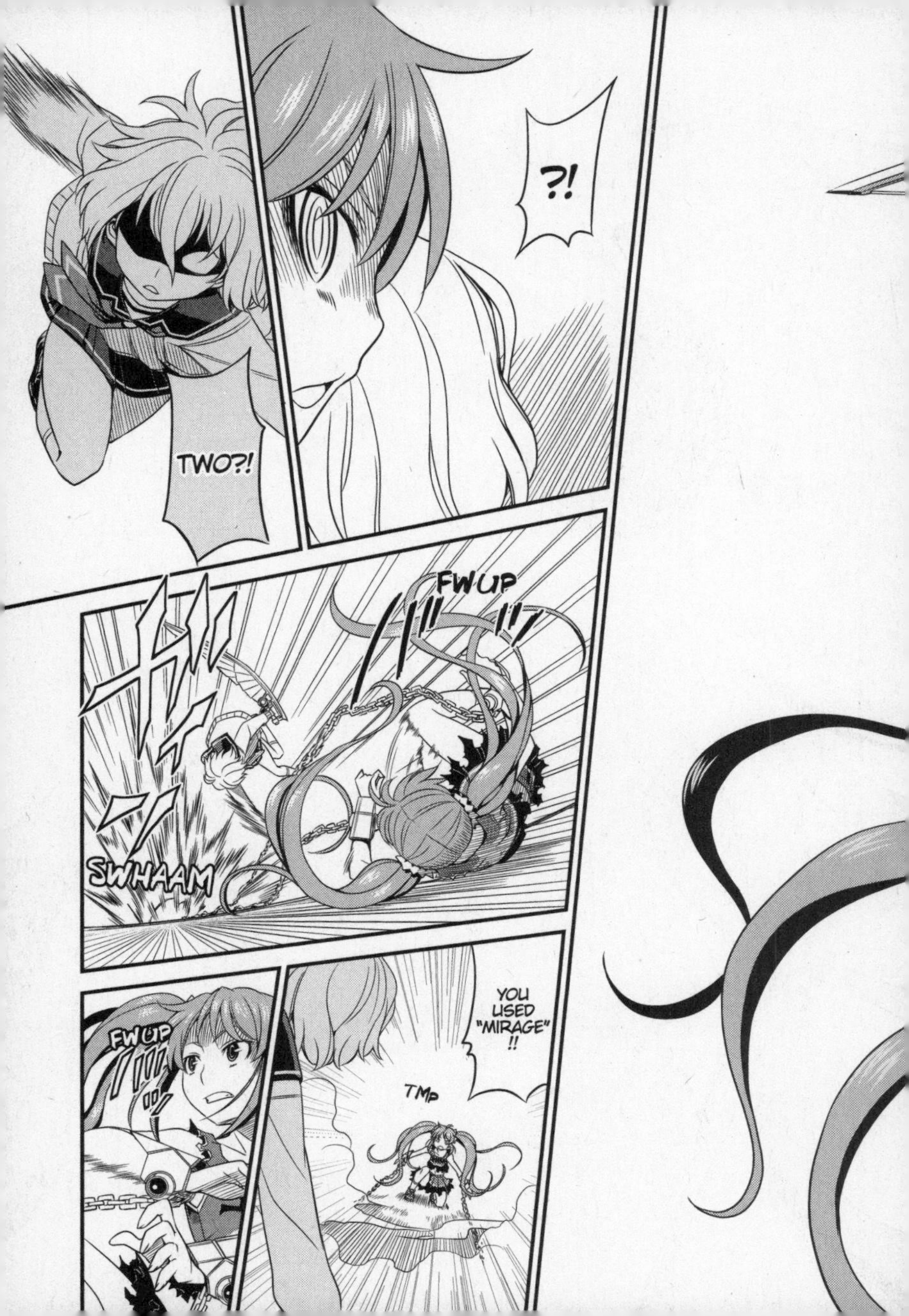
?!
TWO?!
FWUP
SWHAAM
YOU USED "MIRAGE" !!
TMP
FWUP

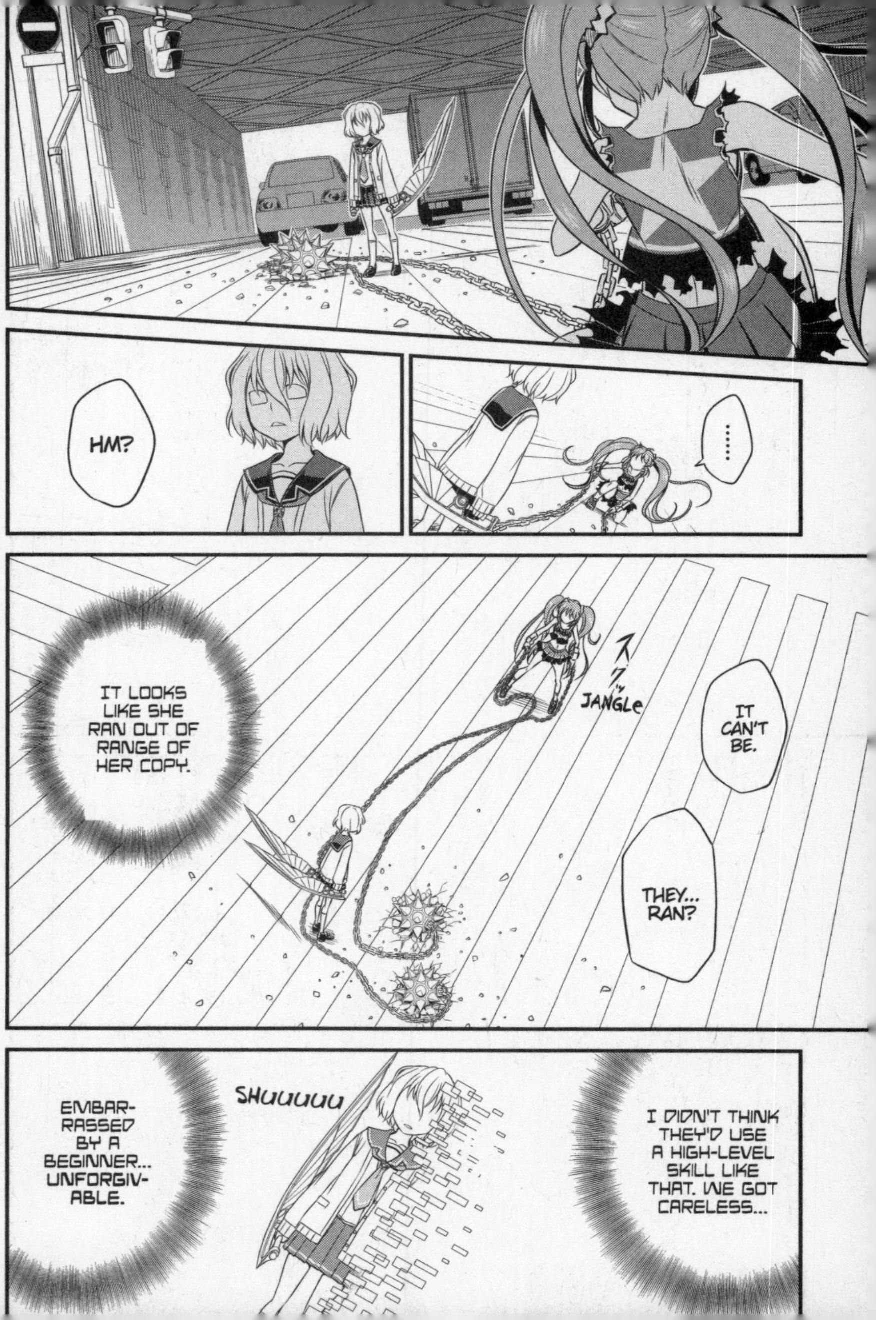
……
HM?
IT CAN'T BE.
THEY... RAN?
JANGLE
IT LOOKS LIKE SHE RAN OUT OF RANGE OF HER COPY.
I DIDN'T THINK THEY'D USE A HIGH-LEVEL SKILL LIKE THAT. WE GOT CARELESS...
SHUUUUU
EMBAR-RASSED BY A BEGINNER... UNFORGIV-ABLE.

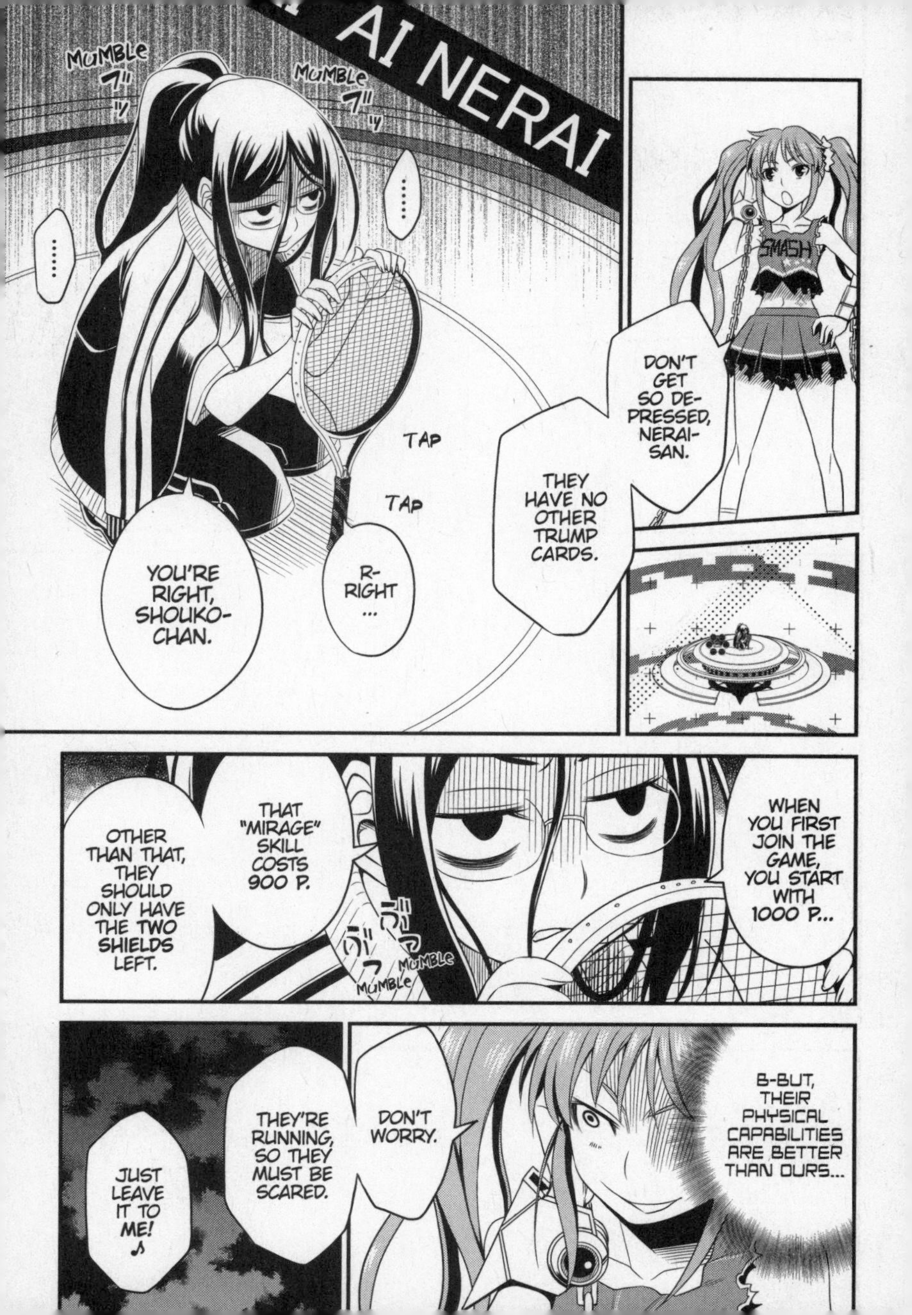
DON'T GET SO DE-PRESSED, NERAI-SAN.
THEY HAVE NO OTHER TRUMP CARDS.
AI NERAI
MUMBLE
MUMBLE
......
......
TAP
TAP
R-RIGHT ...
YOU'RE RIGHT, SHOUKO-CHAN.
WHEN YOU FIRST JOIN THE GAME, YOU START WITH 1000 P...
THAT "MIRAGE" SKILL COSTS 900 P.
MUMBLE
MUMBLE
OTHER THAN THAT, THEY SHOULD ONLY HAVE THE TWO SHIELDS LEFT.
B-BUT, THEIR PHYSICAL CAPABILITIES ARE BETTER THAN OURS...
DON'T WORRY.
THEY'RE RUNNING, SO THEY MUST BE SCARED.
JUST LEAVE IT TO ME! ♪

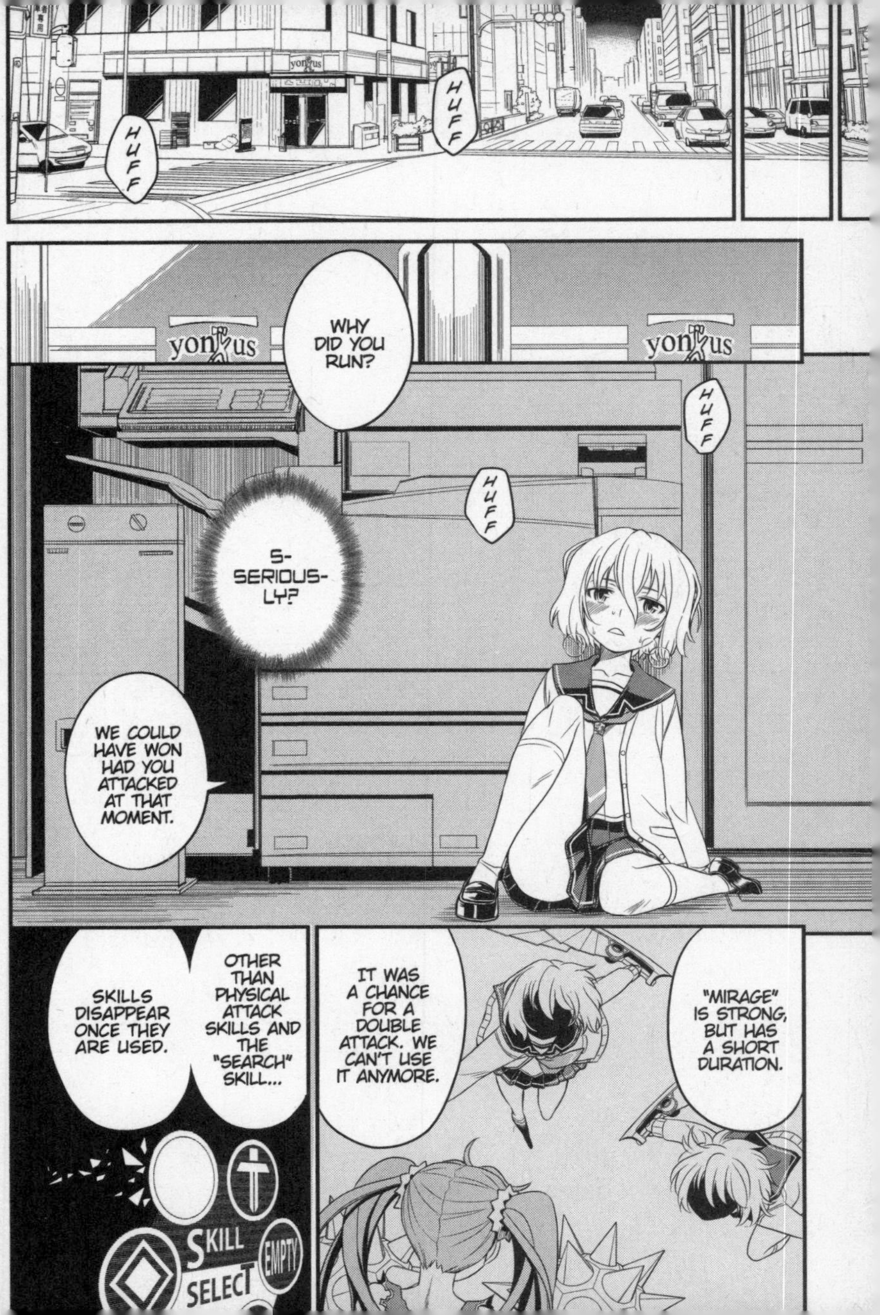
HUFF
HUFF
WHY DID YOU RUN?
HUFF
HUFF
S-SERIOUS-LY?
WE COULD HAVE WON HAD YOU ATTACKED AT THAT MOMENT.
"MIRAGE" IS STRONG, BUT HAS A SHORT DURATION.
IT WAS A CHANCE FOR A DOUBLE ATTACK. WE CAN'T USE IT ANYMORE.
OTHER THAN PHYSICAL ATTACK SKILLS AND THE "SEARCH" SKILL...
SKILLS DISAPPEAR ONCE THEY ARE USED.
EMPTY
SKILL SELECT

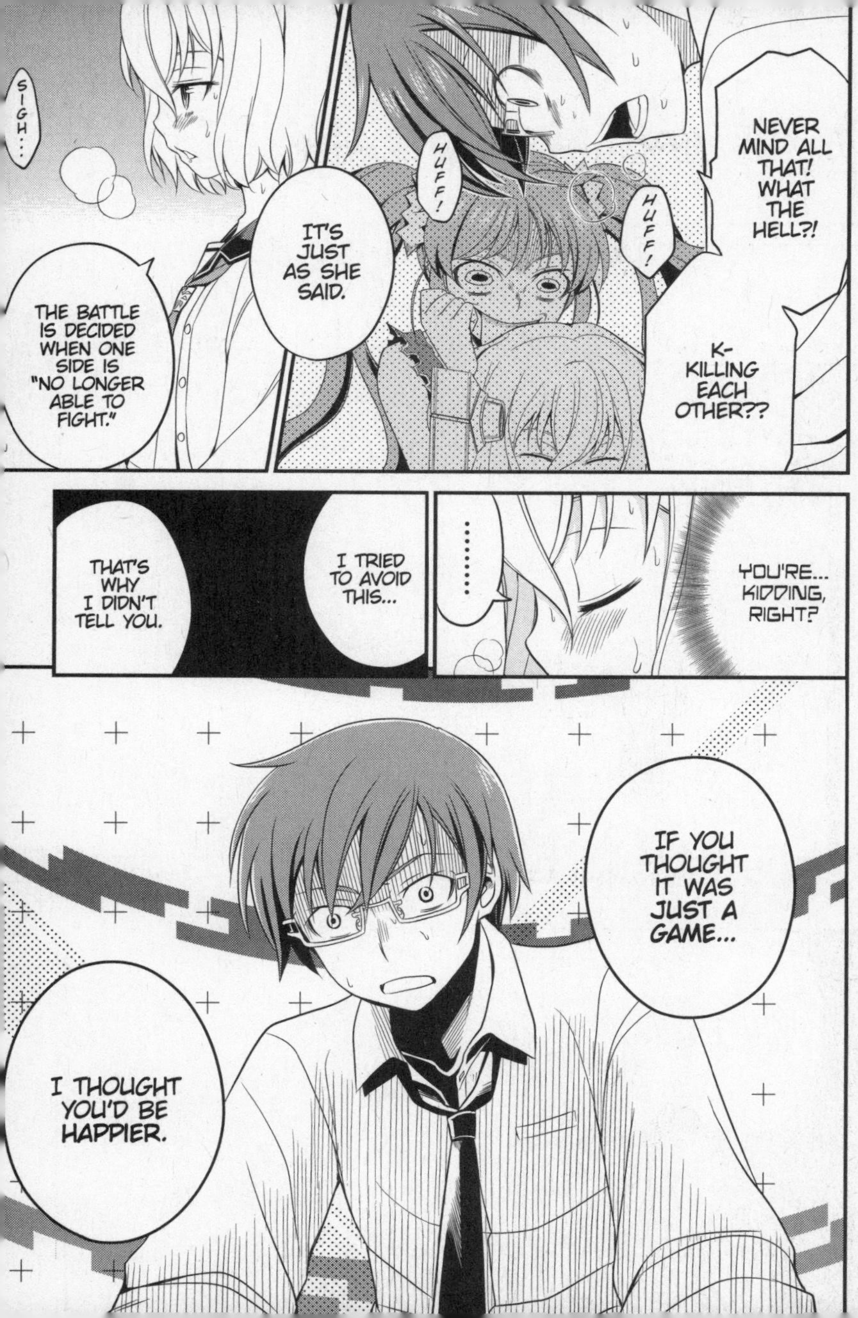
NEVER MIND ALL THAT! WHAT THE HELL?!
K-KILLING EACH OTHER??
HUFF!
HUFF!
IT'S JUST AS SHE SAID.
SIGH...
THE BATTLE IS DECIDED WHEN ONE SIDE IS "NO LONGER ABLE TO FIGHT."
YOU'RE... KIDDING, RIGHT?
......
I TRIED TO AVOID THIS...
THAT'S WHY I DIDN'T TELL YOU.
IF YOU THOUGHT IT WAS JUST A GAME...
I THOUGHT YOU'D BE HAPPIER.

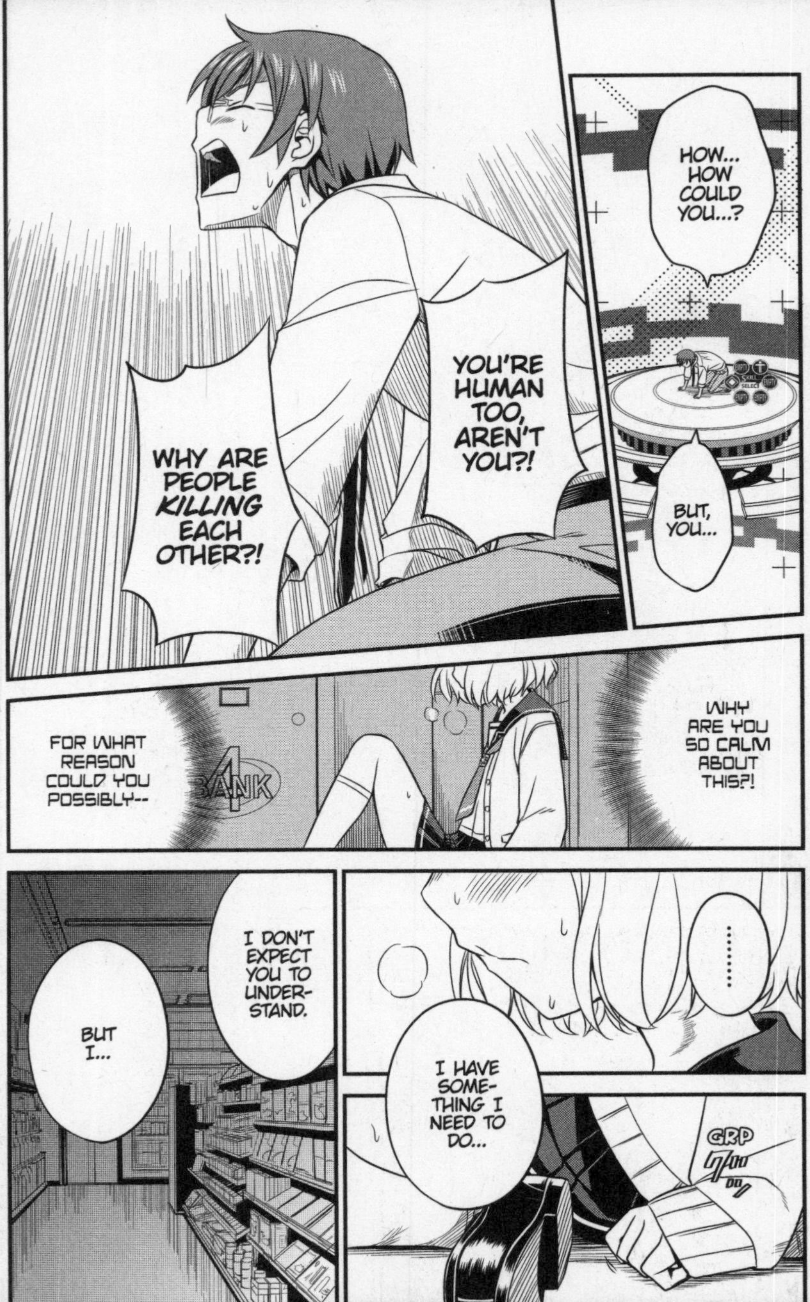
HOW... HOW COULD YOU...?
BUT, YOU...
YOU'RE HUMAN TOO, AREN'T YOU?!
WHY ARE PEOPLE *KILLING* EACH OTHER?!
WHY ARE YOU SO CALM ABOUT THIS?!
BANK
FOR WHAT REASON COULD YOU POSSIBLY--
......
I HAVE SOME-THING I NEED TO DO...
GRP
I DON'T EXPECT YOU TO UNDER-STAND.
BUT I...

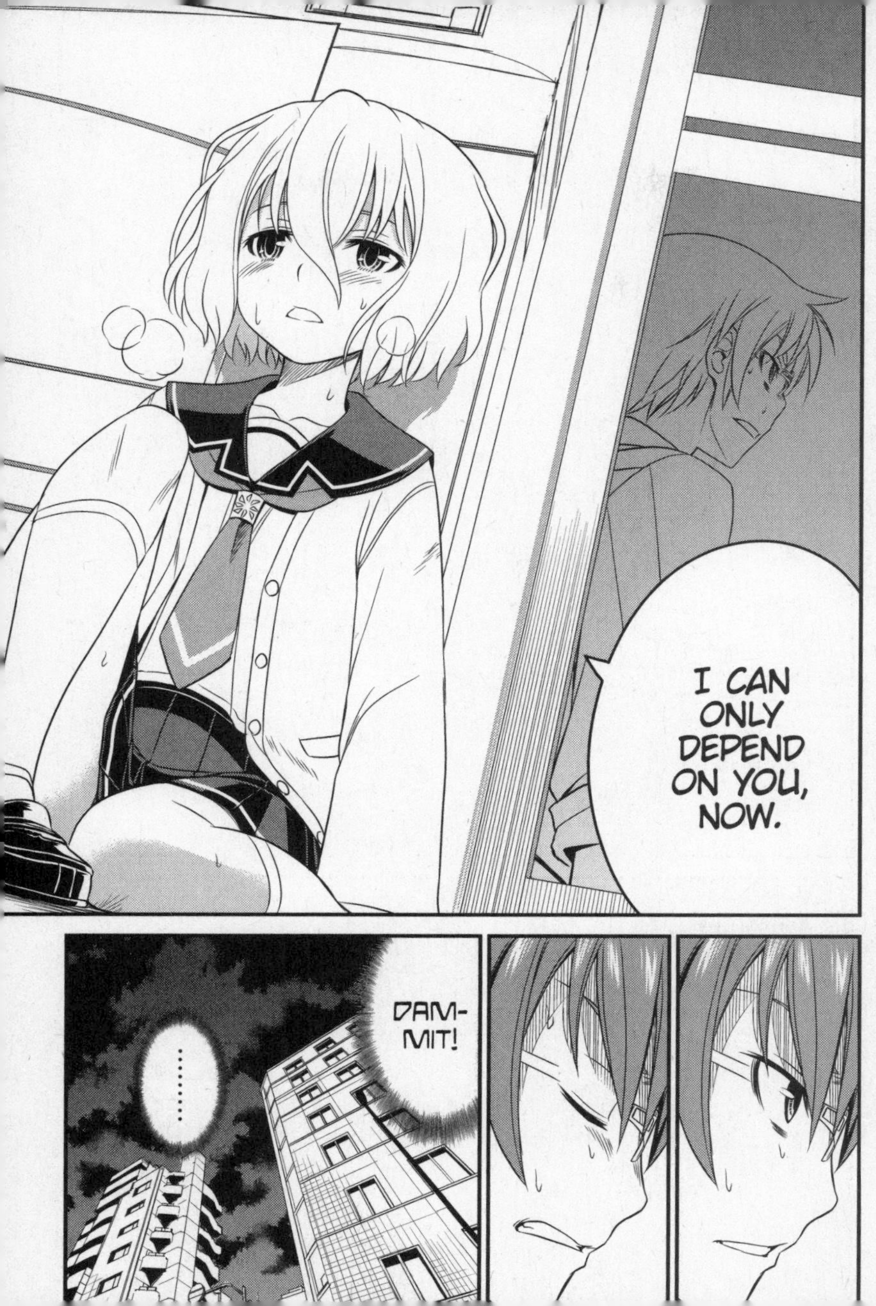
I CAN ONLY DEPEND ON YOU, NOW.
DAM-MIT!
......

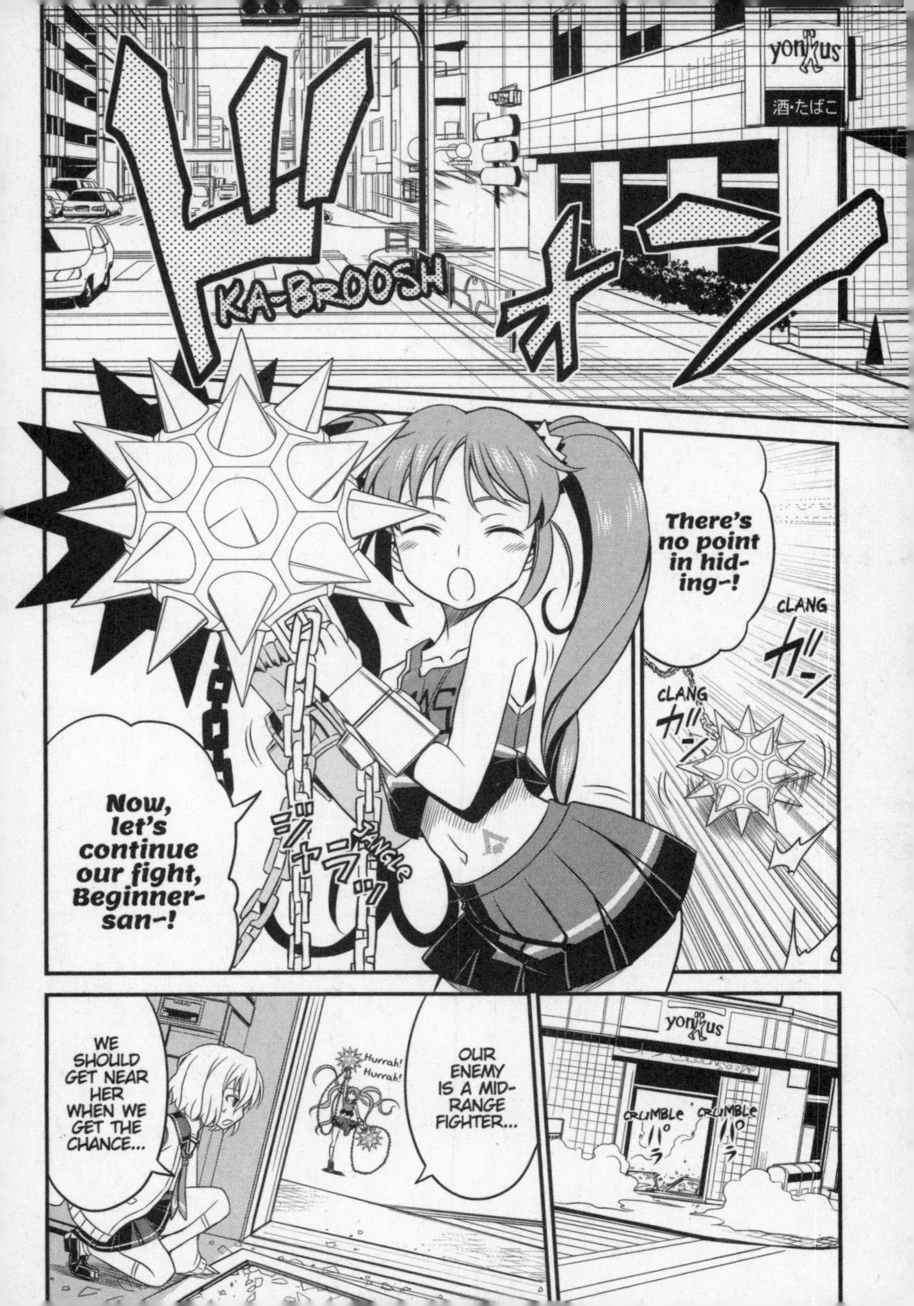
yonkus
酒・たばこ
KA-BROOSH
There's no point in hid-ing-!
CLANG
CLANG
Now, let's continue our fight, Beginner-san-!
JANGLE
yonkus
CRUMBLE
CRUMBLE
OUR ENEMY IS A MID-RANGE FIGHTER...
Hurrah! Hurrah!
WE SHOULD GET NEAR HER WHEN WE GET THE CHANCE...

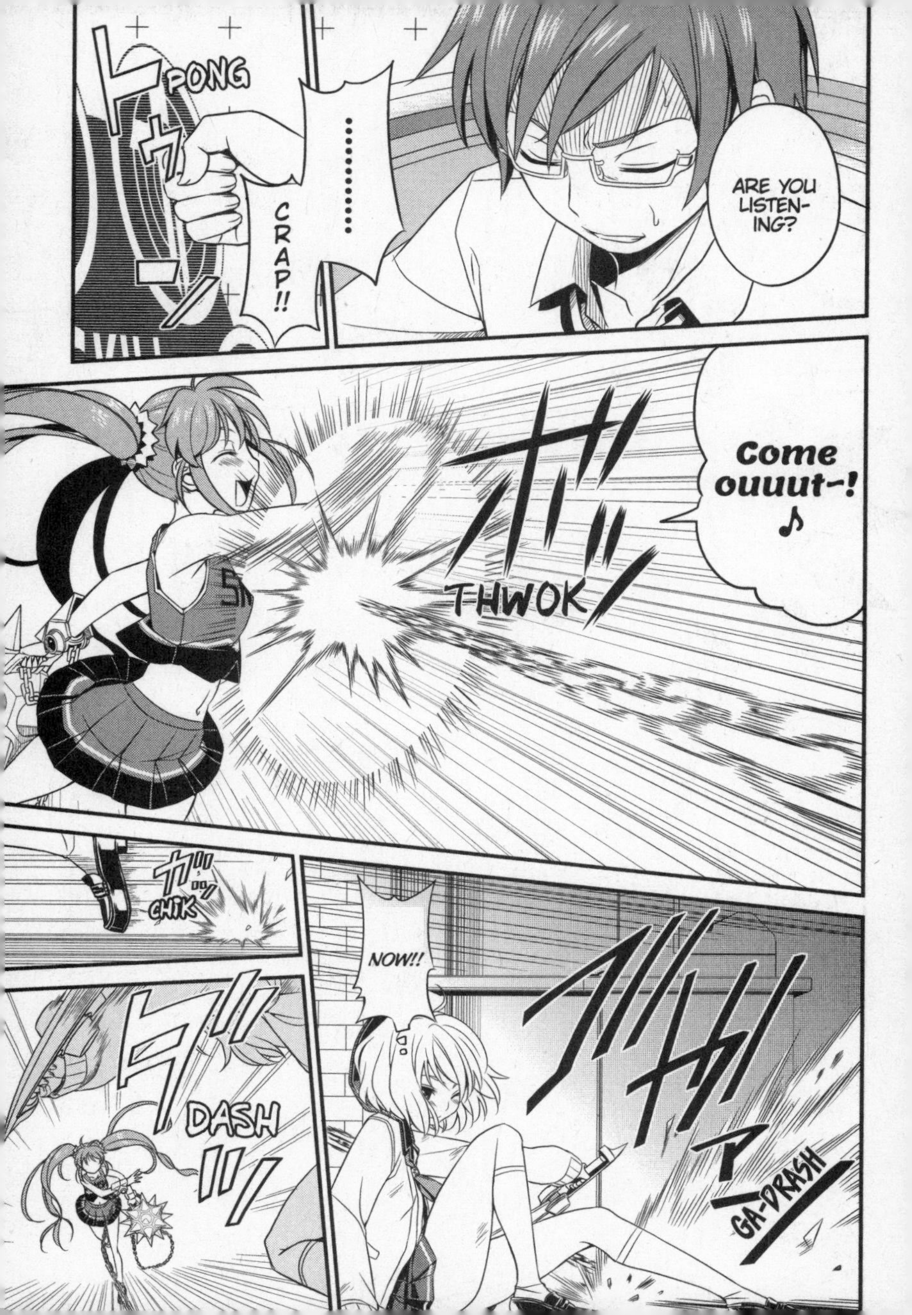
ARE YOU LISTEN-ING?
......
CRAP!!
PONG
Come ouuut-! ♪
THWOK
NOW!!
GA-DRASH
CHIK
DASH

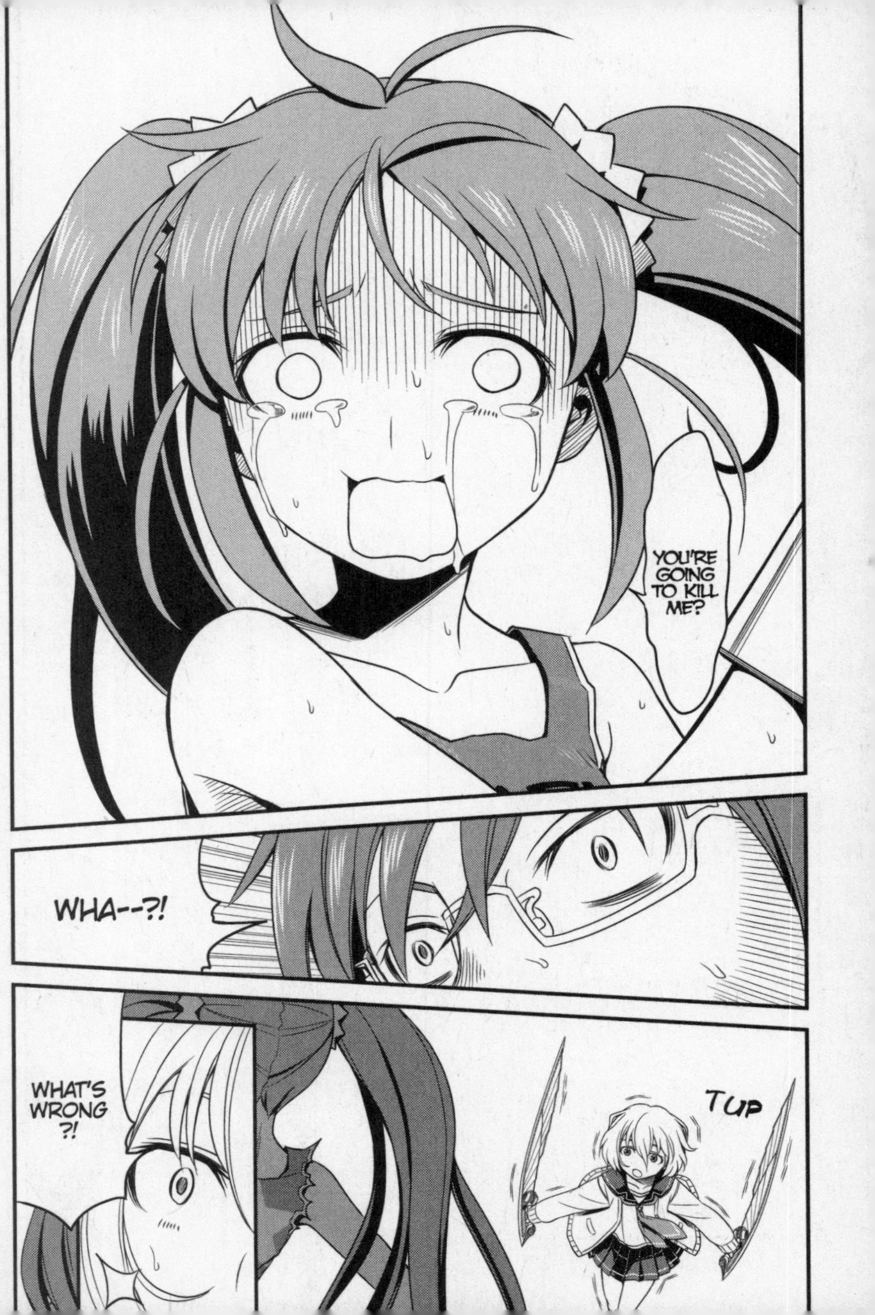
YOU'RE GOING TO KILL ME?
WHA--?!
TUP
WHAT'S WRONG ?!

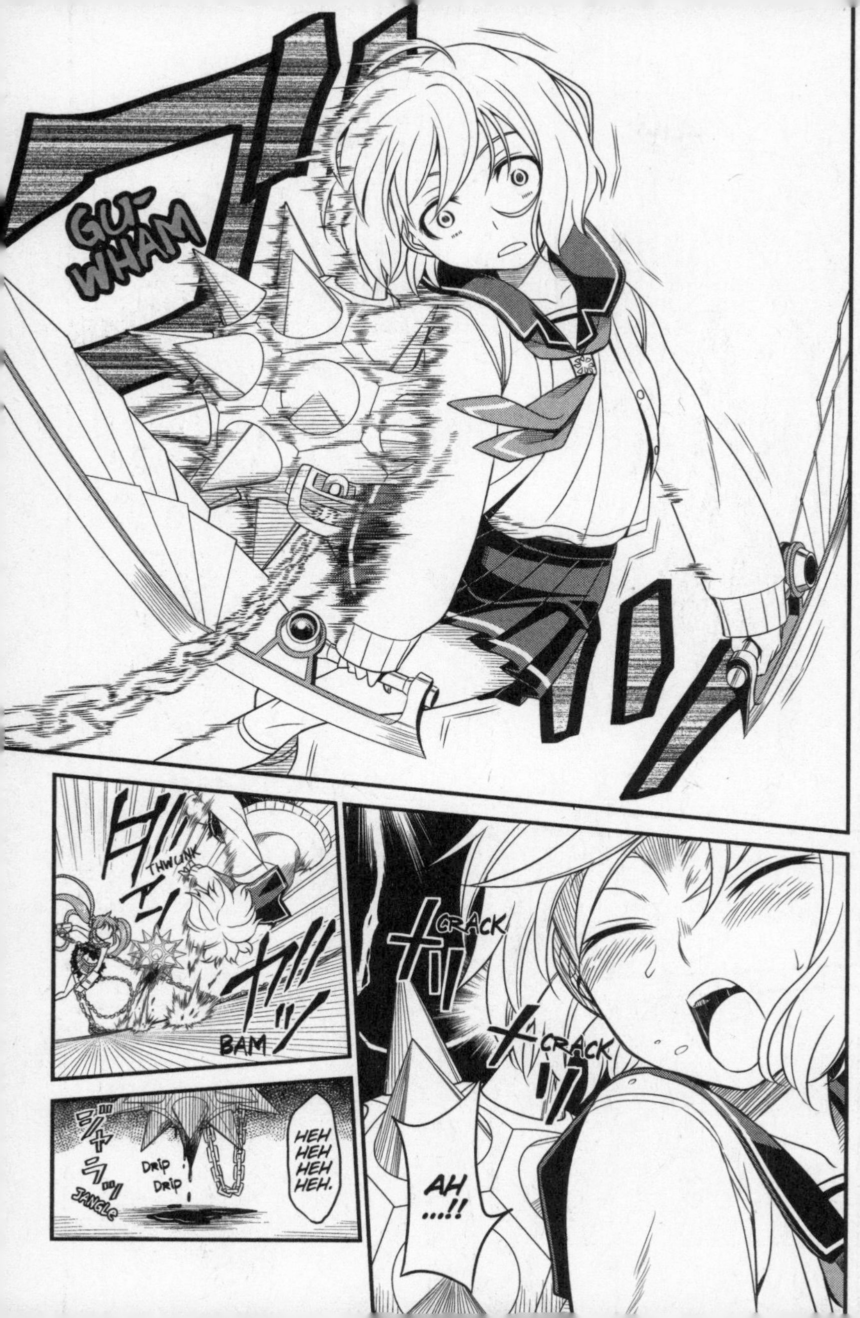
GU-WHAM
CRACK
CRACK
AH ...!!
THWUNK
BAM
HEH HEH HEH HEH.
Drip Drip
JANGLE

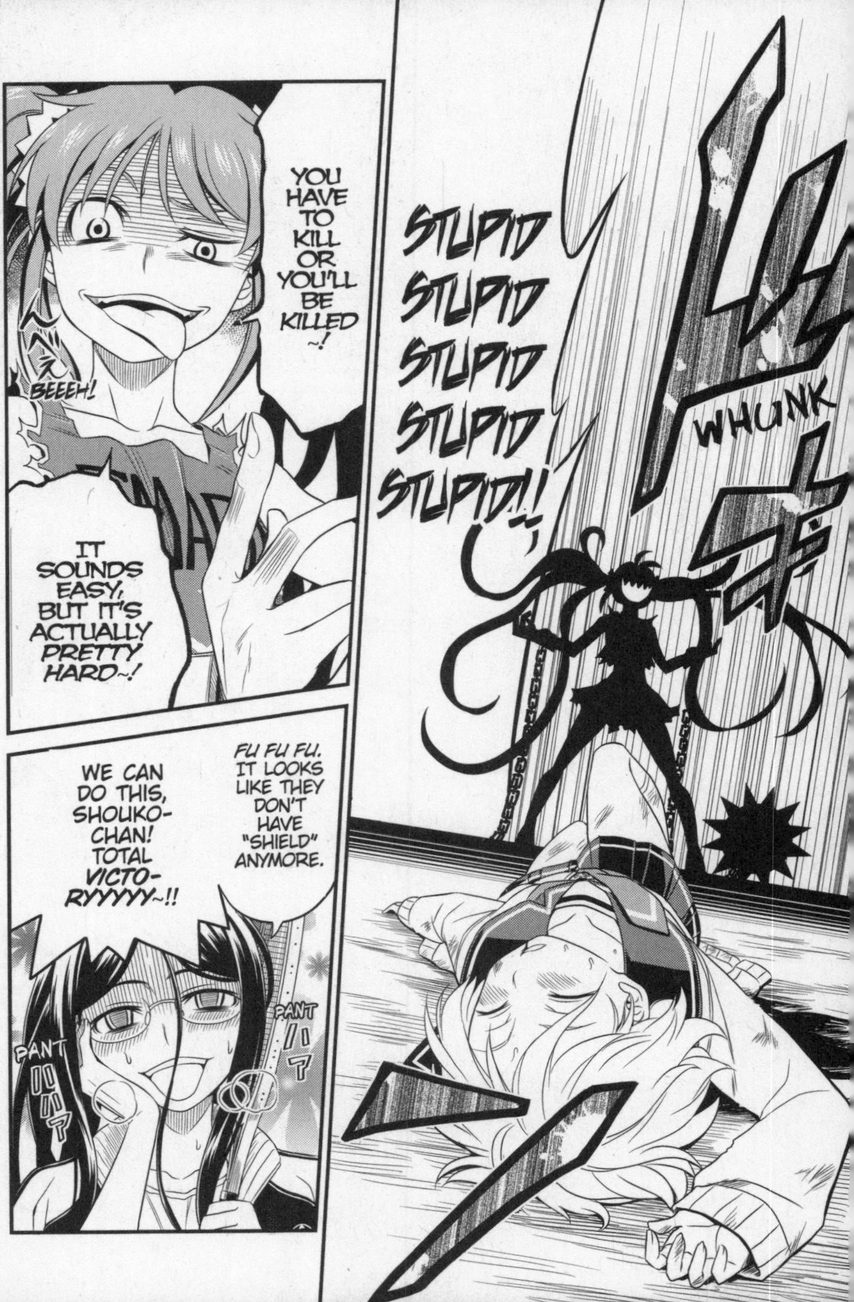
STUPID STUPID STUPID STUPID STUPID!!
WHUNK
YOU HAVE TO KILL OR YOU'LL BE KILLED~!
BEEEH!
IT SOUNDS EASY, BUT IT'S ACTUALLY PRETTY HARD~!
FU FU FU. IT LOOKS LIKE THEY DON'T HAVE "SHIELD" ANYMORE.
WE CAN DO THIS, SHOUKO-CHAN! TOTAL VICTO-RYYYYY~!!
PANT
ハァ
PANT
ハハァ

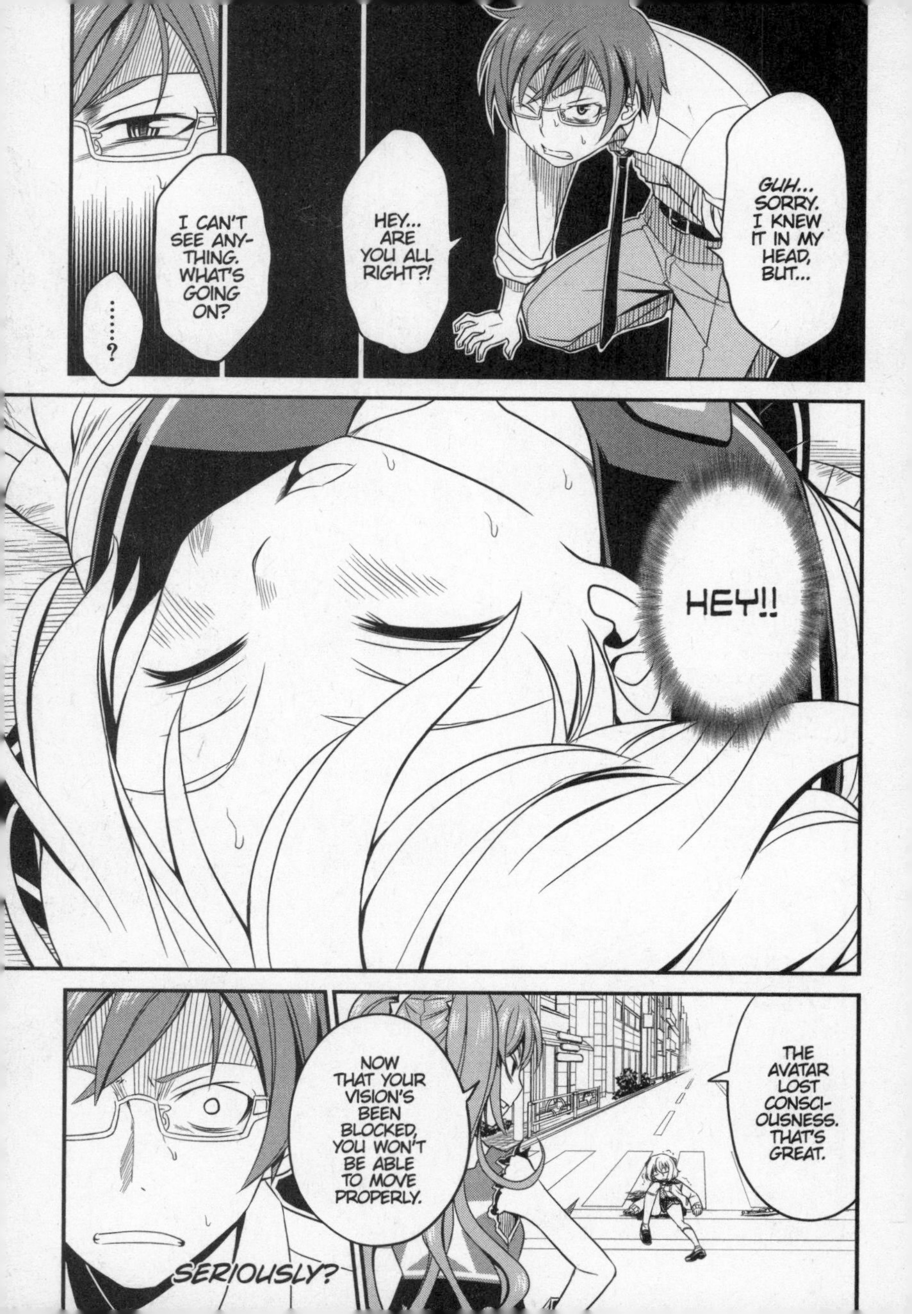
GUH... SORRY. I KNEW IT IN MY HEAD, BUT...
HEY... ARE YOU ALL RIGHT?!
I CAN'T SEE ANYTHING. WHAT'S GOING ON?
......?
HEY!!
THE AVATAR LOST CONSCIOUSNESS. THAT'S GREAT.
NOW THAT YOUR VISION'S BEEN BLOCKED, YOU WON'T BE ABLE TO MOVE PROPERLY.
SERIOUSLY?

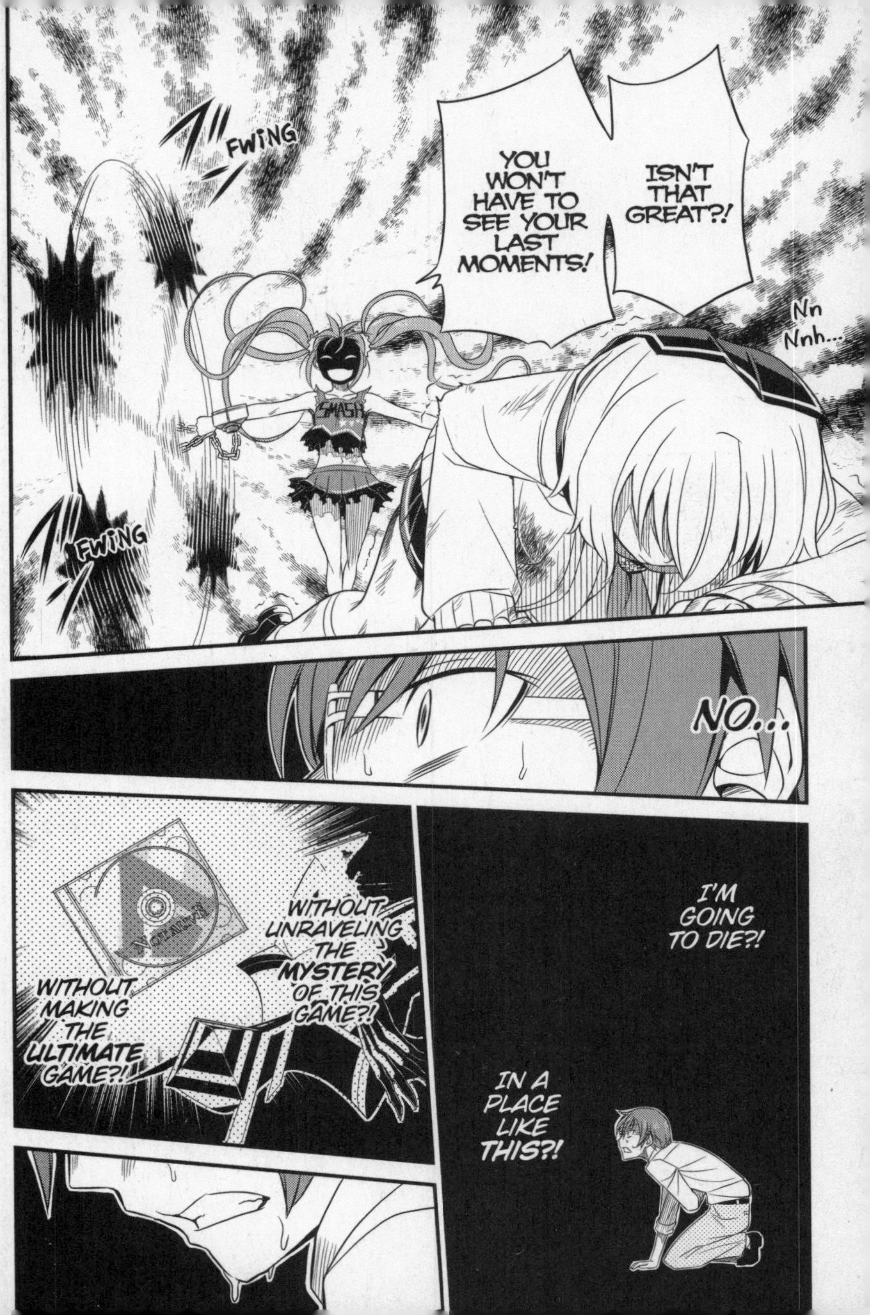
ISN'T THAT GREAT?!
YOU WON'T HAVE TO SEE YOUR LAST MOMENTS!
Nn Nnh...
FWiNG
SMASH
FWiNG
NO...
I'M GOING TO DIE?!
IN A PLACE LIKE THIS?!
WITHOUT UNRAVELING THE MYSTERY OF THIS GAME?!
WITHOUT MAKING THE ULTIMATE GAME?!

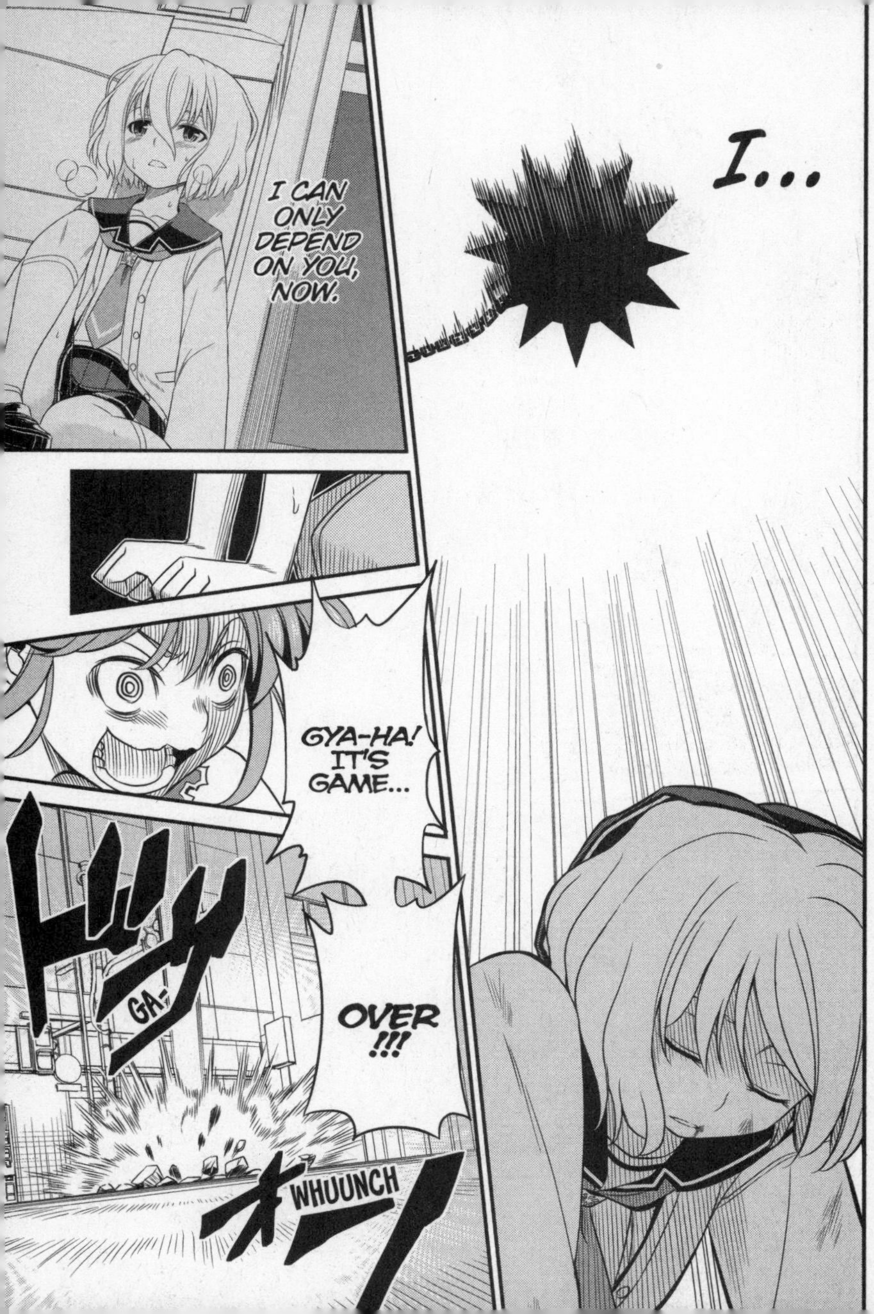
I...
I CAN ONLY DEPEND ON YOU, NOW.
GYA-HA! IT'S GAME...
OVER !!!
GA-
WHUUNCH

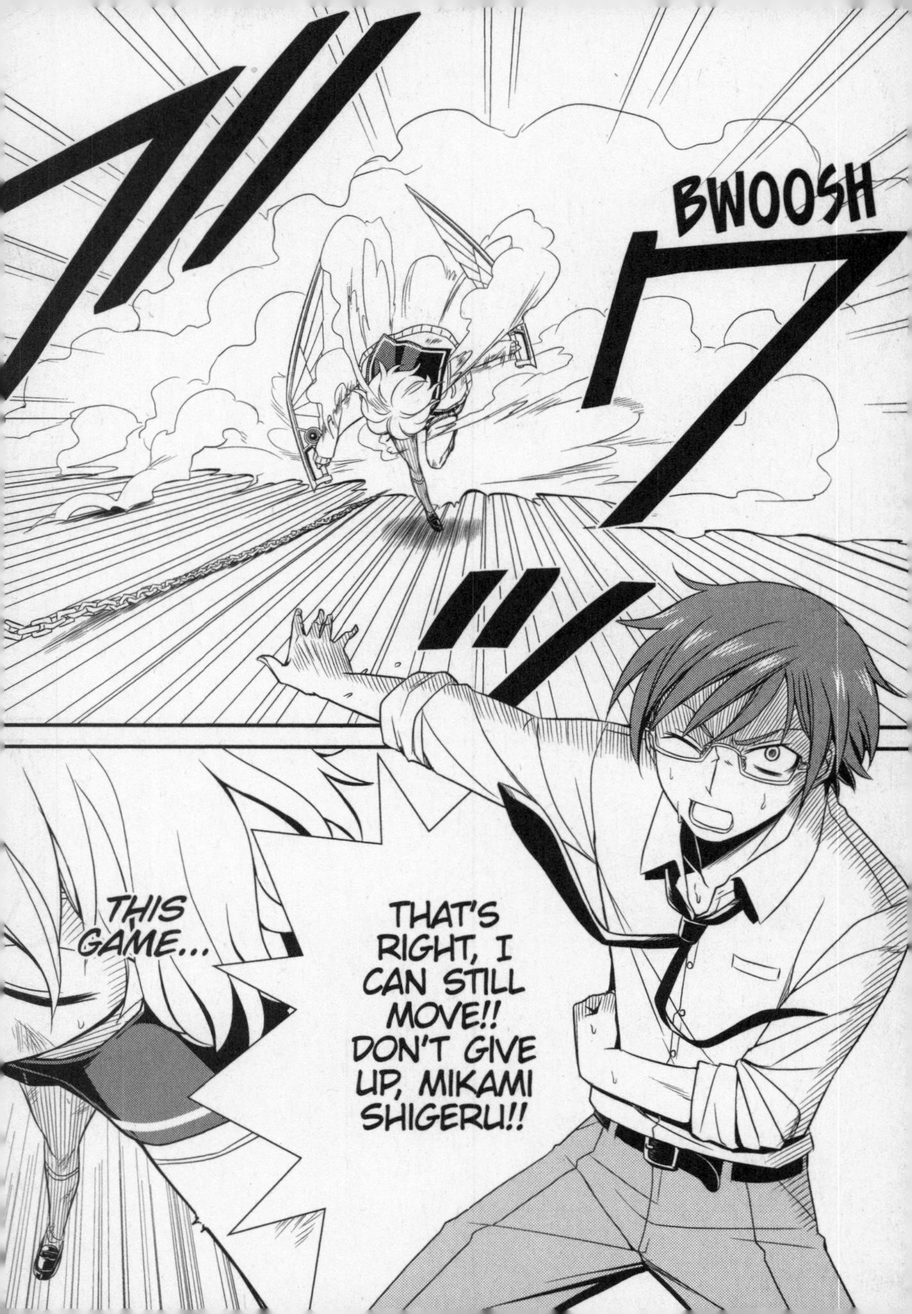
BWOOSH
THAT'S RIGHT, I CAN STILL MOVE!! DON'T GIVE UP, MIKAMI SHIGERU!!
THIS GAME...

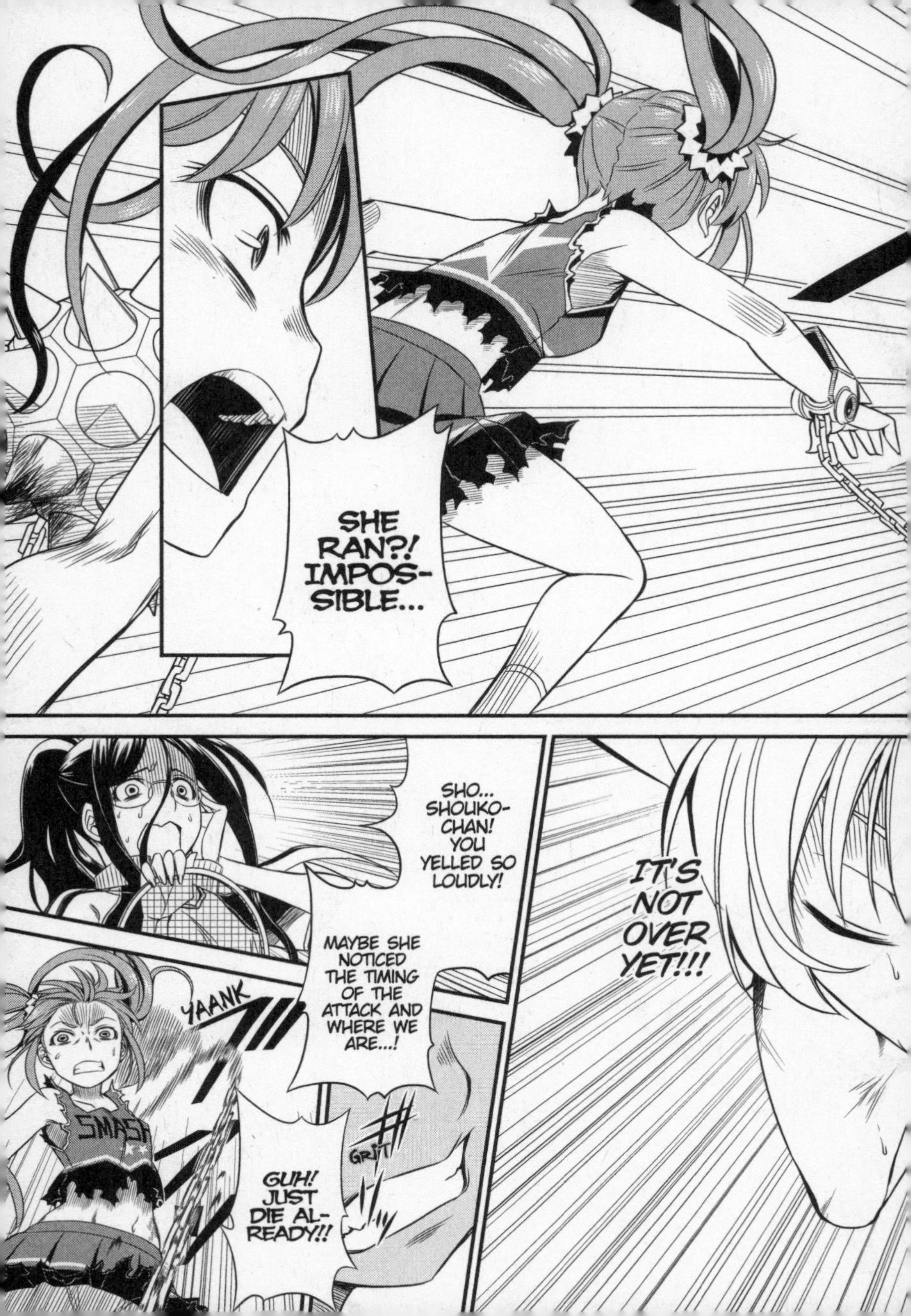
SHE RAN?! IMPOSSIBLE...
IT'S NOT OVER YET!!!
SHO... SHOUKO-CHAN! YOU YELLED SO LOUDLY!
MAYBE SHE NOTICED THE TIMING OF THE ATTACK AND WHERE WE ARE...!
YAANK
SMASH
GRIT
GUH! JUST DIE ALREADY!!

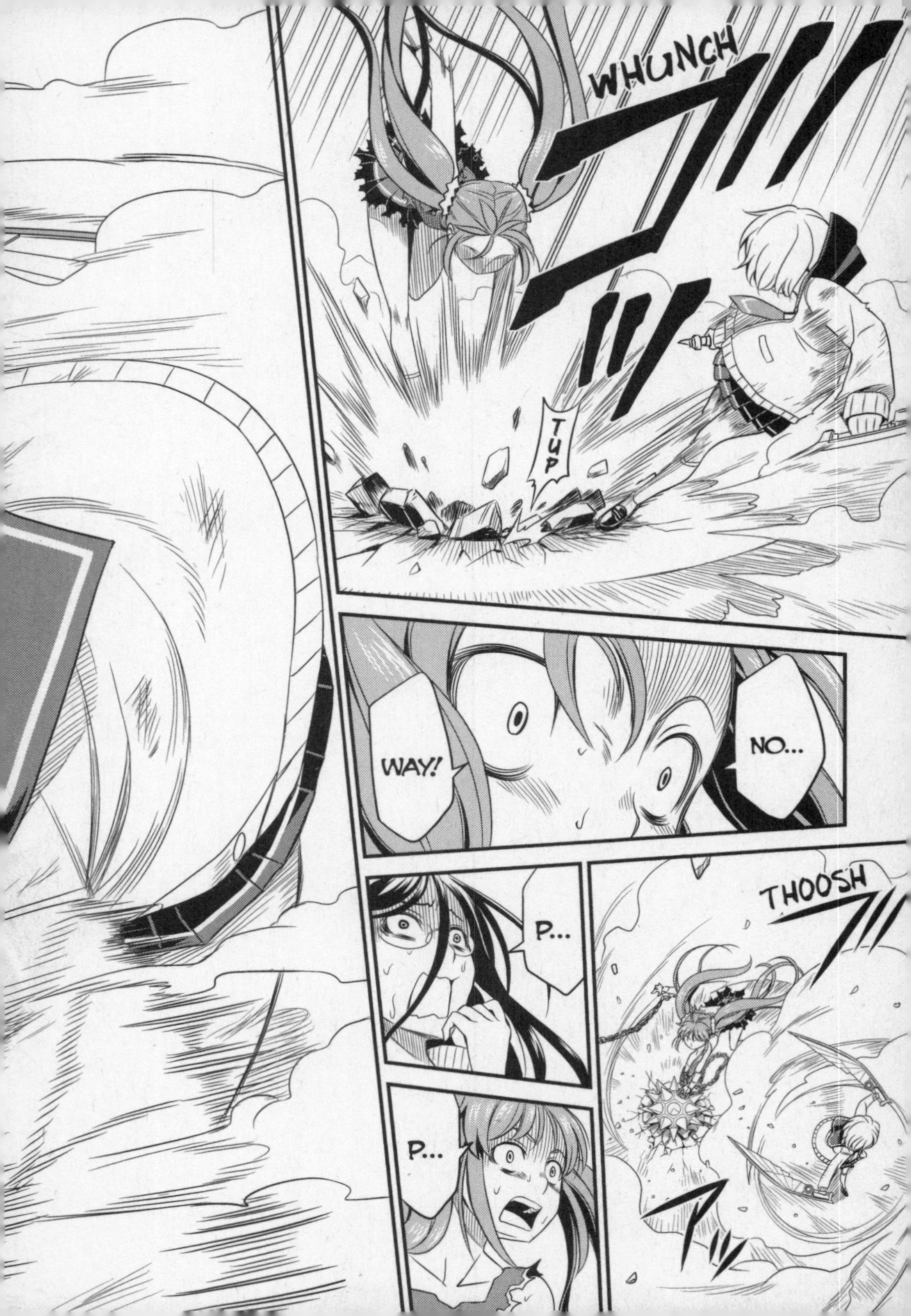
WHUNCH
TUP
NO...
WAY!
THOOSH
P...
P...

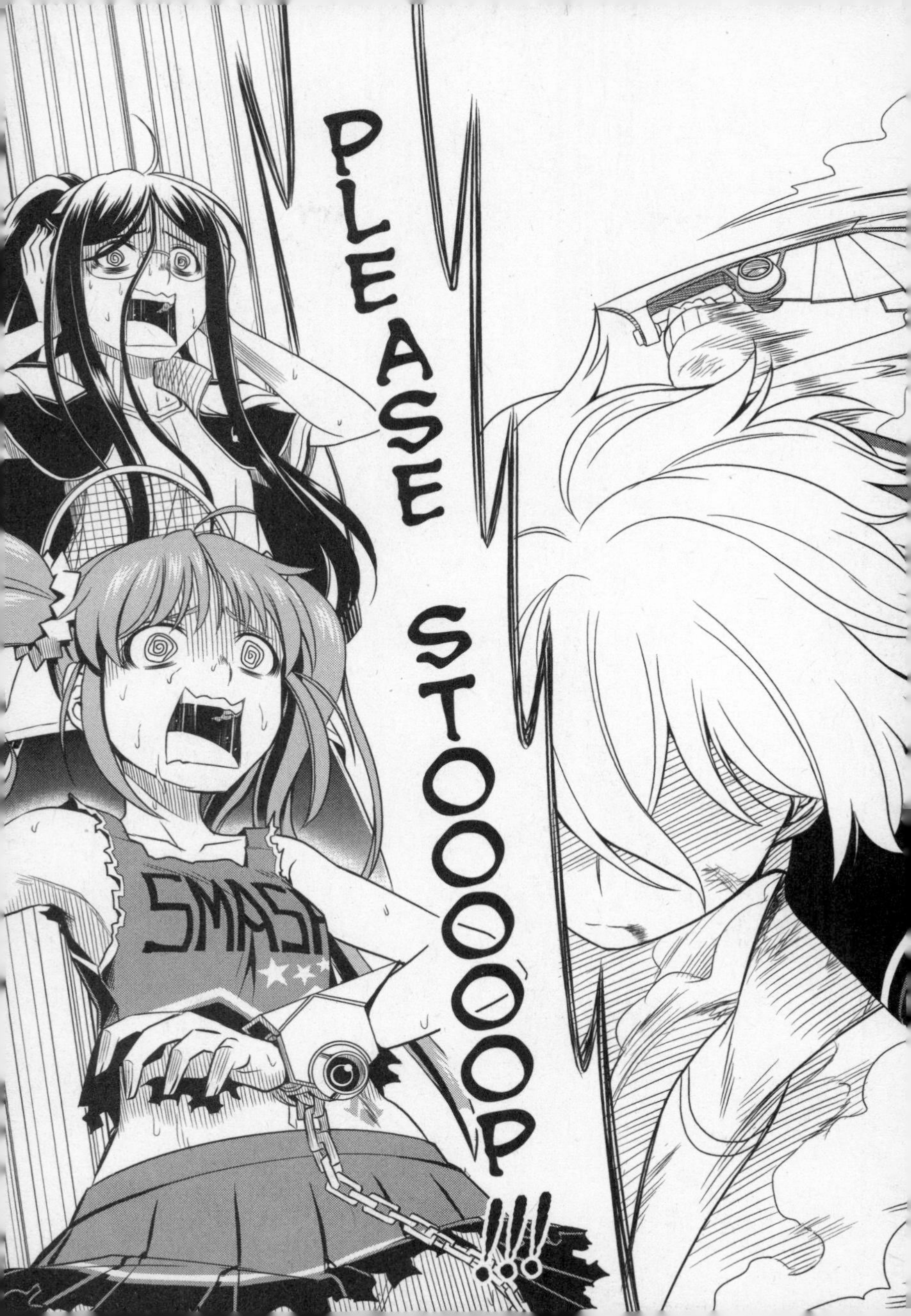
PLEASE STOOOOOP!!!

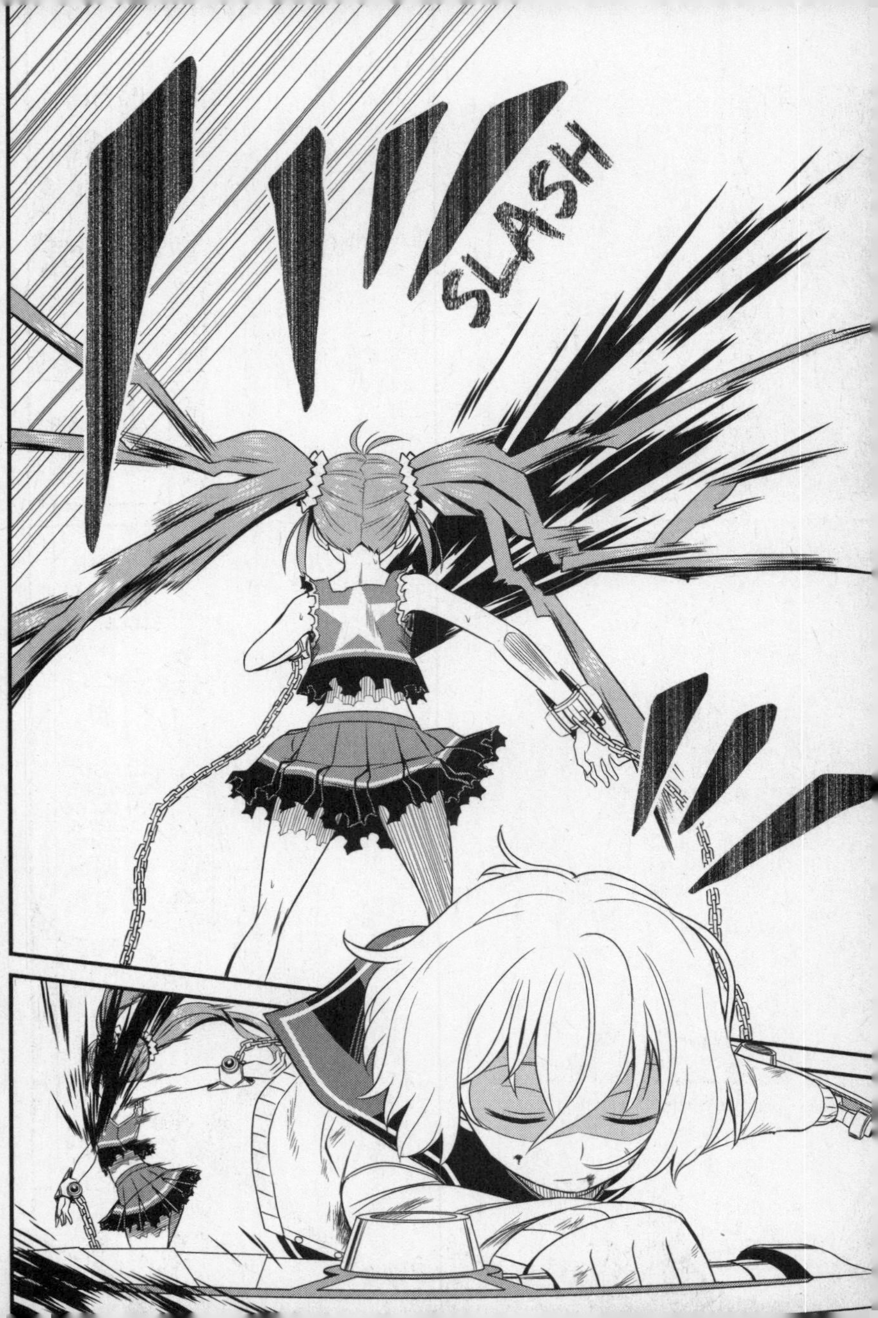
SLASH

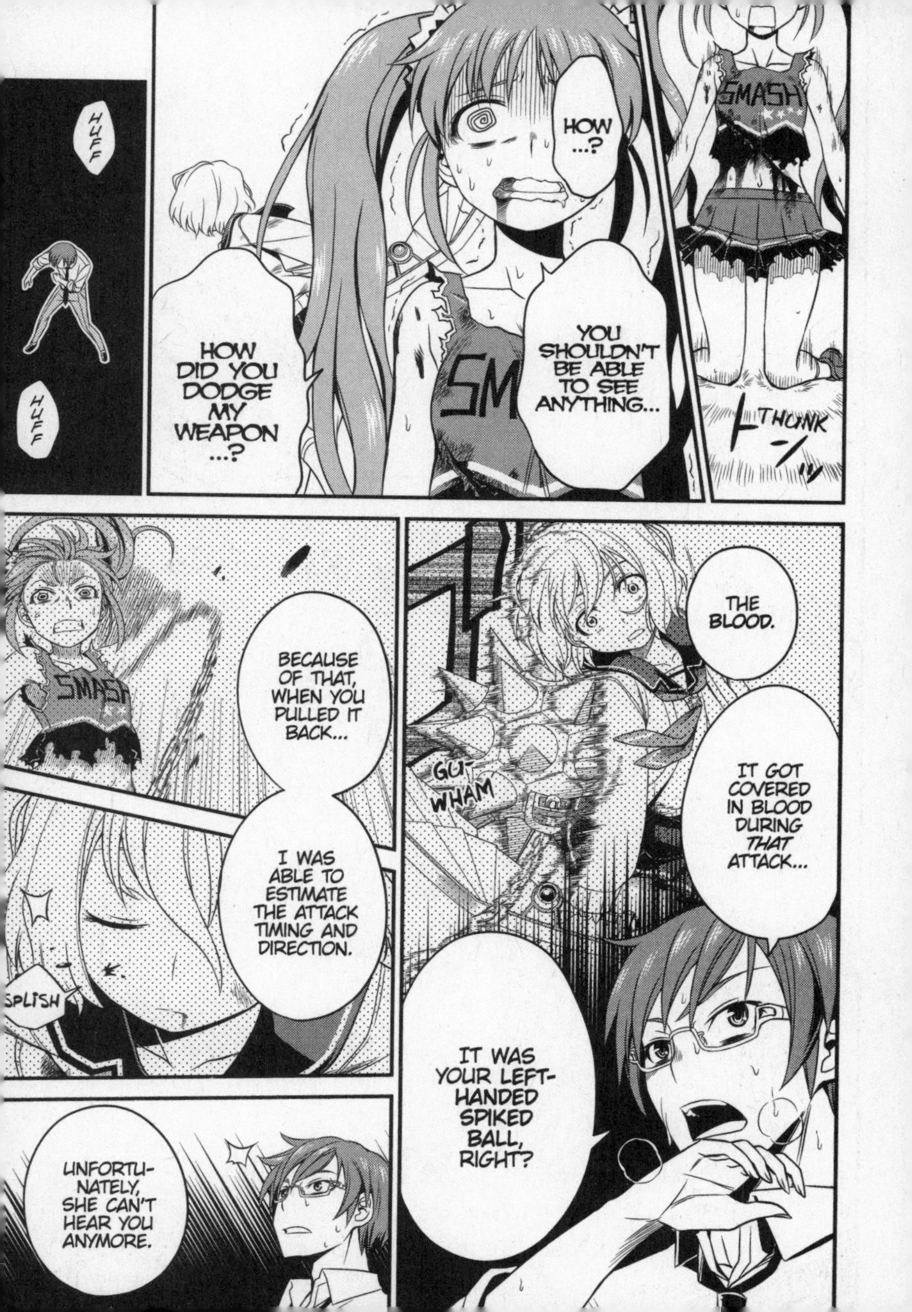
THUNK
HOW ...?
YOU SHOULDN'T BE ABLE TO SEE ANYTHING...
HOW DID YOU DODGE MY WEAPON ...?
HUFF
HUFF
THE BLOOD.
GU-WHAM
IT GOT COVERED IN BLOOD DURING *THAT* ATTACK...
BECAUSE OF THAT, WHEN YOU PULLED IT BACK...
I WAS ABLE TO ESTIMATE THE ATTACK TIMING AND DIRECTION.
SPLISH
IT WAS YOUR LEFT-HANDED SPIKED BALL, RIGHT?
UNFORTUNATELY, SHE CAN'T HEAR YOU ANYMORE.

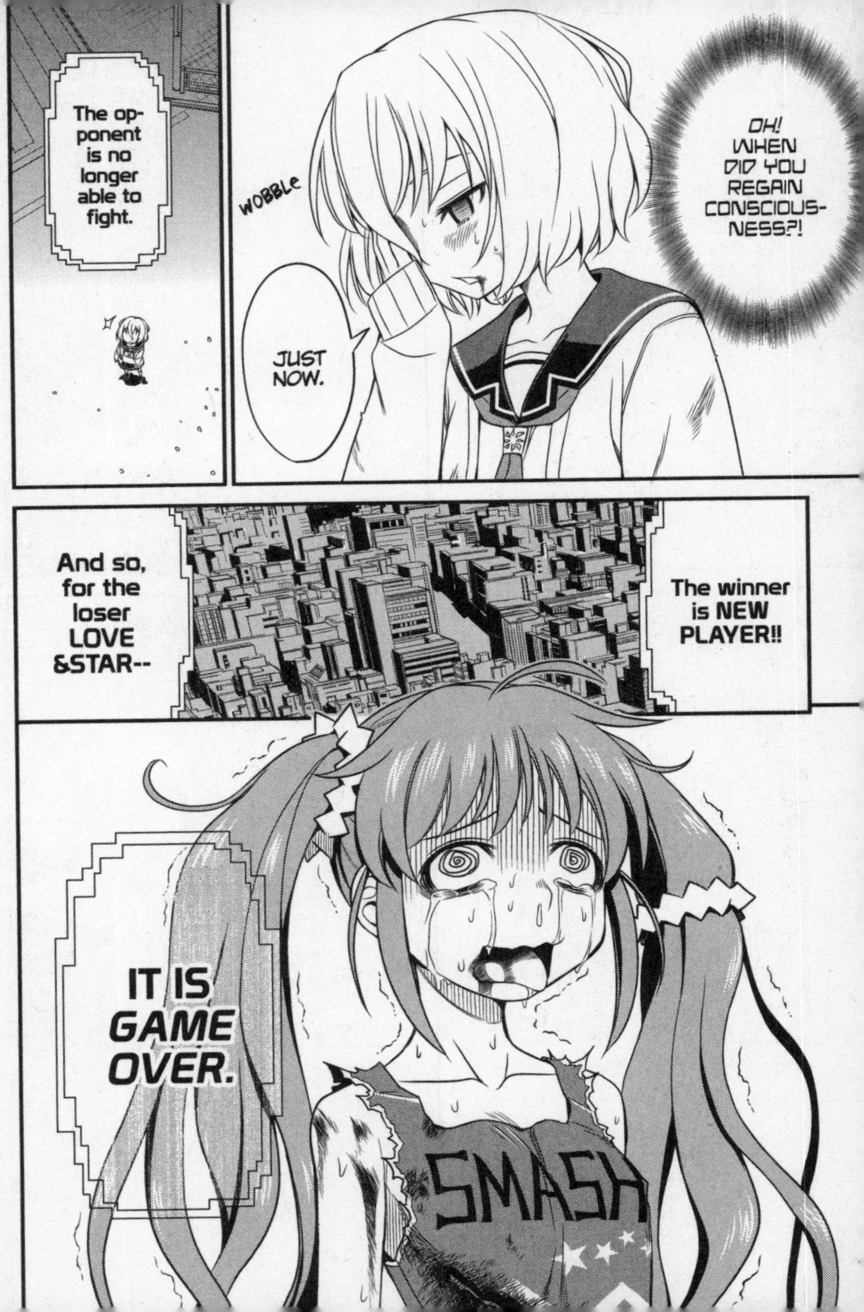

OH! WHEN DID YOU REGAIN CONSCIOUS-NESS?!
WOBBLE
JUST NOW.
The op-ponent is no longer able to fight.
The winner is NEW PLAYER!!
And so, for the loser LOVE &STAR--
IT IS GAME OVER.
SMASH

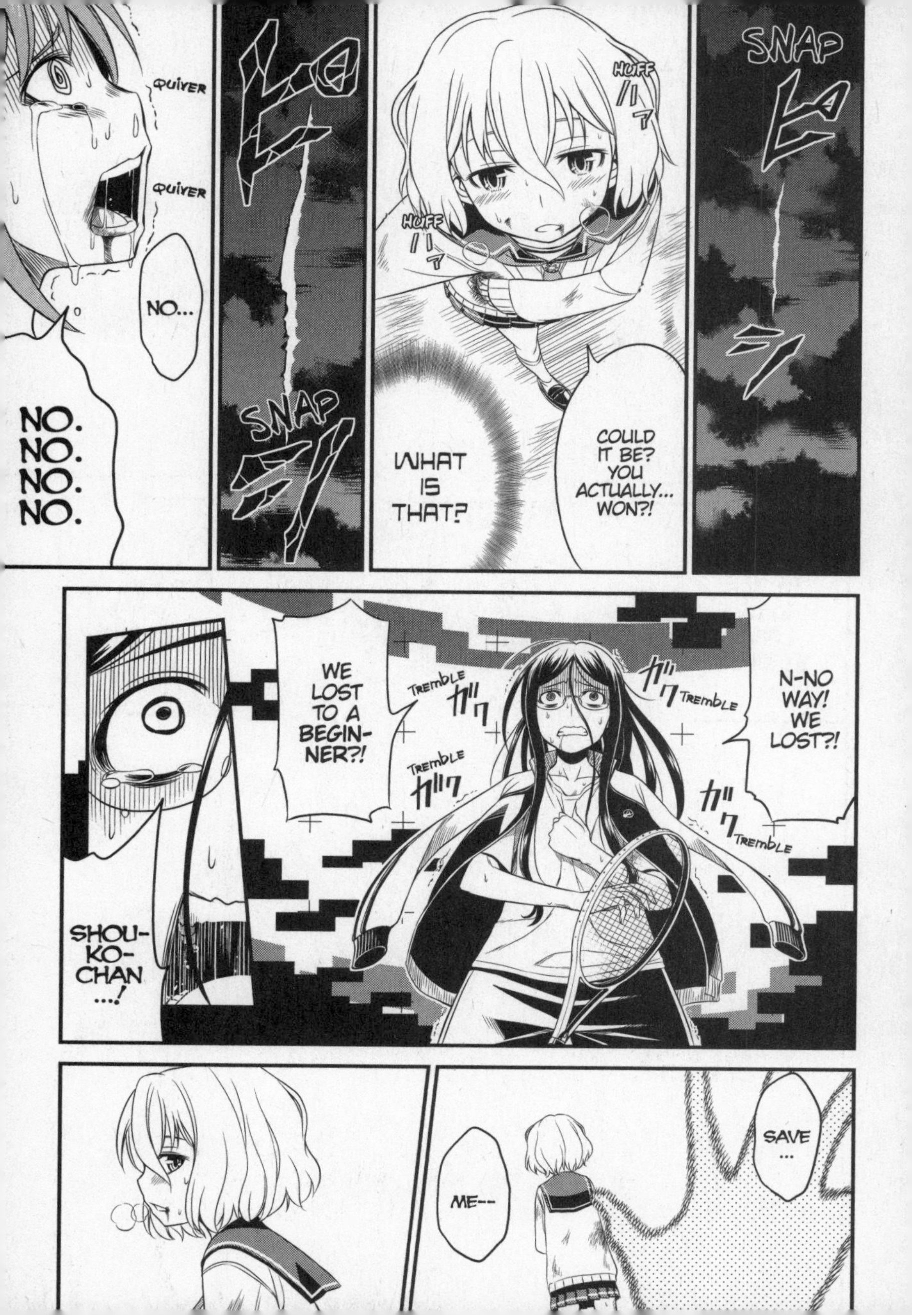
SNAP
HUFF
HUFF
COULD IT BE? YOU ACTUALLY... WON?!
WHAT IS THAT?
SNAP
QUIVER
QUIVER
NO...
NO. NO. NO. NO.
N-NO WAY! WE LOST?!
ガク TREMBLE
ガク TREMBLE
TREMBLE ガク
TREMBLE ガク
WE LOST TO A BEGINNER?!
SHOUKO-CHAN ...!
SAVE ...
ME--

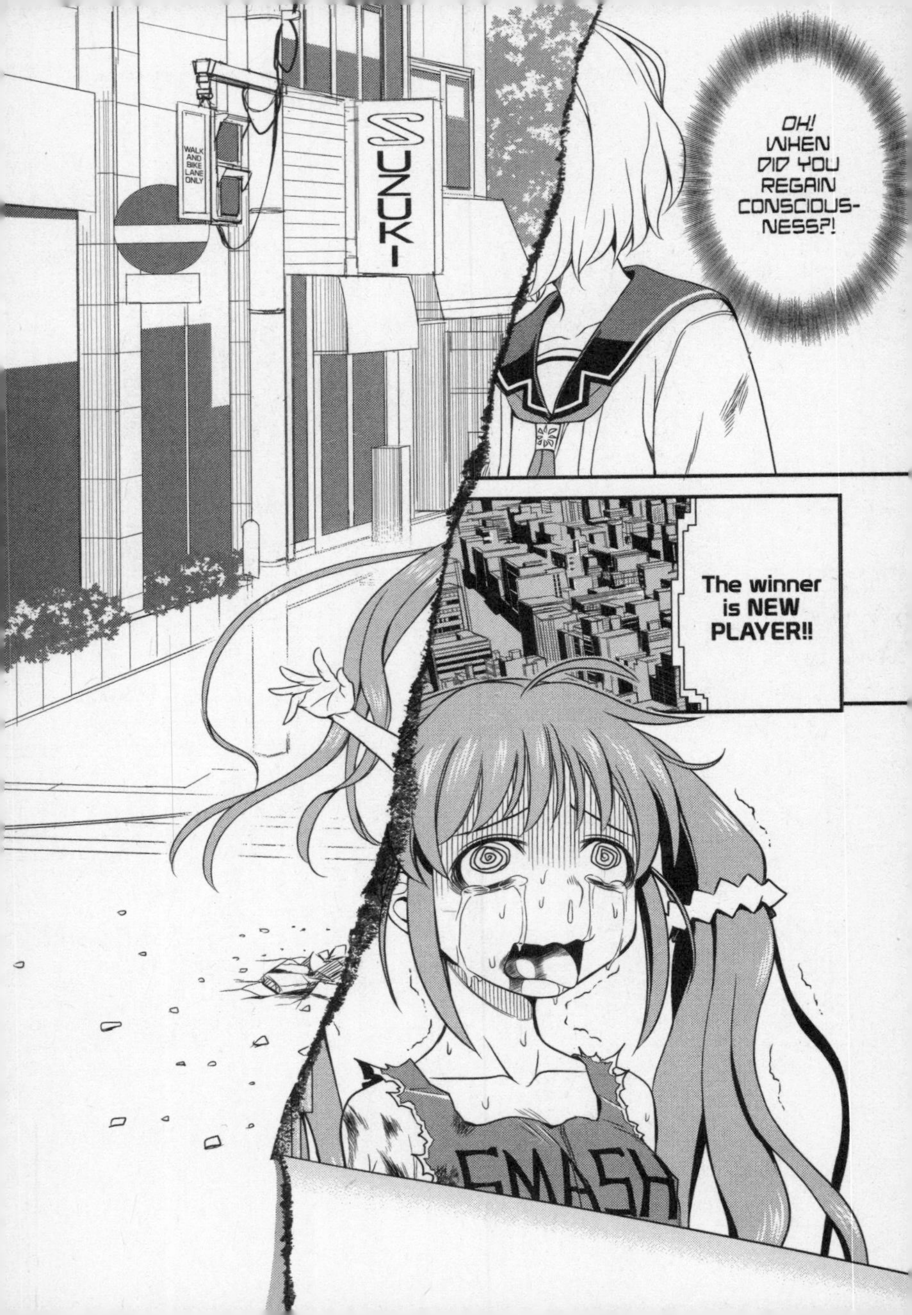
OH! WHEN DID YOU REGAIN CONSCIOUS-NESS?!
SUZUKI
WALK AND BIKE LANE ONLY
The winner is NEW PLAYER!!
SMASH

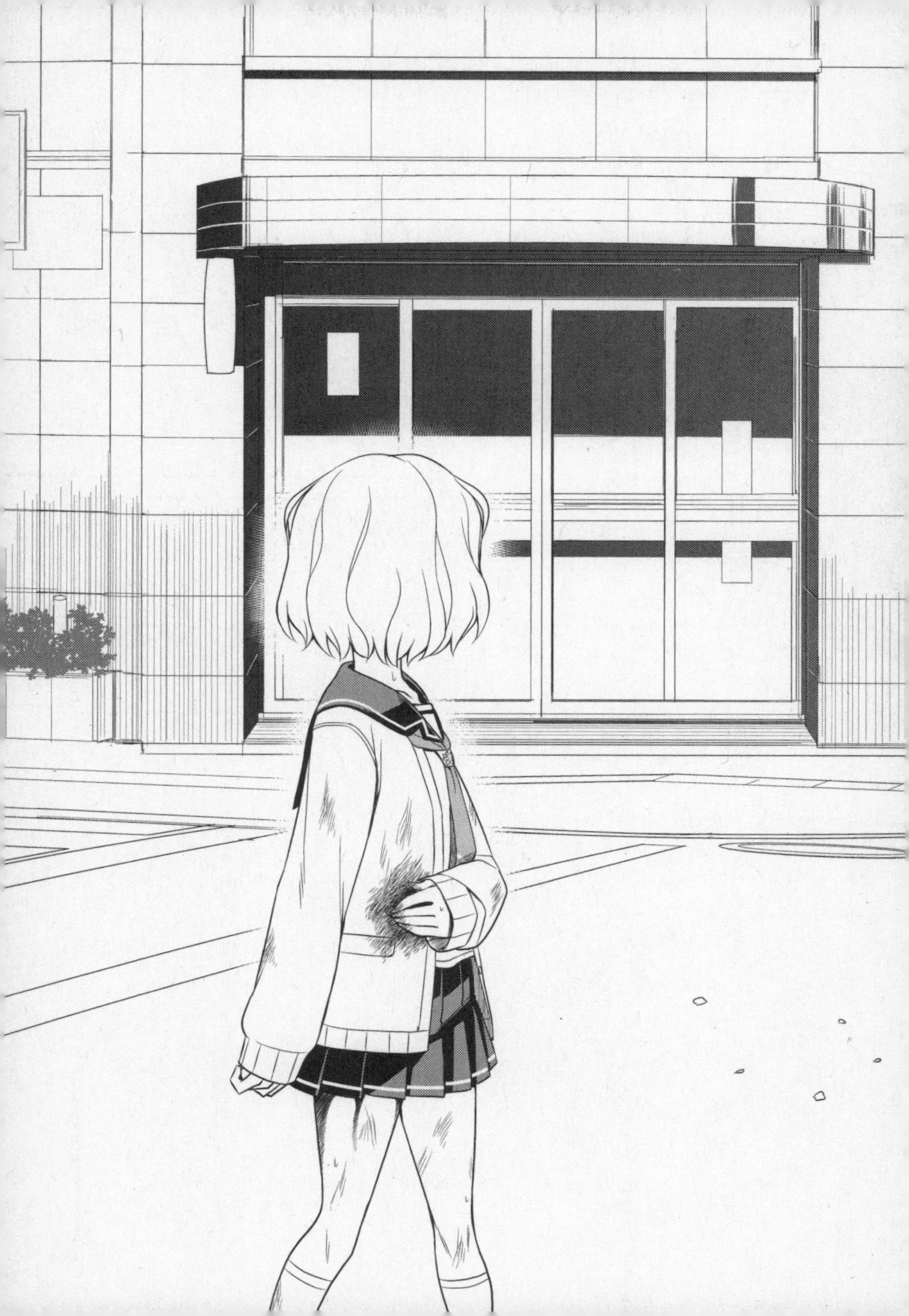

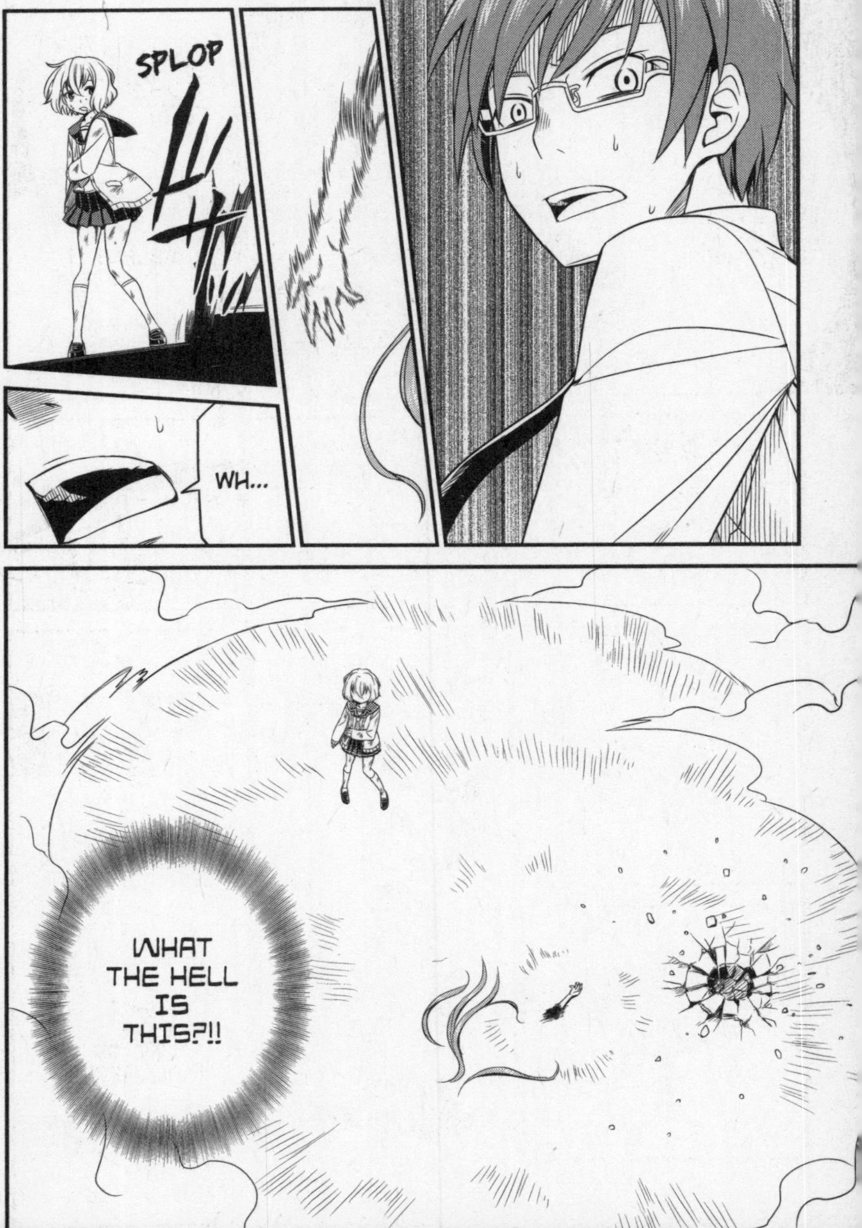
SPLOP
WH...
WHAT THE HELL IS THIS?!!

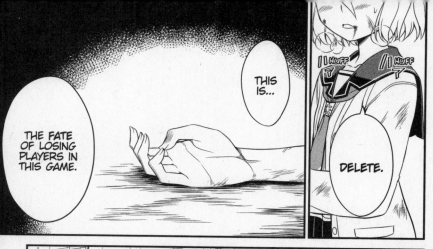

THIS IS...

THE FATE OF LOSING PLAYERS IN THIS GAME.

DELETE.

SHOOOOOOOM

THUMP

HUFF

HUFF

NO.

AM I...

AM *I* THE ONE TO BLAME?!

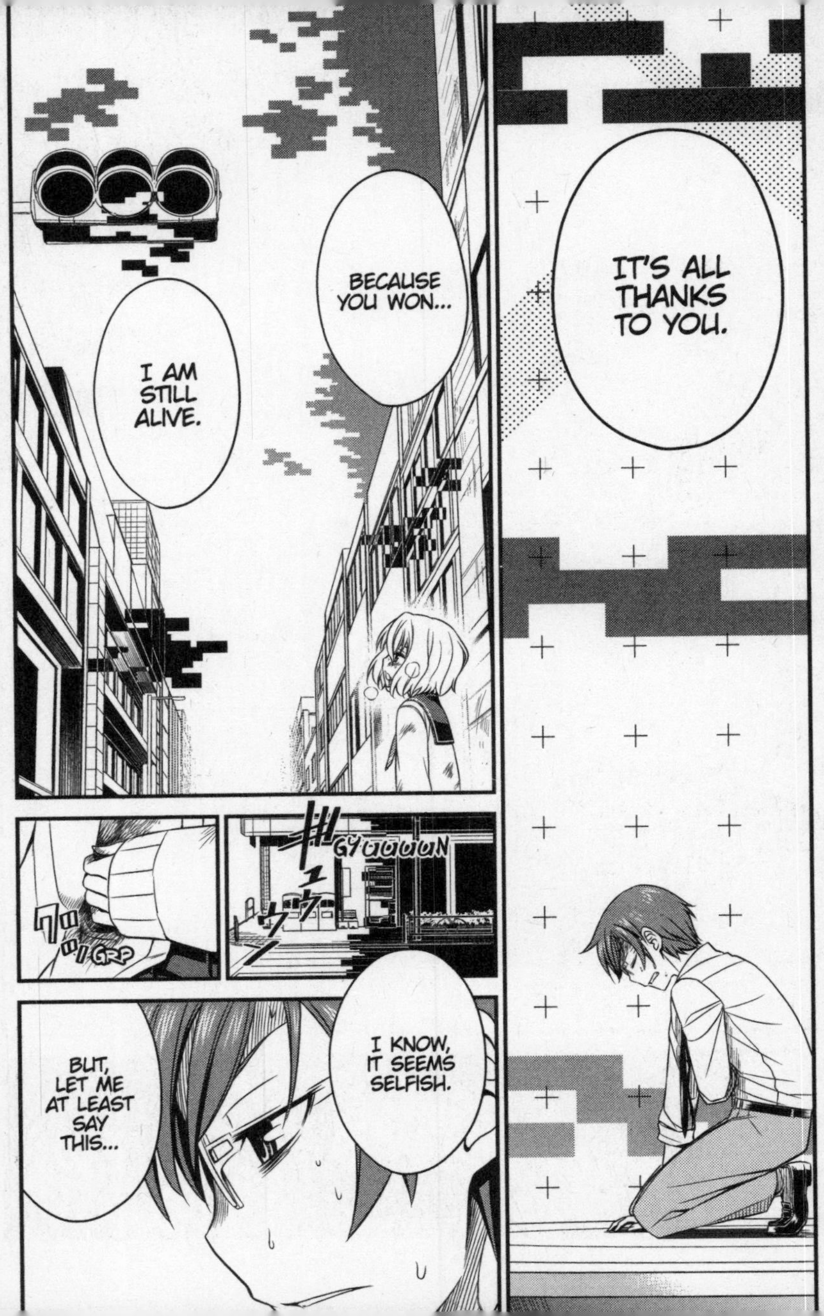
IT'S ALL THANKS TO YOU.
BECAUSE YOU WON...
I AM STILL ALIVE.
GYUUUUUN
GRP
I KNOW, IT SEEMS SELFISH.
BUT, LET ME AT LEAST SAY THIS...

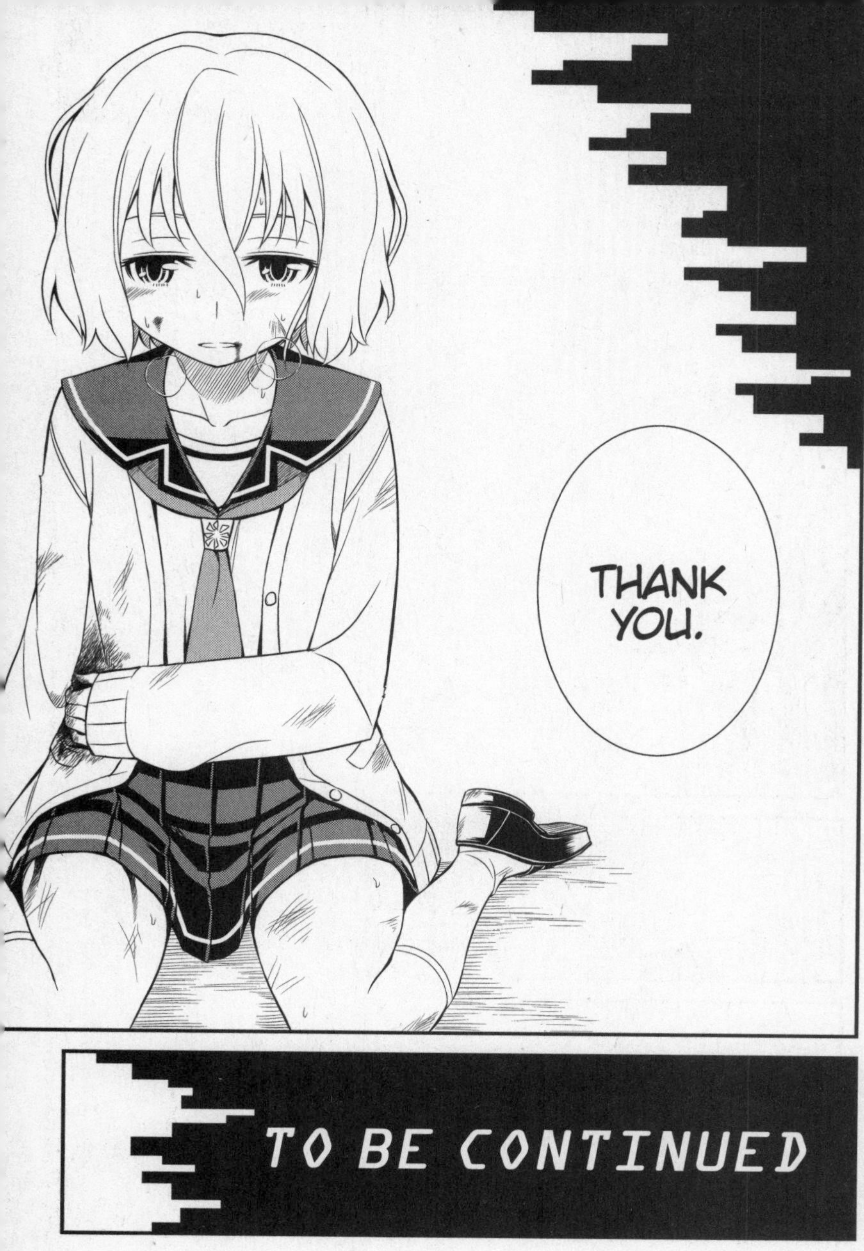
THANK YOU.
TO BE CONTINUED

NOT ALIVE

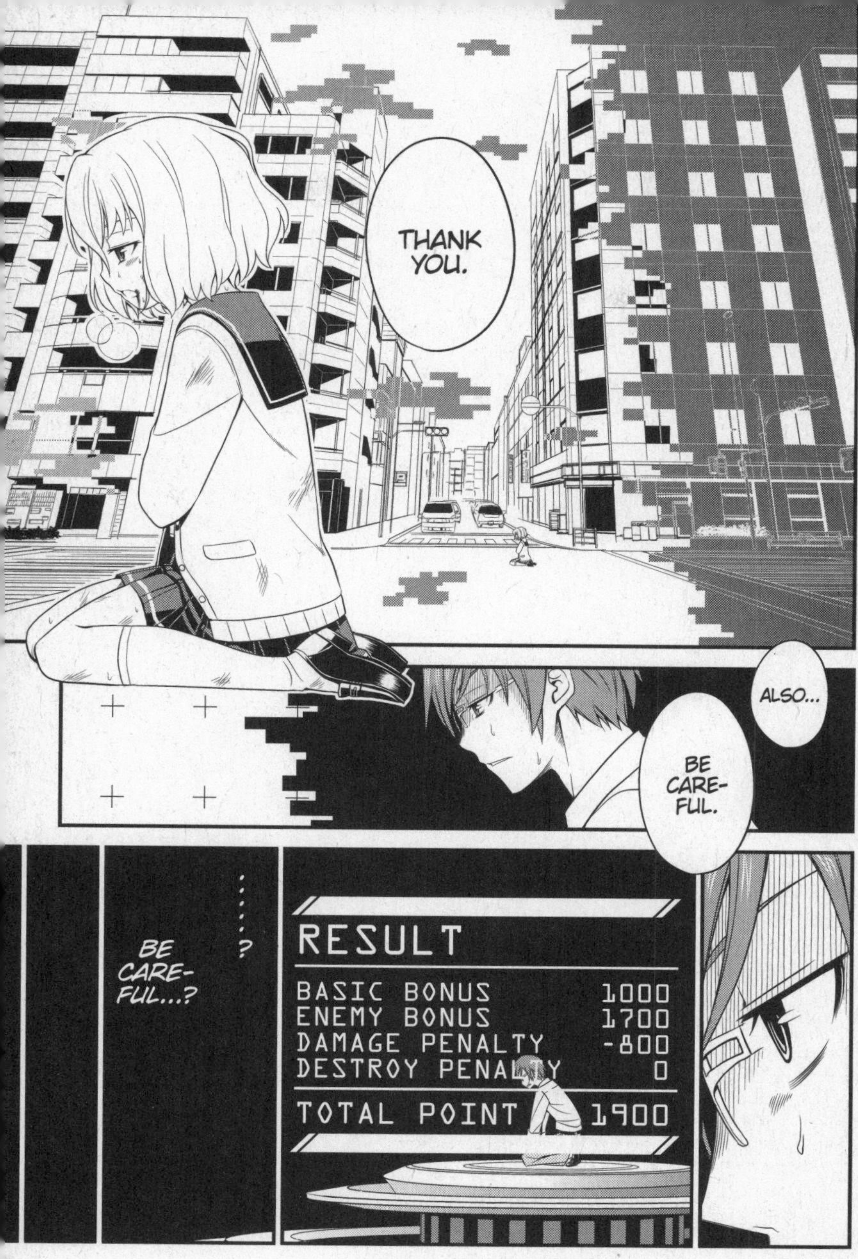
THANK YOU.
ALSO...
BE CARE-FUL.
RESULT
BASIC BONUS 1000
ENEMY BONUS 1700
DAMAGE PENALTY -800
DESTROY PENALTY 0
TOTAL POINT 1900
......?
BE CARE-FUL...?

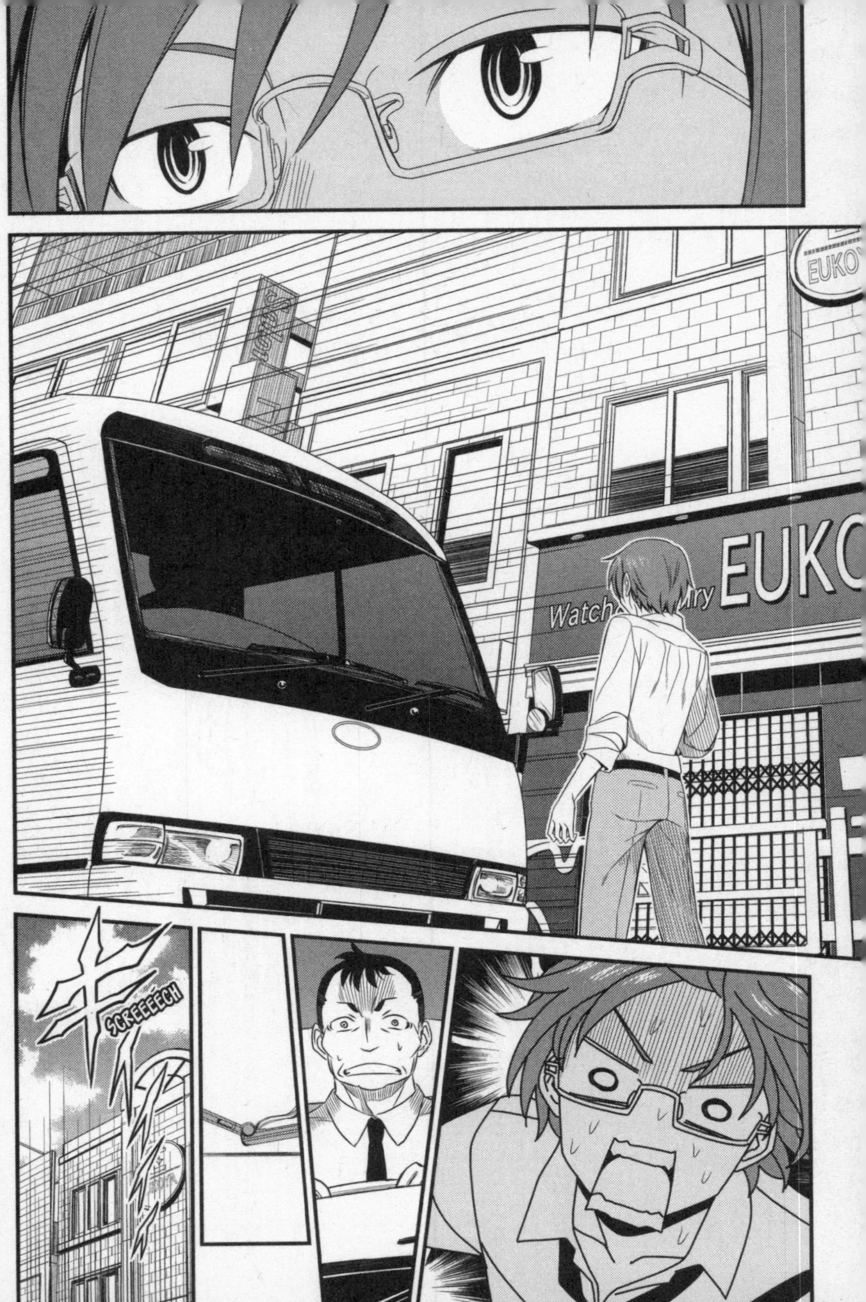
EUKO
Watch
EUKO
SCREEEECH

CHAPTER 4

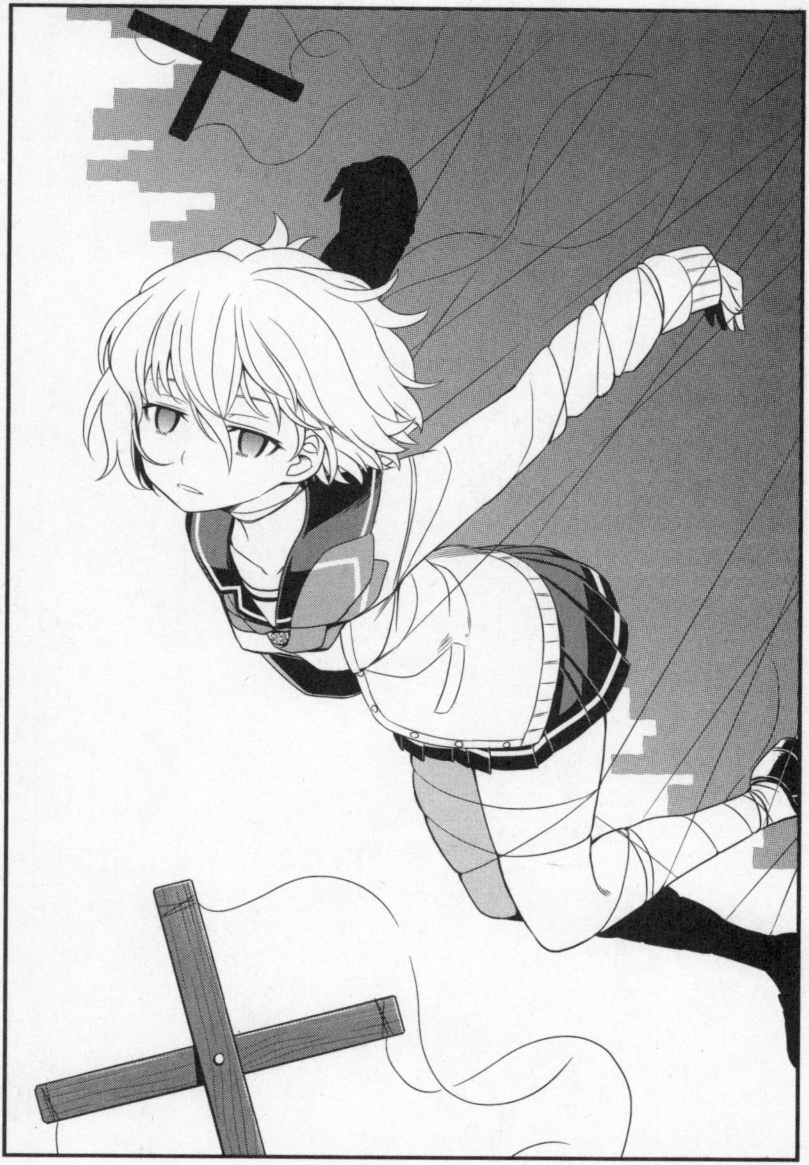

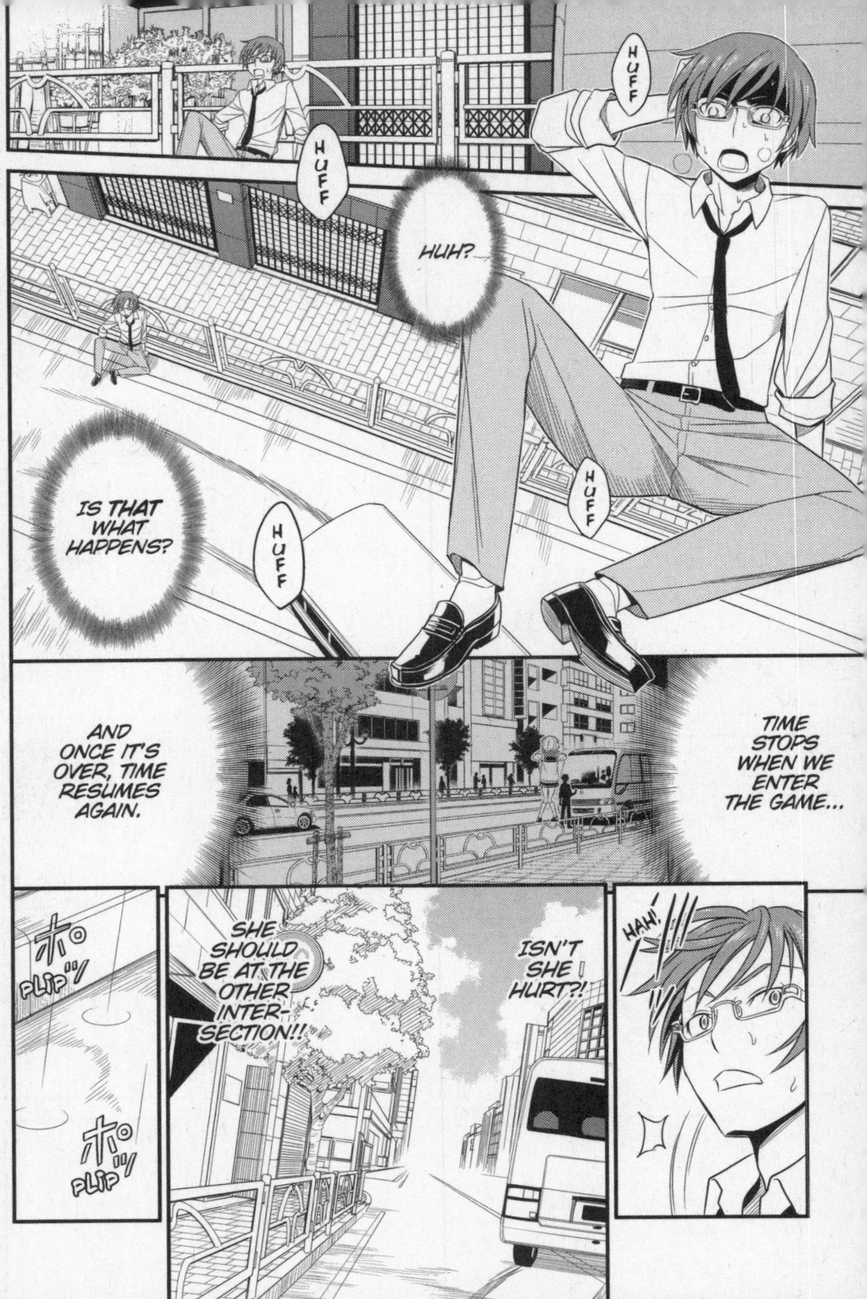
HUFF
HUFF
HUH?
HUFF
HUFF
IS THAT WHAT HAPPENS?
TIME STOPS WHEN WE ENTER THE GAME...
AND ONCE IT'S OVER, TIME RESUMES AGAIN.
HAH!
ISN'T SHE HURT?!
SHE SHOULD BE AT THE OTHER INTER-SECTION!!
ポツ
PLIP
ポツ
PLIP

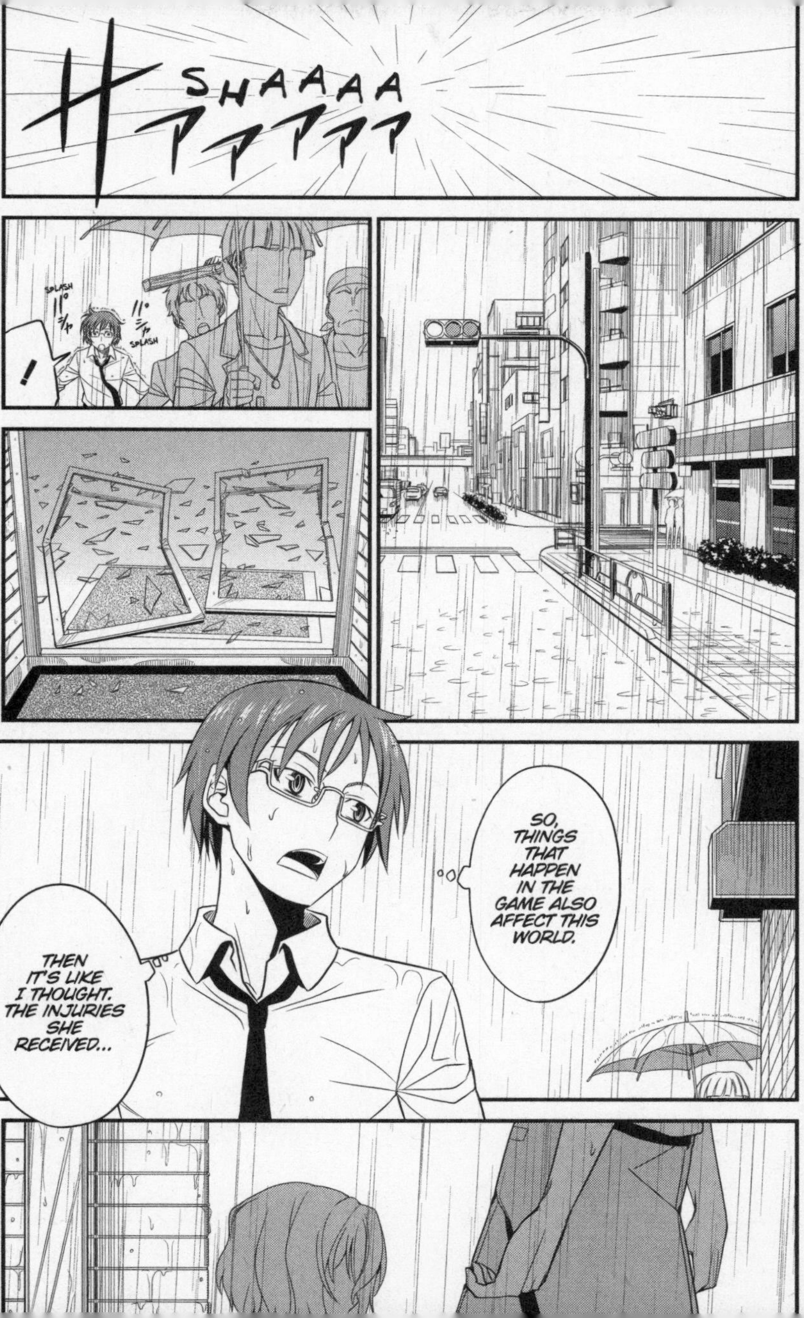
SHAAAA
SPLASH
SPLASH
!
SO, THINGS THAT HAPPEN IN THE GAME ALSO AFFECT THIS WORLD.
THEN IT'S LIKE I THOUGHT. THE INJURIES SHE RECEIVED...

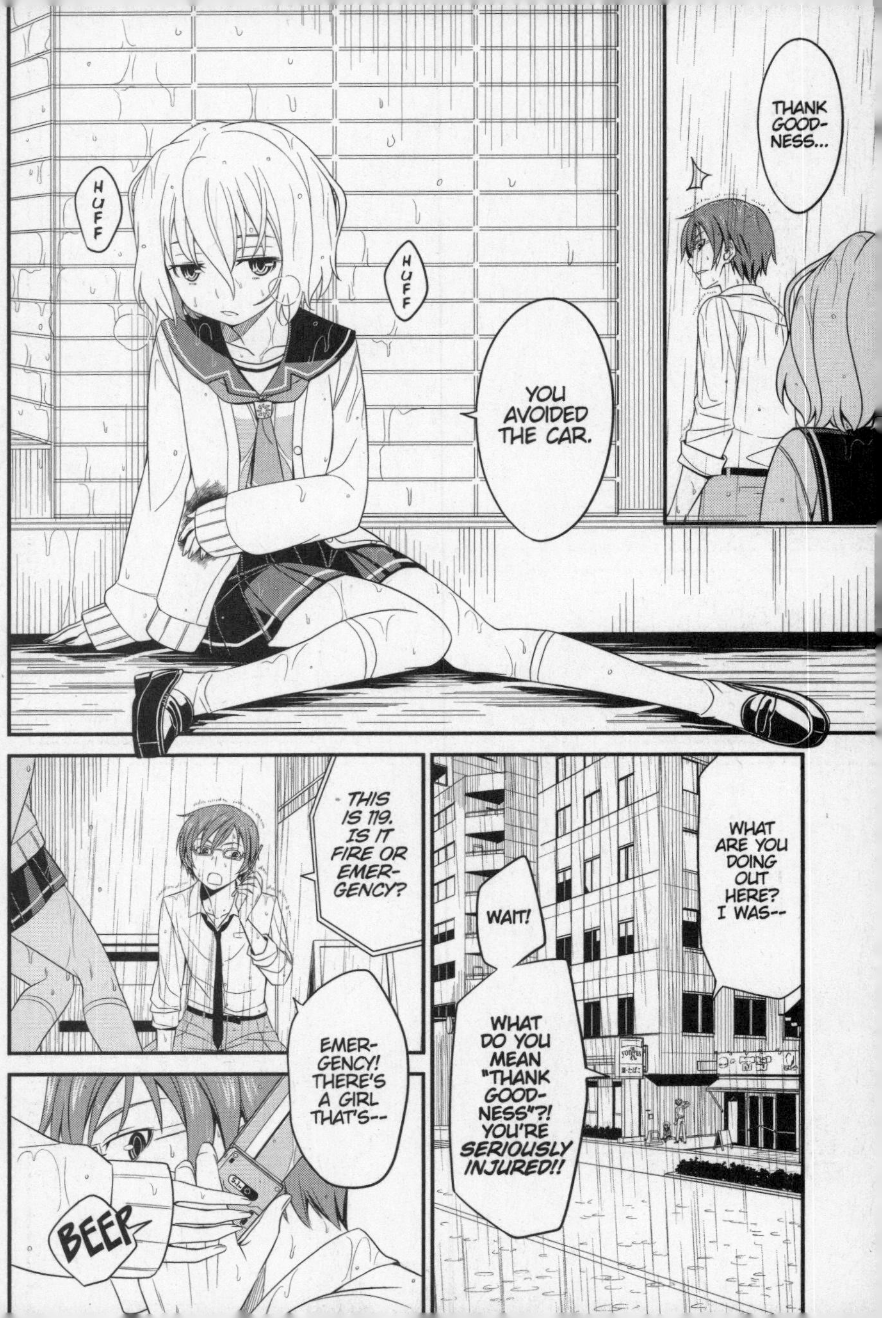
THANK GOODNESS...
YOU AVOIDED THE CAR.
HUFF
HUFF
WHAT ARE YOU DOING OUT HERE? I WAS--
WAIT!
WHAT DO YOU MEAN "THANK GOODNESS"?! YOU'RE SERIOUSLY INJURED!!
THIS IS 119. IS IT FIRE OR EMERGENCY?
EMERGENCY! THERE'S A GIRL THAT'S--
BEEP

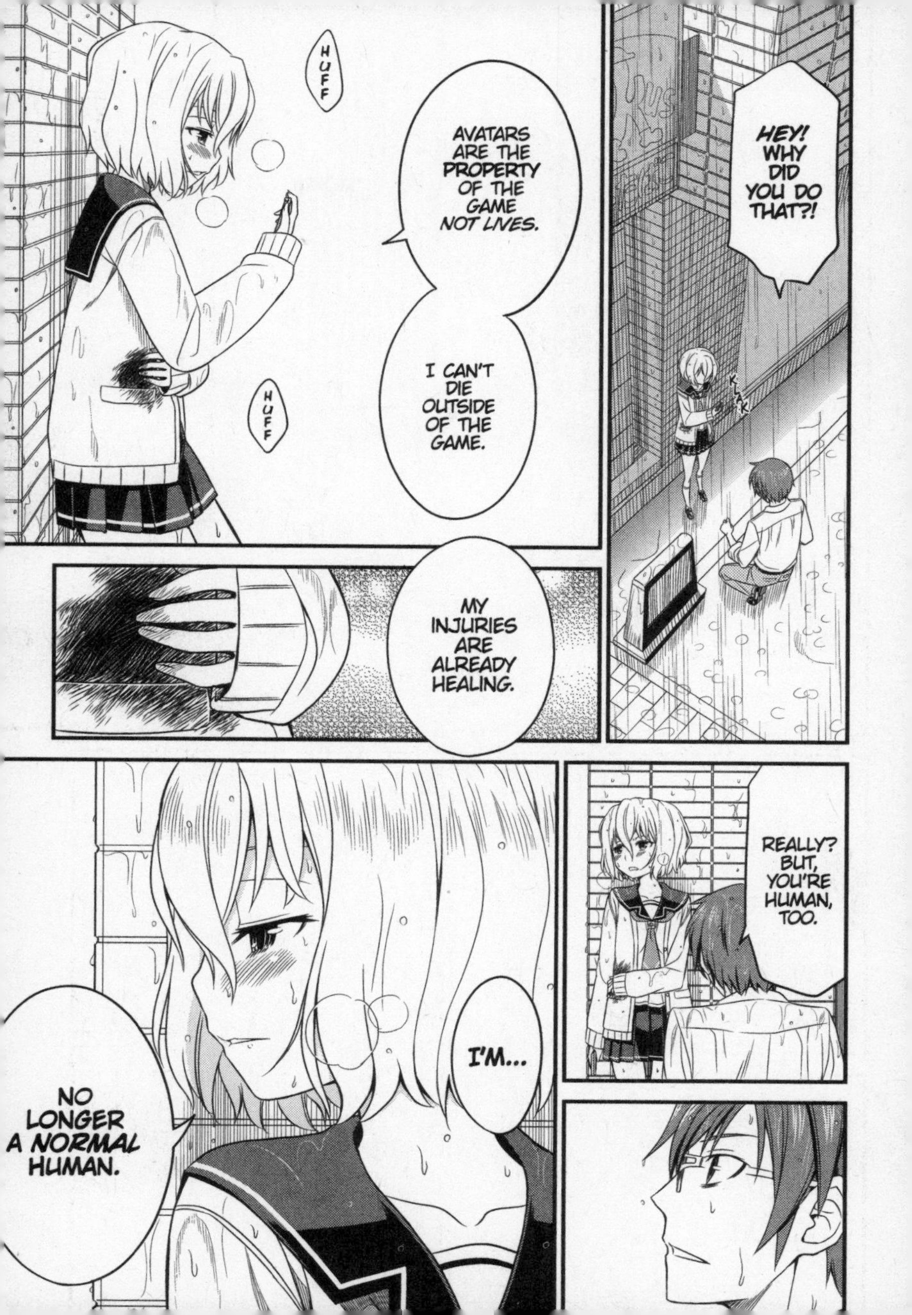
HEY! WHY DID YOU DO THAT?!
KLAK
HUFF
AVATARS ARE THE PROPERTY OF THE GAME NOT LIVES.
I CAN'T DIE OUTSIDE OF THE GAME.
HUFF
MY INJURIES ARE ALREADY HEALING.
REALLY? BUT, YOU'RE HUMAN, TOO.
I'M...
NO LONGER A NORMAL HUMAN.

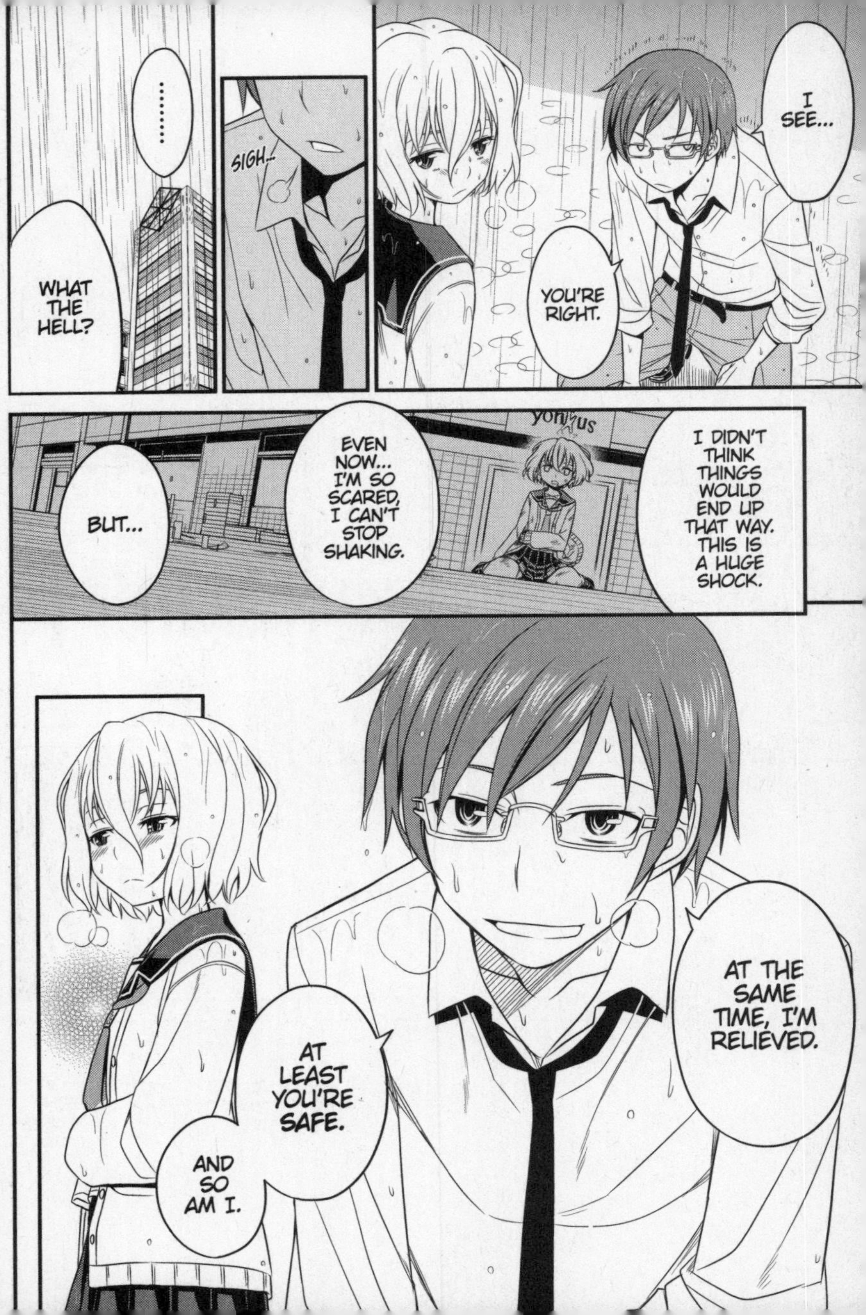
I SEE...
YOU'RE RIGHT.
SIGH...
......
WHAT THE HELL?
I DIDN'T THINK THINGS WOULD END UP THAT WAY. THIS IS A HUGE SHOCK.
EVEN NOW... I'M SO SCARED, I CAN'T STOP SHAKING.
BUT...
AT THE SAME TIME, I'M RELIEVED.
AT LEAST YOU'RE SAFE.
AND SO AM I.

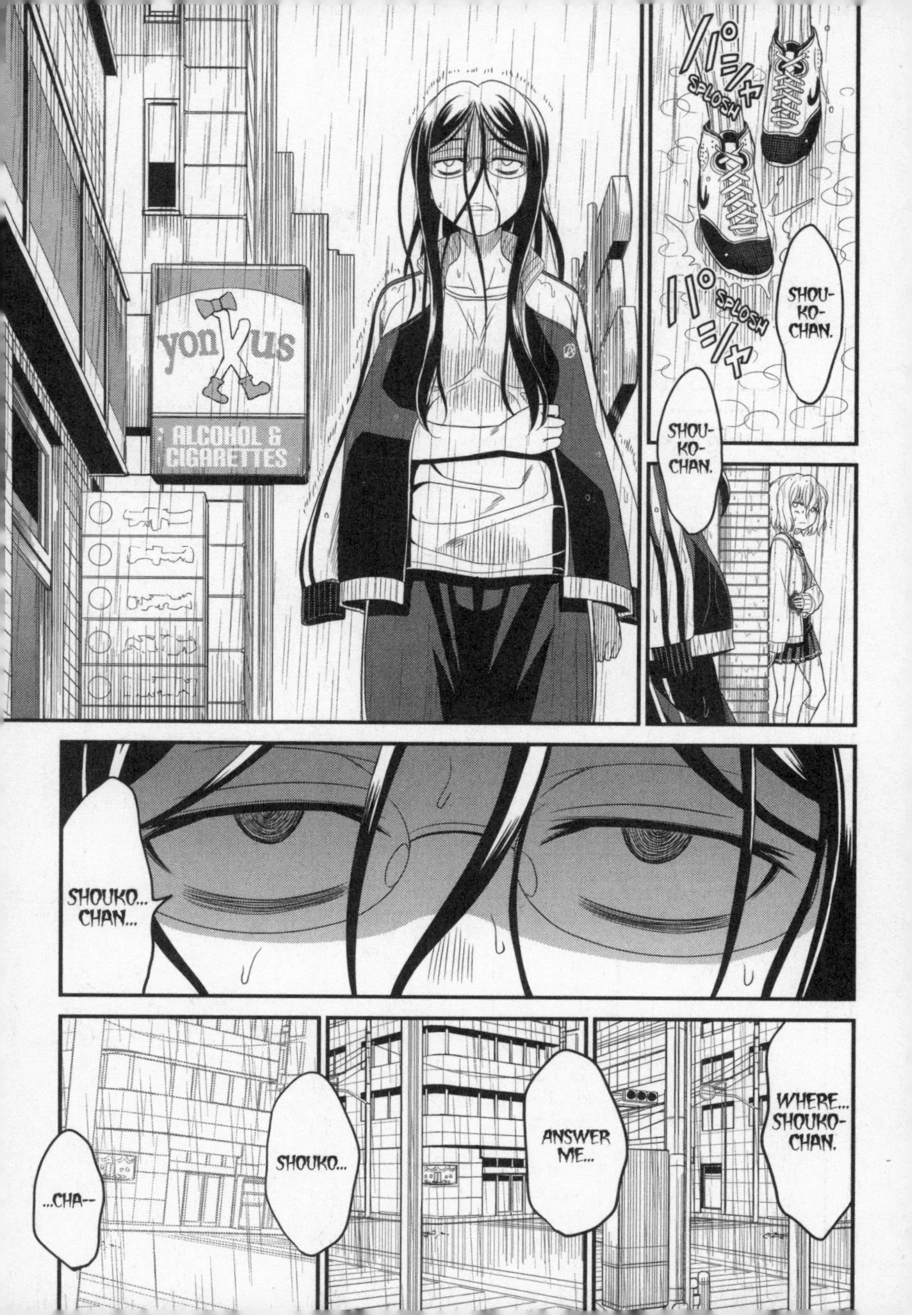
パシャ
SPLOSH
パシャ
SPLOSH
SHOU-KO-CHAN.
SHOU-KO-CHAN.
ALCOHOL & CIGARETTES
SHOUKO... CHAN...
WHERE... SHOUKO-CHAN.
ANSWER ME...
SHOUKO...
...CHA--

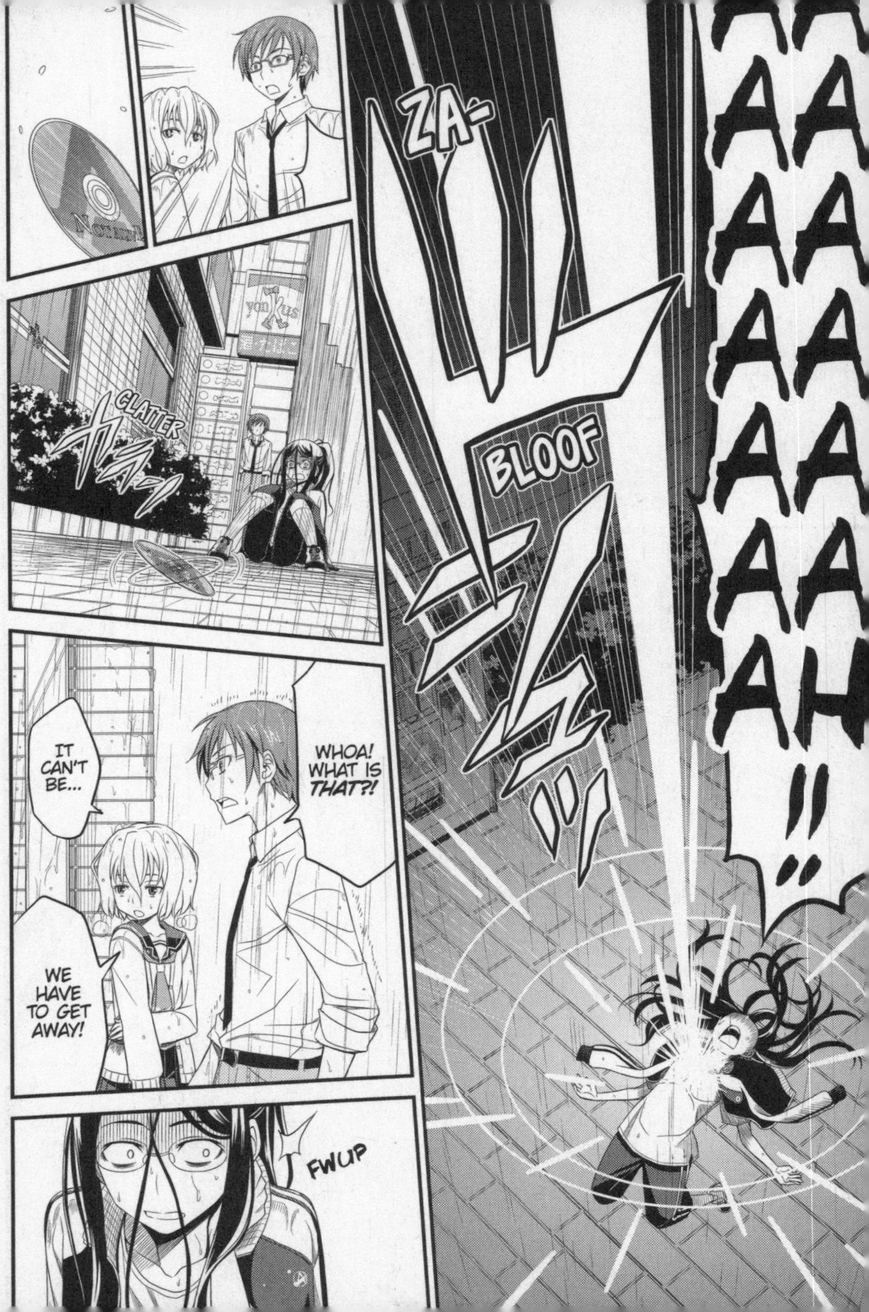
AAAAAAAAAAAAAAH!!
ZA-
BLOOF
CLATTER
WHOA! WHAT IS THAT?!
IT CAN'T BE...
WE HAVE TO GET AWAY!
FWUP

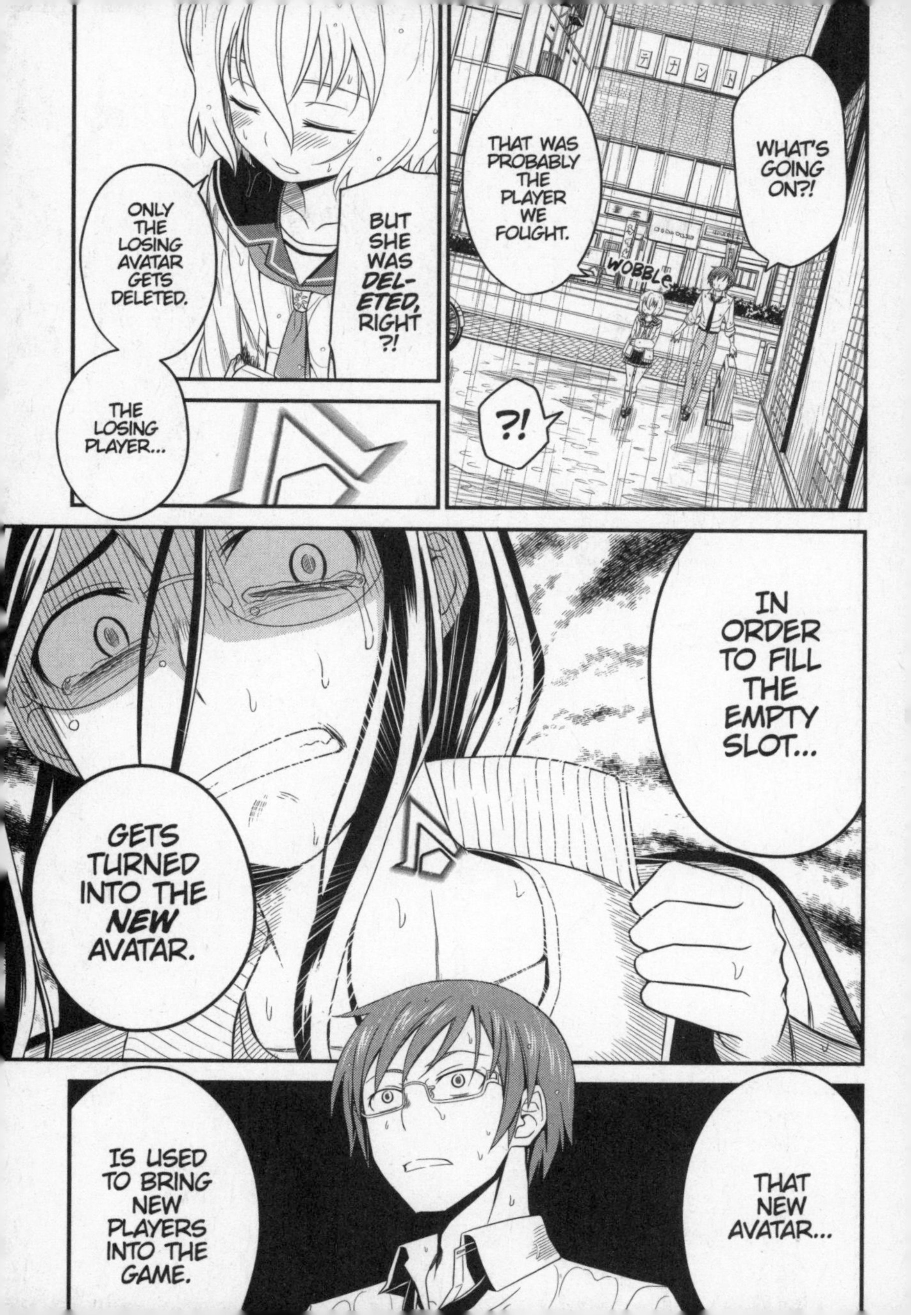
WHAT'S GOING ON?!
THAT WAS PROBABLY THE PLAYER WE FOUGHT.
WOBBLE
?!
BUT SHE WAS *DELETED*, RIGHT?!
ONLY THE LOSING AVATAR GETS DELETED.
THE LOSING PLAYER...
IN ORDER TO FILL THE EMPTY SLOT...
GETS TURNED INTO THE *NEW* AVATAR.
THAT NEW AVATAR...
IS USED TO BRING NEW PLAYERS INTO THE GAME.

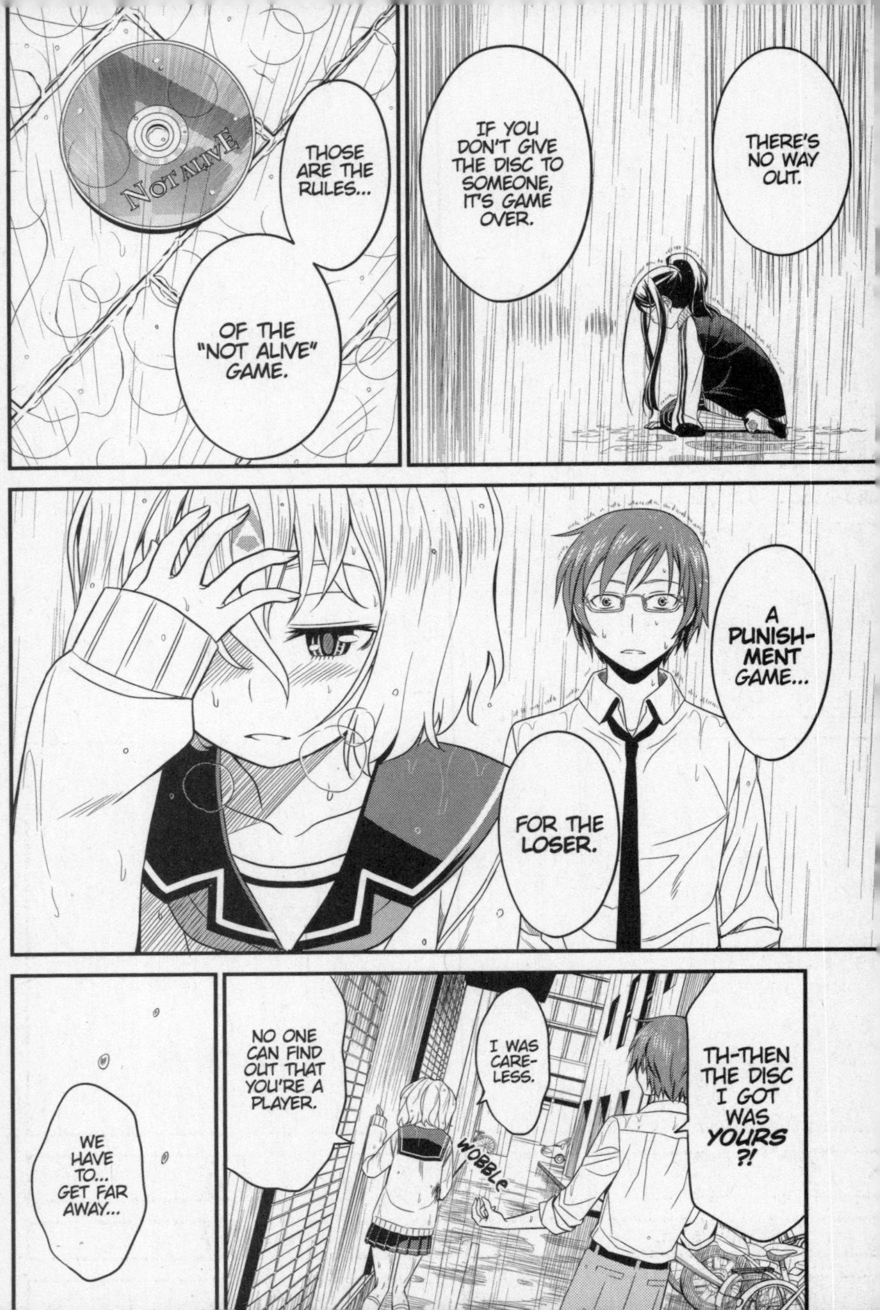
THERE'S NO WAY OUT.
IF YOU DON'T GIVE THE DISC TO SOMEONE, IT'S GAME OVER.
NOT ALIVE
THOSE ARE THE RULES...
OF THE "NOT ALIVE" GAME.
A PUNISHMENT GAME...
FOR THE LOSER.
TH-THEN THE DISC I GOT WAS YOURS?!
I WAS CARELESS.
NO ONE CAN FIND OUT THAT YOU'RE A PLAYER.
WOBBLE
WE HAVE TO... GET FAR AWAY...

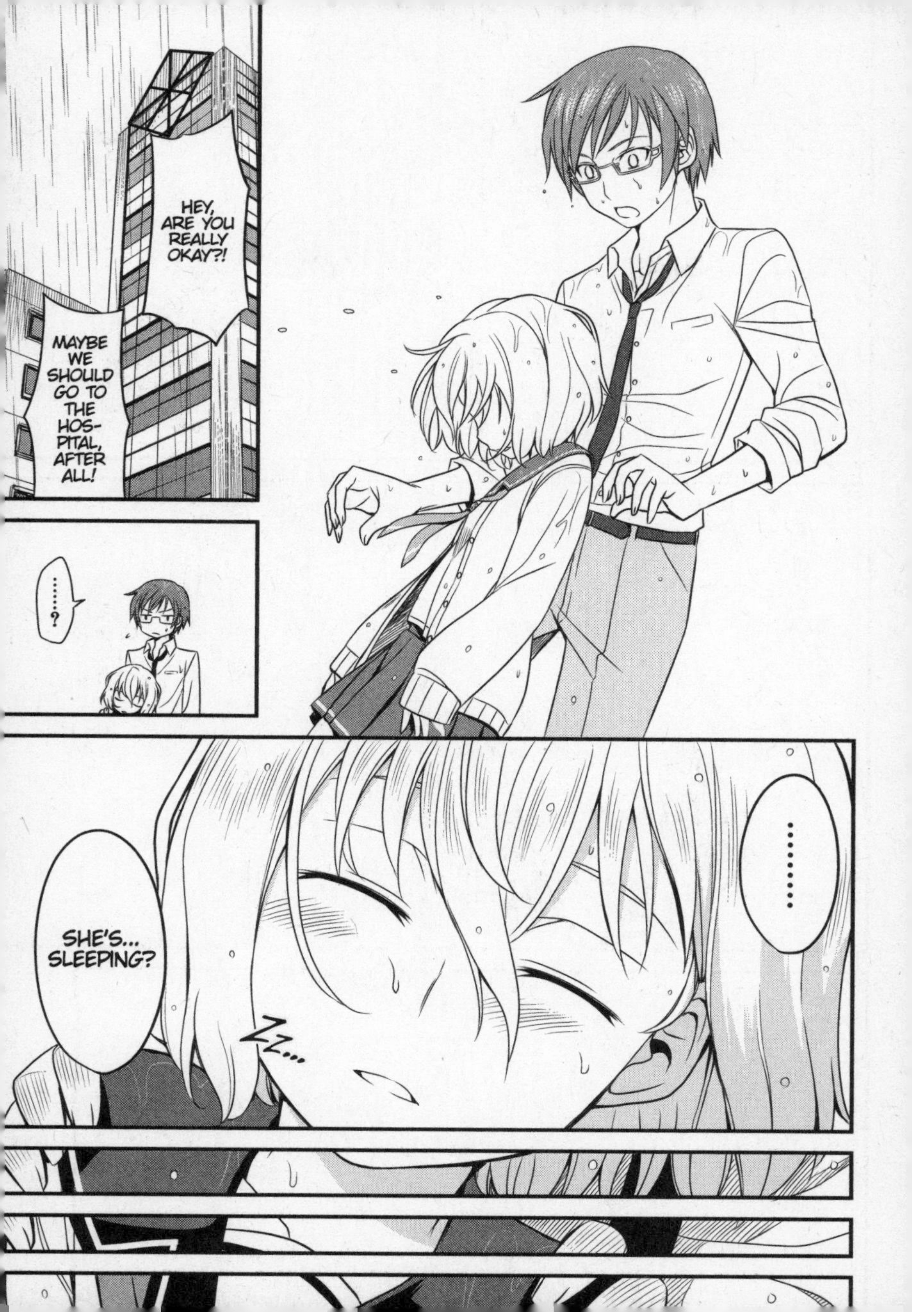
HEY, ARE YOU REALLY OKAY?!
MAYBE WE SHOULD GO TO THE HOS-PITAL, AFTER ALL!
......?
....
SHE'S... SLEEPING?
ZZ...

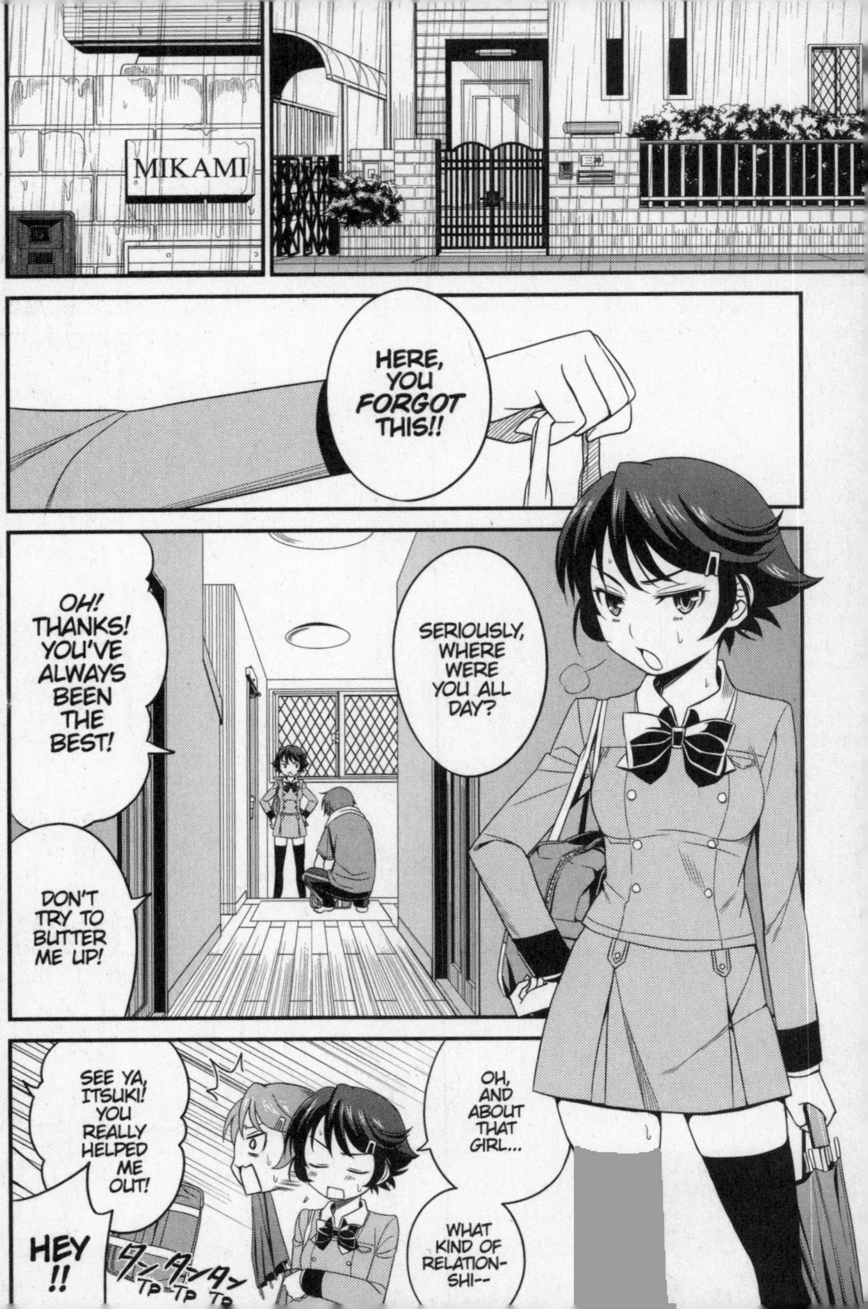
MIKAMI
HERE, YOU FORGOT THIS!!
SERIOUSLY, WHERE WERE YOU ALL DAY?
OH! THANKS! YOU'VE ALWAYS BEEN THE BEST!
DON'T TRY TO BUTTER ME UP!
OH, AND ABOUT THAT GIRL...
WHAT KIND OF RELATION-SHI--
SEE YA, ITSUKI! YOU REALLY HELPED ME OUT!
HEY!!
タンタンタン
TP-TP TP

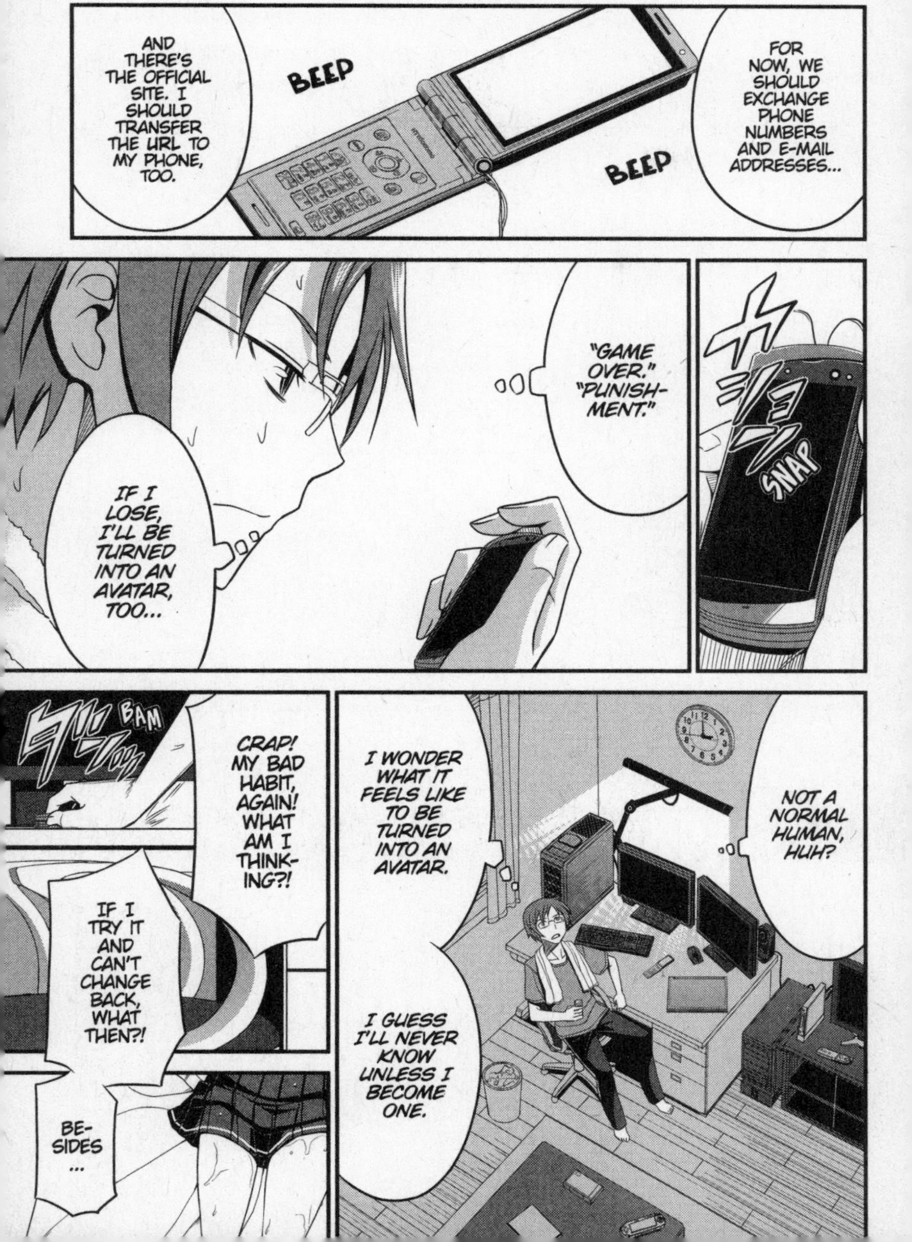
FOR NOW, WE SHOULD EXCHANGE PHONE NUMBERS AND E-MAIL ADDRESSES...
BEEP
BEEP
AND THERE'S THE OFFICIAL SITE. I SHOULD TRANSFER THE URL TO MY PHONE, TOO.
SNAP
"GAME OVER." "PUNISHMENT."
IF I LOSE, I'LL BE TURNED INTO AN AVATAR, TOO...
NOT A NORMAL HUMAN, HUH?
I WONDER WHAT IT FEELS LIKE TO BE TURNED INTO AN AVATAR.
I GUESS I'LL NEVER KNOW UNLESS I BECOME ONE.
BAM
CRAP! MY BAD HABIT, AGAIN! WHAT AM I THINKING?!
IF I TRY IT AND CAN'T CHANGE BACK, WHAT THEN?!
BE-SIDES ...

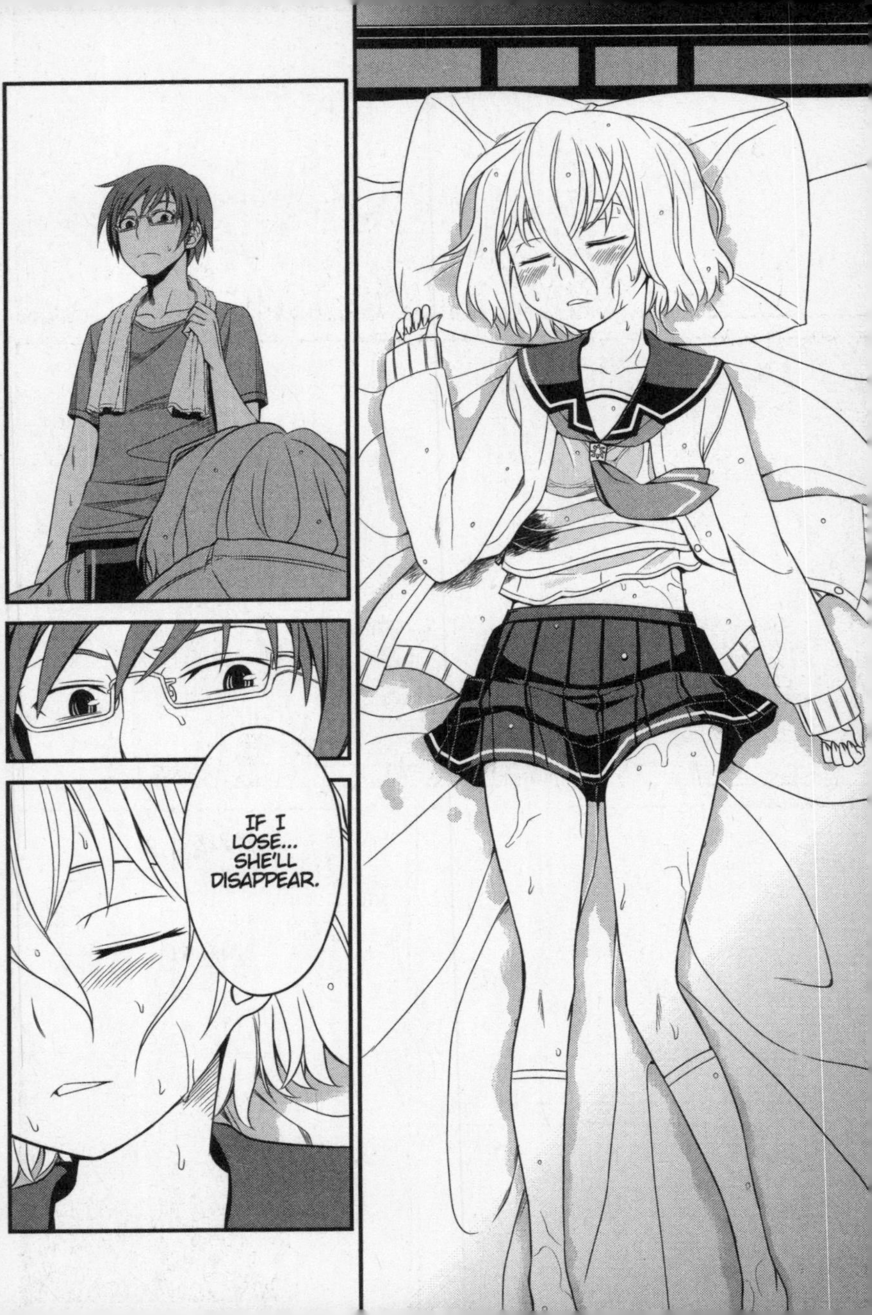
IF I LOSE... SHE'LL DISAPPEAR.

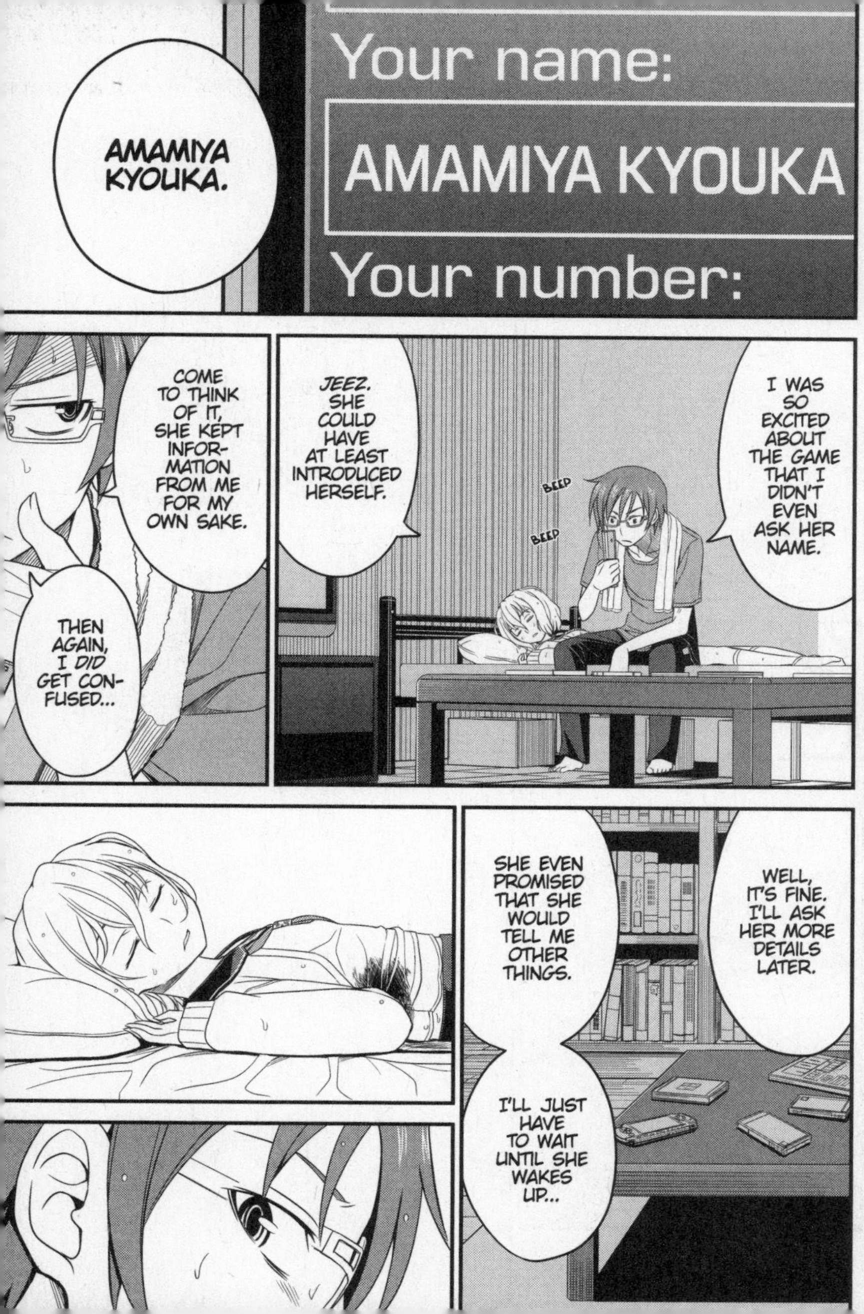

Your name:
AMAMIYA KYOUKA
Your number:
AMAMIYA KYOUKA.
I WAS SO EXCITED ABOUT THE GAME THAT I DIDN'T EVEN ASK HER NAME.
BEEP
BEEP
JEEZ. SHE COULD HAVE AT LEAST INTRODUCED HERSELF.
COME TO THINK OF IT, SHE KEPT INFORMATION FROM ME FOR MY OWN SAKE.
THEN AGAIN, I DID GET CONFUSED...
WELL, IT'S FINE. I'LL ASK HER MORE DETAILS LATER.
SHE EVEN PROMISED THAT SHE WOULD TELL ME OTHER THINGS.
I'LL JUST HAVE TO WAIT UNTIL SHE WAKES UP...

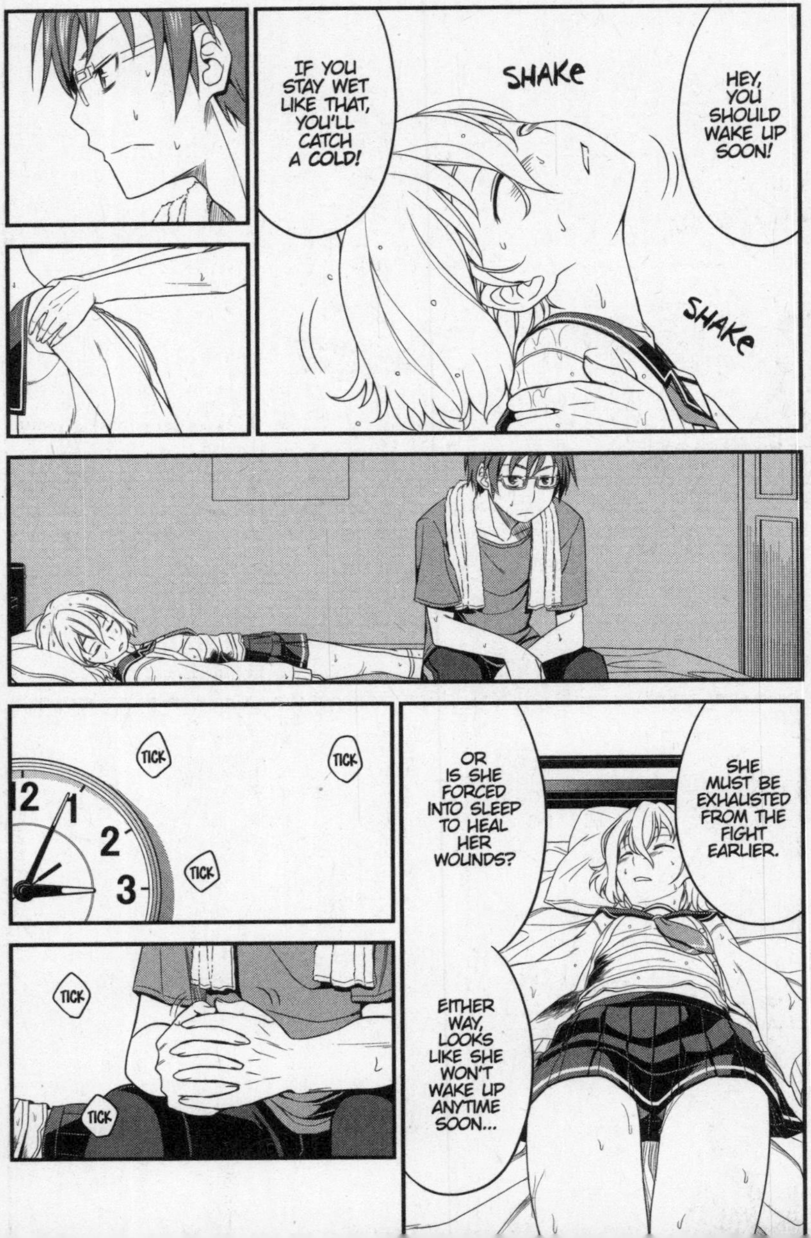
HEY, YOU SHOULD WAKE UP SOON!
SHAKE
IF YOU STAY WET LIKE THAT, YOU'LL CATCH A COLD!
SHAKE
SHE MUST BE EXHAUSTED FROM THE FIGHT EARLIER.
OR IS SHE FORCED INTO SLEEP TO HEAL HER WOUNDS?
EITHER WAY, LOOKS LIKE SHE WON'T WAKE UP ANYTIME SOON...
TICK
TICK
12 1 2 3
TICK
TICK
TICK

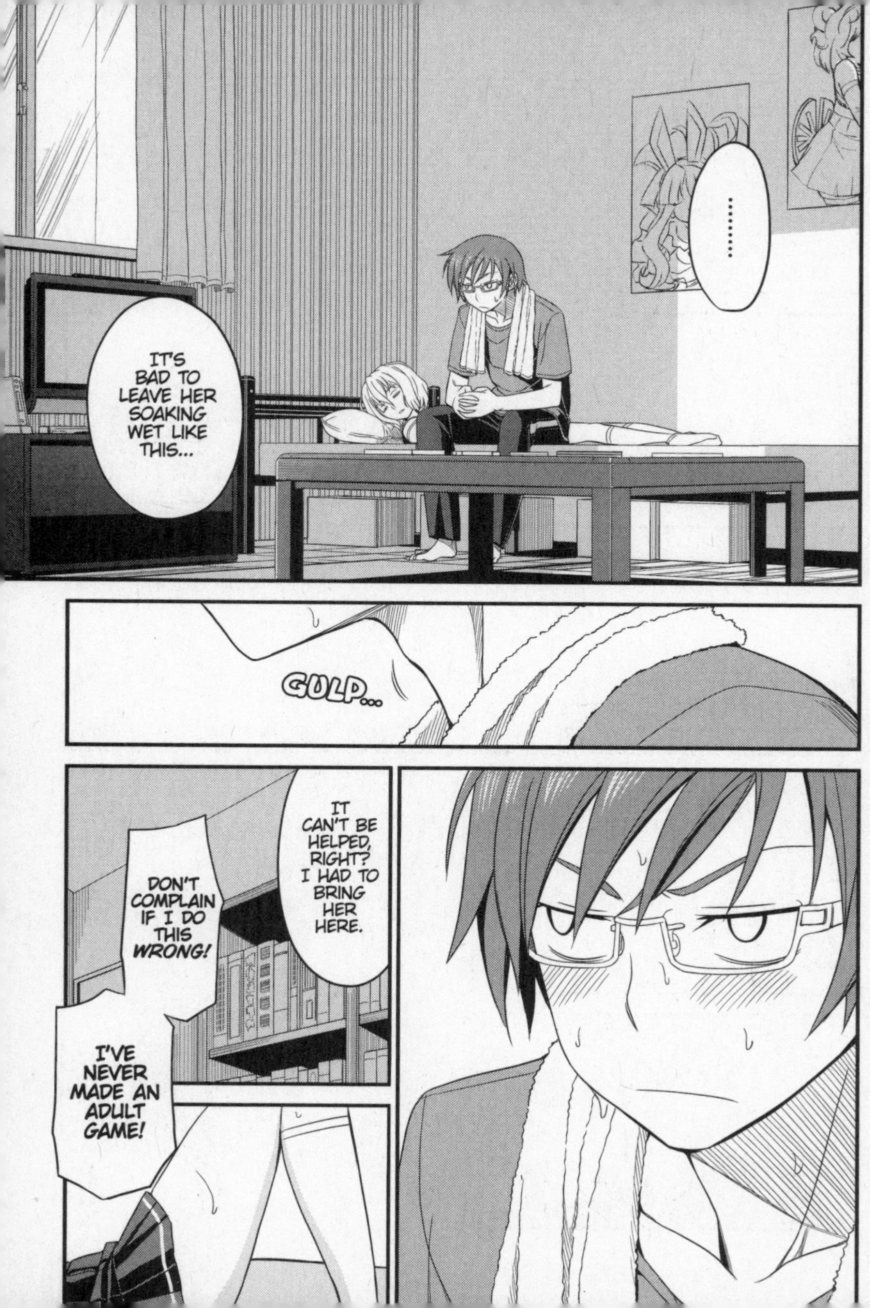
......
IT'S BAD TO LEAVE HER SOAKING WET LIKE THIS...
GULP...
IT CAN'T BE HELPED, RIGHT? I HAD TO BRING HER HERE.
DON'T COMPLAIN IF I DO THIS *WRONG!*
I'VE NEVER MADE AN ADULT GAME!

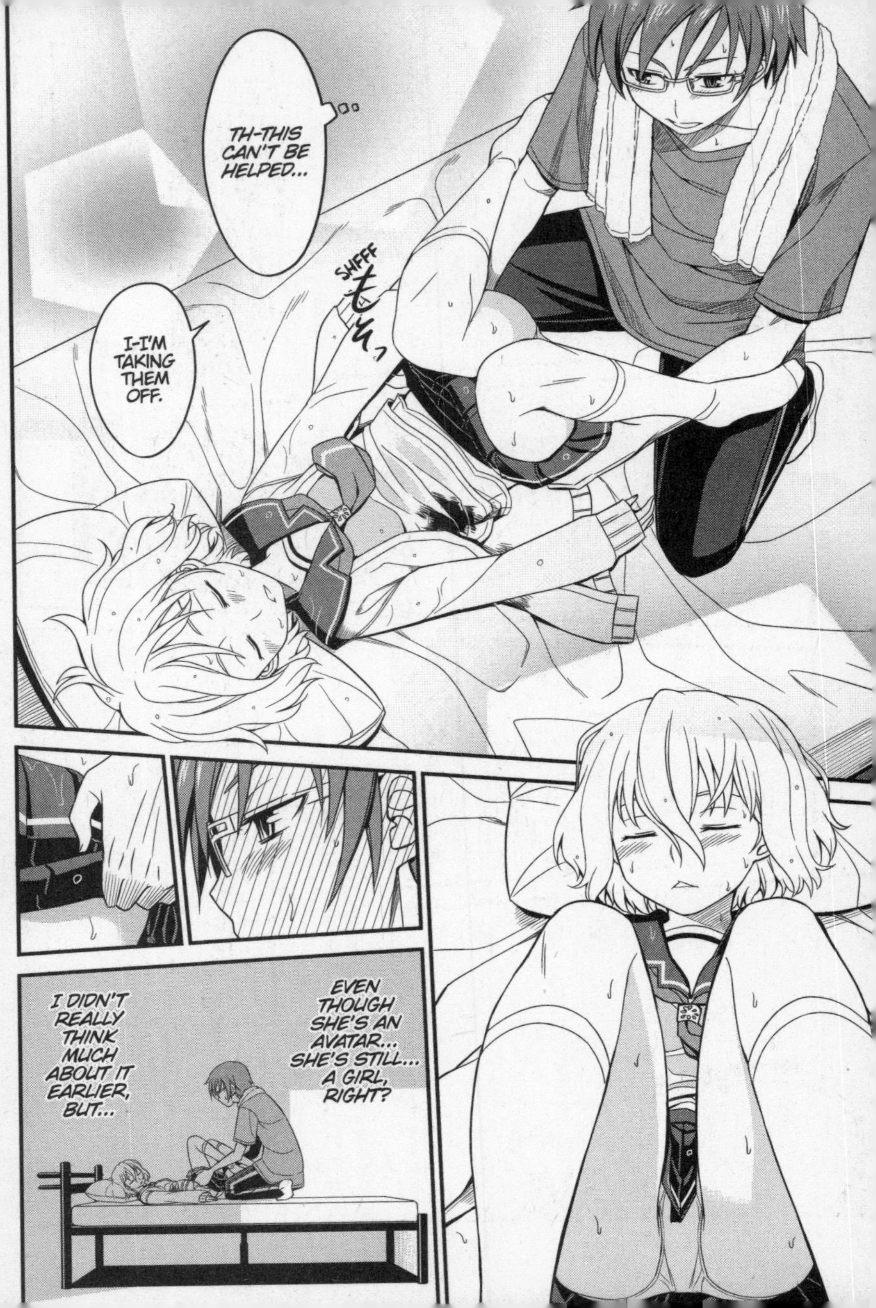
TH-THIS CAN'T BE HELPED...
SHFFF
I-I'M TAKING THEM OFF.
EVEN THOUGH SHE'S AN AVATAR... SHE'S STILL... A GIRL, RIGHT?
I DIDN'T REALLY THINK MUCH ABOUT IT EARLIER, BUT...

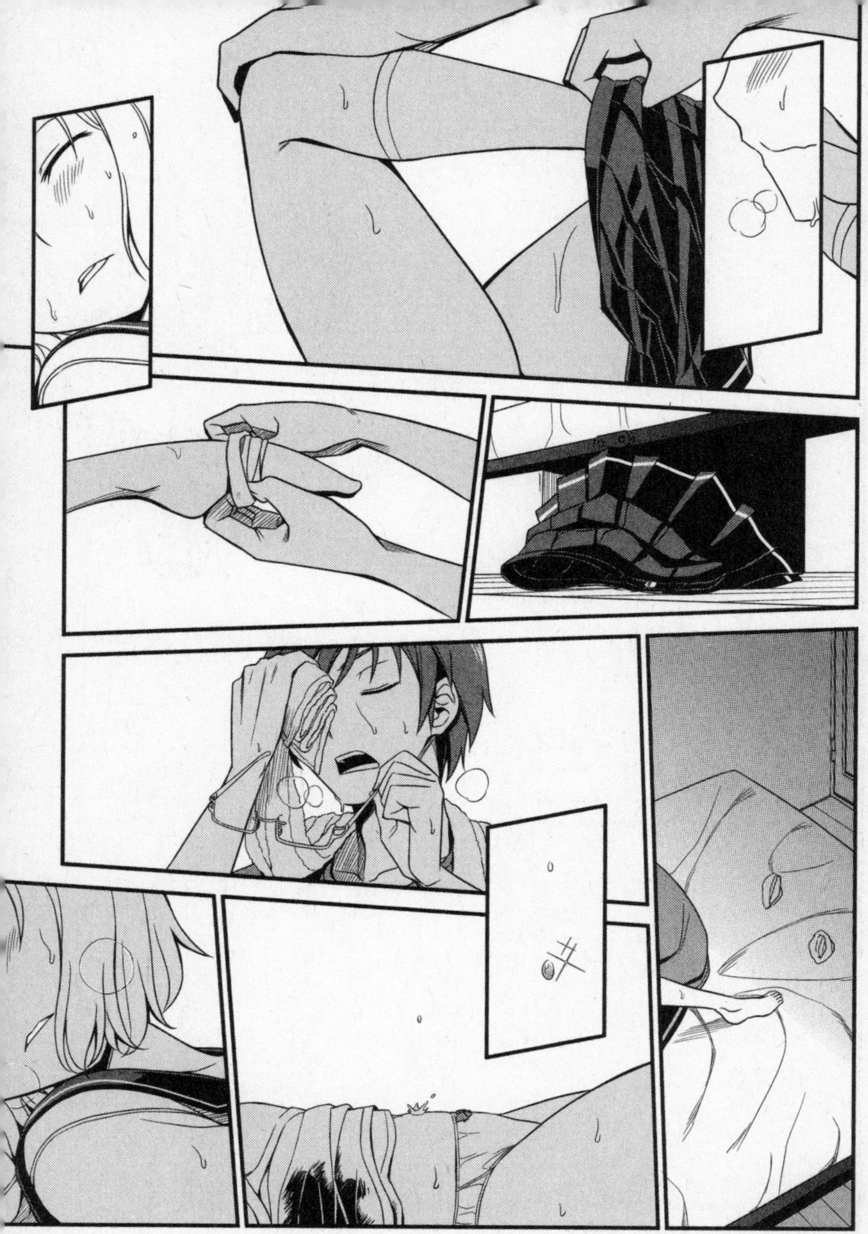

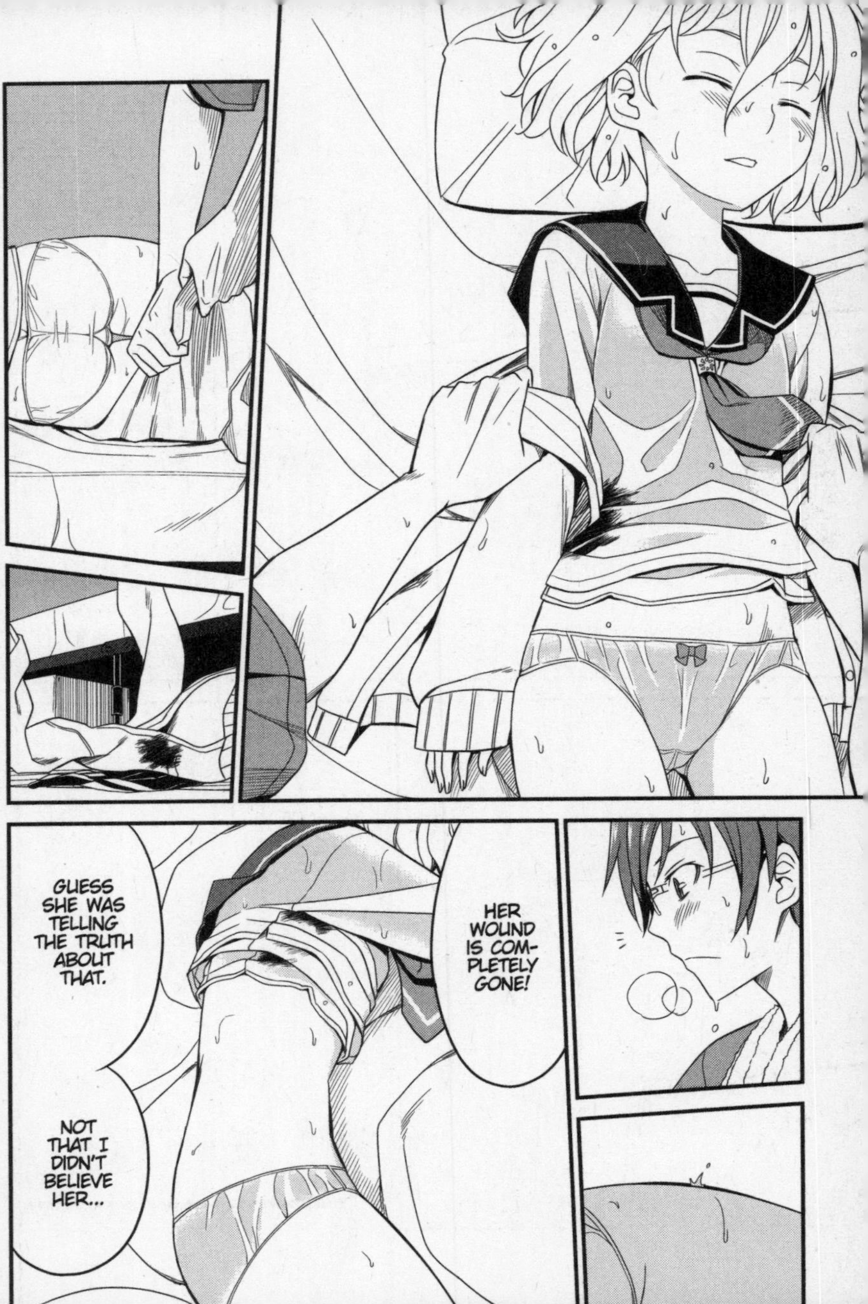
HER WOUND IS COM-PLETELY GONE!
GUESS SHE WAS TELLING THE TRUTH ABOUT THAT.
NOT THAT I DIDN'T BELIEVE HER...

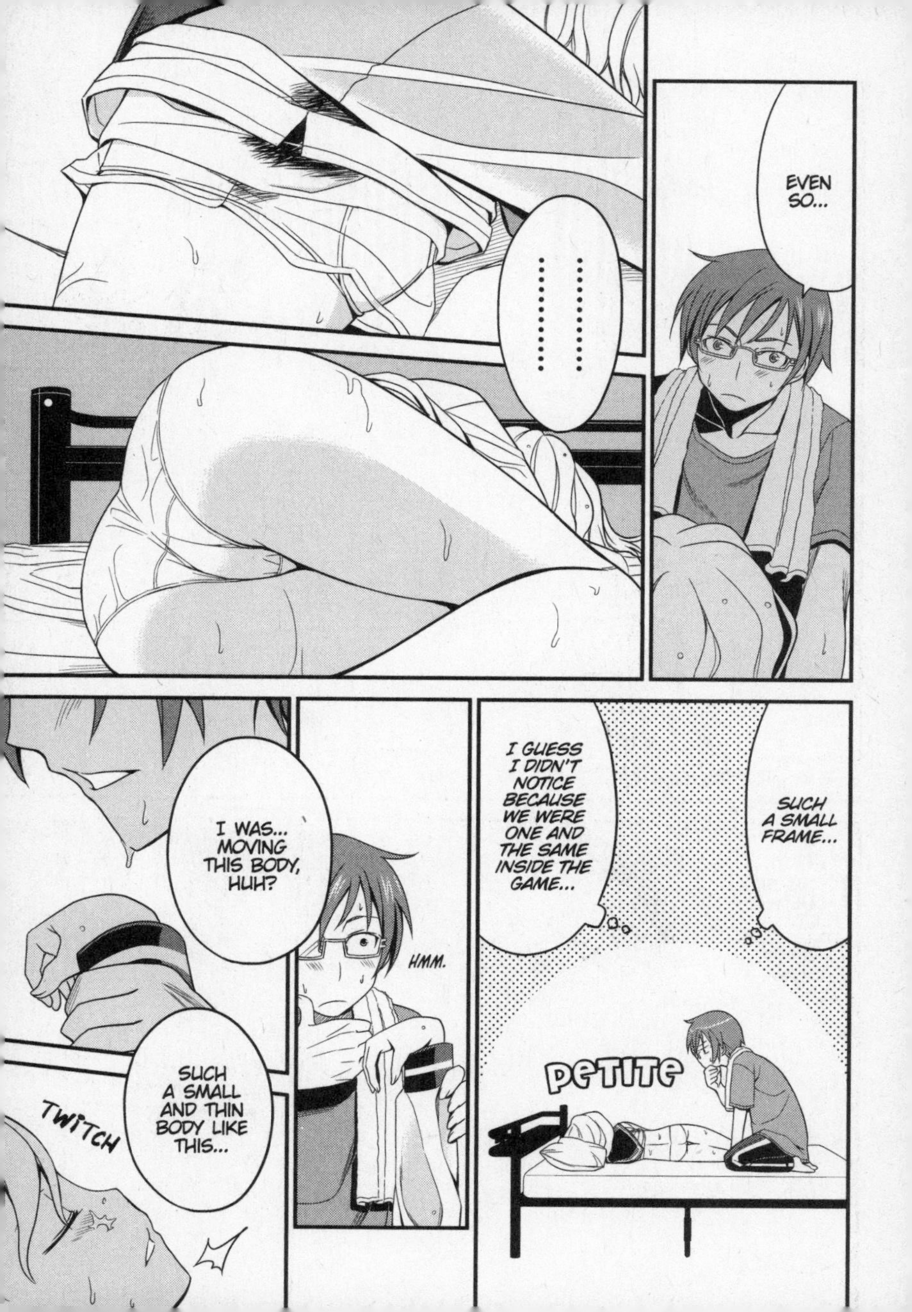
EVEN SO...
......
SUCH A SMALL FRAME...
I GUESS I DIDN'T NOTICE BECAUSE WE WERE ONE AND THE SAME INSIDE THE GAME...
PETITE
I WAS... MOVING THIS BODY, HUH?
HMM.
SUCH A SMALL AND THIN BODY LIKE THIS...
TWITCH

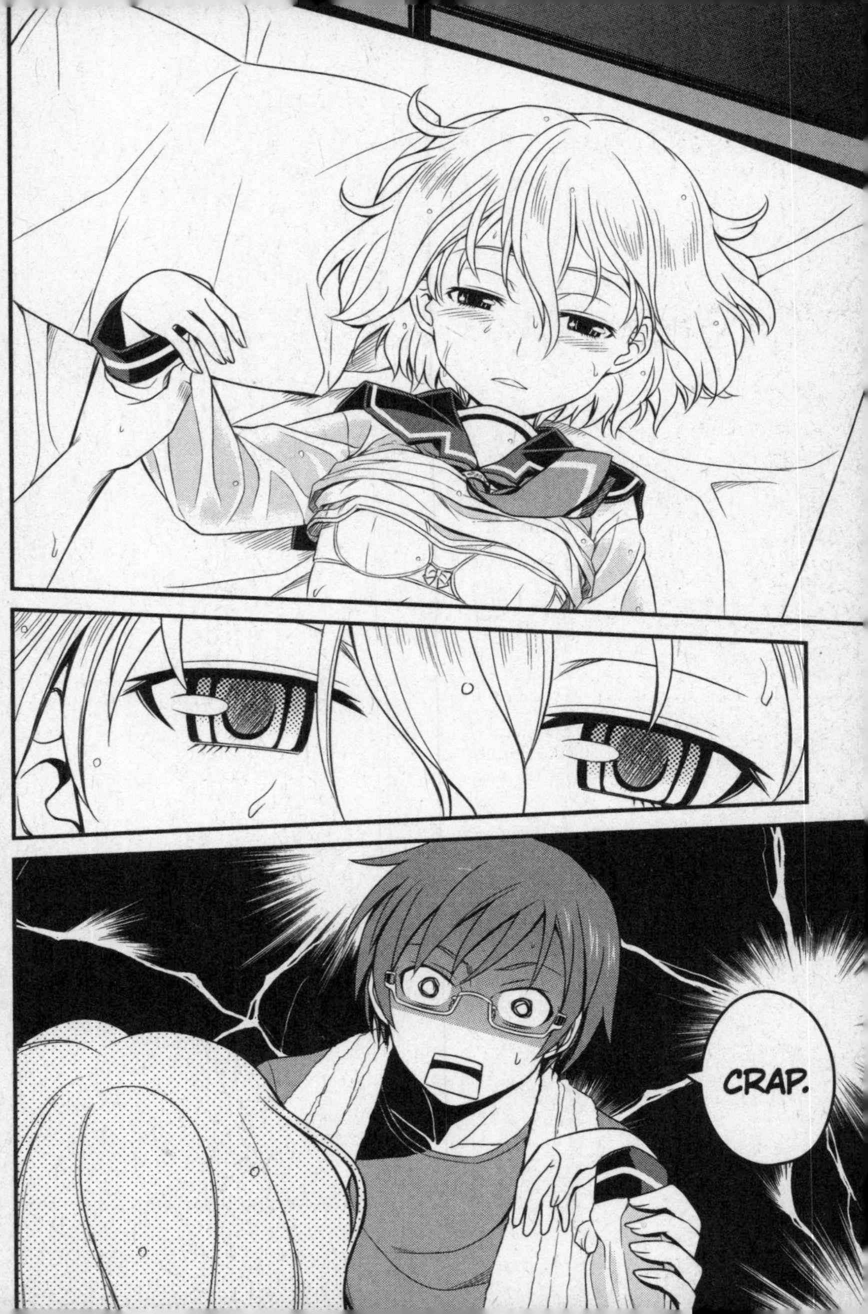
CRAP.

NOT LIVES

ノットライヴス

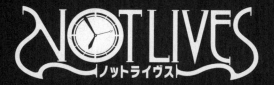

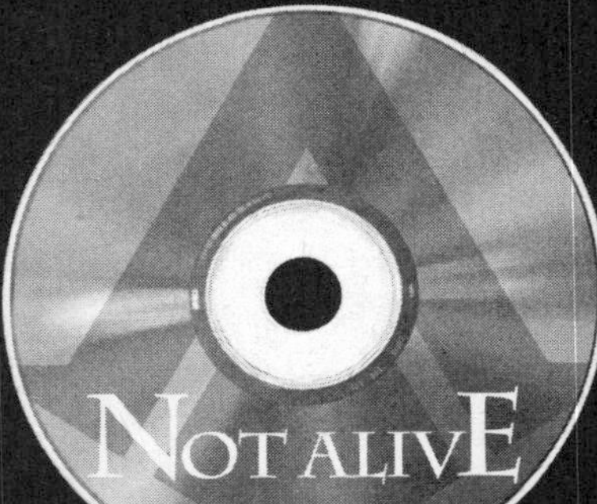
NOT ALIVE

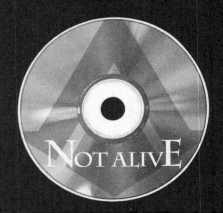

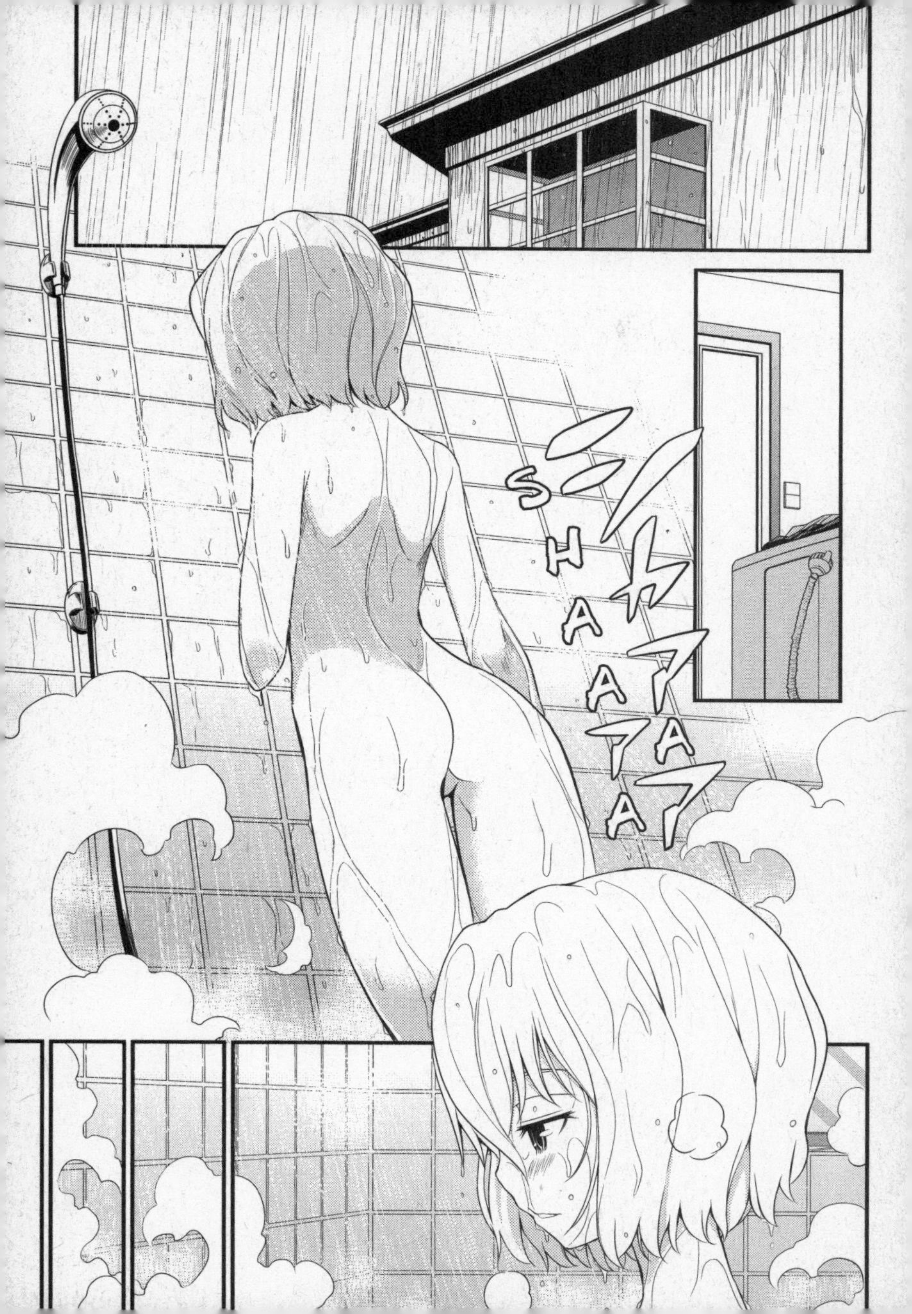
SHAAAAA

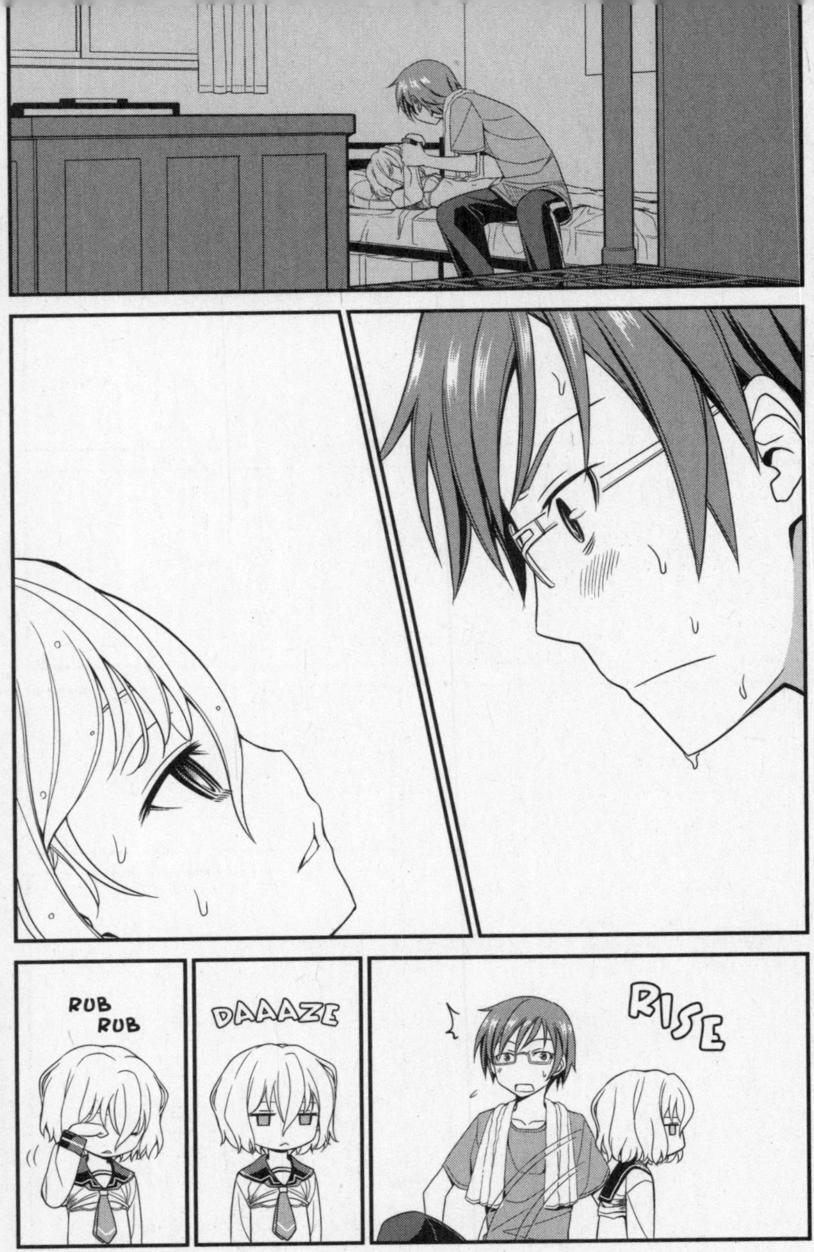
RISE
DAAAZE
RUB RUB

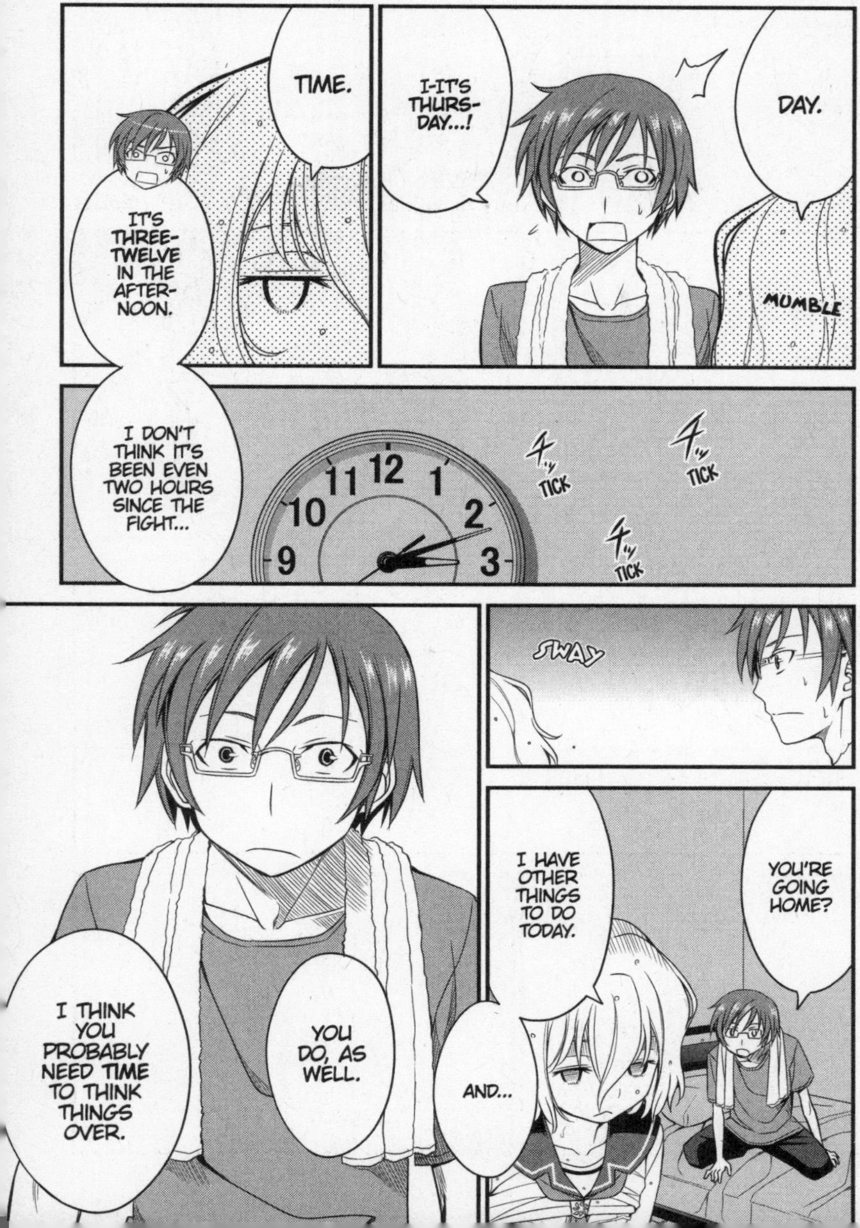
DAY.
I-IT'S THURS-DAY...!
MUMBLE
TIME.
IT'S THREE-TWELVE IN THE AFTER-NOON.
TICK
TICK
TICK
I DON'T THINK IT'S BEEN EVEN TWO HOURS SINCE THE FIGHT...
SWAY
YOU'RE GOING HOME?
I HAVE OTHER THINGS TO DO TODAY.
AND...
YOU DO, AS WELL.
I THINK YOU PROBABLY NEED TIME TO THINK THINGS OVER.

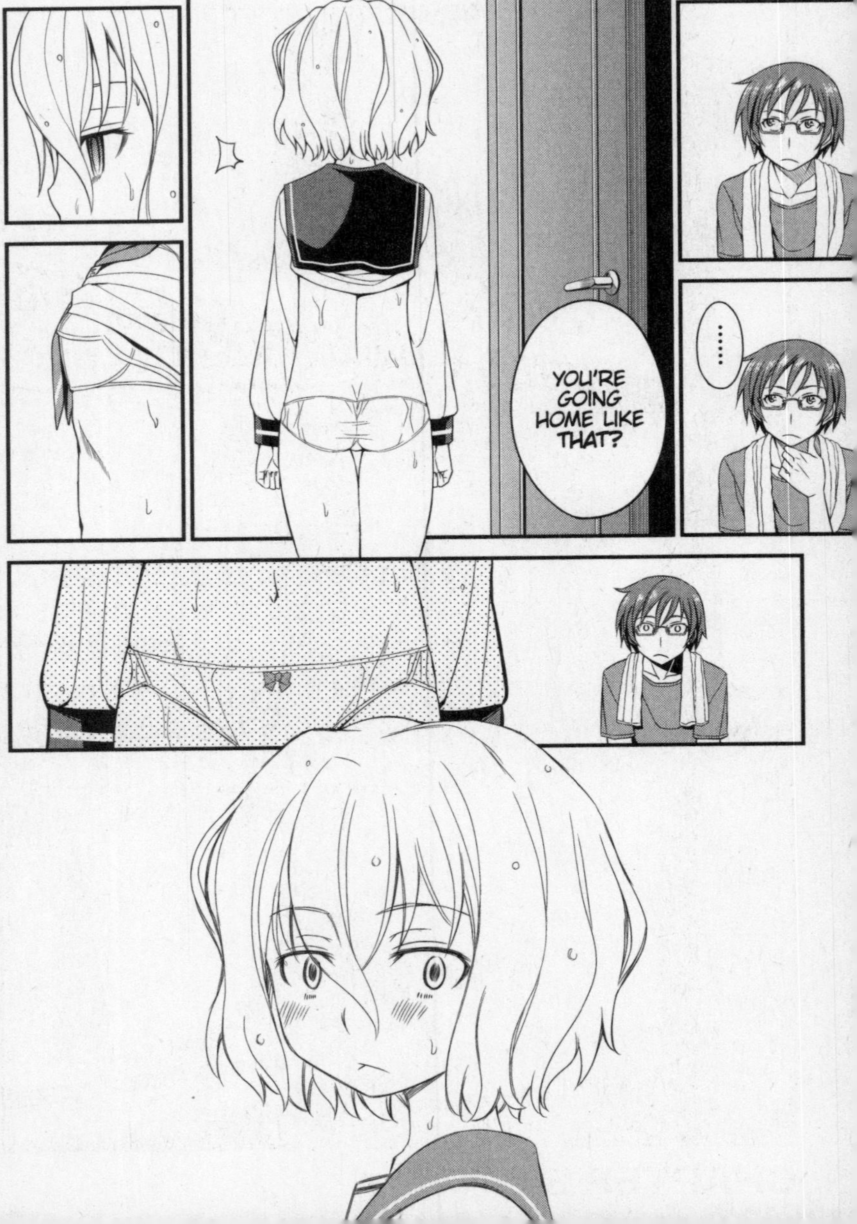
......
YOU'RE GOING HOME LIKE THAT?

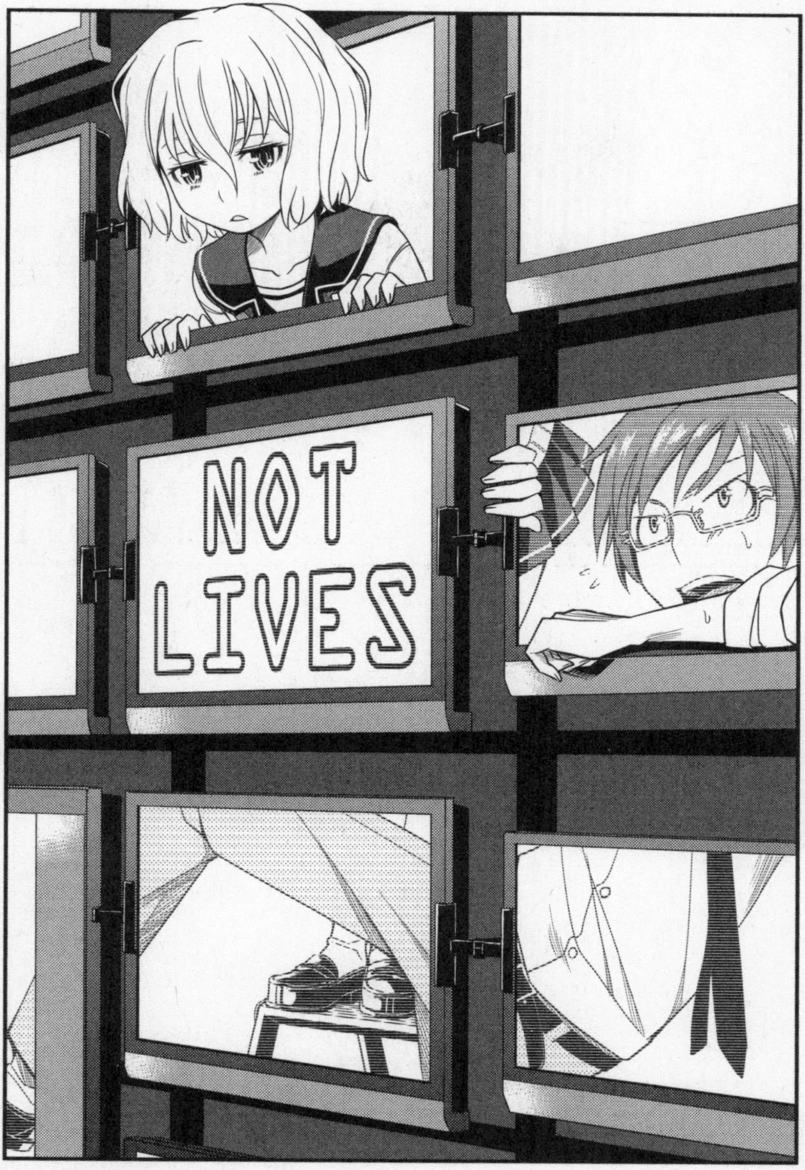
NOT LIVES

CHAPTER 5

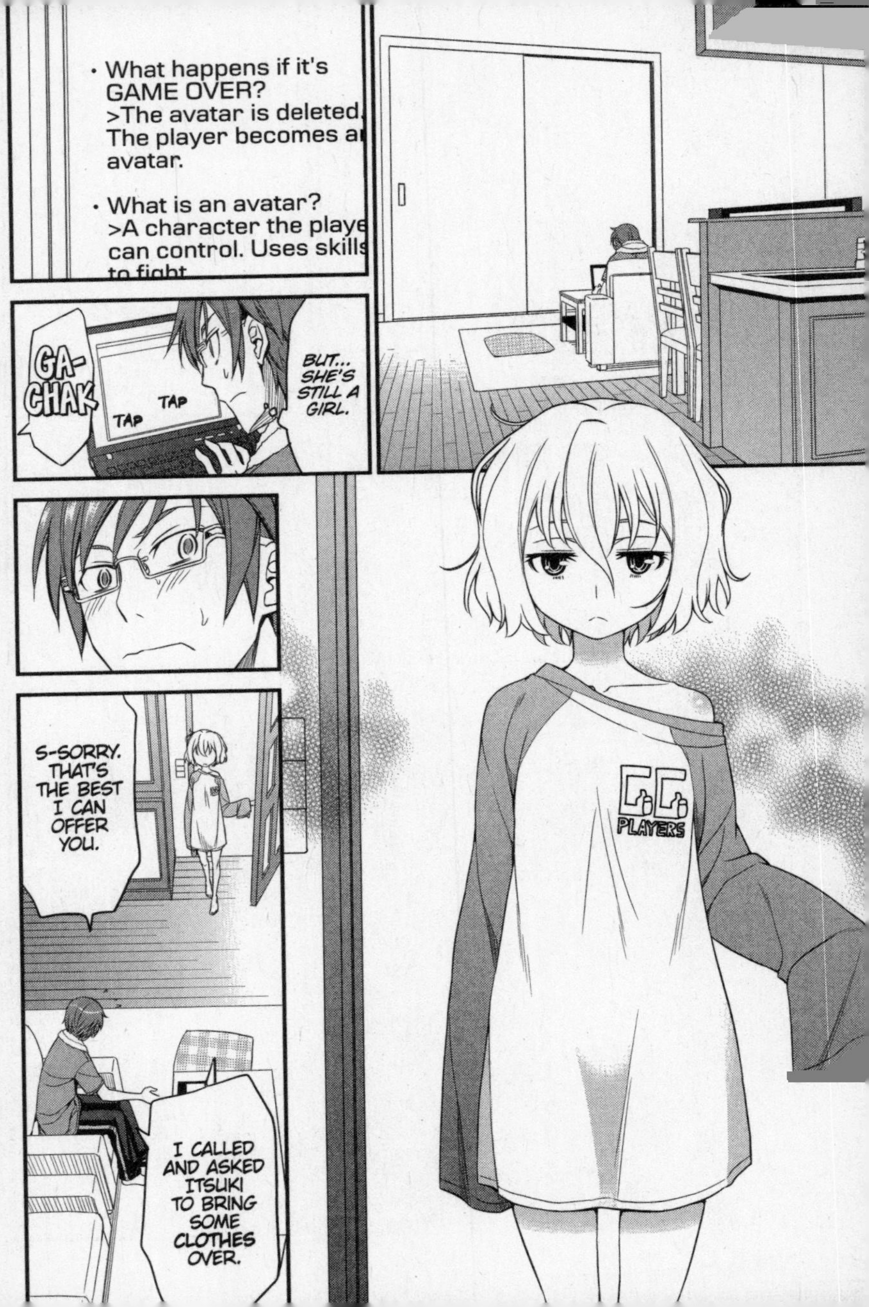
• What happens if it's GAME OVER?
>The avatar is deleted. The player becomes an avatar.
• What is an avatar?
>A character the playe can control. Uses skills to fight
BUT... SHE'S STILL A GIRL.
GA-CHAK
TAP
TAP
S-SORRY. THAT'S THE BEST I CAN OFFER YOU.
I CALLED AND ASKED ITSUKI TO BRING SOME CLOTHES OVER.
PLAYERS

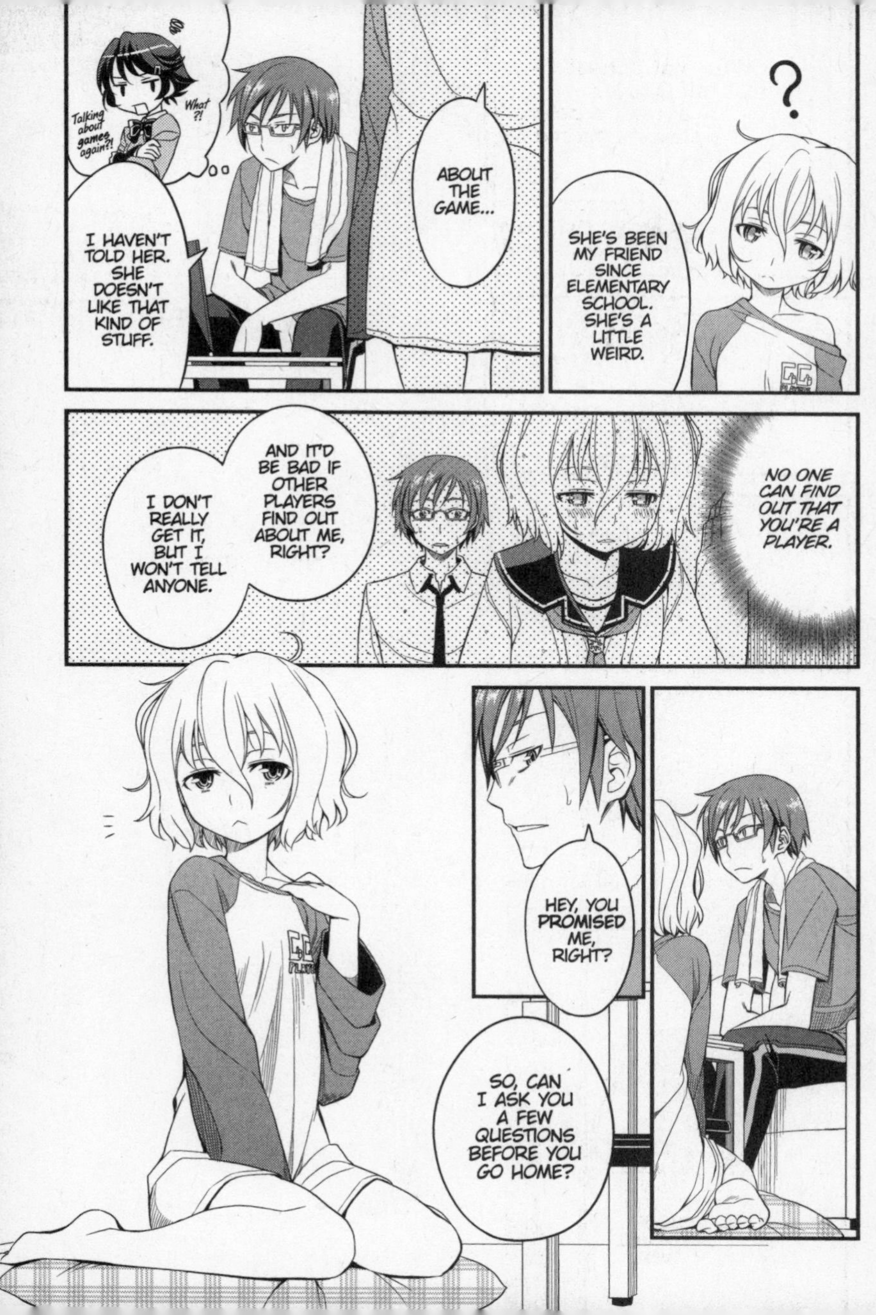
?
SHE'S BEEN MY FRIEND SINCE ELEMENTARY SCHOOL. SHE'S A LITTLE WEIRD.
ABOUT THE GAME...
What ?!
Talking about games again?!
I HAVEN'T TOLD HER. SHE DOESN'T LIKE THAT KIND OF STUFF.
NO ONE CAN FIND OUT THAT YOU'RE A PLAYER.
AND IT'D BE BAD IF OTHER PLAYERS FIND OUT ABOUT ME, RIGHT?
I DON'T REALLY GET IT, BUT I WON'T TELL ANYONE.
HEY, YOU PROMISED ME, RIGHT?
SO, CAN I ASK YOU A FEW QUESTIONS BEFORE YOU GO HOME?

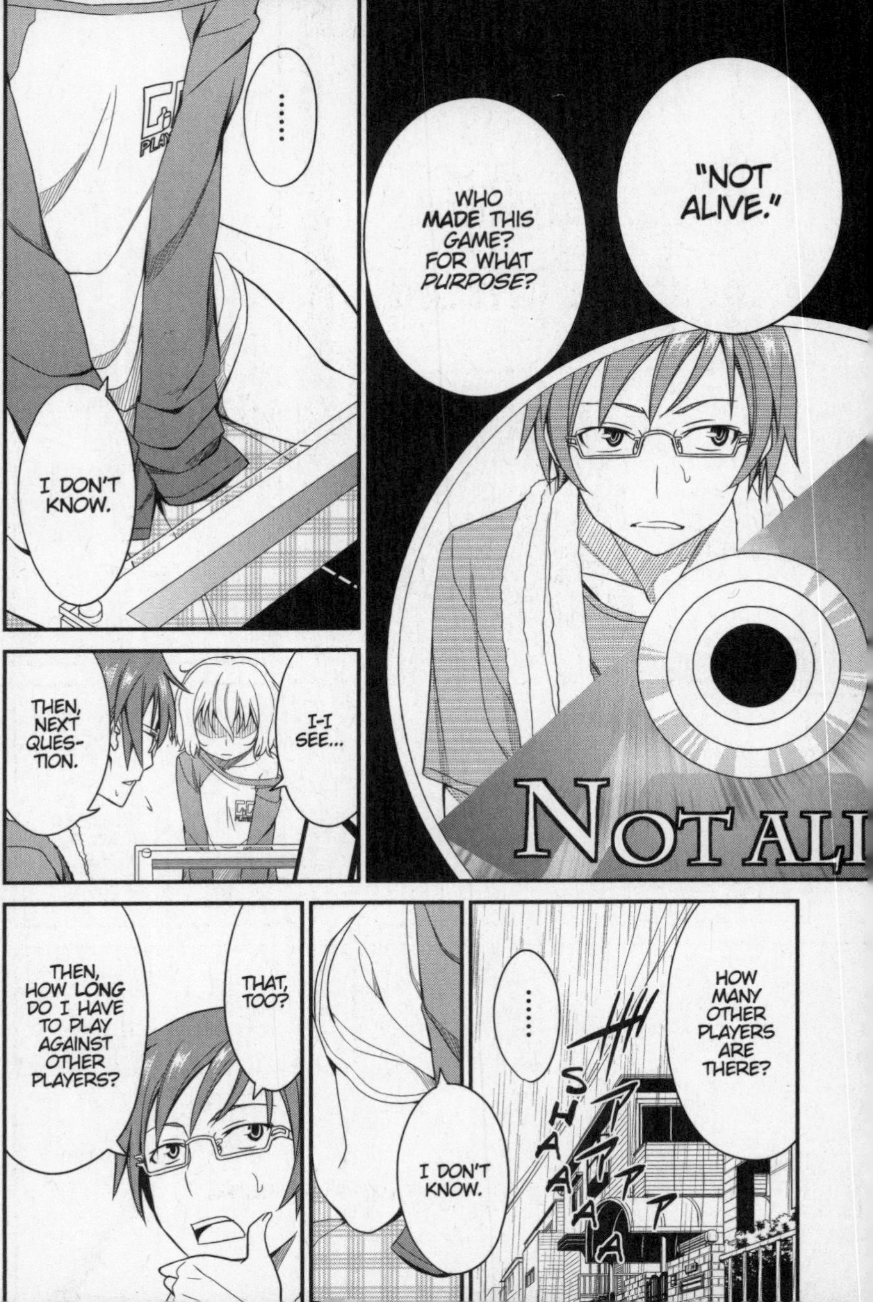
"NOT ALIVE."
WHO MADE THIS GAME? FOR WHAT *PURPOSE?*
NOT ALI
......
I DON'T KNOW.
I-I SEE...
THEN, NEXT QUES-TION.
HOW MANY OTHER PLAYERS ARE THERE?
SHAAAA
TAP TAP
......
I DON'T KNOW.
THAT, TOO?
THEN, HOW LONG DO I HAVE TO PLAY AGAINST OTHER PLAYERS?

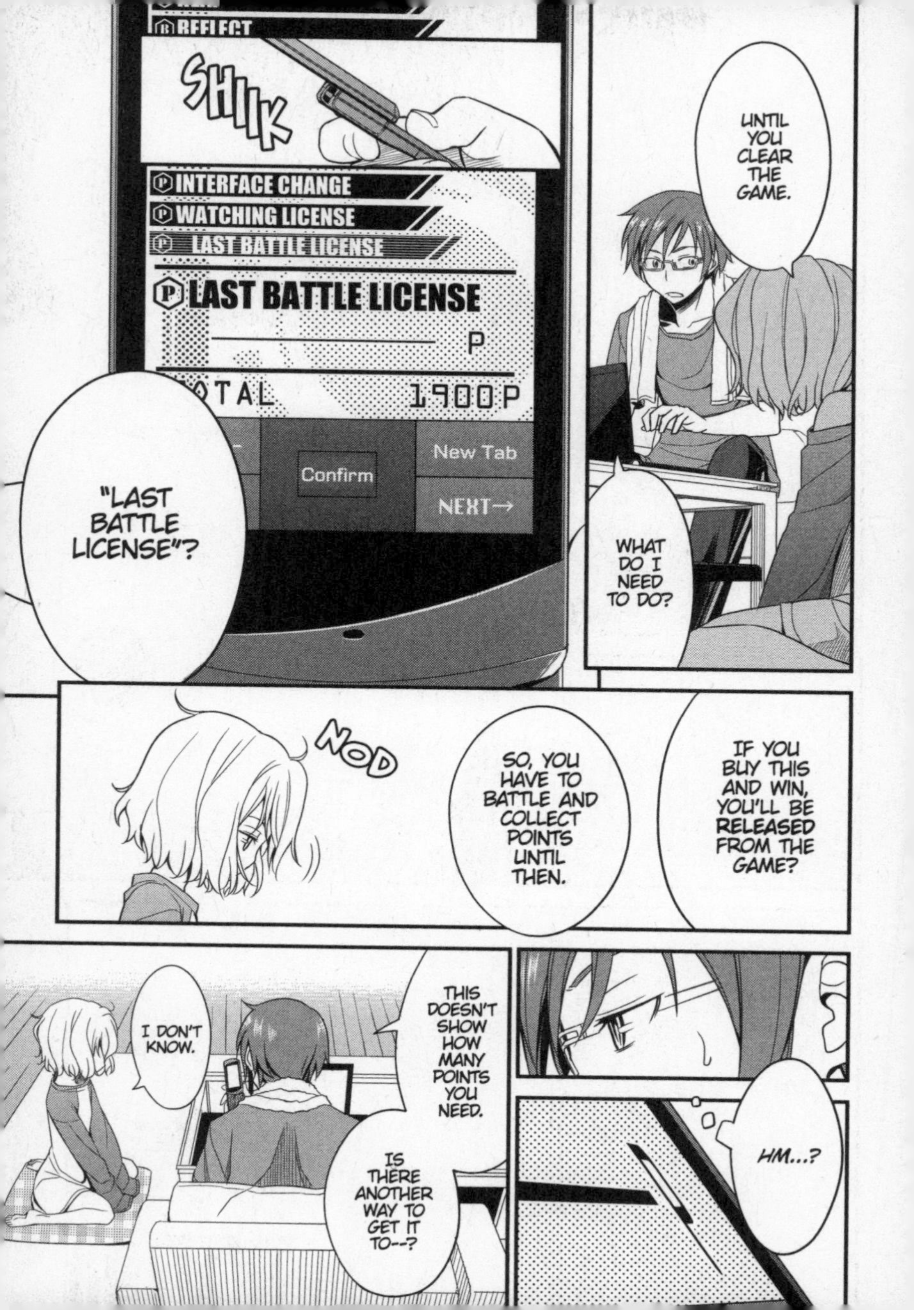
UNTIL YOU CLEAR THE GAME.
WHAT DO I NEED TO DO?
REFLECT
SHIIK
INTERFACE CHANGE
WATCHING LICENSE
LAST BATTLE LICENSE
LAST BATTLE LICENSE
P
TOTAL 1900P
Confirm
New Tab
NEXT→
"LAST BATTLE LICENSE"?
IF YOU BUY THIS AND WIN, YOU'LL BE RELEASED FROM THE GAME?
SO, YOU HAVE TO BATTLE AND COLLECT POINTS UNTIL THEN.
NOD
HM...?
THIS DOESN'T SHOW HOW MANY POINTS YOU NEED.
IS THERE ANOTHER WAY TO GET IT TO--?
I DON'T KNOW.

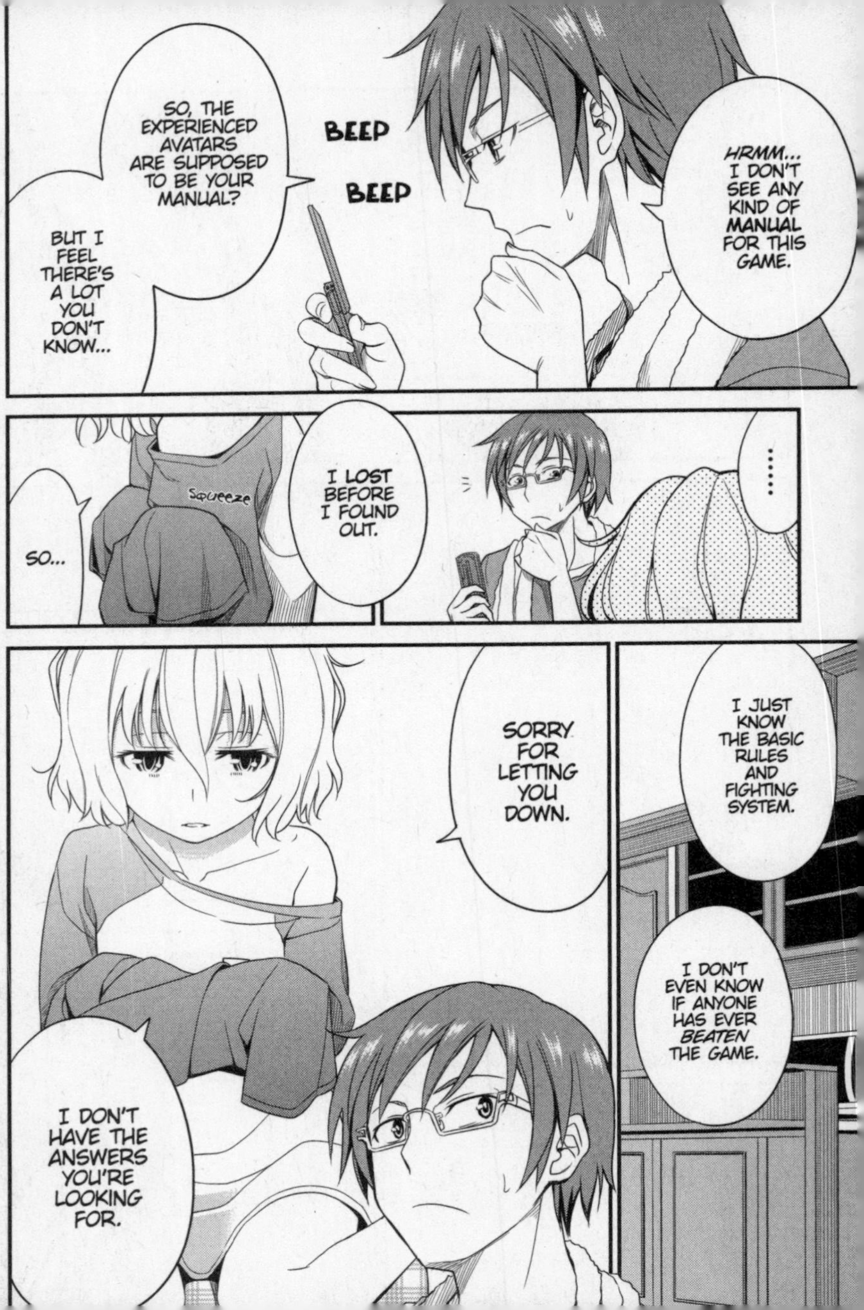
HRMM... I DON'T SEE ANY KIND OF MANUAL FOR THIS GAME.
BEEP
BEEP
SO, THE EXPERIENCED AVATARS ARE SUPPOSED TO BE YOUR MANUAL?
BUT I FEEL THERE'S A LOT YOU DON'T KNOW...
......
I LOST BEFORE I FOUND OUT.
Squeeze
SO...
I JUST KNOW THE BASIC RULES AND FIGHTING SYSTEM.
I DON'T EVEN KNOW IF ANYONE HAS EVER BEATEN THE GAME.
SORRY FOR LETTING YOU DOWN.
I DON'T HAVE THE ANSWERS YOU'RE LOOKING FOR.

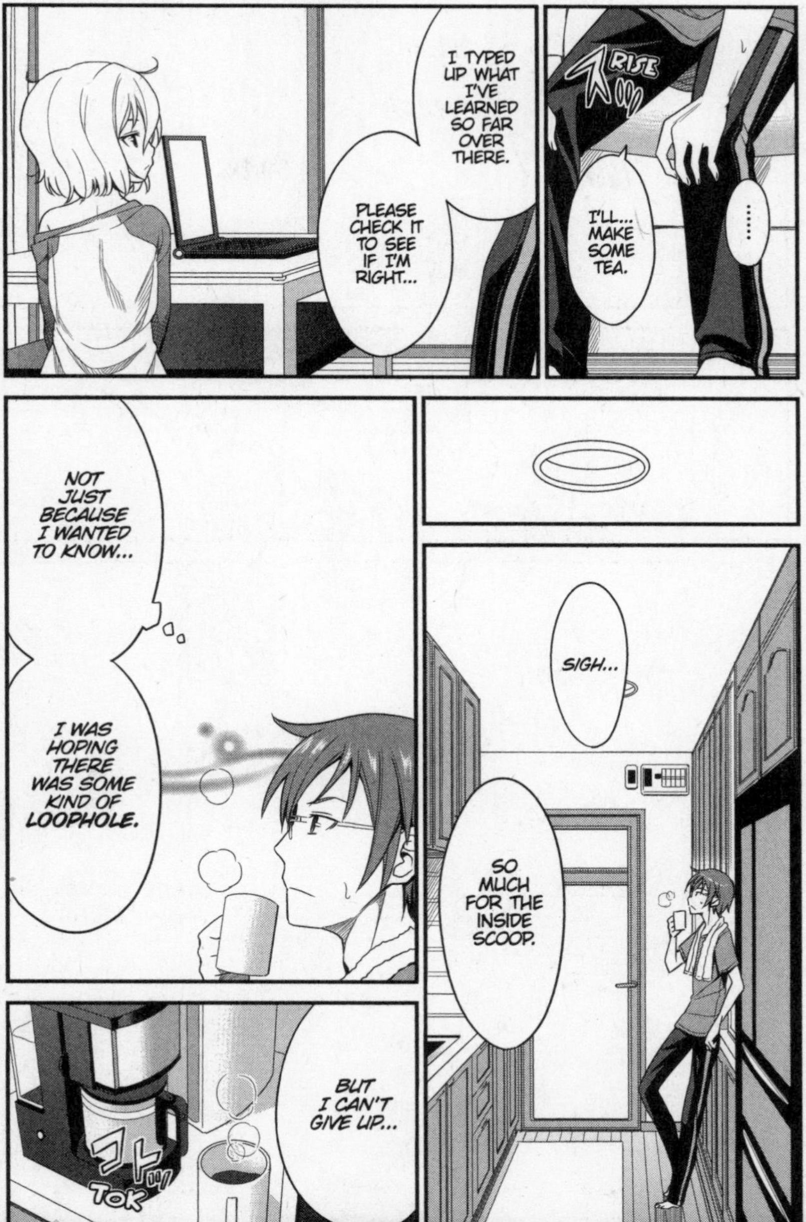
RISE
......
I'LL... MAKE SOME TEA.
I TYPED UP WHAT I'VE LEARNED SO FAR OVER THERE.
PLEASE CHECK IT TO SEE IF I'M RIGHT...
SIGH...
SO MUCH FOR THE INSIDE SCOOP.
NOT JUST BECAUSE I WANTED TO KNOW...
I WAS HOPING THERE WAS SOME KIND OF LOOPHOLE.
BUT I CAN'T GIVE UP...
コトッ
TOK

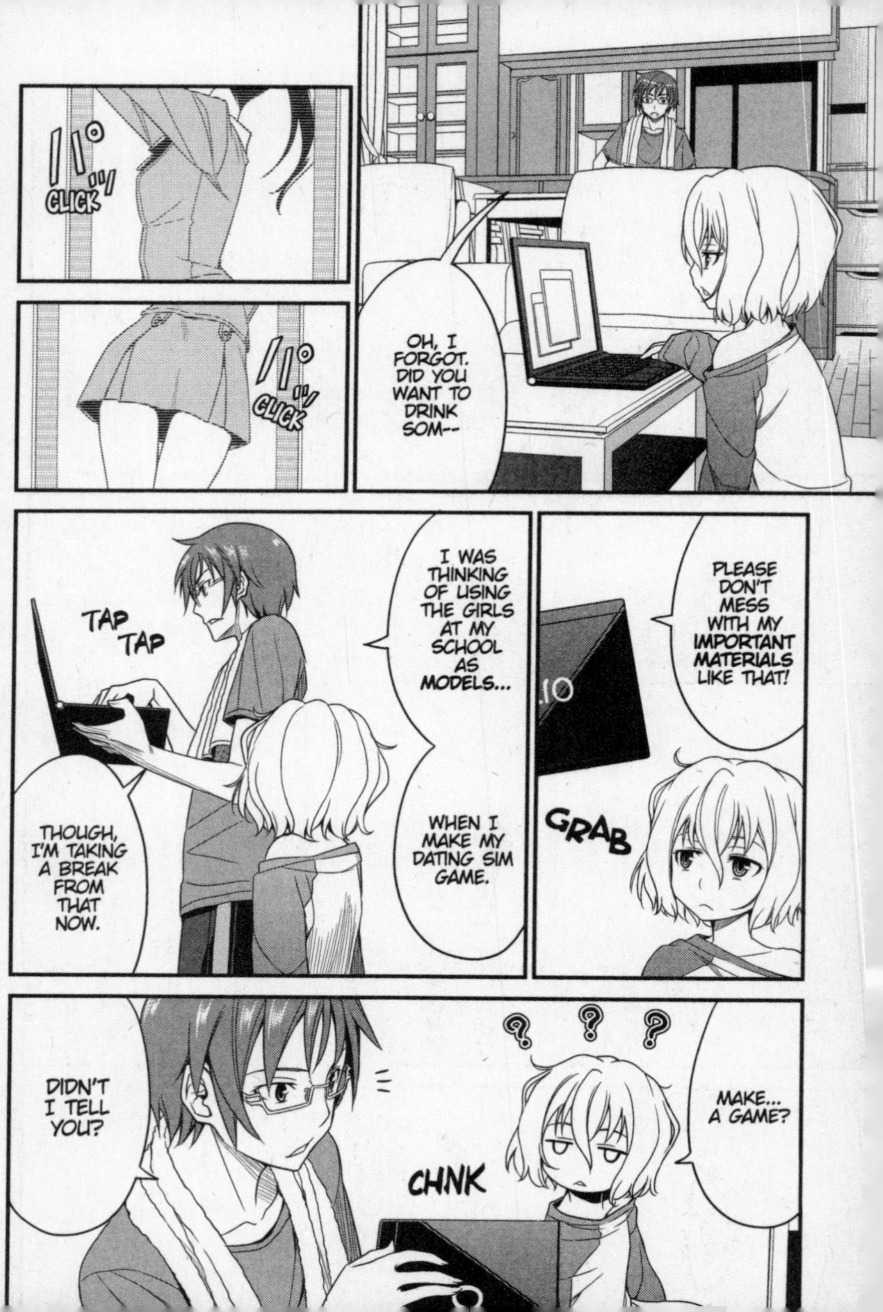
OH, I FORGOT. DID YOU WANT TO DRINK SOM--
CLICK
CLICK
PLEASE DON'T MESS WITH MY IMPORTANT MATERIALS LIKE THAT!
GRAB
I WAS THINKING OF USING THE GIRLS AT MY SCHOOL AS MODELS...
TAP TAP
WHEN I MAKE MY DATING SIM GAME.
THOUGH, I'M TAKING A BREAK FROM THAT NOW.
MAKE... A GAME?
???
CHNK
DIDN'T I TELL YOU?

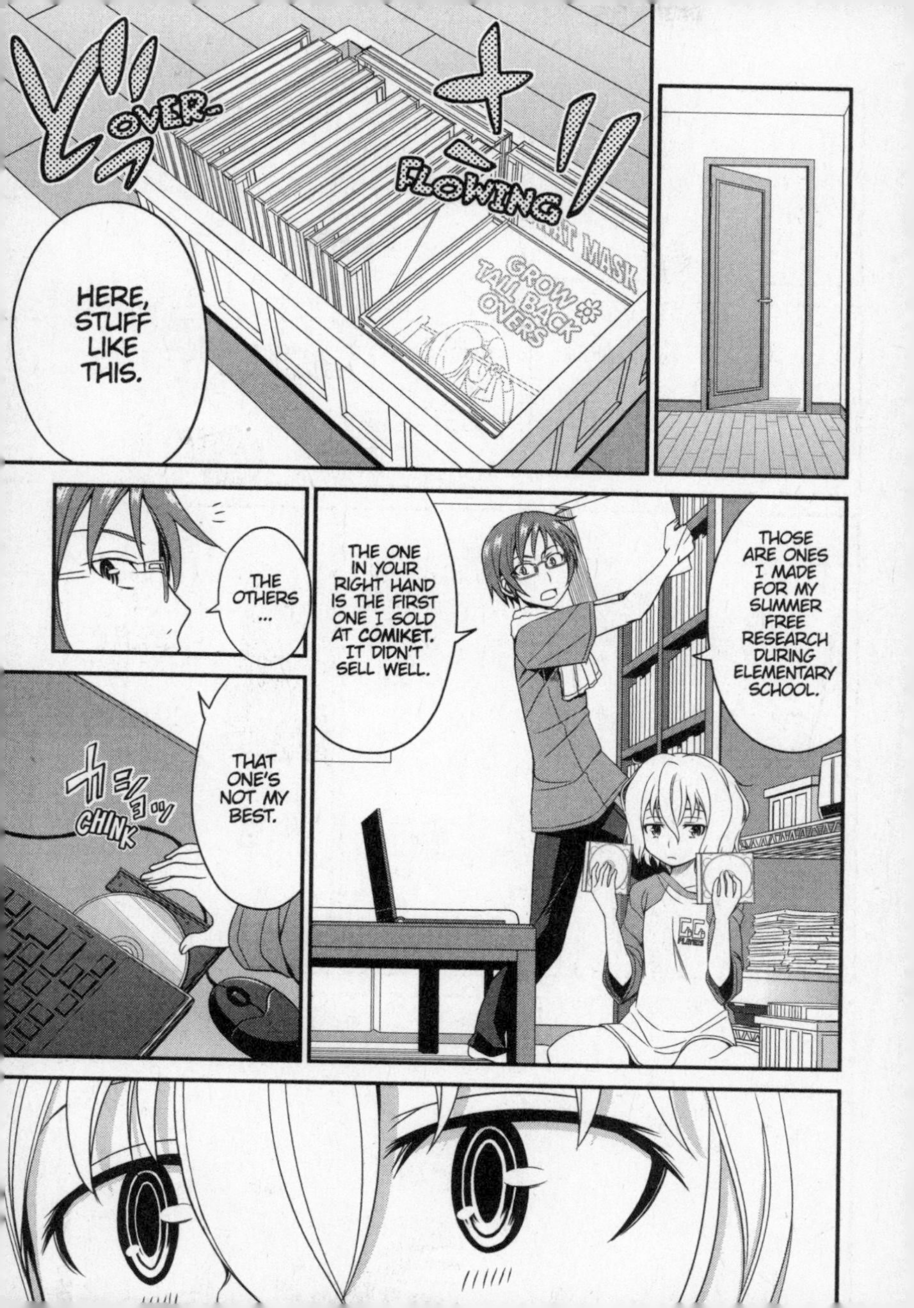
OVER-
FLOWING
GROW TALL BACK OVERS
HERE, STUFF LIKE THIS.
THOSE ARE ONES I MADE FOR MY SUMMER FREE RESEARCH DURING ELEMENTARY SCHOOL.
THE ONE IN YOUR RIGHT HAND IS THE FIRST ONE I SOLD AT COMIKET. IT DIDN'T SELL WELL.
THE OTHERS ...
THAT ONE'S NOT MY BEST.
CHINK

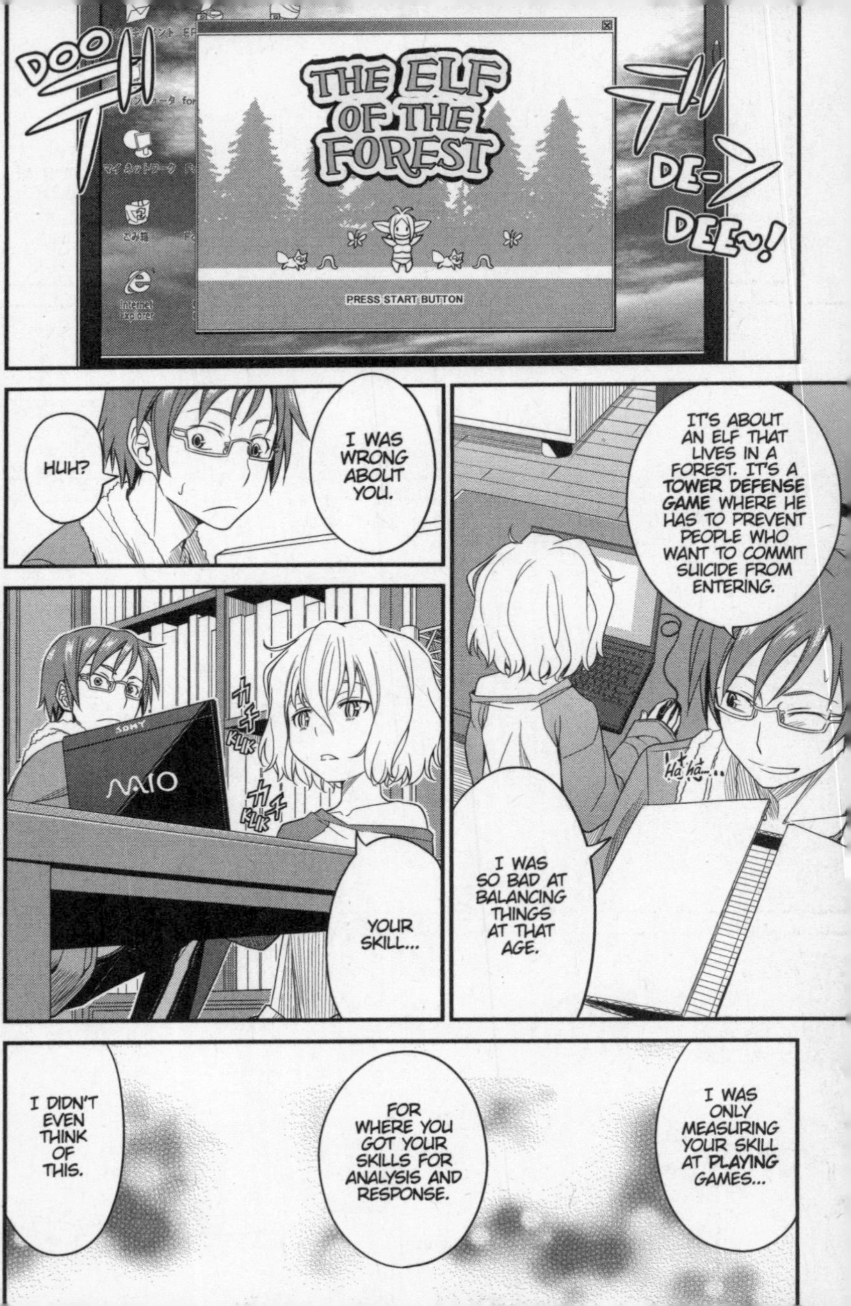
DOO デ
デーン DE-ン DEE~!
THE ELF OF THE FOREST
PRESS START BUTTON
IT'S ABOUT AN ELF THAT LIVES IN A FOREST. IT'S A TOWER DEFENSE GAME WHERE HE HAS TO PREVENT PEOPLE WHO WANT TO COMMIT SUICIDE FROM ENTERING.
Ha ha...
I WAS SO BAD AT BALANCING THINGS AT THAT AGE.
I WAS WRONG ABOUT YOU.
HUH?
カチ KLIK
カチ KLIK
YOUR SKILL...
I WAS ONLY MEASURING YOUR SKILL AT PLAYING GAMES...
FOR WHERE YOU GOT YOUR SKILLS FOR ANALYSIS AND RESPONSE.
I DIDN'T EVEN THINK OF THIS.

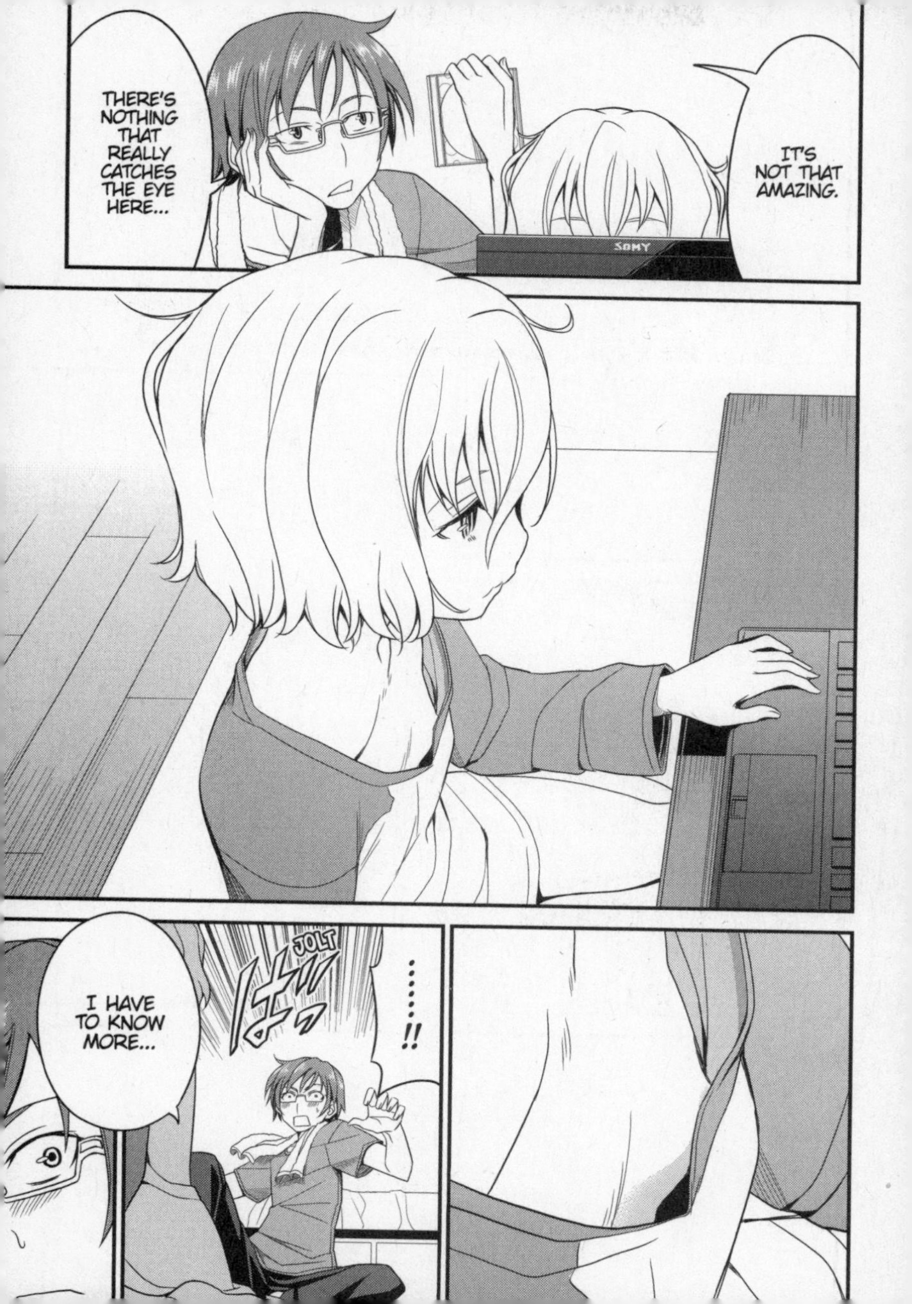
IT'S NOT THAT AMAZING.
THERE'S NOTHING THAT REALLY CATCHES THE EYE HERE...
SOMY
JOLT
......!!
I HAVE TO KNOW MORE...

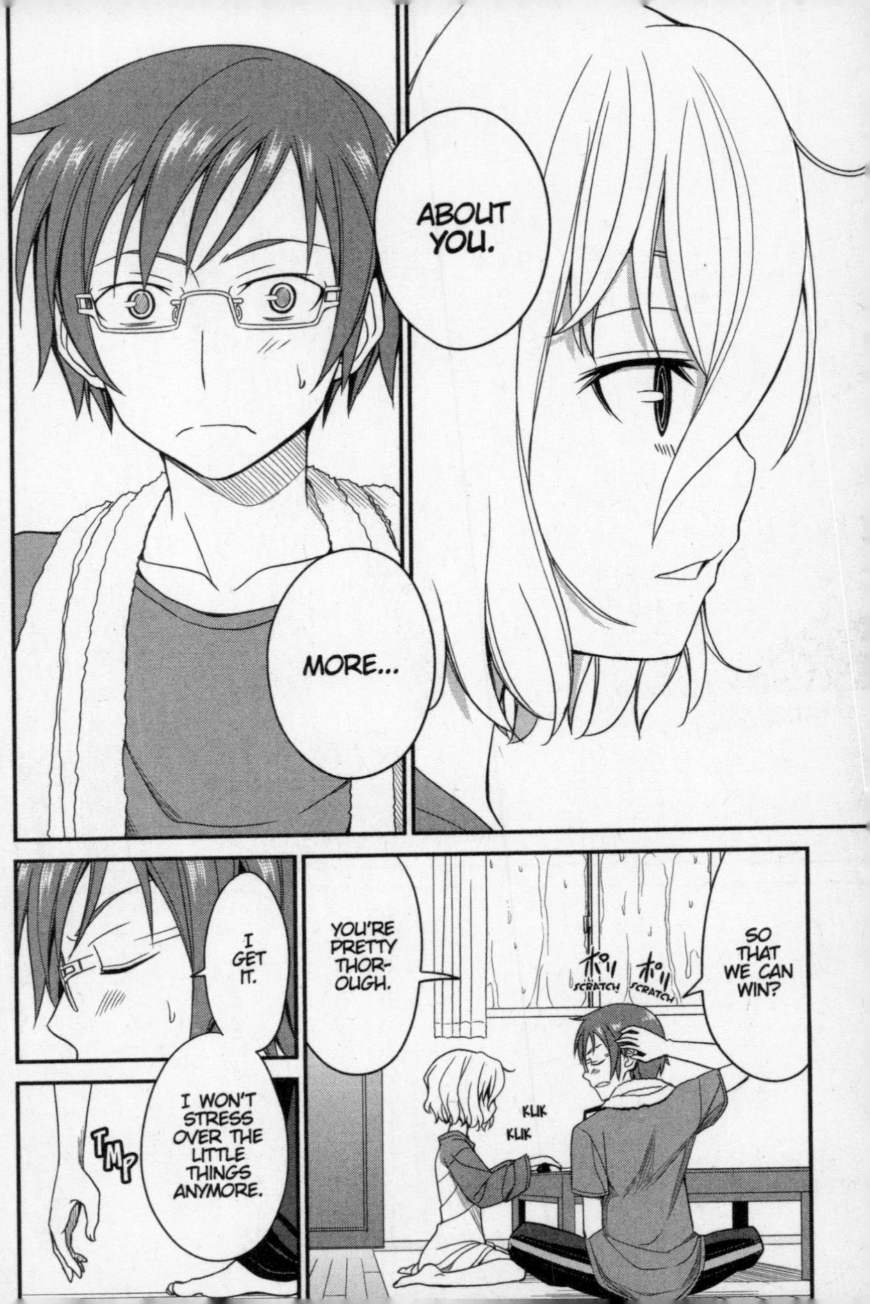
ABOUT YOU.
MORE...
SO THAT WE CAN WIN?
ポリ SCRATCH
ポリ SCRATCH
YOU'RE PRETTY THOR-OUGH.
KLIK
KLIK
I GET IT.
I WON'T STRESS OVER THE LITTLE THINGS ANYMORE.
TMP

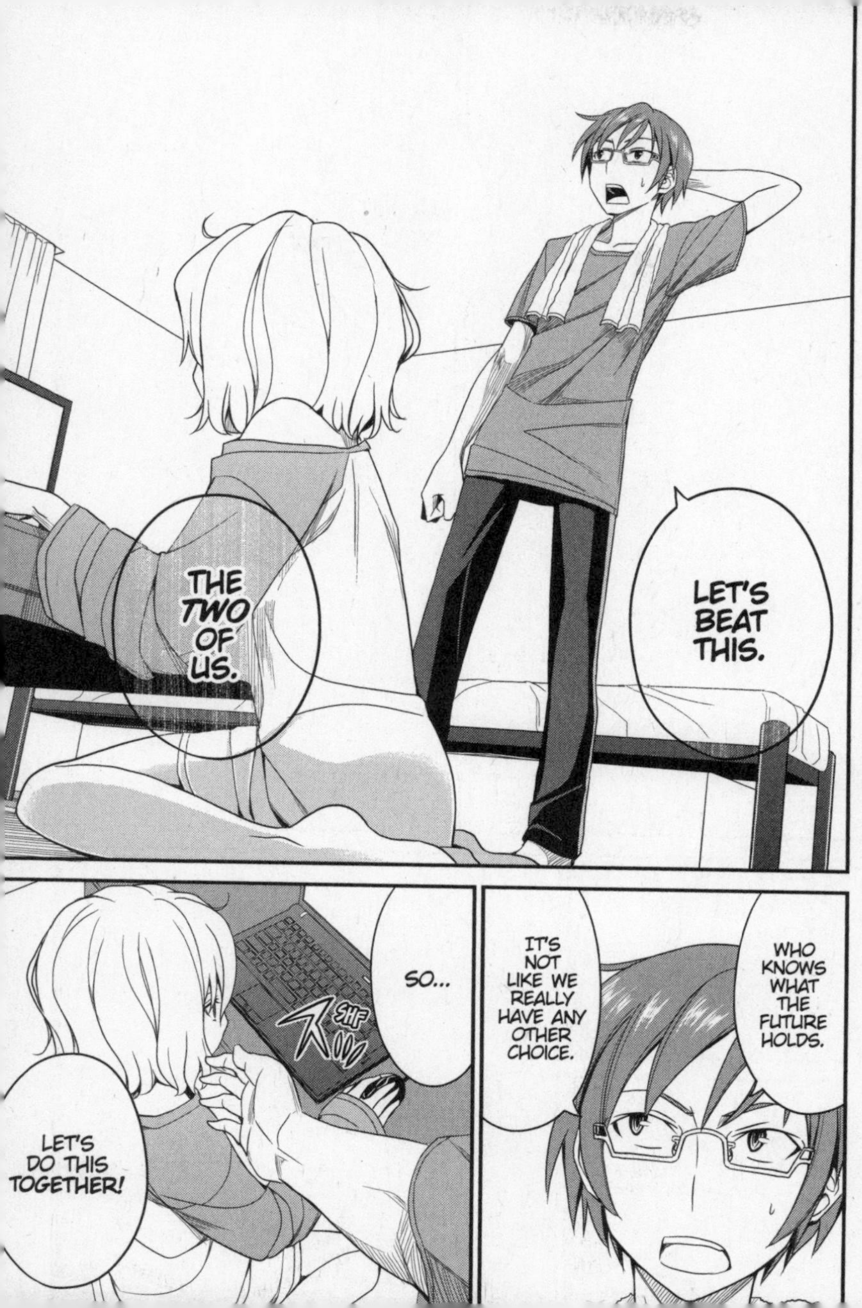
LET'S BEAT THIS.
THE TWO OF US.
WHO KNOWS WHAT THE FUTURE HOLDS.
IT'S NOT LIKE WE REALLY HAVE ANY OTHER CHOICE.
SO...
SHF
LET'S DO THIS TOGETHER!

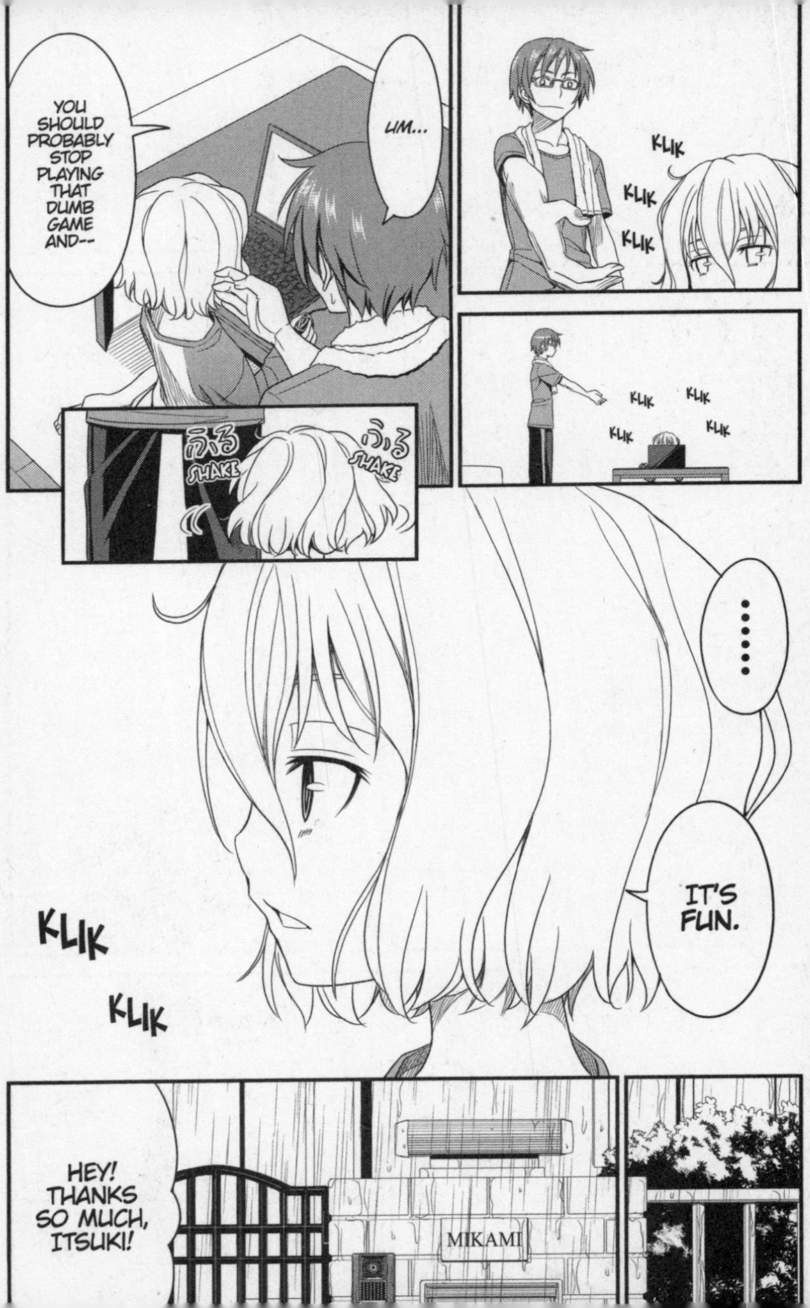
KLIK
KLIK
KLIK
KLIK
KLIK
KLIK
KLIK
UM...
YOU SHOULD PROBABLY STOP PLAYING THAT DUMB GAME AND--
ふる
SHAKE
ふる
SHAKE
......
IT'S FUN.
KLIK
KLIK
HEY! THANKS SO MUCH, ITSUKI!
MIKAMI

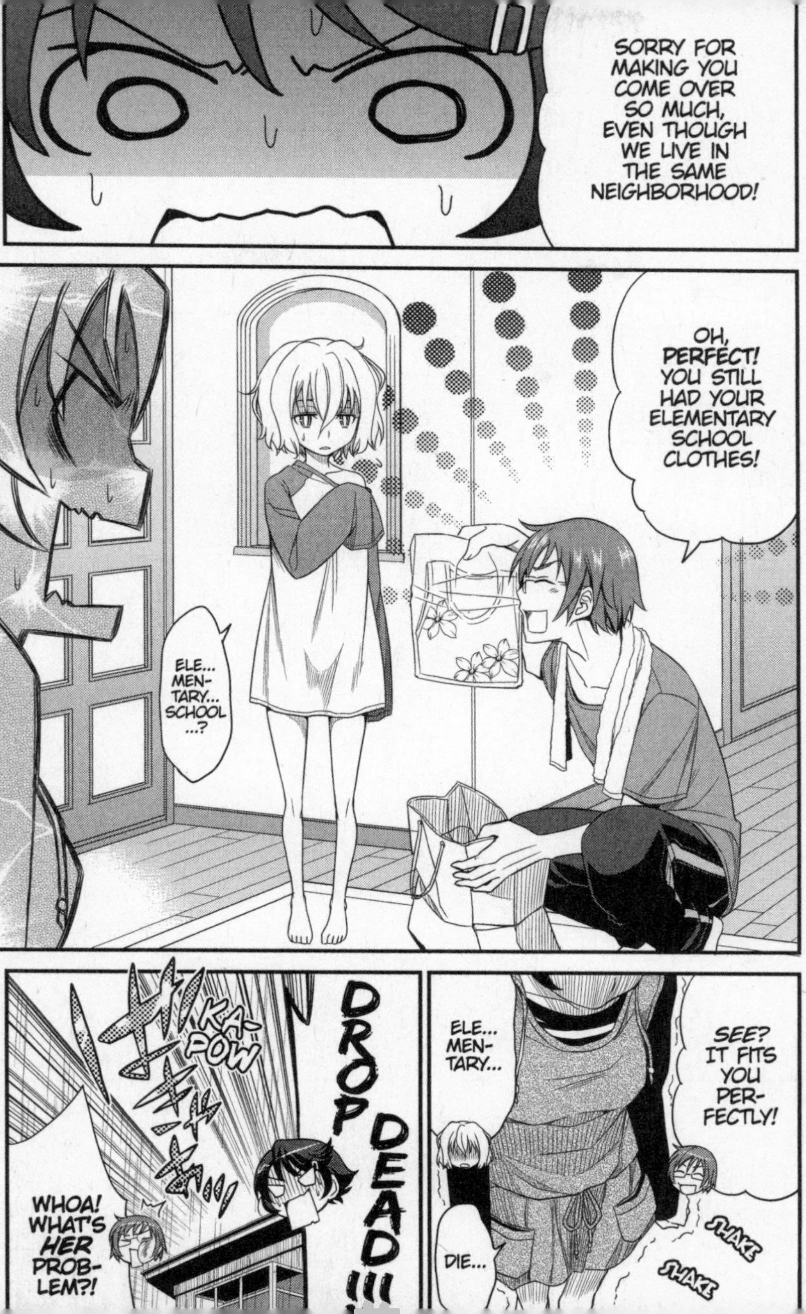
SORRY FOR MAKING YOU COME OVER SO MUCH, EVEN THOUGH WE LIVE IN THE SAME NEIGHBORHOOD!
OH, PERFECT! YOU STILL HAD YOUR ELEMENTARY SCHOOL CLOTHES!
ELE... MEN-TARY... SCHOOL ...?
SEE? IT FITS YOU PER-FECTLY!
ELE... MEN-TARY...
SHAKE
SHAKE
DIE...
KA-POW
DROP DEAD!!!
WHOA! WHAT'S HER PROB-LEM?!

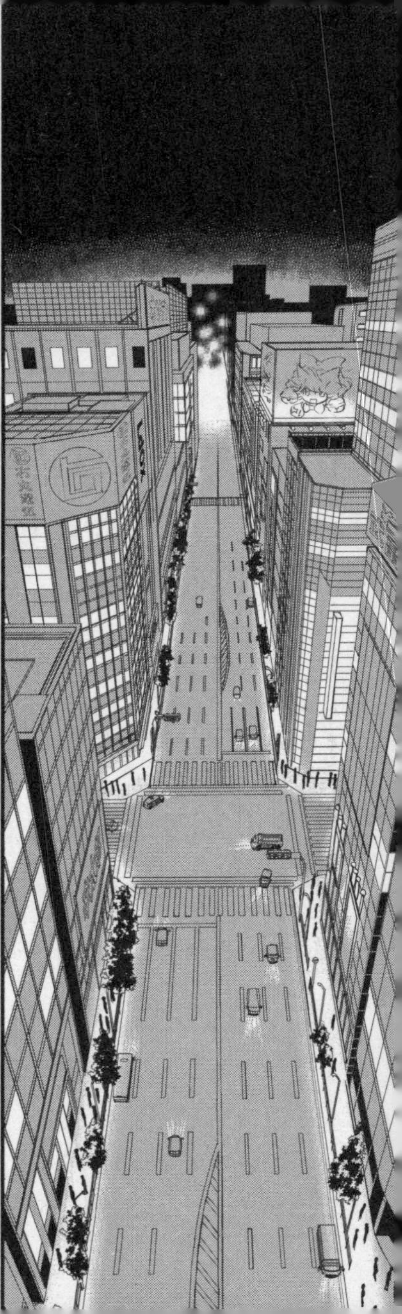

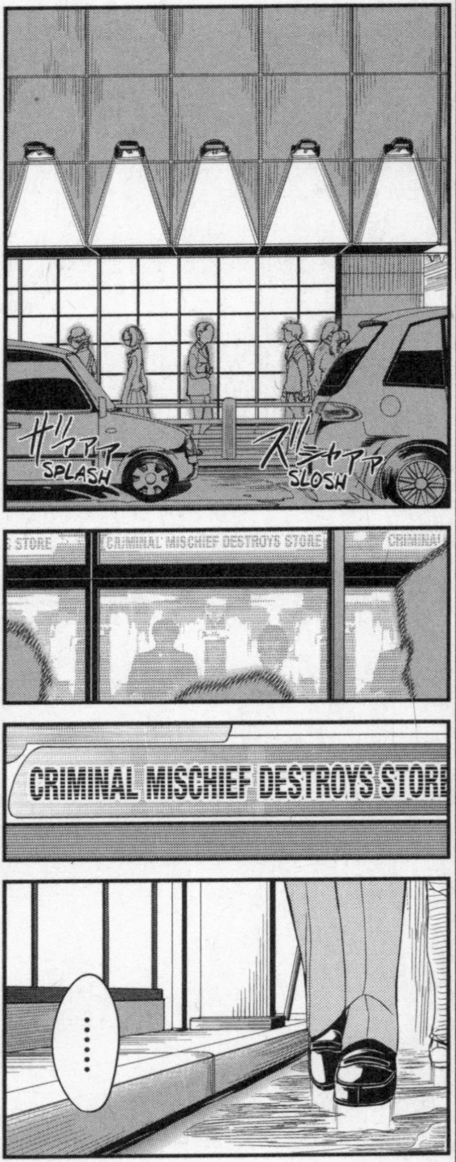
ズシャアア
SLOSH
ザァァァ
SPLASH
S STORE
CRIMINAL MISCHIEF DESTROYS STORE
CRIMINAL
CRIMINAL MISCHIEF DESTROYS STORE
……

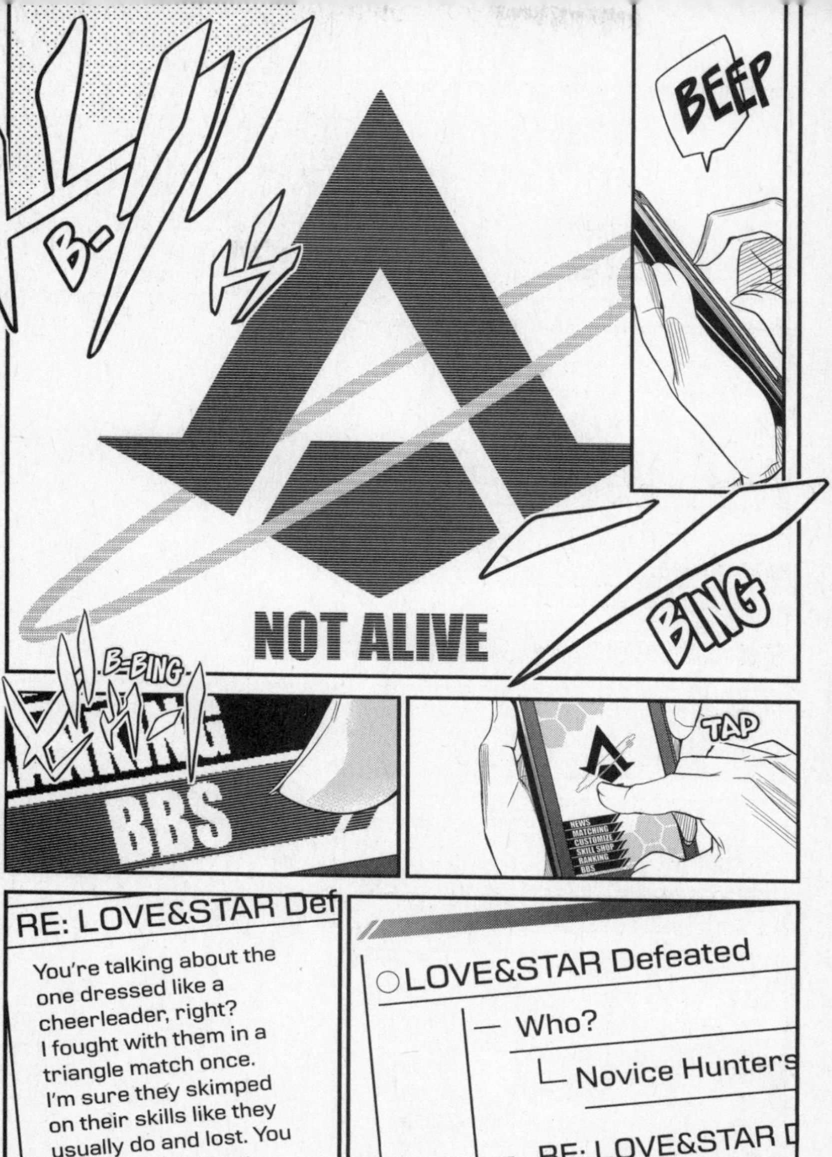
BEEP
B-
NOT ALIVE
BING
TAP
NEWS
MATCHING
CUSTOMIZE
SKILL SHOP
RANKING
BBS
B-BING
BBS
LOVE&STAR Defeated
Who?
Novice Hunters
RE: LOVE&STAR D
RE: LOVE&STAR
RE: LOVE&STAR Def
You're talking about the one dressed like a cheerleader, right? I fought with them in a triangle match once. I'm sure they skimped on their skills like they usually do and lost. You reap what you sow.

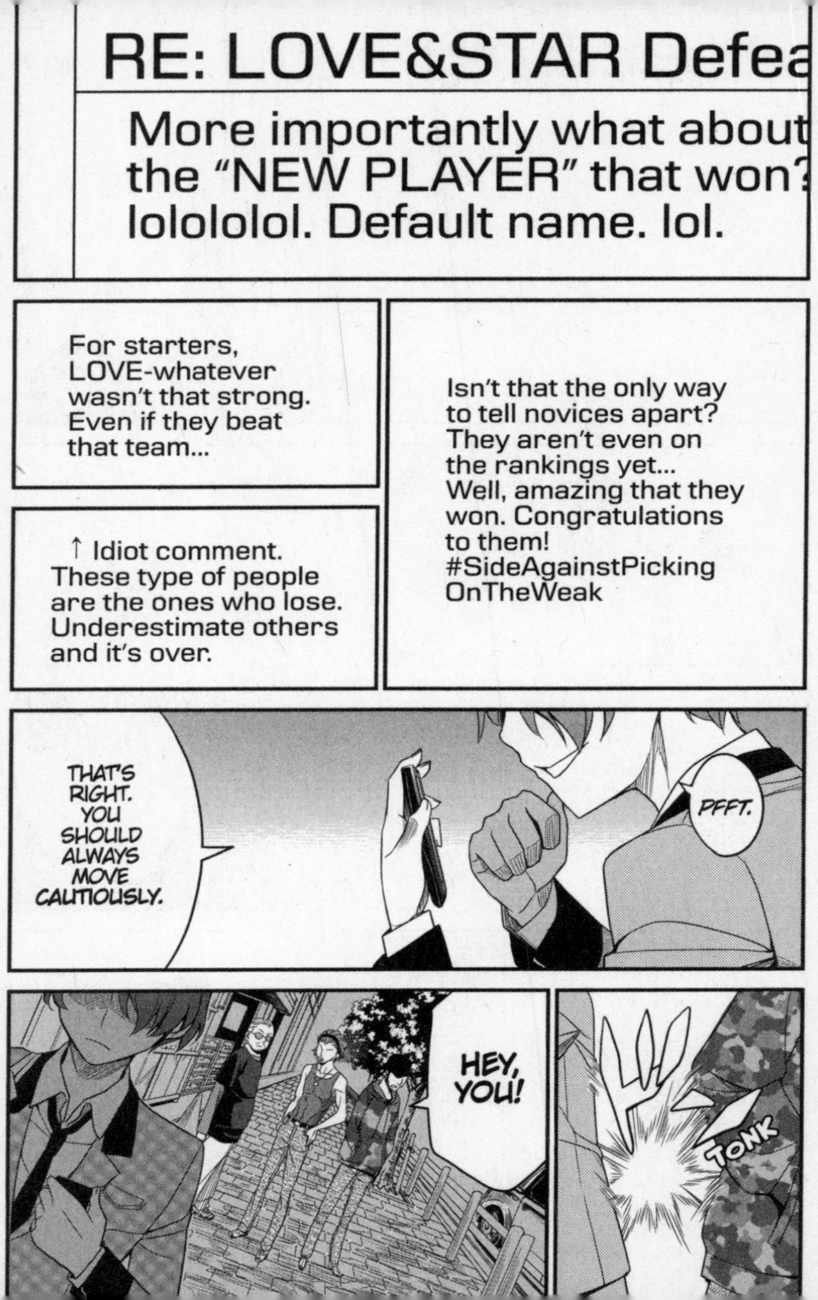
RE: LOVE&STAR Defea
More importantly what about the "NEW PLAYER" that won? lolololol. Default name. lol.
Isn't that the only way to tell novices apart? They aren't even on the rankings yet... Well, amazing that they won. Congratulations to them! #SideAgainstPickingOnTheWeak
For starters, LOVE-whatever wasn't that strong. Even if they beat that team...
↑ Idiot comment. These type of people are the ones who lose. Underestimate others and it's over.
PFFT.
THAT'S RIGHT. YOU SHOULD ALWAYS MOVE CAUTIOUSLY.
TONK
HEY, YOU!

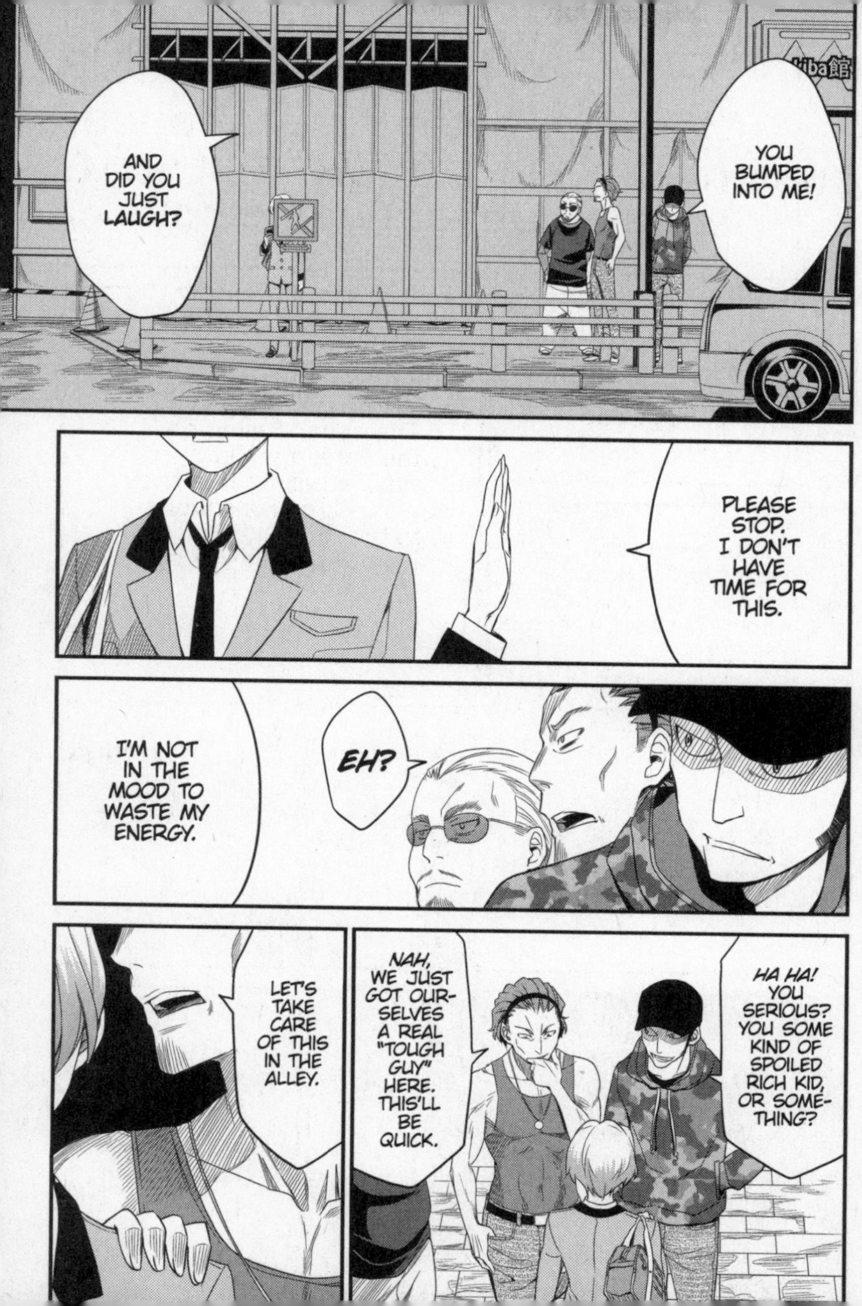
YOU BUMPED INTO ME!
AND DID YOU JUST LAUGH?
PLEASE STOP. I DON'T HAVE TIME FOR THIS.
EH?
I'M NOT IN THE MOOD TO WASTE MY ENERGY.
HA HA! YOU SERIOUS? YOU SOME KIND OF SPOILED RICH KID, OR SOME-THING?
NAH, WE JUST GOT OUR-SELVES A REAL "TOUGH GUY" HERE. THIS'LL BE QUICK.
LET'S TAKE CARE OF THIS IN THE ALLEY.

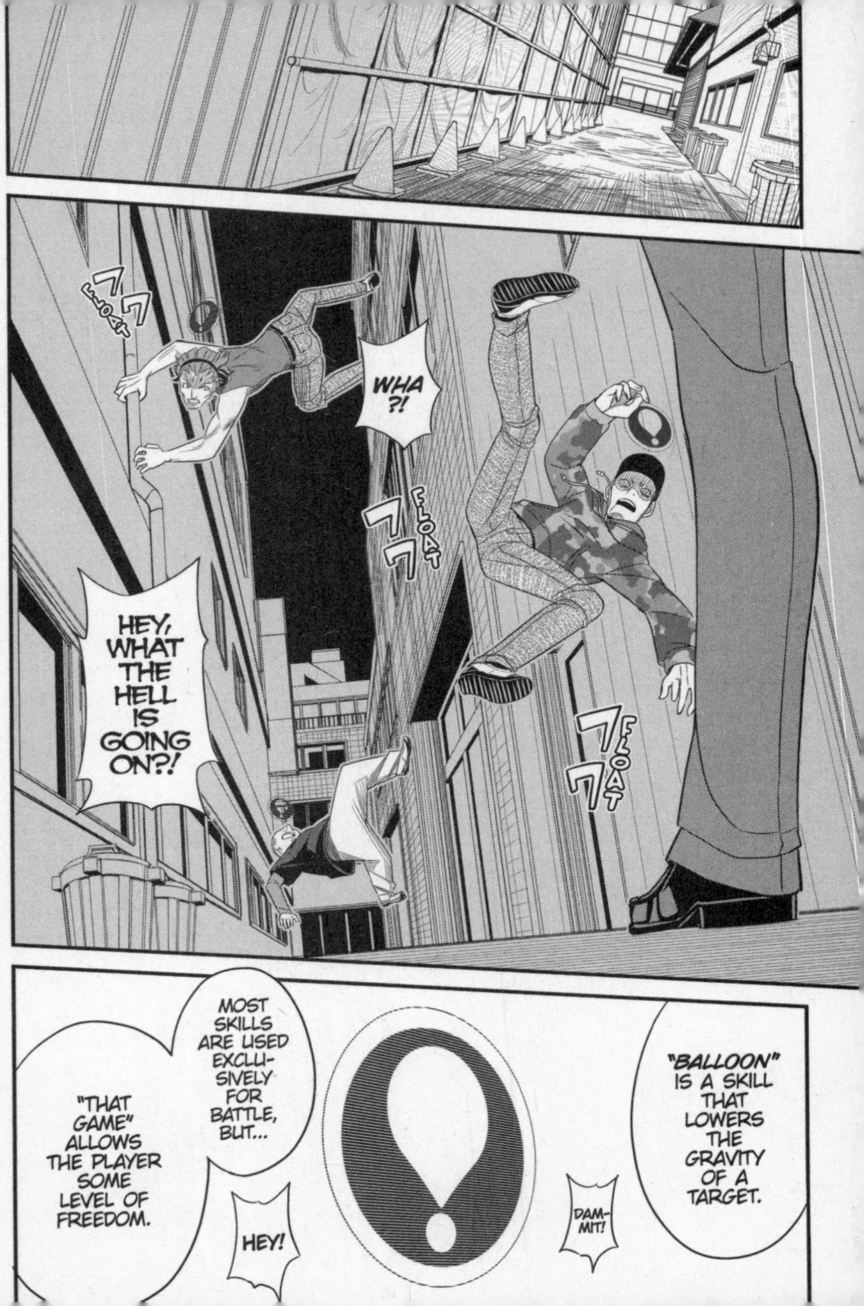

FLOAT
FLOAT
WHA ?!
FLOAT
HEY, WHAT THE HELL IS GOING ON?!
"BALLOON" IS A SKILL THAT LOWERS THE GRAVITY OF A TARGET.
DAM-MIT!
HEY!
MOST SKILLS ARE USED EXCLUSIVELY FOR BATTLE, BUT...
"THAT GAME" ALLOWS THE PLAYER SOME LEVEL OF FREEDOM.

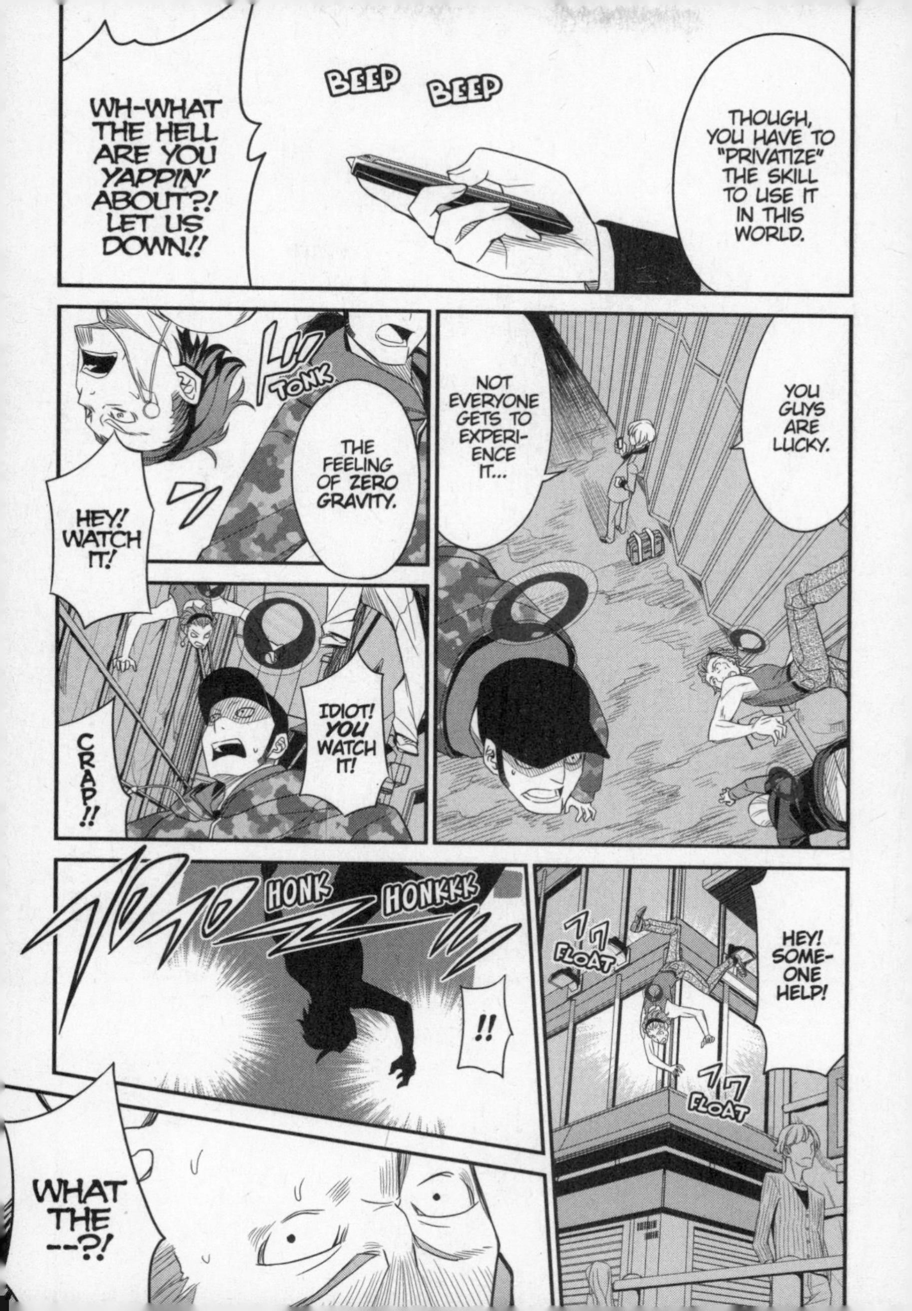
THOUGH, YOU HAVE TO "PRIVATIZE" THE SKILL TO USE IT IN THIS WORLD.
BEEP
BEEP
WH-WHAT THE HELL ARE YOU *YAPPIN'* ABOUT?! LET US DOWN!!
YOU GUYS ARE LUCKY.
NOT EVERYONE GETS TO EXPERIENCE IT...
TONK
THE FEELING OF ZERO GRAVITY.
HEY! WATCH IT!
IDIOT! *YOU* WATCH IT!
CRAP!!
HEY! SOMEONE HELP!
FLOAT
FLOAT
HONKKK
HONK
!!
WHAT THE--?!

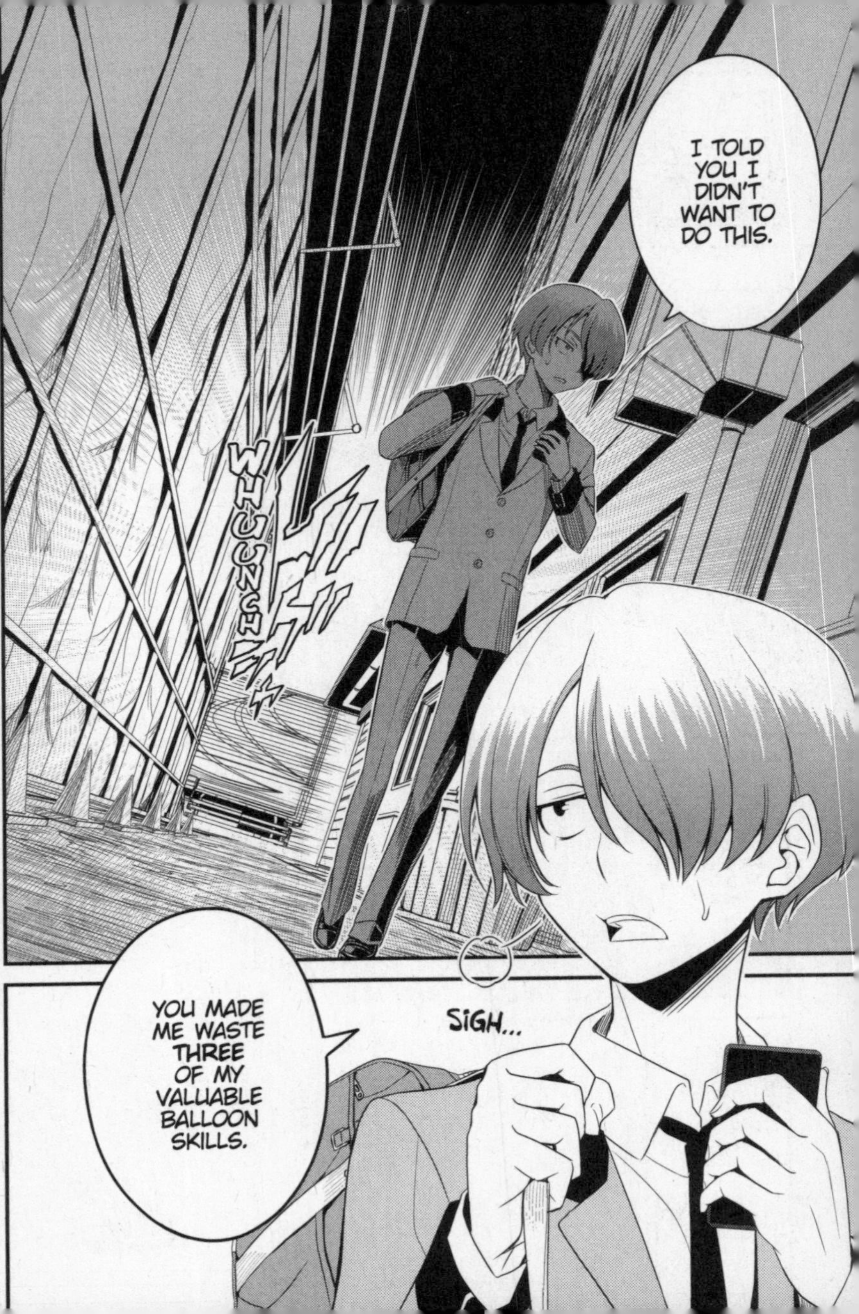
I TOLD YOU I DIDN'T WANT TO DO THIS.
WHUUNCH
SIGH...
YOU MADE ME WASTE THREE OF MY VALUABLE BALLOON SKILLS.

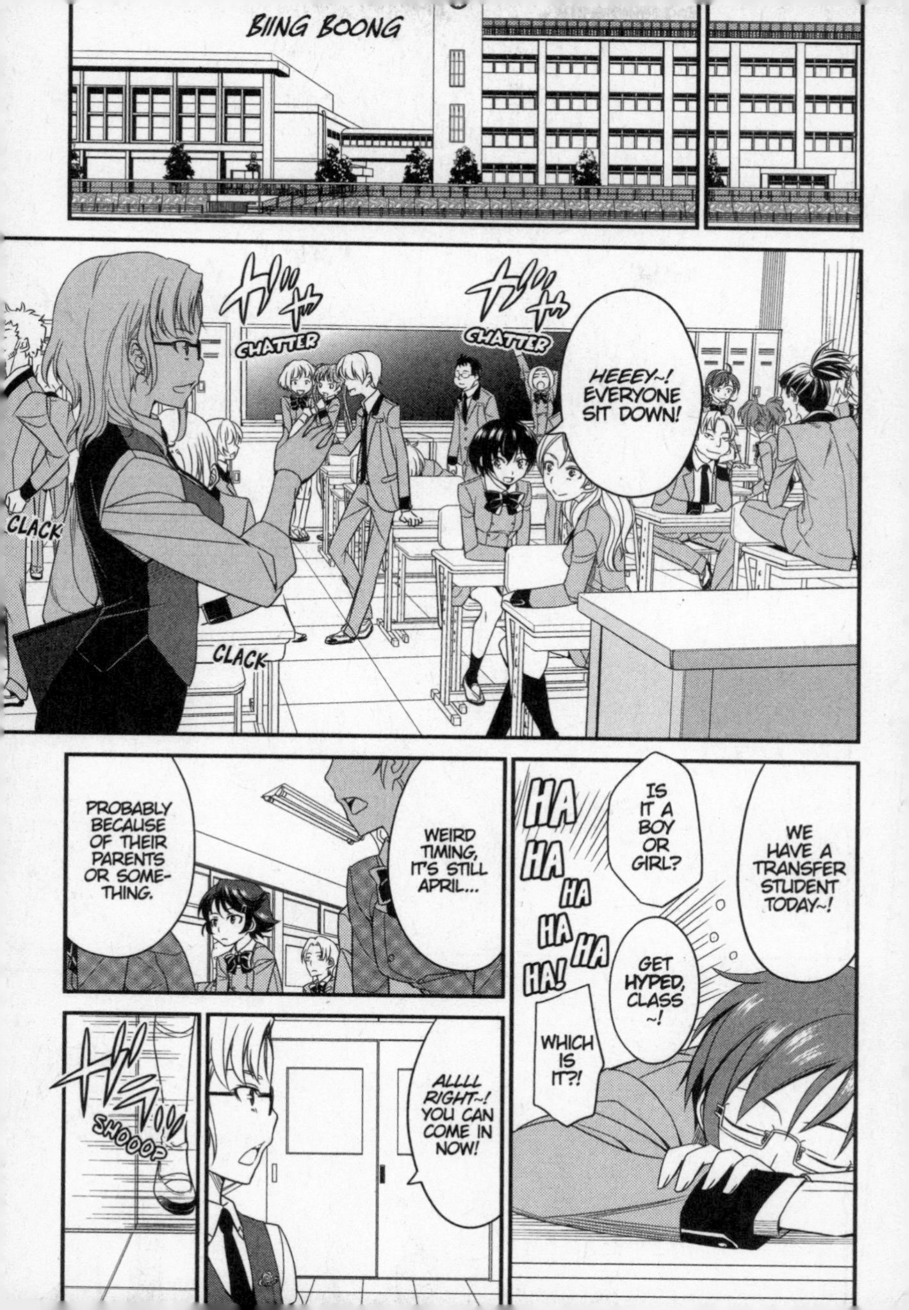
BIING BOONG
CHATTER
HEEEY~! EVERYONE SIT DOWN!
CHATTER
CLACK
CLACK
WE HAVE A TRANSFER STUDENT TODAY~!
IS IT A BOY OR GIRL?
HA HA HA HA HA HA!
GET HYPED, CLASS ~!
WHICH IS IT?!
WEIRD TIMING, IT'S STILL APRIL...
PROBABLY BECAUSE OF THEIR PARENTS OR SOME-THING.
ALLLL RIGHT~! YOU CAN COME IN NOW!
SHOOOP

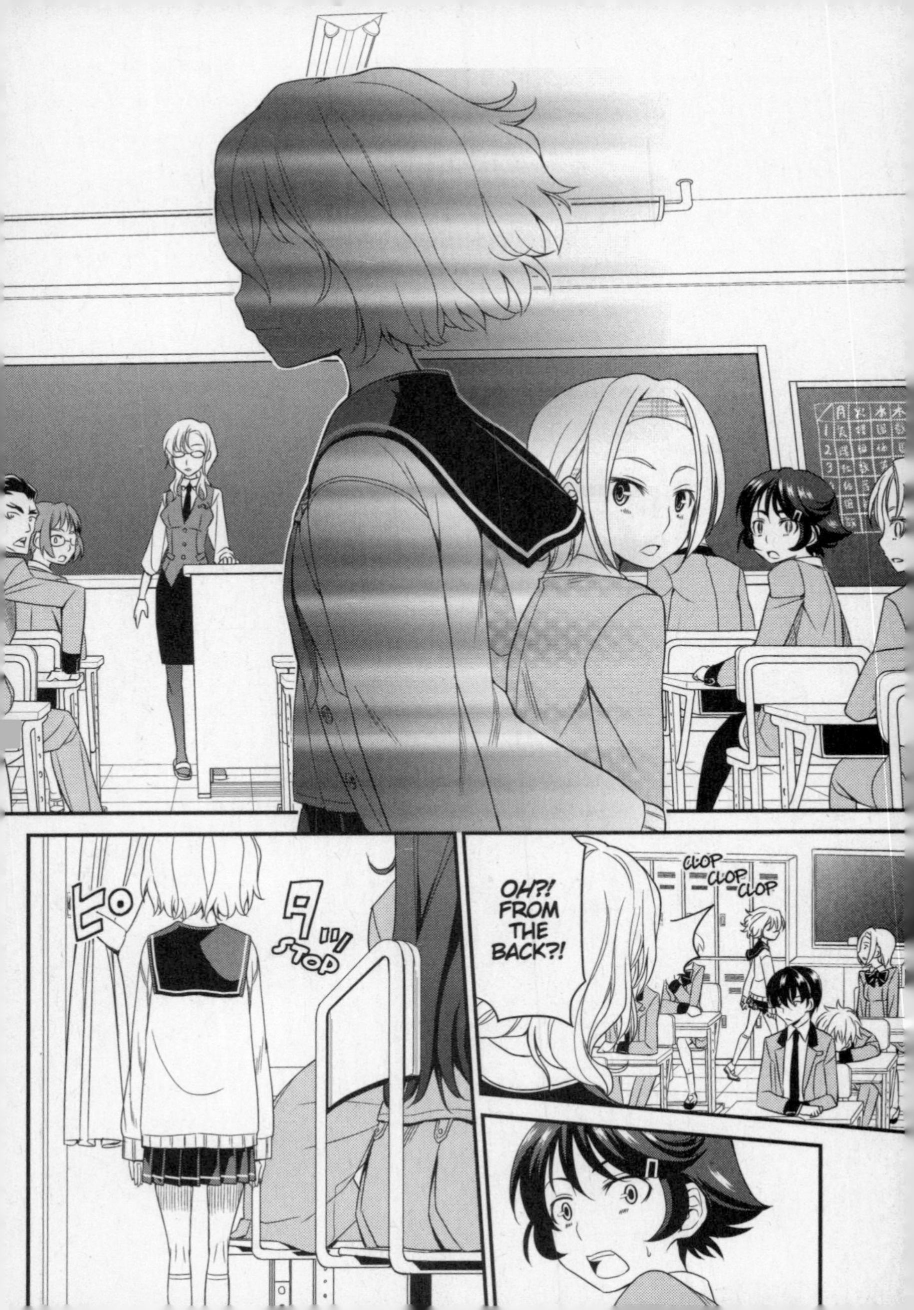
CLOP CLOP CLOP
OH?! FROM THE BACK?!
ピタッ
STOP

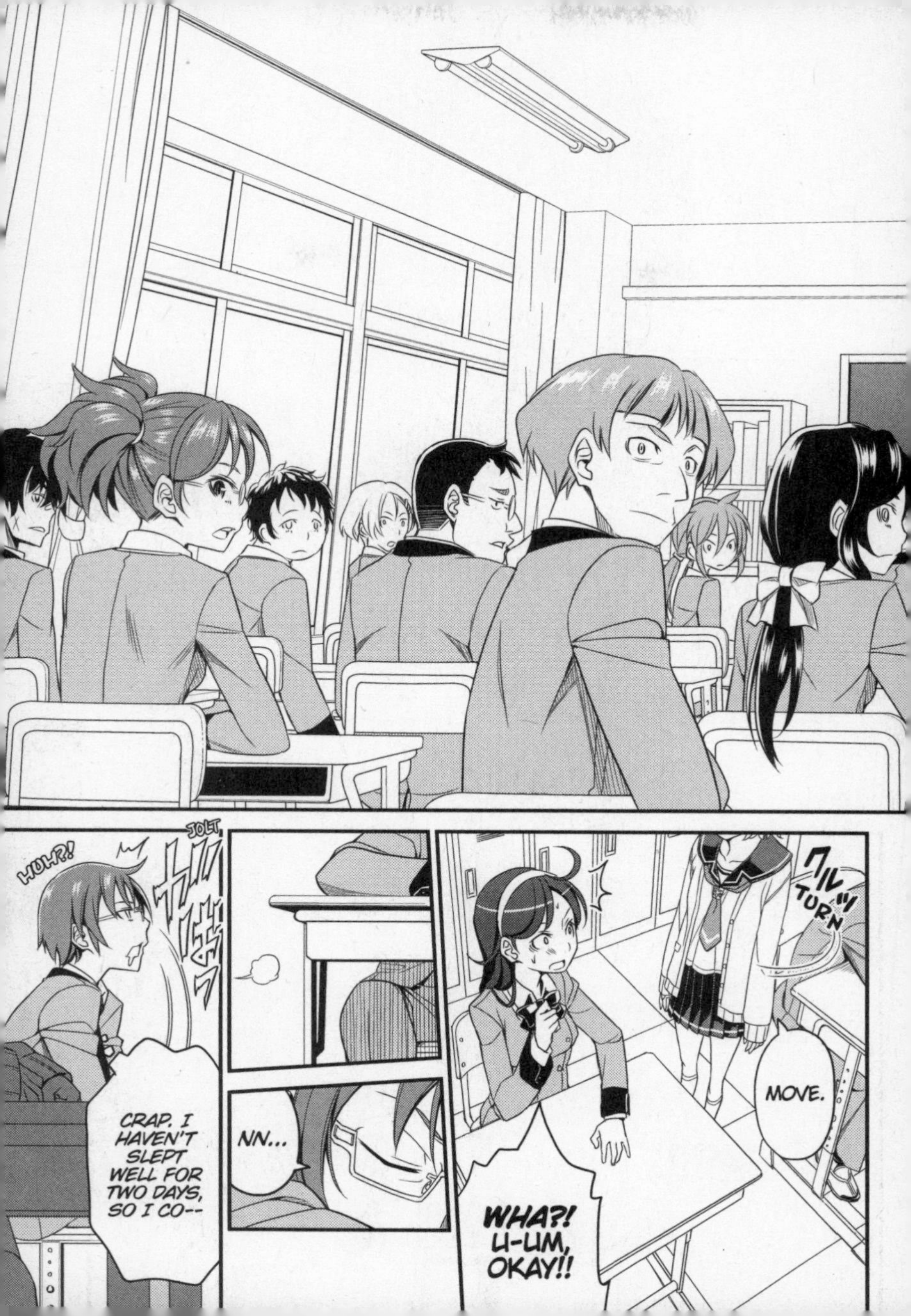
TURN
MOVE.
WHA?! U-UM, OKAY!!
NN...
JOLT
HUH?!
CRAP. I HAVEN'T SLEPT WELL FOR TWO DAYS, SO I CO--

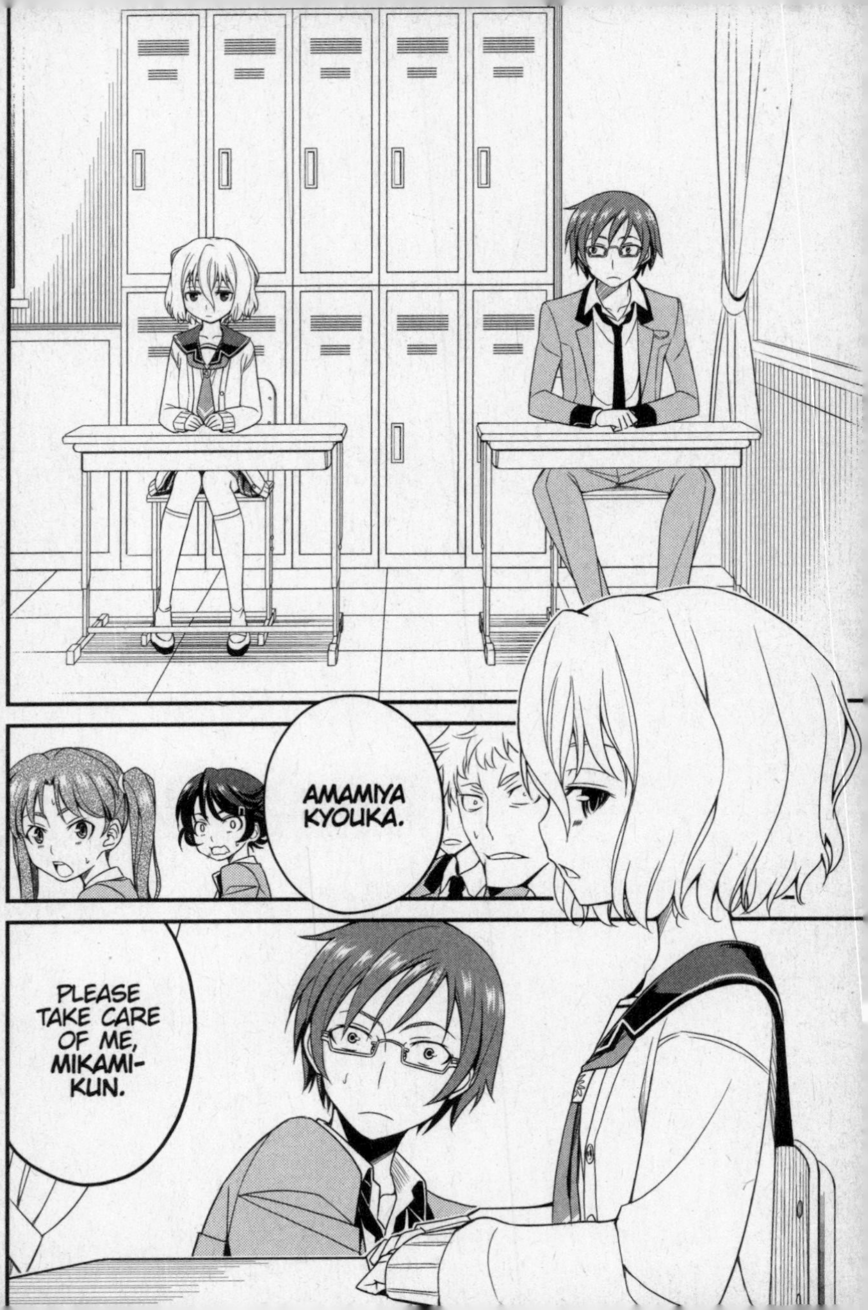
AMAMIYA KYOUKA.
PLEASE TAKE CARE OF ME, MIKAMI-KUN.

NOT LIVES
ノットライヴスト

NOT LIVES: Side Story

Let's Play With the Avatar

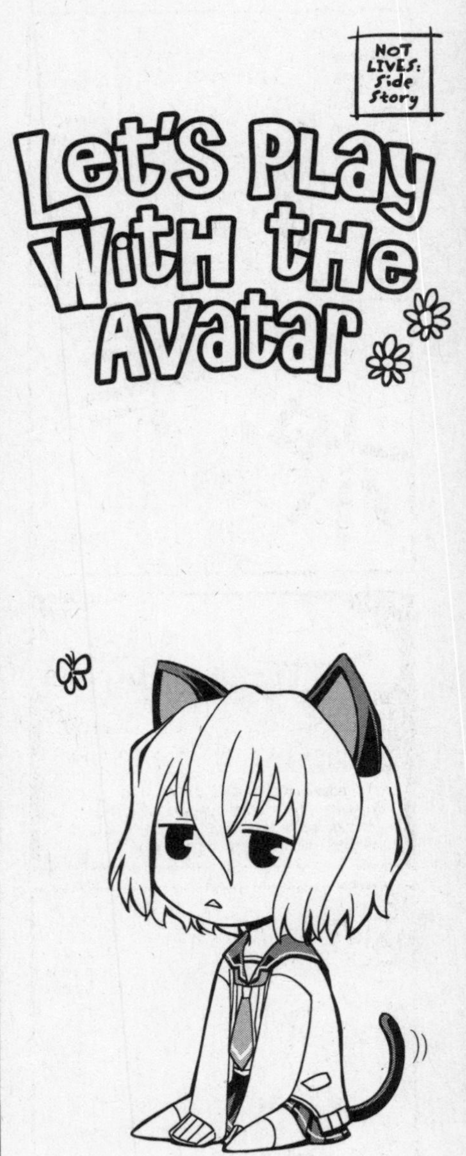

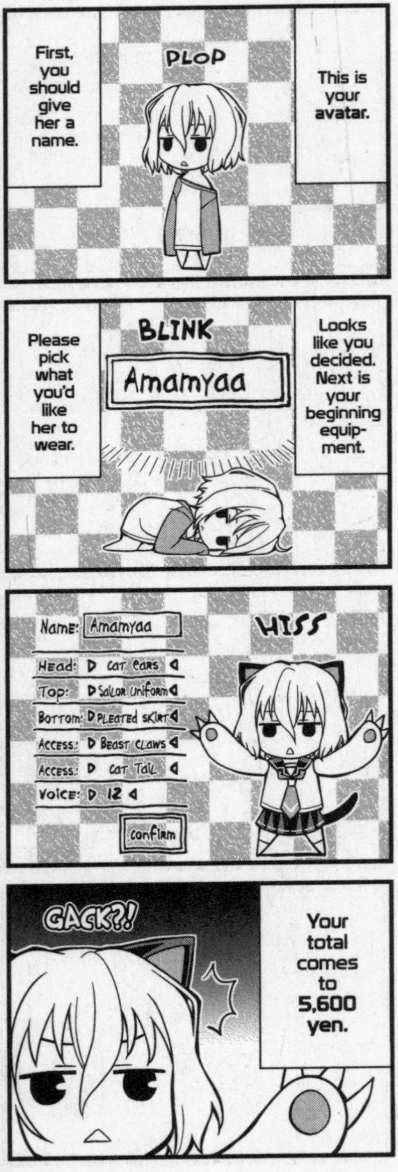
This is your avatar.
PLOP
First, you should give her a name.
Looks like you decided. Next is your beginning equipment.
BLINK
Amamyaa
Please pick what you'd like her to wear.
HISS
Name: Amamyaa
Head: cat ears
Top: Sailor uniform
Bottom: pleated skirt
Access.: Beast claws
Access.: cat tail
Voice: 12
confirm
Your total comes to 5,600 yen.
GACK?!

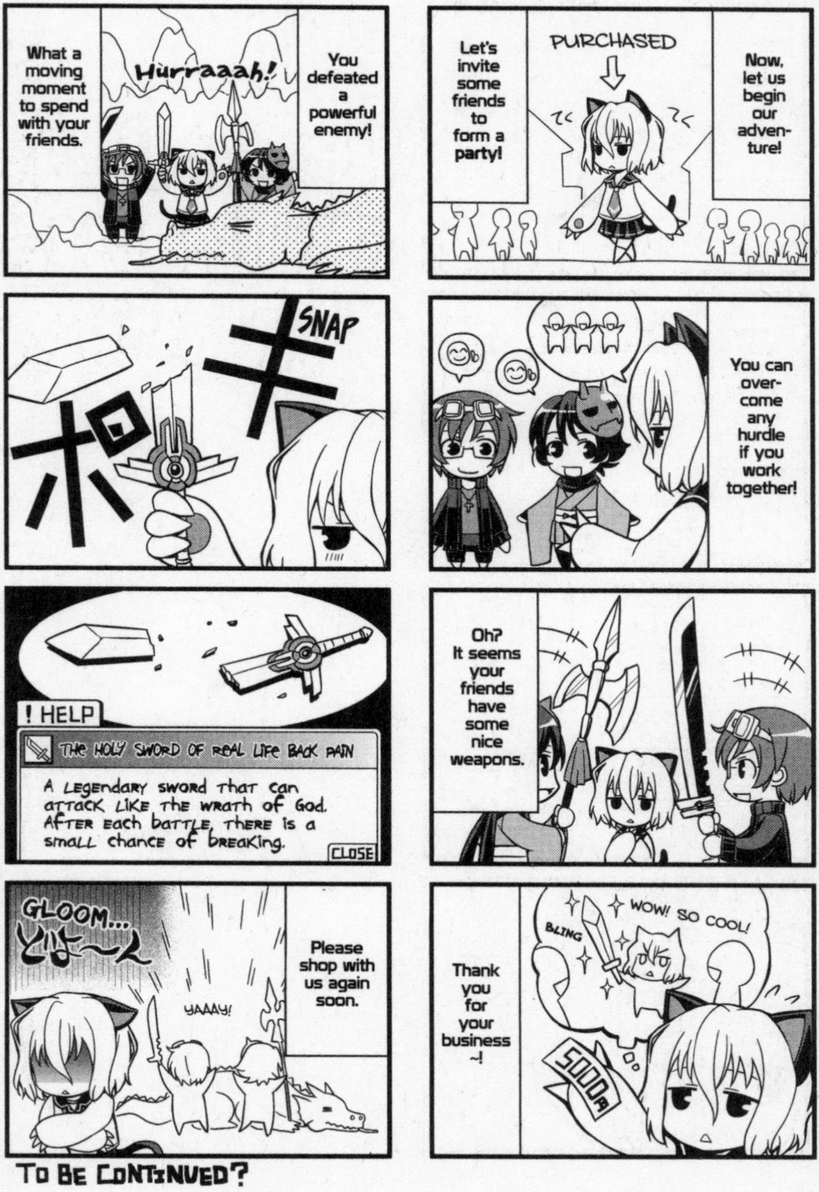
Now, let us begin our adventure!
PURCHASED
Let's invite some friends to form a party!
You can overcome any hurdle if you work together!
Oh? It seems your friends have some nice weapons.
WOW! SO COOL!
BLING
5000
Thank you for your business~!
You defeated a powerful enemy!
Hurraaah!
What a moving moment to spend with your friends.
SNAP
ポキ
! HELP
THE HOLY SWORD OF REAL LIFE BACK PAIN
A LEGENDARY SWORD THAT CAN ATTACK LIKE THE WRATH OF GOD. AFTER EACH BATTLE, THERE IS A SMALL CHANCE OF BREAKING.
CLOSE
Please shop with us again soon.
YAAAY!
GLOOM... どよ~ん

TO BE CONTINUED?

...THE DISTANCE BETWEEN MIKAMI AND AMAMIYA CHANGES...?!!

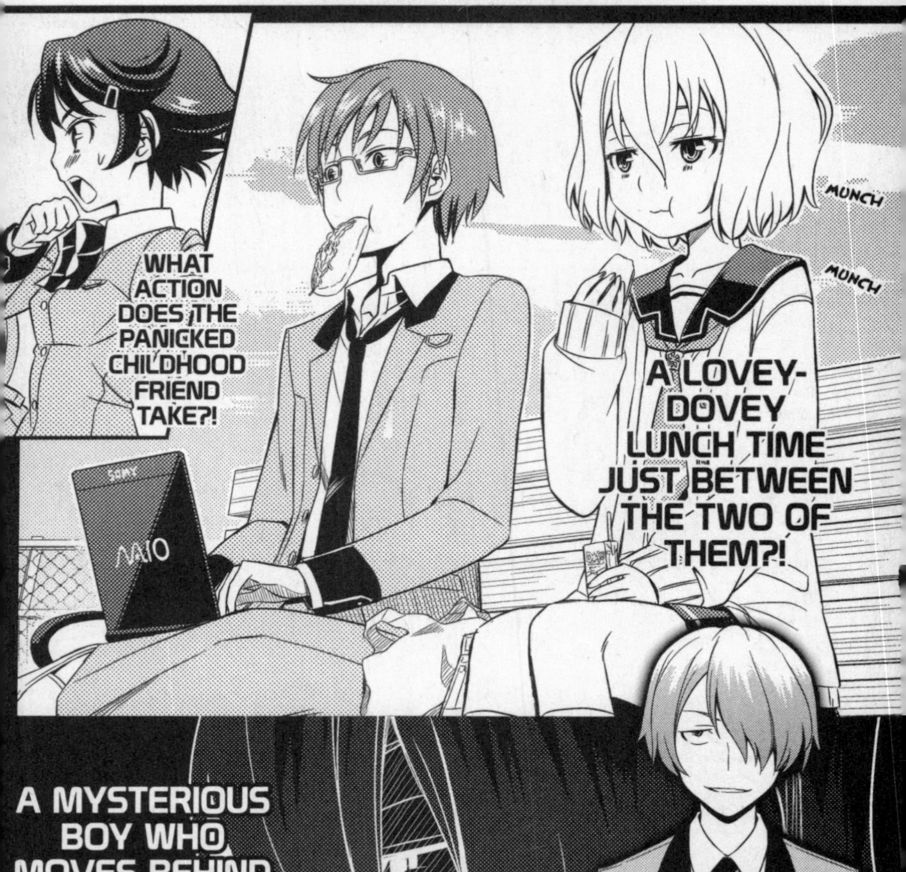
MUNCH
MUNCH
A LOVEY-DOVEY LUNCH TIME JUST BETWEEN THE TWO OF THEM?!
WHAT ACTION DOES THE PANICKED CHILDHOOD FRIEND TAKE?!

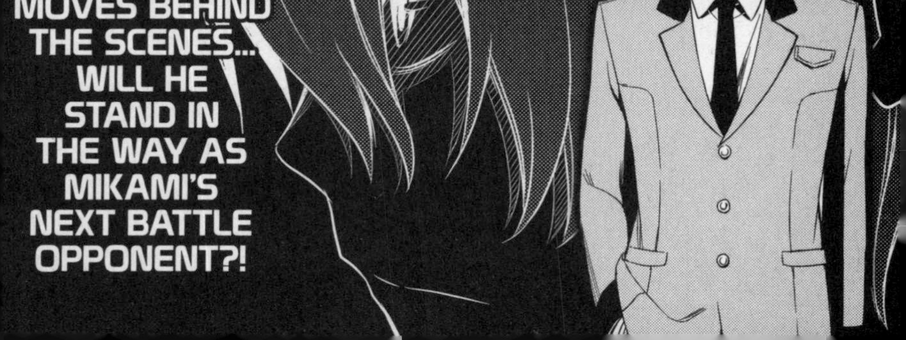
A MYSTERIOUS BOY WHO MOVES BEHIND THE SCENES... WILL HE STAND IN THE WAY AS MIKAMI'S NEXT BATTLE OPPONENT?!

NEXT VOLUME!!

ON THE NEW STAGE KNOWN AS SCHOOL...

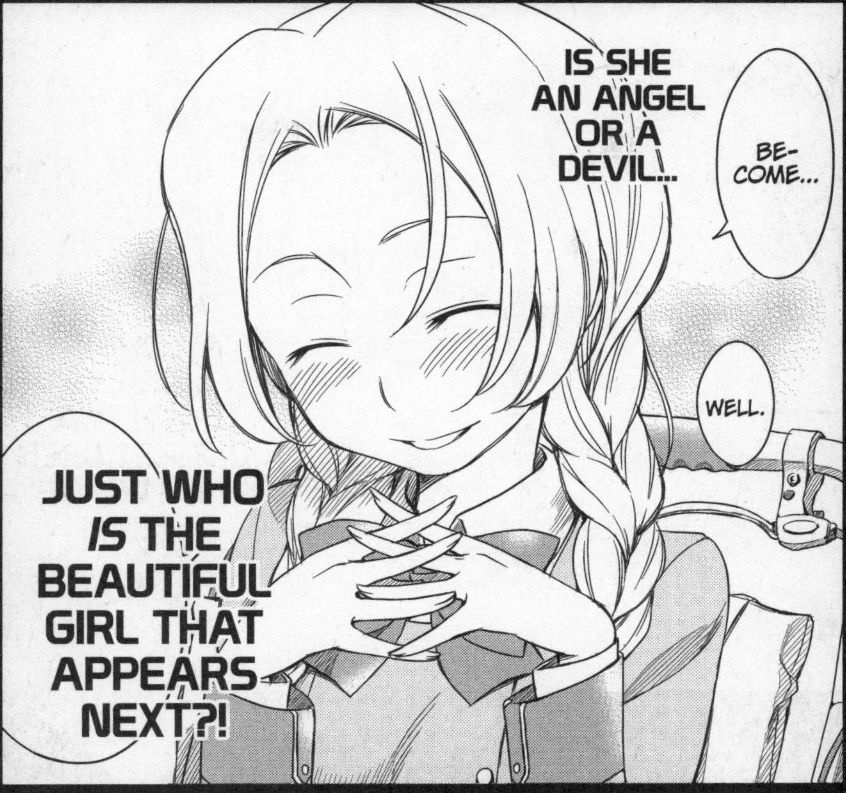
BE-COME...
IS SHE AN ANGEL OR A DEVIL...
WELL.
JUST WHO *IS* THE BEAUTIFUL GIRL THAT APPEARS NEXT?!

MEETING WITH A PRETTY GIRL WILL DRAG OUR PLAYER INTO THE MOST STIMULATING GAME YET!!

NØT LIVES 02

COMING SOON!!

SEVEN SEAS ENTERTAINMENT PRESENTS

NOT LIVES

story and art by **Wataru Karasuma**   **VOLUME 1**

TRANSLATION
Angela Liu

ADAPTATION
Steven Golebiewski

LETTERING AND LAYOUT
James Adams

COVER DESIGN
Nicky Lim

PROOFREADER
Danielle King
Tim Roddy

PRODUCTION MANAGER
Lissa Pattillo

EDITOR-IN-CHIEF
Adam Arnold

PUBLISHER
Jason DeAngelis

NOT LIVES VOL. 1
© WATARU KARASUMA 2012
Edited by ASCII MEDIA WORKS.
First published in Japan in 2012 by KADOKAWA CORPORATION, Tokyo.
English translation rights arranged with KADOKAWA CORPORATION, Tokyo.

Seven Seas books may be purchased in bulk for educational, business, or
promotional use. For information on bulk purchases, please contact Macmillan
Corporate & Premium Sales Department at 1-800-221-7945 (ext 5442)
or write specialmarkets@macmillan.com.

Seven Seas and the Seven Seas logo are trademarks of
Seven Seas Entertainment, LLC. All rights reserved.

ISBN: 978-1-626923-07-2

Printed in Canada

First Printing: March 2016

10 9 8 7 6 5 4 3 2 1

FOLLOW US ONLINE: *www.gomanga.com*

READING DIRECTIONS

This book reads from *right to left*, Japanese style. If
this is your first time reading manga, you start
reading from the top right panel on each page and
take it from there. If you get lost, just follow the
numbered diagram here. It may seem backwards at
first, but you'll get the hang of it! Have fun!!

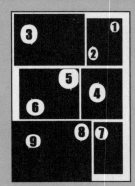

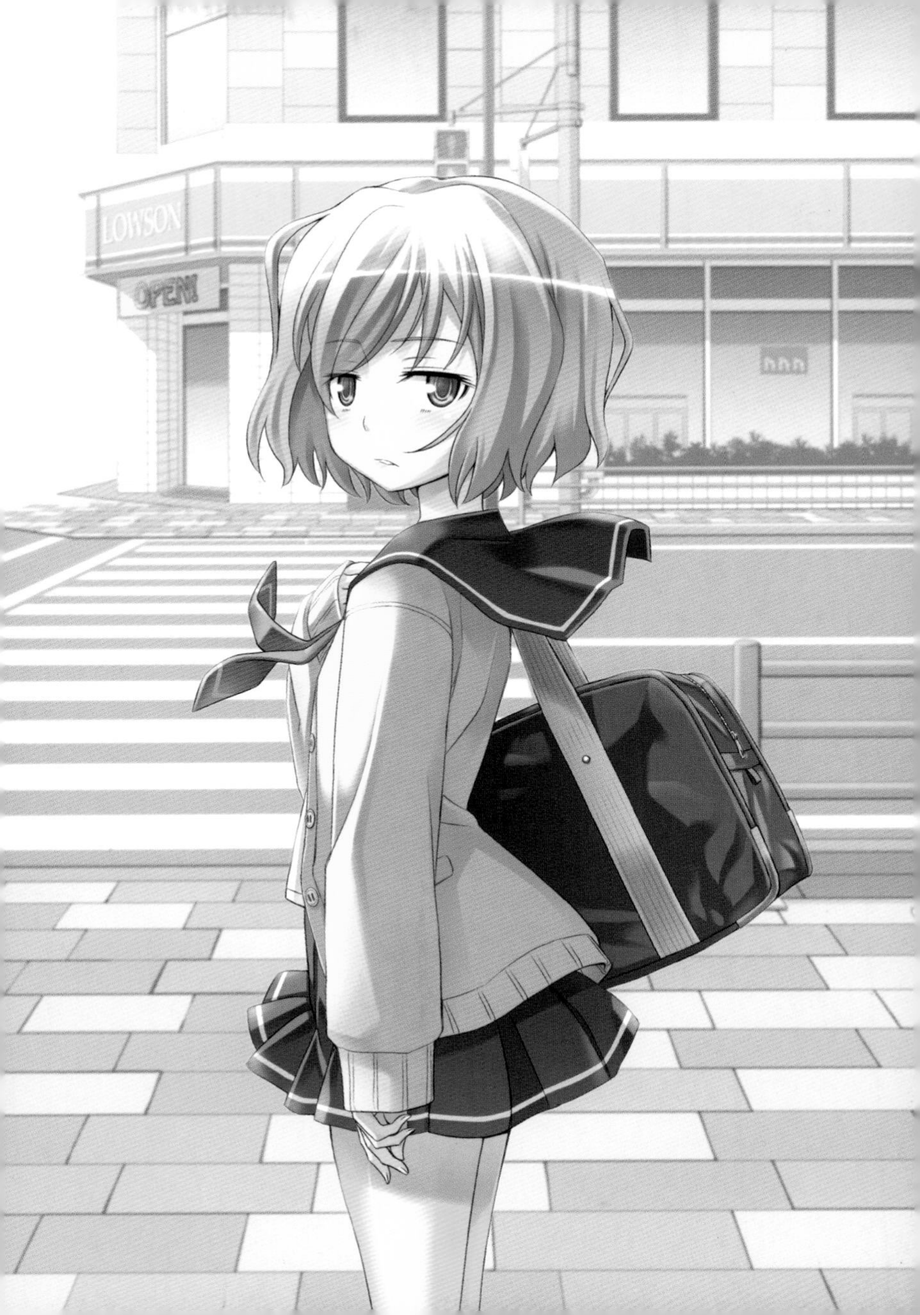
LOWSON
OPEN!

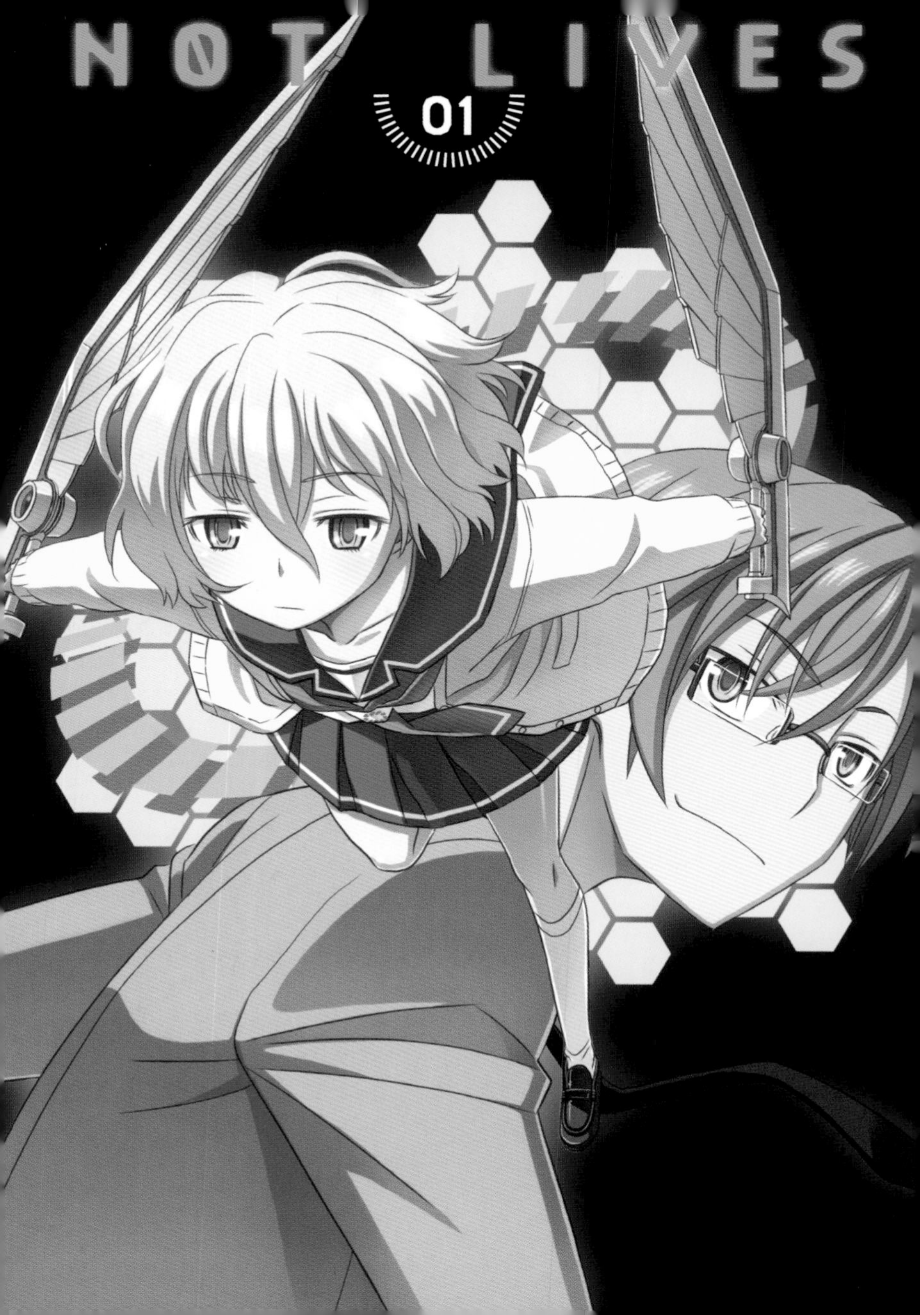
NOT LIVES
01